P9-CCW-255

The
PHANTOM
of FIFTH
AVENUE

The
PHANTOM
of FIFTH
AVENUE

THE MYSTERIOUS LIFE AND
SCANDALOUS DEATH OF HEIRESS
HUGUETTE CLARK

MERYL GORDON

GRAND CENTRAL
PUBLISHING

NEW YORK   BOSTON

Photo on page ii reproduced with the permission
of the Estate of Huguette M. Clark

Grand Central Publishing
Hachette Book Group
237 Park Avenue
New York, NY 10017

www.HachetteBookGroup.com

Printed in the United States of America

RRD-C

First Edition: May 2014

10 9 8 7 6 5 4 3

Grand Central Publishing is a division of Hachette Book Group, Inc.
The Grand Central Publishing name and logo is a trademark of
Hachette Book Group, Inc.

The publisher is not responsible for websites (or their content) that are not owned
by the publisher.

Library of Congress Cataloging-in-Publication Data

Gordon, Meryl.
   The phantom of Fifth Avenue : the mysterious life and scandalous death of
heiress Huguette Clark / Meryl Gordon. —First edition.
     pages cm
   Includes bibliographical references and index.
   ISBN 978-1-4555-1263-8 (hardcover) — ISBN 978-1-4789-5339-5 (audio
download)   1. Clark, Huguette, 1906–2011.   2. Heiresses—United
States—Biography.   3. Recluses—United States—Biography.   4. Collectors and collecting—United States—Biography.   5. Clark, William Andrews,
1839–1925—Family.   6. Clark, Huguette, 1906–2011—Homes and haunts—
United States.   7. Mansions—United States—History.   I. Title.   II. Title:
Mysterious life and scandalous death of heiress Huguette Clark.
   CT275.C6273G67 2014
   973.9092—dc23
   [B]

2014002852

To Walter
For Everything

To my parents
Spirited, Indomitable, Ever Curious

William Andrews Clark spent $7 million building his 121-room mansion, the largest private home in Manhattan. It was torn down in 1926, eleven years after it was completed. *(Collection of the New York Historical Society, George P. Hall & Son Photograph Collection, negative #58976)*

Contents

CONTENTS

Character List

Huguette Clark: Born in France in 1906, died 2011. Talented artist (painter, photographer, miniaturist), played the violin, attended Spence School, exhibited her work at the Corcoran Gallery, passionate doll collector, became a recluse in later years.

Anna La Chapelle's siblings

Amelia La Chapelle: (1881–1969) Married three times, no children. Frequently traveled with Anna and the senator, very close to Huguette.

Arthur La Chapelle: (1883–1946) Based in California. His daughter, Anna La Chapelle, was supported by Huguette, her first cousin. Sued Huguette to break a trust.

THE FRIENDS AND SUITORS

Tadé Styka: (1889–1954) Polish artist, child prodigy in Paris. His portrait of Teddy Roosevelt hangs in the White House. Painted eleven portraits of Senator Clark. Huguette Clark's painting instructor for thirty years, frequent escort during the 1930s, closest man in her life.

Doris (Ford) Styka: Fashion model who walked into Tadé's studio during Huguette's painting lesson and stole his heart. Married the artist in 1942.

Wanda Styka: Their daughter. Huguette's goddaughter, museum archivist.

William M. Gower: (1905–1976) Huguette's only husband. Married in August 1928, separated in April 1929, divorced in 1930. Received $1 million to marry Huguette. Moved to France with second wife, Constance Baxter Tevis McKee Toulmin. Later reestablished affectionate connection with Huguette.

Etienne de Villermont: (1904–1982) French marquis and childhood family friend of the Clarks. In 1938, Walter Winchell announced the marquis's engagement to Huguette. Etienne married a Frenchwoman instead but conducted a decades-long flirtation with Huguette, who wrote him checks.

Edward FitzGerald: Duke of Leinster. Bankrupt Irish duke, briefly courted Huguette for her money.

Edward "Major" Bowes: (1874–1946) Radio pioneer, host of NBC's *Original Amateur Hour*, popular culture sensation in the 1930s, famous for his gong. Widower, began dating Anna Clark in 1935.

Dr. William Gordon Lyle: Family physician to the Clarks. Wife Leontine was a Spence classmate of Huguette. Their children: Gordon Lyle Jr. and Leontine "Tina" Lyle Harrower (goddaughter of Anna Clark).

Suzanne Pierre: French, widow of Dr. Jules Pierre, also a Clark family physician. Huguette's best friend dating from the mid-1970s, saved Huguette's life. Died in 2011.

Agnes Clark Albert: Daughter of Huguette's half brother Charles Clark. Family member who had the closest relationship by far with Huguette and Anna Clark. Died in 2002.

HUGUETTE'S RETAINERS

Donald Wallace: Lawyer, worked for Huguette from 1976 to 1997. Exasperated by her failure to update her will. Died in 2002.

Wallace Bock: Attorney who inherited Huguette as a client from Donald Wallace, worked for her from 1997 until her 2011 death. Wrote her controversial final will, named an executor.

Irving Kamsler: Accountant, worked for Huguette from 1979 to 2011, visited often and held her medical proxy, executor of her will. Pled guilty to online sex offenses in 2008.

Christopher Sattler: Huguette's assistant from 1991 to 2011. Worked on her artistic photography projects, maintained her three apartments at 907 Fifth Avenue.

THE NURSES

Hadassah Peri: Filipino immigrant married to an Israeli cabdriver, Peri was Huguette's principal nurse from 1991 to 2011. Received $31 million in gifts from Huguette including extensive real estate, antique jewelry, and a Stradivarius.

Geraldine Coffey: Irish immigrant, private night nurse, worked for Huguette from 1991 to 2011.

Marie Pompei: Hospital staff nurse, one of the first people to treat Huguette, became her close friend.

THE HOSPITAL PERSONNEL

Dr. Robert Newman: Chief executive officer of Beth Israel Hospital, where Huguette lived for two decades. Repeatedly solicited gifts from Huguette, even had his mother visit the heiress in an effort to secure donations.

Dr. Jack Rudick: Surgeon who treated Huguette for skin cancer, later received $2.1 million in gifts from Huguette.

Dr. Henry Singman: Chief personal physician to Huguette. He made the 1991 house call that led to her admission to the hospital. Received more than $1 million in gifts from Huguette.

THE LEGAL FIGHT

Clark family members who launched original guardianship lawsuit

Karine McCall: Granddaughter of Charles Clark.
Ian Devine: Great-grandson of Mary Clark.
Carla Hall: Great-granddaughter of Katherine Clark.

The lawyers in the estate fight

Harvey Corn: Represented Hadassah Peri.
John Dadakis: Represented Wallace Bock and Huguette Clark estate.
John Graziano: Represented Wanda Styka.
Jason Lilien and Carl Distefano: New York State Attorney General's office.
John Morken: Represented Clark relatives.
Peter Schram: Appointed by the court to represent public administrator's office.

The judges

Kristin Glen: Tart-tongued Surrogate's Court justice.
Nora Anderson: Assigned Clark probate case in 2013 after Glen retired.

The Descendants of

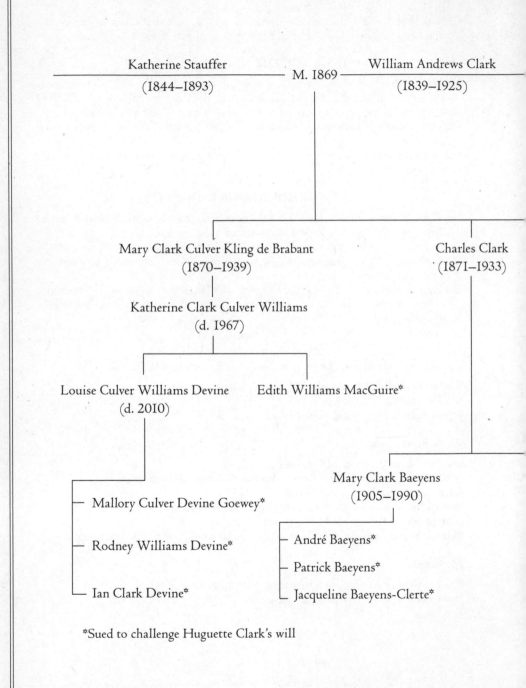

Katherine Stauffer (1844–1893) —— M. 1869 —— William Andrews Clark (1839–1925)

Mary Clark Culver Kling de Brabant (1870–1939)

Charles Clark (1871–1933)

Katherine Clark Culver Williams (d. 1967)

Louise Culver Williams Devine (d. 2010)

Edith Williams MacGuire*

Mary Clark Baeyens (1905–1990)

— Mallory Culver Devine Goewey*

— Rodney Williams Devine*

— Ian Clark Devine*

— André Baeyens*

— Patrick Baeyens*

— Jacqueline Baeyens-Clerte*

*Sued to challenge Huguette Clark's will

Senator William Andrews Clark

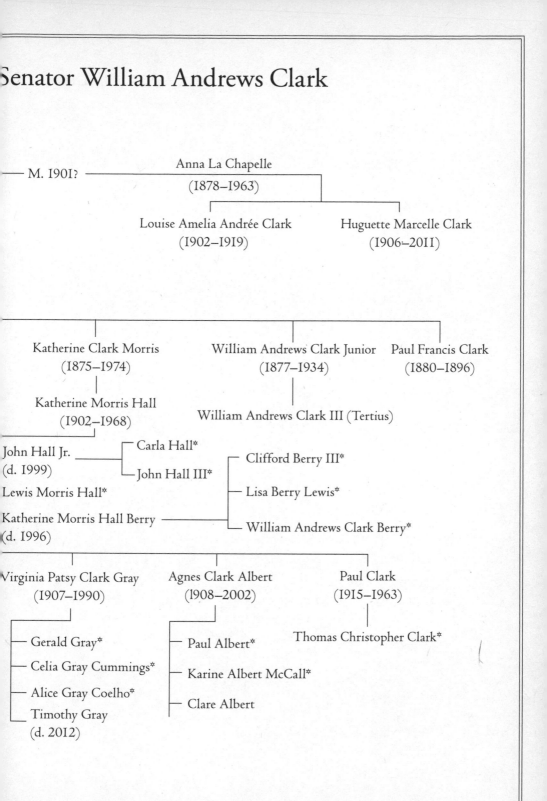

M. 1901? ——————— Anna La Chapelle
(1878–1963)

Louise Amelia Andrée Clark   Huguette Marcelle Clark
(1902–1919)   (1906–2011)

Katherine Clark Morris   William Andrews Clark Junior   Paul Francis Clark
(1875–1974)   (1877–1934)   (1880–1896)

Katherine Morris Hall   William Andrews Clark III (Tertius)
(1902–1968)

John Hall Jr. ——— Carla Hall*
(d. 1999)   Clifford Berry III*
     —— John Hall III*

Lewis Morris Hall*   Lisa Berry Lewis*

Katherine Morris Hall Berry ——— William Andrews Clark Berry*
(d. 1996)

Virginia Patsy Clark Gray   Agnes Clark Albert   Paul Clark
(1907–1990)   (1908–2002)   (1915–1963)

     Thomas Christopher Clark*

— Gerald Gray*   — Paul Albert*

— Celia Gray Cummings*   — Karine Albert McCall*

— Alice Gray Coelho*   — Clare Albert

— Timothy Gray
(d. 2012)

The
PHANTOM
of FIFTH
AVENUE

Chapter One

The Clark Family Reunion at the Corcoran

Located just two blocks from the White House, the Corcoran Gallery of Art feels as if it is off the beaten path in Washington, drawing just a fraction of the city's tourist throngs. The white marble 1897 Beaux Arts colossus usually closes promptly at 5 p.m. on Fridays. But on the rainy night of October 24, 2008, the lights were ablaze well into the evening. With a two-story atrium sporting forty Doric columns and a sweeping staircase to a grand balcony, the perennially cash-strapped private museum is often rented out for weddings and parties. However, tonight's more than seventy-five guests, who had flown in from Paris, London, Florida, Texas, California, and New York, had a personal connection to the museum and its paintings by Corot, Gainsborough, and Delacroix.

In his invitation, Corcoran director Paul Greenhalgh had described the two days of events as "a gathering of the Clark Family." Not just any family named Clark, but a reunion of the descendants and relatives of William Andrews Clark, who in 1907 was described as the second richest man in America, after John D. Rockefeller, with a personal fortune worth more than $3 billion in today's dollars. The copper mogul and Montana senator had been born in 1839 and died in 1925. A Corcoran benefactor, Clark's name is prominently featured in gold leaf on the museum's interior wall and credited in small type beside the many sculptures and paintings that he donated to the permanent collection.

The idea for the Clark family get-together had been jointly hatched by Greenhalgh, a British decorative arts scholar with a mop of brown hair, and Katherine Hall Friedman, known professionally as Carla Hall, a great-great-granddaughter of William Andrews Clark, whose father and grandmother had served on the Corcoran board. Ever since he had joined the Corcoran two years earlier, Greenhalgh, the former head of research at the Victoria and Albert Museum in London, had been wooing potential donors, and he was eager to establish a stronger relationship to the Clarks. As Greenhalgh recalls, "It was clear a lot of the family had never been to the museum before."

The relatives of William Andrews Clark were a far-flung family and many had never met prior to the reunion. Some siblings were estranged and had not seen or spoken to one another in decades. In an e-mail that Carla Hall sent a month before the reunion, she seemed hopeful that the event would change the family dynamics: "We are all eager to get to know one another and learn more about the Clark family, with a specific focus on the life of WA Clark and his legacy that is reflected in the Corcoran's exquisite collection."

This night would prove to be a turning point in the tangled history of the Clarks, although not in a way that the organizers could have imagined. Four years later, the party guests would be quizzed by teams of lawyers about their memories of the evening and who said what to whom. In the whispered asides at the Corcoran party, one could hear the battle lines of a future family feud taking shape. The Clarks in attendance that night included descendants of three branches of the family tree and a representative from the fourth. The senator had sired seven children during his first marriage, and then as a widower married a much younger woman and produced two daughters. As a result, there was a thirty-six-year age gap between his oldest and youngest children: his grandchildren and young daughters were nearly the same age.

Three children from his first marriage—the scandal-prone Manhattan divorcée Mary (known as May), the booze- and racetrack-loving California bon vivant Charles, and the prim and proper

Katherine—had produced seven children, and many of their descendants were in attendance this evening.

Strolling past the snarling bronze lions guarding the Corcoran's entrance, Karine Albert McCall, a petite and slender sixty-eight-year-old blonde, arrived with her husband, Donald McCall, a retired cellist. The grandchild of Charles Clark and his banking heiress wife, Celia, Karine had grown up in luxury at her grandmother's San Francisco Tudor castle, "House-on-Hill," a 35,000-square-foot estate on six acres with a fifty-five-foot-long music room, twelve bedrooms, and lush gardens.

An artist who painted colorful abstracts, the mother of three children, Karine had spent most of the previous forty years living in Europe, but she and her husband had just moved from London to Washington, D.C. She had recently discovered worrisome information about an elderly Clark relative and had been obsessing about what, if anything, to do. She had confided in her first cousin Jacqueline Baeyens-Clerte, who had flown in from her home in Paris to attend the reunion and give Karine moral support. Tonight Karine had a mission: finding allies to discuss her concerns. Karine had never met many of her Clark relatives. As she and Donald and Jacqueline circulated through the cocktail hour at the Corcoran, introducing themselves and making small talk, there was a subtext to the conversations. As Karine recalls, "We were trying to figure out, who can we trust?"

Karine's newfound worries centered on her great-aunt, a woman she had known all her life as "Tante Huguette." The frail and monied Manhattan centenarian had a haunting hold on the imaginations of several generations of Clark relatives.

Huguette Marcelle Clark, the sole surviving child of William Andrews Clark, was now 102 years old and resided in Beth Israel Hospital in New York. No family member had seen her in forty years. Born in 1906 in Paris to Clark's second wife, Anna, Huguette (pronounced you-GET) had been instantly famous for her wealth and constantly chased by photographers as a pretty child and desirable debutante, reluctantly starring in the society pages. Divorced in 1930 after a brief marriage, she never wed again or had children and cut herself off from the social whirl, deliberately cultivating an air of mystery. The gossip columnists of her era, Walter Winchell and Cholly Knickerbocker, had periodically run whatever-happened-to items about Huguette.

Several third-generation Clark relatives like Karine, now in their sixties and seventies, had met Huguette during their childhoods, but to the younger generation she was a cipher, an eccentric curiosity. The family members speculated about her life, and several had repeatedly asked to meet her to no avail, which only made them even more curious. She haunted the imaginations of three generations of Clark relatives, an elusive, reclusive figure. "Talking with the family, none of them knew her," says Corcoran director Greenhalgh. "I'm sure they were desperate to get an audience but none of them did." The professional photographer who had been hired to capture the reunion, Martha FitzSimon, had been briefed about Huguette in advance, recalling, "Carla told me that nobody had been able to talk to her for years."

The last time any family member could remember actually seeing Huguette was at the funeral of Carla Hall's grandmother in March 1968 at St. Thomas Church in Manhattan. "After the funeral, we all were together for a short while, greeting each other and expressing condolences," recalls Erika Hall, Carla's mother and the widow of Huguette's great-nephew John Hall. "Huguette was there also and did the same thing, very sweet, and disappeared rather soon."

Disappeared was an apt word to describe Huguette's behavior. She maintained sporadic phone contact for many years with a few Clark relatives, speaking in a soft voice with a hint of a French accent. When Erika Hall and her husband sent flowers once or twice a year, Huguette would call to say a brief thank-you. But even these kinds of communications had tapered off in recent years. Huguette had repeatedly declined to give out her phone number and had always taken a standoffish don't-call-me-I'll-call-you approach to her relatives. Most did not know that she was in the hospital and assumed she still resided at her sprawling complex of three apartments at 907 Fifth Avenue, with forty-two rooms.

Her two gatekeepers were Irving Kamsler, an accountant who had worked for her since 1979, and attorney Wallace Bock, a real estate tax specialist who had inherited Huguette as a client when her veteran lawyer became ill in 1997. At age seventy-six, Bock still handled Huguette's legal affairs and served as an intermediary between Huguette and her relatives. An Orthodox Jew, Bock had been invited to the Corcoran event as Huguette's representative, but the Friday-Saturday schedule conflicted with the Sabbath. He sent his colleague Kamsler to attend in his stead.

Huguette was, in fact, closer to the deferential sixty-one-year-old Kamsler, who visited her frequently and coordinated her medical care with her private nurses and doctors at Beth Israel Hospital. Bock and Kamsler viewed themselves as Huguette's protectors: they paid her bills, handled her taxes, supervised her staff, and even ran errands. "I found them very easy to deal with," says Greenhalgh of Kamsler and Bock. "My impression is what Huguette did is get faithful people who would stand by her and she would stand by them."

Paid generous monthly retainers (Bock received $15,000 per month; Kamsler got $5,000 per month plus a standard yearly $50,000 bonus), the men made themselves constantly available to their most important client. As Cynthia Garcia, a paralegal at Bock's firm from 1999 to 2002, recalls, "If Mr. Bock was in the men's room when she called, I had to put her on hold and run to the men's room and knock on the door. If he was smoking his pipe by the air shaft, I'd get him. I knew where he ate lunch, a kosher luncheonette. If she called, I'd run out to get him. She would call ten times a day." But Huguette Clark was older now and her hearing was fading; the calls had become much less frequent.

The Corcoran Gallery had been the recipient of William Andrews Clark's vast art collection, including nearly two hundred paintings, Rodin marble nudes, Oriental rugs, Egyptian antiquities, and majolica. His collection featured Corot landscapes and Degas ballet paintings, a Gilbert Stuart portrait of George Washington, and works by Chardin and Cazin. The Salon Doré, an ornate 1770s gilded room that Clark had imported from Paris to install in his turn-of-the-century robber-baron Fifth Avenue mansion, gleamed as the result of a recent restoration.

As William Andrews Clark's distant relations peered admiringly at the art, one implicit thought floated through the air: if only these valuable works of art had stayed in the family. Imagine the cachet of a Corot in one's very own living room. Or better yet, consider the millions of dollars that these artworks would fetch now at auction. A Sickle-Leaf Persian carpet that had once belonged to Clark was subsequently sold by the museum for $33.7 million.

William Andrews Clark, who made his fortune in mining and banking in Montana, expanded into building railroads. Clark showered his children with gifts, bragging in nouveau riche fashion about his generosity. On May 29, 1900, the *New York Times* recited the senator's wedding presents to his daughter Katherine, including $100,000 worth of jewelry—a diamond-and-ruby bodice ornament and diamond-and-emerald tiara—plus $4 million in securities and real estate. Just in case that sum did not convey his enduring fatherly love, the story noted that Clark had previously given his daughter $10 million.

Upon his death, the senator bequeathed an estimated $15 million each (inflation-adjusted, the equivalent of $200 million today) to his surviving children: two adult sons and two adult daughters from his first marriage, and the teenage Huguette. But fortunes have a way of dwindling as the money passes through several generations, especially in a family like the Clarks, with multiple marriages and divorces. Some of tonight's guests were trust funders, but others lived off their salaries. As the Corcoran's Greenhalgh recalls, "My impression was that a significant portion of the people at the reunion were not wealthy people. I think there was a range."

On the Corcoran's second floor, the tables were decorated with red-and-gold tablecloths and set with gold-rimmed glasses and gold-rimmed dinnerware. With just a half hour left before the seated dinner was to begin, Carla Hall, wearing a fitted navy cocktail dress with short sleeves, could be seen rearranging place cards. And she did not look happy about it.

A five-foot-ten, imposing fifty-six-year-old blonde with a take-charge personality, Carla had embraced her Clark heritage with pride. She ran a corporate branding business out of her Upper West Side brownstone in Manhattan, creating annual reports and marketing materials for clients such as the Ford Foundation and Morgan Stanley. Carla's great-grandmother, Katherine Clark Morris, had been the only one of William Andrews Clark's children to make a socially fortuitous marriage, to a descendant of one of the signers of the Declaration of Independence, Lewis Morris.

Carla had been working on the arrangements for the Corcoran party for months with Ian Devine, another fourth-generation Clark descendant. A preppy-looking fifty-five-year-old consultant, Devine advised financial firms on how to market their services to wealthy families. His great-grandmother, Mary Clark Culver Kling de Brabant, had been the bad girl of her generation. Married three times, Mary, the oldest child of William Andrews Clark, was a darling of the gossip columns of her era for her acrimonious divorces and exotic galas.

Carla and Ian had only discovered by serendipity that they were related. In 2001, a business associate arranged for the duo to meet at Carla's home office to discuss a potential work project. Ian's brother had recently given him a family tree and certain names sounded familiar: his great-grandmother Mary and Carla's great-grandmother Katherine had been sisters. As Ian recalls, "At the end of our business meeting, I asked if her parents were John and Erika. She said yes, and we took it from there." Both of their families owned portraits of William Andrews Clark by Polish painter Tadé Styka (pronounced TAH-day STEE-ka), an artist popular in Washington and Hollywood, who had been commissioned by the senator to create an excessive eleven paintings.

Carla Hall had never met or spoken to her "Tante Huguette," but she had frequently been in touch by phone in recent years with Huguette's lawyer, Wallace Bock. Acting in 2006 as a self-appointed family liaison to the Corcoran, Carla had asked Bock to pass along a request to Huguette to donate archival Clark family material (letters, photos, documents) to the museum. Huguette declined to do so. Curious about William Andrews Clark's historic estate, Bellosguardo, in Santa

Barbara, still owned by Huguette but vacant, Carla had requested and received permission, via Wallace Bock, to visit in 2007. She sent Huguette a thank-you note afterward but did not receive a reply.

As soon as Carla began planning the Corcoran party, she consulted Bock and then sent Huguette an invitation to the event with a request for a donation to underwrite expenses. It was cheeky to write to a distant relative and ask for money, but everyone in the family assumed, correctly, that Huguette could easily afford it. Huguette contributed $10,000 but, as expected, declined to attend. As her accountant, Irving Kamsler, recalls telling her, "If you want to go, we can absolutely arrange it, get you there in a luxury limousine." He adds, "But she had no desire to meet her family." Her absence was a disappointment. Beverly Bonner McCord, a descendant of one of the senator's sisters, says, "We would have loved to have met Huguette, even for just a few minutes."

The centenarian represented a living link to the most glittering era of family history. Huguette and her mother, Anna Clark, attended the opening of the Clark wing at the Corcoran in 1928—President Calvin Coolidge cut the silken cord—and she had an emotional attachment to the artworks. She had played with her older sister, Andrée, in the Salon Doré back when it was part of her father's Fifth Avenue house. The paintings and sculptures at the Corcoran had been the backdrop to her daily life. She had accompanied her father to museums in Europe and Manhattan. Art was a way that this shy girl could connect with her formidable father. Inspired to become an artist herself, she had taken private lessons for many years with Tadé Styka. The Corcoran had even mounted a show of Huguette Clark's artwork in 1929, which received favorable attention. With intricate brushwork, she created a striking self-portrait and romantic depictions of flowers.

Proud of her father's legacy as an art collector, she had been a loyal supporter of the Corcoran for many decades. "I talked to Huguette a number of times, she was very sweet," recalls David Levy, former Corcoran Gallery director. "She loved things that were French and she loved the Salon Doré. We were restoring that and she contributed." But he also thought her behavior was strange, to say the least. "She had some huge aversion to anyone seeing her. She would send me group photos, historic stuff, a group of people standing in front of a building. She would take a black magic marker and cross out her face. It was pretty weird. She never explained it and I never asked." Freed now from the diplomatic requirements of being a museum head, Levy adds, "She was a nutcase. If you have a nutcase giving you between $25,000 and $100,000 per year, you've got to let it ride."

Huguette's long-standing relationship with the Corcoran unraveled when Levy championed a new addition to the museum designed by Frank Gehry, which would have sliced into the Clark wing and destroyed the rotunda. She cut her contributions. When the board canceled the Gehry addition, Levy quit as director. Greenhalgh, his successor, had worked to smooth the waters, although he was never able to speak to Huguette Clark directly. "I went to see Wallace Bock, and he was extremely cold at first, because Huguette's experience with the museum had been bad for many years," Greenhalgh recalls. "We reassured Wallace Bock that the Clark wing and Clark collections were extremely important to the museum."

The strategy worked. When Greenhalgh wrote to Huguette in 2007 to tell her about the museum's precarious financial condition— it was running a $2 million yearly deficit—she responded by pledging $1 million, to be paid in four installments. The new director was understandably eager to keep her, and her advisers, feeling warmly toward the museum.

———

Carla Hall had been happily chatting with guests that evening and accepting congratulations when she was abruptly interrupted by the Corcoran director's assistant with an urgent request to change the seating arrangements at the head table. The table needed new additions for the emissaries from Tante Huguette: her accountant, Irving Kamsler, and his wife, Judith.

Short and overweight, wearing a dark suit, white shirt, and striped navy tie, Kamsler and his red-headed wife, Judi, did seem like interlopers as they mingled with the Clark descendants. A graduate of Baruch College, Kamsler and his second wife lived in a modest condominium in Riverdale, and until recently he had been president of his Bronx temple. After working at several different accounting firms, he was now a sole practitioner and Huguette Clark was his most important client. As her representative, he enjoyed the reflected glory at the party, recalling that the family members were eager for news: "Everyone was interested, people were asking me questions, what was Mrs. Clark like? How is she? I didn't say very much."

Even in absentia, Huguette Clark was present at the party. A Clark family photo display included pictures of Huguette and her sister Andrée, pretty young girls with long hair, dressed up for an outing. But Kamsler had become perturbed upon seeing a Clark family tree that did not mention either Huguette or her mother, Anna. He did not realize that the tree had been created as a seating chart for those actually in attendance that night.

Upset by what he perceived as a lack of respect for Huguette, Kamsler tracked down Greenhalgh's executive assistant and angrily complained. As Kamsler recalls, "I said I'm not going to make a scene, but they are asking her to come and underwrite the cost and they're ignoring her in this thing." His rant sparked the last-minute seating change: the Corcoran staffer had taken it upon herself to ask Carla Hall to move Kamsler and his wife from Siberia in the hope of appeasing them.

Carla was visibly upset by the request to upgrade the Kamslers. "I had to reorchestrate all the table arrangements and accommodate the elder members of the family that had traveled far and wide," Carla recalled with irritation. "I was shaken by that, and I didn't understand."

Once the family members were seated, as the mistress of ceremonies, Carla stood up and took to the microphone to welcome her relatives, noting that this was the first time the extended family had come together in a century. She told the group that she hoped the reunion would "begin a new era of Clark cousin connections." Toward the end of her prepared remarks, Carla expressed her gratitude to Tante Huguette for her "tremendous generosity toward making this weekend reunion possible." Carla had placed note cards on each table, and suggested that people write to Huguette, with the promise that the comments would be sent along. But her remarks irked Irving Kamsler, or as he put it, "Carla did make a point to thank Mrs. Clark, and in my opinion, I thought it was an afterthought."

At the end of the evening, as waiters cleared the tables and the crowd began to disperse, Carla went up to the accountant and his wife and asked, "How did you enjoy the evening?" She was startled by Kamsler's response. "He grimaced, which I didn't quite expect, and then I said, 'How would you think my great-aunt would have liked and enjoyed the evening?' He became very belligerent and used words that felt very harsh to me... He said, 'She would have been disgusted at this event, that it was disrespectful of her.' Then he huffed off. My next conversation was with Ian, because he and his wife, Kerri, were coming toward me and I was quite shaken up."

Ian Devine overheard a commotion and raced over to Carla to see what was going on. After hearing her account, he was furious about what he perceived as "this out-of-place attack" and "verbal assault on Carla."

Paul Greenhalgh witnessed the confrontation. "Definitely, Irving was put out," he says. "My memory was that on the various boards and posters put around, Huguette was not thanked for supporting the evening, and he was upset." Word quickly spread that Kamsler had criticized the festivities.

The contretemps ended the evening on a jarring note. The next morning, the guests gathered at the museum again, starting with a brunch. Irving and Judi Kamsler received a decidedly chilly reaction from the family. "They treated us like lepers," he recalled.

After touring the Clark collection, the guests wound up at a luncheon, with featured speaker Stanley Pitts, an amateur historian. Pitts, an airline safety administrator based in Alaska, had written his master's thesis on William Andrews Clark at the University of Northern Texas. Back in 1899, Clark had been charged with bribing Montana legislators to win his Senate seat; Pitts's thesis was an attempt to clear the senator's name. Clark's descendants were well aware of the controversies swirling around their patriarch and sought Pitts out to tell him their tales. "They'd been told that he was a rascal and tight-fisted," Pitts says, recalling that one Clark relative confessed, " 'My great-aunt would not let us speak his name in the house, they were so ashamed. We thought he was a criminal.'"

Even though Pitts had a dramatic story to tell, the senator's great-granddaughter Karine McCall had trouble paying attention during his remarks. Karine, who had come to the family reunion on a mission, needed to make a quick decision. Who could she trust in this roomful of relatives? The hyperorganized Carla Hall appeared to be plugged into the family history. Karine passed her a note, inviting Carla over to her town house in Georgetown later that afternoon. She had urgent matters to discuss.

Chapter Two

The Quest for "Tante Huguette"

On this rainy Saturday afternoon, Carla Hall arrived at Karine's Georgetown house with Ian Devine in tow. Karine's houseguest and cousin, Jacqueline Baeyens-Clerte, a French baron's daughter, joined them as well. The white 1820s four-story town house on P Street NW in Georgetown, located on a prime corner lot, had been meticulously restored, with marble fireplaces on each floor and a small, sunny backyard. Karine and Donald McCall had purchased the showplace just weeks before the family reunion at the Corcoran and were still unpacking the final boxes.

They had decorated in eclectic fashion with African masks, colorful Oriental rugs, Russian icons mixed with antique furniture, and paintings that Karine had inherited from her mother, Agnes Clark Albert. A San Francisco philanthropist and granddaughter of William Andrews Clark, Agnes had attended the Spence School in Manhattan with Huguette back in the early 1920s.

The events that had triggered Karine's newfound curiosity about her great-aunt Huguette began with a rekindled romance. In 1967, Karine, a divorced single mother, had married Donald, a musician nine years her senior. The couple amicably divorced in 1987 and settled in separate countries (Karine in England, Donald in Italy) but had recently gotten back together and remarried. Earlier this year, as they tried to decide where to live together as a couple, a bit of information emerged that inadvertently related to Huguette.

After Karine ushered her relatives into her new living room, she explained that her trip down the rabbit hole began with the enactment of a new British tax on foreigners that she and Donald feared might be ruinous to their finances. As they considered their options, an adviser inquired: Would Karine inherit money in the future? "I don't know," she replied, but then began to wonder about the odds.

The first name that came to Karine's mind was an aging and wealthy family member who just might be generous: Tante Huguette. It was plausible. Karine's mother had been friendly with Huguette, and Karine recalled visits to her relatives' Fifth Avenue apartments and Santa Barbara estate. "Huguette was always sitting next to her mother [Anna], but she never said anything," Karine remembers. "Anna was so much fun, she was an original. She did what she wanted. She had married for money, and she spent it too." Huguette and Karine's mother, Agnes Albert, spoke regularly even though they lived on opposite sides of the country. As Karine recalls, "My mother used to phone Tante Huguette every month."

But a few years before Agnes died in 2002, she told her daughter Karine that she was concerned about Huguette. "My mother was not well," Karine recalled. "She called me into her room and said she wanted to speak to me about something important. She said, 'I tried to call Huguette to say hello, and instead spoke to her lawyer. He told me not to phone any longer, if Huguette wanted to talk to me, she would call. But that's not the way it's always been.'"

After Agnes Albert died, Karine's older brother, Paul Albert, sent Tante Huguette a note informing her of the death. Huguette replied with a heartfelt handwritten condolence note:

September 22nd, 2002

Dear Paul,

Your kind letter regarding your dear Mother deeply touched me.

Your Mother was a very remarkable person and had such great talent as a musician. I admired her greatly and was very fond of her.

You had reason to be very proud of her.

With my very deepest sympathies, dear Paul, and much love, Tante Huguette.

With no children of her own, it was possible that Huguette might leave a bequest to Agnes's children. Karine asked her lawyer to get in touch with Wallace Bock to inquire about whether she was in Huguette's will, for tax planning purposes. Word came back that Karine and her siblings were not among the future recipients of Huguette Clark's generosity.

Recalling her mother's request to look out for Huguette and seized with a nagging sense of guilt, Karine did a Google search on Huguette's closest known associates, Bock and accountant Irving Kamsler. She was astonished to discover that Kamsler was a convicted felon: "What I found out was his arrest for pedophilia."

On September 6, 2007, Kamsler had been arrested and charged with exchanging sexually explicit e-mails with a fifteen-year-old girl in an AOL chat room. As the *Riverdale Press* story noted, the "girl" was an undercover cop; this was a sex sting. Kamsler used an e-mail address that was not even remotely incognito for an accountant trolling for underage girls: IRV1040@aol.com.

Freed on $20,000 bond, Kamsler was forced to resign from the presidency of his temple, Congregation Shaarei Shalom. A law enforcement officer who investigated the case recalls, "He was really nasty and domineering, very explicit about what he would do to these girls." Yet the official also noted that Kamsler "wanted a 'girlfriend' experience. He wanted a more refined girl who would dress up a little bit and meet him in a hotel." Newspaper photos show Kamsler's wife, Judi, at his side for the court hearings.

Just three weeks before the Corcoran party, Kamsler pled guilty on October 2 to attempting to disseminate indecent material to a minor. (Sentenced several months later, he received a $5,000 fine and five years probation, and was required to register as a sex offender. He received a dispensation from the judge to continue to practice as an accountant.) Karine had been horrified by the prospect of sitting near Kamsler at the Clark reunion. Now she asked Carla and Ian: did they think Tante Huguette's finances should be handled by a convicted felon?

"Carla and I were pretty much speechless," Ian recalls. "I'm a pretty jaded guy, but this was horrifying."

But this was not the first time that he and Carla had wondered whether anything was amiss with Huguette's financial affairs. Five years earlier, Ian had seen an article in the *New York Times* announcing that Sotheby's was auctioning off a Renoir, *Dans Les Roses (Madame Leon Clapisson)*, a portrait of an aristocratic Parisian in a garden. The owner was listed as Mrs. Huguette M. Clark. Ian alerted Carla, and they went to Sotheby's together for a closer look. It was a bonding experience, cementing their mutual Clark roots and trying to satisfy their mutual curiosity about their relative.

"It took us by surprise that this painting was up for sale," Carla said. "Why is this huge painting, very valuable painting, being sold? What's going on? A woman who is of a substantial asset base, the daughter of Senator Clark, why is it being sold now?" (The Renoir was purchased for $23.5 million by casino owner Steve Wynn.) Carla fired off a letter to Dare Hartwell, a Corcoran curator, writing, "We were as shocked as anyone by the sale and she must have been truly horrified to see her name in print."

Carla had also had a disconcerting back-and-forth with David Levy, the Corcoran's former director, who mentioned that Huguette's contributions to the museum had dropped substantially. He had heard that she had given a large sum of money instead to an Israeli project to help out Wallace Bock's daughter. (Carla would later learn that at Bock's behest, Huguette, who was Catholic, had donated $1.85 million to build a security system in Efrat, Israel.) David Levy wrote Carla an e-mail: "In truth, I've had some disturbing thoughts about the whole matter and in particular, Mrs. Clark's relationship to Wallace Bock, the current lawyer, who may have his own agenda (which would be a big legal no-no.)"

Carla reported this development to her mother and to her uncle Lewis Hall, but both urged caution. "I brought this to the family's attention and the answer was . . . if Mrs. Clark wanted to give to Israel, it's her free will to give to Israel and it's none of our business," Carla recalls. "They advised me not to speak to anybody and to respect Mrs. Clark's privacy."

But this new information—that Huguette's accountant was a convicted sex offender—was impossible to ignore. Sitting in Karine's living room, the family members strategized over how to proceed. They had no proof of any wrongdoing, but their questions were multiplying by the second. Was she in good health and of sound mind, or was someone else making financial decisions on her behalf? Was she well cared for? As the meeting broke up, they agreed to do more research and make a plan.

Although Ian Devine's great-grandmother Mary and Huguette had been half sisters, he had never met the oldest living Clark. He sent her two cards in the 1970s that went unanswered. Now Ian went home and searched online for information about Kamsler. What turned up was odd. A friend of the accountant had posted purported advice from Kamsler about the repercussions of an upcoming tax law change. As Ian recalls, the quotes "seemed to indicate that Irving Kamsler was in favor of getting clients to agree to be kept on life support, kept alive by any means possible, until 2010, when estate taxes dropped to zero because of a quirk in the law." These kinds of comments were actually common in accounting circles at the time because of the oddities of the 2001 Bush tax cut. (The family of Yankees owner George Steinbrenner saved an estimated $600 million in federal taxes because he died in 2010, rather than a year earlier or later.) Karine had found the same online reference to Kamsler's supposed thoughts about estate taxes. The trio worried that Huguette might be in physical danger.

———

Unaware that the Clark relatives were marshaling their forces against him, Irving Kamsler went to Beth Israel Hospital to tell Huguette about the reunion. At 102, she remained mentally sharp, although she suffered from severe hearing loss. She was capable of having a conversation if people stood near her good left ear; familiar voices were easier for her to understand. Kamsler portrayed himself as acting as her champion at the event, challenging her family members on her behalf. Brutally honest, he told Huguette that in his opinion, her relatives were ingrates: "I was upset on your behalf that the family diagram and tree didn't have your name on it." For Huguette, this brought back painful memories of being treated dismissively by her half siblings in the 1930s and '40s. Kamsler did tell her that many relatives had expressed interest in her, but the accountant insisted that he had been circumspect. As he recalls, "She was glad that I had gone to represent her but upset that I had gotten into a tiff with Carla."

Carla Hall called Wallace Bock to complain that Kamsler had been rude at the reunion, saying that she was "upset and concerned." Bock recalls, "I tried to gloss it over and smooth it out." Carla asked Bock to arrange a call between Huguette and her mother, Erika—the women had not spoken in several years—and he turned her down. Carla then talked things over with her mother, who decided to make the case herself. On November 24, Erika Hall phoned Wallace Bock to reiterate her request to speak to Huguette and received an equally frosty response. "He was very noncommittal and closed the door," says Erika Hall. "That was the feeling, you had the door shut in to your face."

Bock insists that he was only following Huguette's instructions. "Mrs. Clark wasn't talking to anyone on the telephone. She wouldn't talk to any strangers," he said. "One of the problems was her hearing. People had to shout at her, and she didn't enjoy the conversations anymore."

Erika was so angry that she wrote to Corcoran director Paul Greenhalgh, complaining about Bock and describing Kamsler's criminal conviction. "As you may have heard, several of us are very disturbed and worried about the condition and financial situation of Huguette Clark," she wrote. "After meeting the Kamslers, this became very apparent...We are exploring what legal rights we have and if there could be 'elder abuse.'"

But the museum officials already knew about the accountant's legal troubles. "Irving came to us personally and confessed he had this conviction," Greenhalgh says. His reaction was that Kamsler had used poor judgment in one part of his life, but there was no evidence that he had done anything wrong in a professional context. Greenhalgh decided this should be seen as an isolated incident, explaining in an interview with me, "As far as I was concerned, it had nothing to do with the family and it was done, over and finished."

Feeling increasingly frustrated, Carla and Ian decided to take direct action and actually go visit Huguette Clark. One relative mentioned that Huguette had supposedly been at Doctors Hospital in the

1990s, which had been taken over by Beth Israel. A telephone operator at Beth Israel confirmed to Ian that they did have a patient with the right name. He insists that they wanted "to make sure that our aunt was not being kept alive by artificial means in some inhumane fashion."

Before heading to the hospital, Carla asked for advice from one of the few family members who had been in touch with Huguette. California Realtor Paul Clark Newell Jr., a descendant of William Andrews Clark's younger sister Ella, had been working for a decade on an unpublished biography of Senator Clark. He had interviewed Huguette, although they had last spoken four years earlier in 2004. The go-between who arranged his calls was Suzanne Pierre, the widow of Huguette's physician and the heiress's best friend.

At Carla's behest, Newell called Suzanne Pierre, who told him that Huguette was "well taken care of" and was "always in a good mood." Newell then sent Carla a lengthy e-mail, describing the conversation and cautioning Carla to keep her distance.

> *She said also that Huguette doesn't get out much anymore—which seems to suggest that she may leave the hospital from time to time... Who knows? Perhaps she's passed you unrecognized while shopping at Macy's? My conclusion is that Huguette is simply an unusual person... for reasons which we may never fully understand she has chosen to further insulate herself from nearly everyone...*

Newell summarized what he had learned about Huguette's family history on her mother's side—that she had no living relatives—and wrote that Huguette's attorney, Wallace Bock, had been consistently "pleasant" to him. Newell recalled that Huguette had been alert and lucid during their last conversation. But the Realtor noted that he was not privy to information about her finances.

> *None of this addresses your concern as to whether she is getting the best financial counsel and that her assets are being managed ethically and responsibly. But absent compelling indications to the contrary, I don't see how you can probe this issue... Further, there*

is the question as to who has the necessary "standing" to file a complaint or seek an investigation, and on what grounds???…

I feel that calling at the hospital is not a good idea, that your chances of a friendly reception there are from slim to none and that such "good will" as you may now enjoy vis-à-vis Huguette might be irreparably damaged by making an unwelcome approach…Fond regards, Paul

———

The bright blue sign over the entryway at Beth Israel Medical Center looks garish against the backdrop of the sweeping white concrete columns of the silolike structure, which sits on the busy corner of First Avenue and Sixteenth Street. Inside the bustling ten-floor, 1,100-bed hospital, one serene third-floor area has been set aside to cater to well-to-do patients. The suites offer views overlooking Stuyvesant Square, concierge service, flat-screen televisions, fluffy bathrobes, unrestricted visiting hours, and in-room sleep sofas for family members. "The unit is more reminiscent of a luxury hotel than a hospital," notes the facility's promotional material. Nonetheless, this teaching hospital, located in a noisy commercial neighborhood, lacks the cachet of its Upper East Side competitors.

Founded in 1890 as a clinic for poor Jewish immigrants working in the sweatshops of the Lower East Side and living in tenements, Beth Israel was for many decades a charity hospital. From that inauspicious beginning, the hospital has morphed into a busy urban modern medical facility with such gritty units as a methadone clinic for drug addicts. This is not the kind of place where William Andrews Clark could have imagined one of his descendants spending the night, even in an emergency. If by some accident of fate an heiress to one of the great American fortunes was admitted to Beth Israel, the obvious place for her would be the VIP floor, where a chef creates gourmet meals and suites begin at $450 per night on top of regular hospital costs.

On Friday, December 5, 2008, Ian and Carla arrived at the hospital and headed toward the upscale third-floor wing. But Huguette Clark was not there. Instead, William Clark's youngest child was right around the corner in the Karpas Pavilion, down a dreary corridor to Room 3K01, next to a utility closet. Huguette's room had an old-fashioned radiator with peeling paint and a window overlooking the industrial air-conditioning unit.

Ian and Carla knocked on the door. The private nurse on duty, Christie Ysit, a Filipino immigrant, came out to greet them. Christie was chatty and told them that Huguette was sleeping but was doing well for her age. The nurse reported that Huguette still had a good appetite and was able to get up and walk around the room, albeit with assistance. Looking for an excuse to enter, Carla seized on a friendly mention of religion. "I asked if I could go in and give her a blessing," Carla said. "Ian and I entered the room. She was sleeping peacefully." They stayed for scarcely a minute, standing at the foot of Huguette's bed. Ysit suggested that if they wanted more information, they might want to return the following day to talk to Huguette Clark's primary nurse, Hadassah Peri.

A Filipino immigrant married to an Israeli cabdriver, Hadassah Peri was so devoted to her patient that she sometimes put in twelve-hour days taking care of Huguette. Her own children complained that the nurse was never home. Her maiden name had been Gicela Oloroso, but after moving to New York and marrying Daniel Peri, she had converted to Judaism and changed her name. Hadassah's native language was Tagalog, and although she had lived in the United States since 1972, she still spoke in fractured English, with lapses in grammar and awkward sentence structure.

At Beth Israel, the doctors were aware that the patient and her chief nurse were unusually close. "Mrs. Peri was very caring, and she couldn't do enough for Mrs. Clark," says Dr. Jack Rudick, a surgeon, adding that the heiress "related to her as her very best friend." Every night when Hadassah returned to her home in the unfashionable Brooklyn neighborhood of Manhattan Beach, within minutes after she walked in the door she would get a phone call from her patient. Huguette wanted to make sure the nurse got home safely. Sometimes Hadassah would get another call later in the evening. Huguette wanted to say, "Good night."

When Carla and Ian arrived for their second visit to the hospital twenty-four hours later, they were hoping to see Huguette and brought a bouquet of flowers. This time, when they knocked on Huguette's door, Hadassah Peri came out to speak to them in the hallway. The pint-sized nurse was furious. She told them that Huguette Clark was "very upset" that they had turned up uninvited on Sunday and barged into her room. Carla and Ian could not see into the hospital room but heard Huguette in the background, calling out for Hadassah in a shrill, high-pitched voice. The nurse demanded that they leave the hospital immediately.

For scions of a WASP family who had attended elite schools—Ian was a product of the Palm Beach Day School, Deerfield Academy, and the University of Pennsylvania; Carla had attended the Ethel Walker boarding school followed by Middlebury College—it was quite a turnabout to be ordered out by a paid-by-the-hour immigrant employee. "We were worried," says Ian. Carla was startled by the nurse's behavior, saying, "Hadassah Peri was very belligerent." These two well-connected New Yorkers had been joking between themselves about feeling like Nancy Drew or the Hardy Boys as they tried to learn more about Huguette, but this confrontation made them feel like they had stepped into something noir.

As soon as the uninvited duo left, Hadassah picked up the phone and called Irving Kamsler, who immediately got in touch with Wallace Bock. By the time Carla returned to her Upper West Side office, a threatening e-mail awaited her from Bock, warning her and Ian that if they tried to visit Huguette Clark again, they would be removed by force. "Your attempt to invade her privacy, which she guards so carefully and is guarded so scrupulously by those of us on whom she relies on a daily basis, was not appreciated," he wrote. "In fact, she was quite disturbed about it."

Carla asked to meet with Bock, to explain why they had gone to the hospital. "We had never met but we had been conversing for years and with this e-mail and the situation, we thought it best to sit down face-to-face," she says. The next day, she and Ian went to Bock's office on Lexington Avenue. Rather than the gleaming premises of a high-end Manhattan law firm, the place exuded a frayed-around-the-edges quality, with worn carpeting and furniture.

A rotund Brooklyn native whose father had worked in the garment business ("He was a schmatta dealer," Bock says), the lawyer had served in the Army during the Korean War and attended Columbia Law School on the GI Bill. Bock's original specialty was an obscure area of real estate law. He had shared office space with Huguette's longtime attorney Donald Wallace, who suffered a serious heart attack in 1997. As a result, Bock took over Huguette Clark's legal affairs, making himself so indispensable that she did not seek other counsel.

For Wallace Bock, dealing with the Clark descendants was yet another part of his mandate to shelter his client from outsiders. Huguette Clark had repeatedly told him that she did not want direct contact with these relatives. During a back-and-forth of letters with Clark family members in 2007 about repairs to the William Andrews Clark mausoleum, Bock came away with the strong impression that they were not genuinely interested in Huguette. "I don't think anyone really inquired other than saying, 'I didn't think she was still alive,'" he says. Bock has a personality that runs hot and cold: he can be grandfatherly with a wry sense of humor or acerbic and adversarial.

Given the angry tone of Bock's e-mail to Carla, she was surprised to discover that in their face-to-face meeting the lawyer was initially quite friendly and open in discussing Huguette's life, her finances, and her friendships. "We found out about Madame Pierre, that Huguette wrote many checks much to his chagrin," Carla recalls. "We found out what her days were like."

But his tone changed when the duo handed the lawyer a newspaper account of Kamsler's criminal conviction. "He turned many shades whiter," says Carla. "We said, 'Step into the shoes of her father—would you be proud to have a convicted felon representing your daughter?'" Bock appeared to them to be unconcerned, saying it was just a sting. "He made the decision to cover on the spot for Kamsler," says Ian. "I knew in my bones that there was something rotten going on."

The lawyer admits that he was taken aback by Carla and Ian's insistence that he fire the accountant. "I was upset they were raising it," Bock said. He takes pains to add that he was unhappy about the accountant's conviction but did not want to take punitive action. "There was no question that Kamsler was in the wrong, but to what extent was he in the wrong? He claims he was just playing around on the computer and had no intention of going through with it," Bock explains. "As far as I was concerned, he was a good accountant and concerned about Mrs. Clark. It didn't interfere with his functioning as her accountant."

At the end of the meeting, Carla penned a note of apology to Huguette, saying that they did not intend to invade her privacy and just wanted to make sure she was well taken care of. She asked Bock to deliver it.

The lawyer was aware that Huguette Clark relied on Irving Kamsler and their relationship went beyond the client-accountant hierarchy. For the first twenty years that Kamsler handled her taxes, she refused to even speak to him and conducted all business by mail. But she had finally relented and now saw and spoke to Kamsler on a regular basis. He was such an integral part of her life that she had given him control of her day-to-day well-being. "I believe that she trusted me implicitly," Kamsler says, "because over the course of time she named me as the medical proxy to make health-care decisions for her or to carry out the ones that she expressed."

Now that the Clark family members were aroused, they were determined not to back down. They saw themselves as Huguette's saviors—whether or not she needed or wanted to be saved. The circle of those family members involved kept getting larger, well beyond the original group who met at Karine McCall's house in Washington. The initial conspirators brought in their siblings, and the group would eventually expand to include nineteen descendants of William Andrews Clark.

Karine McCall's older brother Paul Albert, a retired California lawyer, had skipped the family reunion but he now joined the e-mail chain, writing to Ian Devine. "I agree with what you said that Huguette wants nothing in her life to change...She has chosen to be a recluse her entire life and to cut herself off from the family."

A month after the hospital incident, Carla wrote to Wallace Bock, demanding that he draft a notice to Huguette Clark that described Irving Kamsler's conviction. She wanted an "unbiased witness" to present the document to Huguette, and request her signature to confirm that she still wanted to employ Kamsler. The lawyer acceded to

Carla's request, although the witness who handled the next stage—
Kamsler himself—was not exactly unbiased.

Irving Kamsler hand-delivered a letter, dated February 9, 2009, to
Huguette Clark.

> *Dear Mrs. Clark,*
>
> *I recently visited with you and explained my legal situation con-
> cerning my pleading guilty to one single felony charge involving the
> use of my computer to attempt to communicate with minors, who in
> fact were not minors but undercover agents.*
>
> *Although I do not believe I had committed any crime, I accepted
> this plea in order to put this incident behind me and enable me not
> to have to put my family or myself through the risks and agony of a
> trial, as well as the high financial costs involved.*
>
> *The judge believed that this in no way should affect my ability to
> serve my clients and continue as a professional. He therefore granted
> me a Certificate of Relief from Civil Disabilities.*
>
> *You have indicated that you want me to serve as your accountant
> and representative and as one of your Executors and Trustees and in
> any other capacity you desire.*
>
> *Please indicate your agreement by signing below.*

With shaky handwriting, Huguette signed: H. M. Clark, 3-5-2009.

Executor? What an interesting title. A position that would undoubtedly involve huge fees to probate a multimillion-dollar estate. This
letter, once circulated to the Clark clan, set off new alarm bells about
the future of Huguette's fortune and the integrity of her accountant
and lawyer.

As the relatives' suspicions intensified, they pressed the Corcoran
to get involved. Corcoran director Paul Greenhalgh talked things
over with the museum's chairman, and the two of them agreed to stay
out of this familial dispute. They sent Wallace Bock a note saying that
the museum would not take sides. "Our view was that if Huguette
Clark wished to retain Irving Kamsler, we would do business with
him," explains Greenhalgh. "In terms of the family, I'm sure that
Carla is a lovely person and they were quite anxious that the family

heritage was done properly. But clearly there was a lot of money there, and those two men were the gatekeepers."

Since Huguette had passed the century mark and was believed to be worth hundreds of millions of dollars, the museum officials also suspected that this was the opening shot of what could become a full-fledged war. Why get involved and do anything that might upset Huguette Clark? The Corcoran hoped to be a beneficiary of her estate, too. Of course, for now, she was still among the living.

Chapter Three

Huguette's Walk
in Central Park

S he was fearless as a girl. Accompanied by her older sister Andrée, Huguette Clark gleefully sledded down a snowy hillside in Central Park near their father's Fifth Avenue mansion. At the Château de Petit-Bourg, the eighteenth-century estate her parents rented on the outskirts of Paris, she spent her days galloping about on horseback. On vacation in Hawaii, the well-traveled Huguette frolicked in the waves with Olympic swimming gold medalist Duke Kahanamoku. Afterward, the fifteen-year-old wrote to her father from Honolulu, "The surfing here is wonderful. I am learning to stand on those boards. I am so tan, I almost look like a Hawaiian."

Gordon Lyle Jr., a childhood friend who joined Huguettte at her family's Santa Barbara oceanfront estate, Bellosguardo, recalls, "She loved to swim." Now in a South Carolina nursing home, Lyle can still describe one beach scene when he was a young boy and witnessed Huguette, fourteen years his senior, in the water. "There was a big wave, she jumped up to avoid being rolled. That's where I saw her." What made the sight so memorable? The uninhibited Huguette was skinny-dipping.

But now as a centenarian, Huguette Clark scarcely had the energy to leave her bed. A genteel white-haired woman with blue eyes, she now requested warm milk at bedtime, embracing the calming comforts of childhood. Her weight had dropped below one hundred pounds. Each night she recited the Lord's Prayer out loud—impressing her caregivers by doing so in French, Spanish, and English. Born into the kind of wealth that allowed her to dictate the terms of her life rather than bow to the wishes of others, she was used to getting her way.

"She wanted to be in control," says Geraldine Lehane Coffey, an Irish immigrant who worked for Huguette as the night nurse. "She would only do what she wanted to do." But the doctors had been adamant in their instructions: the patient had to stand up and move to keep her heart active and muscles from atrophying. It was up to the nurses to make it happen.

These responsibilities fell on the shoulders of Hadassah Peri, who had a knack for cajoling her recalcitrant patient to comply with medical directives. But this time Hadassah turned for help to Huguette's longtime assistant, Christopher Sattler. Stationed at his employer's warren of apartments at 907 Fifth Avenue, Chris usually stopped by the hospital at 4 p.m. to bring items that she requested such as magazines, art and architecture books, and antique dolls from her collection. He always stayed to visit for at least a half hour to entertain "Mrs. Clark," as he called her, with news from the outside world.

The 102-year-old Huguette brightened when the handsome fifty-four-year-old with the rakish smile turned up. A graduate of Fairfield University with a passion for history, Chris had been working for her ever since his family's construction firm renovated her apartment in 1991 and Chris had been assigned to inventory her possessions. As the years passed, Huguette had watched with pleasure as he became a father, and he occasionally brought his wife, Joan, and two daughters to the hospital to see her. Her primary physician, Dr. Henry Singman, noted approvingly that Huguette and Chris Sattler had a "very nice relationship. He got along very well with her. He would sit down with her and start talking or musing and telling her stories."

With this convivial relationship in mind, Hadassah came up with the idea of converting Chris's daily arrival at the hospital into a new ritual. She asked him to come by earlier in the day, closer to noon, when her patient was likely to have more energy. When he knocked on the door of Huguette's room, Hadassah would announce, "Chris is here. It's time to go for a walk in Central Park."

The park was more than two miles away, and there was no limo waiting downstairs to whisk them there. Instead, Chris, nearly six feet tall and brawny, would help Huguette out of bed and, holding her frail arm, carefully escort her around the room, doing at least three laps. He would offer descriptive commentary as if they actually were taking a walk in the park: "Now we're going in at Sixty-Seventh Street, we're going to see the Obelisk."

Amused by the ruse, Huguette looked forward to these strolls. She wore a regulation-issued cotton hospital gown topped with one of her cashmere cardigans, white or a variation of blue to complement her eyes. Each day, Chris charted a different route based on the Central Park landmarks that his employer used to see from the windows of her apartment. "Maybe we should go to the bridle path? Now we're going up to Seventy-Ninth Street, then we'll have seven blocks to get back to your apartment." He would gently tease her, saying, "I hope you're not too tired from this long walk, Mrs. Clark."

She would circle her room, slowly, very slowly, but smiling as she traced the paths of her youth in her imagination. The hospital quarters, with white walls and a window without a view, served as a blank backdrop. Ever since her family had moved into her father's newly built 121-room Fifth Avenue mansion in 1911, the largest private residence in Manhattan, Central Park had been a constant in her life. Her vantage point changed after her father died and the house was sold. Twenty-year-old Huguette and her mother, Anna, moved five blocks south to a twelfth-floor apartment on Fifth Avenue at Seventy-Second Street, but the park vista remained a source of pleasure and inspiration.

Huguette had equipped one room in her apartment with a series of Rolleiflex cameras mounted on tripods facing Central Park. With telephoto lenses, she could zoom in to people watch, taking photos of children sailing their toy boats or couples seated on park benches. She had painted a striking picture of Central Park at night, lights twin-kling as seen from her apartment, with a Tiffany-style lamp glowing on a table by the windowsill. The painting expressed two contradic-tory juxtaposed longings that defined the artist: the beckoning eve-ning and the excitement of the city, set against the quiet allure and safety of staying at home.

Before she entered the hospital, Huguette had often rhapsodized during phone calls with her goddaughter, Wanda Styka, about the glorious park views and the statues whose names she knew by heart. The daughter of Huguette's painting instructor, Tadé Styka, Wanda called her godmother "Marraine," the French version of the honorific. "Marraine talked about how she could see the statue of the Pilgrim from her window," says Wanda, describing the 1884 bronze by sculptor John Quincy Adams Ward of a man leaning on a musket. Concerned that Huguette might miss that view, Wanda says, "I sent her a book on Central Park."

In the shorthand slang of a hospital ward, the other nurses quickly picked up on this new walking ritual. Whenever they wanted Huguette to get out of bed, they'd say, "It's time to do your Central Park." These strolls would spark memories, a century's worth of his-tory from a woman who remembered being evacuated from France by ship in 1914 after the outbreak of World War I. The heiress would regale Chris Sattler and her nurses with selected stories, giving them a glimpse of the formative years of her life. As an eighteen-year-old, she had relished the sight of twentieth-century progress, writing to her father on October 15, 1924, from Manhattan:

Dear Daddy,

...As I was having breakfast this morning, I happened to see a huge thing flying through the air that resembled a whale. It was a zeppelin, it ended its journey of 5,066 miles in 81 hours and 17 minutes. Isn't it marvelous when we come to think that a nine day trip on a ship can be made in three days by a zeppelin. Below her the city held its breath and gazed upward. She circled so low that it seemed she must impale her fragile sides on the spires of the highest buildings.

Now Huguette kept the blinds closed in her hospital room, shutting out the world. She had changed in the intervening years from an engaging and curious young girl to a mysterious recluse. It was not just age that had caused her to retreat to solitude. So much had happened, love but also heartbreak and betrayal, notoriety in the gossip columns, visits from the FBI—so many thrilling and terrifying memories that she did not choose to discuss, a lifetime of secrets.

But when she did reveal slivers of information about the past, her recall was remarkable. Even after Huguette entered her nineties, virtually everyone who encountered her noted that she was easily able to summon up dates and places, in better mental shape than her contemporaries. "Her memory was good, she was conversational," said her relative Paul Newell. "Unless there were issues of possibly not hearing something correctly, it was as if you were talking with a person who was maybe twenty or thirty years younger than she." Her night nurse, Geraldine Coffey, said, "Physically, she was very strong, for her age, she was incredible. Mentally, she was very strong, very smart—she was clever, she really was."

These days Huguette time traveled between the present and the past. Giggling like a mischievous schoolgirl, she described to Chris Sattler how she and her older sister Andrée played hide-and-seek in their father's mansion, hiding from their nannies in their favorite place, the bell tower. She often asked to look at her favorite photo album, focusing on childhood snapshots of family visits to Butte, Montana, that rough-and-tumble Western mining city where her parents first met.

She confided to the nurses that she sometimes thought she heard the strains of someone playing the piano. It was only in her mind. But music had been important throughout her life. Her mother, who studied the harp in Paris and Manhattan, practiced regularly at home, her older sister, Andrée, had played the piano, and Huguette had taken violin lessons and tried her hand at the harp. As a young woman, Huguette and her mother maintained their own box at the Metropolitan Opera. Her sparkling accoutrements for the opera— magnificent diamond-and-emerald necklaces and bracelets from Van Cleef and Arpels and Cartier—were now stored in a bank vault. These days, the radio in Huguette's room was usually tuned to the all-news station 1010 WINS, but sometimes she listened to classical music. She could still pick up fragments of melody.

————

The average patient stay at Beth Israel is five days, according to the hospital's statistics. Patients who need continued care are transferred to rehabilitation facilities or released to return home and to rely on private nursing care. But by 2008, Huguette Clark had been living at a Beth Israel–run hospital—initially at Doctors Hospital, the premier society medical facility on the Upper East Side, and now at Beth Israel's main building downtown—for seventeen years. Seventeen years! In that entire time, she had gone outside only twice: first to a dentist's appointment, and later, when Doctors Hospital closed in 2004, on a trip to the Sixteenth Street facility. The sun had not touched her face in more than a decade, and she never evinced a desire to go outdoors.

The curious thing was that for most of those seventeen years, Huguette Clark had been in good health. Only in recent years had she begun to suffer from the vicissitudes of extreme old age. She could have walked out of the hospital at any time or even left for just a few hours to go to a restaurant, see an opera, visit an art gallery, or take a chauffeur-driven jaunt around the city—all the pleasurable pastimes that she had enjoyed as a young woman. Instead, she turned down every invitation or suggestion to leave. Simply put, she was done with all that.

She had entered the hospital in 1991 to be treated for a serious case of skin cancer. Once she recovered, she decided that she wanted to stay in the hospital. This was a rich woman's whim, but the startling thing was that the hospital chose to accommodate her wishes. She did not have insurance but was willing to pay the going rate, plus donate substantial funds to the hospital.

Her admitting physician, Dr. Henry Singman, later wrote in a memo that he "strongly urged her to go home, talking with her nurses and with the promise that I would visit her home. This was never an acceptable option for her." Singman wrote his memo in 1996, belatedly putting his thoughts on paper five years later to justify the unprecedented decision to let Huguette remain in the hospital. "I already knew that we were dealing with a very wealthy woman who didn't appear to have any relatives or anybody else around her, and I suspected sooner or later there was going to be a problem," he later explained. He wanted a record because he thought there might be "relatives coming out of the woodwork, relatives that she didn't know coming out to look for her or to try to get money from her."

She was hiding in the hospital; it signified safety. She told her lawyer, accountant, and assistant not to tell anyone she was there. Her doormen at 907 Fifth Avenue were instructed to accept packages and flower deliveries as if she was still on the premises; Chris Sattler would bring mail and other items to the hospital. Huguette had no outside visitors other than her friend Suzanne Pierre. Despite how much Huguette cared for her goddaughter, Wanda, she did not even inform her that she was in the hospital, although they were in regular telephone contact. "She probably didn't tell me because she thought I'd be alarmed," says Wanda, a museum archivist based in the Berkshires. Wanda eventually learned about Huguette's whereabouts from Suzanne Pierre, but did not press her godmother for information out of respect for her privacy.

The situation was unorthodox. Huguette's living expenses ballooned as the years went by. The tab in 2007 alone was nearly $5 million: $850 per day for room and board at Beth Israel for a total of $3.1 million a year; and an additional $300,000 for round-the-clock private nurses plus doctors' bills. Huguette held on to three luxury properties, paying $260,000 a year in maintenance for her Fifth Avenue apartment complex, more than $1.2 million a year on her Santa Barbara estate, and $150,000 a year on her secluded twenty-two-room mansion in New Canaan, Connecticut. In noblesse oblige fashion, Huguette was still sending generous Christmas tips to the doormen at her apartment building even though she had never met most of them.

After her first few years in residence at the hospital, staffers no longer asked why she was still there—it was simply a fact of life. Thousands of patients rotated through Beth Israel, but Huguette was that rare constant, the woman who never left. She had become an urban legend. Dr. Louise Klebanoff, a neurologist at Beth Israel, had heard about this phantom figure for many years before she was asked by another doctor to examine Huguette in 2005. As Klebanoff recalled, when she met her patient, "I put two and two together, that the person I was consulting on was, in fact, the little old lady who lives in the hospital." Her impression of the patient? "She seemed, you know, cute as pie, little old lady, perfectly content..."

———

Life in a hospital room could have been dreary and claustrophobic. But Huguette had created a self-contained and busy life within these four walls. Ever since her parents had given her Jumeau and Bru dolls from France as a child, she had been a passionate doll and toy collector. She owned more than six hundred antique French porcelain dolls, and her interests had expanded to include wind-up antique automatons, Japanese Hina dolls, toy soldiers, Smurfs, and even Barbie dolls, plus all available accessories. Her collection encompassed nearly 1,200 dolls. She relished the thrill of the chase, the acquisitive urge. When catalogues arrived from Theriault's, the premier American doll auction house, she would page through them with anticipation, and then instruct her lawyer, Wallace Bock, to bid, spending up to $120,000 for a single doll. Auction days were exciting, and her staff got caught up in the drama, too. "She would wait by the phone for the outcome," says Chris Sattler. "She really enjoyed the outcome."

Bock found the bidding to be an unusual experience, since his client refused to specify a price limit. "Whatever it was, that was what we were going to pay for it," says Bock. He recalls Huguette's reaction when he put in an offer to Sotheby's for three times the asking price for a Japanese screen and was nonetheless outbid. "She was very upset. I had to go buy it from the person who bought it at the auction." Yet once her craving for possession had been satisfied, she usually did not feel the need to see what she had bought. "The screen was sent right to her apartment," Bock says. "All she saw was the picture in the catalogue. But she knew what she wanted."

Huguette had become the patron of an unusual art form: commissioning miniature historical French châteaus and Japanese castles. These complex projects could take years to finish, since Huguette had an idealized idea of perfection. "We were taking a real castle in Japan, which is a fortified building, and making it to scale down to one-sixteenth of an inch and everything had to be accurate," says Caterina Marsh, who runs the California import firm that Huguette used to hire artisans in Japan for this specialized work. Huguette scrutinized photos of works-in-progress and requested changes. "There were some interior panels in a Japanese home which are called fusuma," Marsh explained. "So we hired an artist to paint the fusuma, and Mrs. Clark didn't like the particular design on these doors, so we had to send drawings and find out which particular pattern she would like."

As part of her historical research for these projects, Huguette would ask Chris Sattler to bring her books from her vast home library or purchase new ones. She was perfectly happy spending hours reading her books or perusing the *New York Times*, *Newsweek*, and French magazines like *Paris Match* to stay au courant. Her interests were eclectic: she followed the Olympics but also had an ongoing interest in Japanese and European royalty, especially Princess Grace. As Chris Sattler marvels, "She never appeared bored."

With twenty-four-hour shifts of private nurses, Huguette was never alone and had turned her caretakers into a surrogate family. She would pepper the nurses and doctors with questions about their children. "She is the one always asking about our family," recalls Hadassah Peri. Huguette initially kept to herself when she first entered the hospital in 1991 but had become more outgoing as the years passed, taking an interest in anyone in the vicinity. As Peri added, "Not only us, everybody who is involved with Madame, even the housekeeper, even the person who come just to fix Madame television and keyboard."

For Huguette, her hospital room was her sanctuary. She wanted advance notice and control over who was allowed to cross the threshold. Dr. Henry Singman noted with a mixture of admiration and exasperation that she would refuse to meet hospital personnel—from medical specialists to interns—if she wasn't in the mood. "She would chase them away, she wouldn't see anybody," he said. "She was very particular who she allowed to talk to [her] and who she wouldn't."

So the surprise visit to Huguette's room by Ian Devine and Carla Hall was as welcome to her as a screeching car alarm. They had breached her fortress. Huguette was upset, and her protectors felt responsible for letting her down. She viewed the sudden interest in her by Carla and Ian as suspect. William Andrews Clark had bequeathed money to all of his children, but now Huguette was the only one left, and she believed these distant family members had an ulterior motive. Or as Huguette plaintively said to Chris Sattler, "They got their money. Why do they want mine?"

The money, it always came back to the money, that coppery patina that cast a shadow over William Andrews Clark's family, their friends, and their associates. The millions amassed by this American buccaneer had a life of their own, spawning tentacles of greed and corruption, multiple lawsuits over a century, and so many dysfunctional relationships that the boughs of the family tree had splintered. It sometimes seemed as if anyone who had even come into proximity to the Clark millions experienced an adverse reaction.

Rather than be grateful for any largesse, recipients consistently wheedled for more. Huguette had experienced money grabs before. She had established a $750,000 trust in 1964 ($5.6 million in today's inflation-adjusted terms) to support a California cousin on her mother's side of the family—Anna La Chapelle, her mother's namesake. The divorced cousin sent Huguette frequent letters asking for more cash and finally showed her appreciation in the late 1980s by hiring lawyers to try, albeit unsuccessfully, to break the trust. The heiress wrote frequent checks to Beth Israel's development office, but staffers also constantly cajoled her for more.

"She was a soft touch," says her lawyer, Wallace Bock. "Nobody ever asked her for money, but they would come with a hard-luck story and she would volunteer." Sharing her wealth was a bittersweet experience. Each year she gave large bonuses to her nurses for their loyalty but responded awkwardly when they expressed gratitude. As her night nurse, Geraldine Coffey, recalls, Huguette would always say the same thing: "Don't thank me, thank my father. I never earned a cent."

Chapter Four

The Copper King

The fortune that would become twenty-first-century tabloid fodder came into being some 150 years earlier in Montana, nearly two thousand miles away from Huguette's New York hospital bed. It tells you everything that you need to know about a played-out Western mining town when one of its major tourist attractions, complete with a $2 admission fee, is America's largest toxic waste site. The Berkeley Pit, the grim environmental legacy of open-pit copper mining, sits less than a mile from Butte's downtown city center. The vast mile-long man-made lake is filled with 40 billion poisonous gallons of metal residue and chemicals that continue to rise every year.

As seen from the viewing platform, the scene is ominously beautiful: the mysterious, murky depths that drop down a quarter of a mile, the striated rock outcroppings etched by explosives, the snow-tipped mountains in the distance. Muted clanking sounds can be heard from the operations of a copper mine nearby, still exploiting the earth's bounty.

Mining camps sprouted up here in the 1860s, and the street names attest to the city's metalcentric history: Gold Street, Copper Street, Quartz Street, Mercury Street, Silver Street, Platinum Street, Aluminum Street, and Iron Street. Walk around downtown and it's quiet—very quiet. Butte's population peaked at 100,000 in 1910, but now there are fewer than 34,000 residents. It is not a ghost town, but it feels that way after dark. Many street lots are eerily empty, abandoned and strewn with weeds, the result of suspicious fires during tough times when businesses were torched for the insurance money.

William Andrews Clark once reigned in Butte, controlling every vital city service. He came here in 1872 to inspect several mines believed to be played out and made fortuitous purchases that produced millions in copper riches. He became the city's dominant employer. He built the trolleys and owned the water system, the electric light company, prime real estate, and the newspaper, the *Butte Miner*. His merchant bank doled out loans on favorable terms to friends and denied them to enemies. Clark built and ran Columbia Gardens, a sixty-eight-acre amusement park with a carousel, a zoo, and greenhouses. Butte citizens might draw a salary from Clark's operations as his employees, but they paid it back to him for city services. His influence extended statewide as he spent lavishly to convince the Montana legislature to embrace his goals.

Clark's power—and how he used and abused it—made him an irresistible character not only for newspaper writers but for novelists. Clark is portrayed as the ill-concealed villain in Dashiell Hammett's 1929 novel *Red Harvest*, in which Butte is named "Poisonville." Hammett describes the smelters that had "yellow-smoked everything into uniform dinginess. The result was an ugly city...between two ugly mountains that had been all dirtied up by mining." Clark's doppelganger owns the town "heart, soul, skin and guts."

Residues of Clark's past still endure in modern-day Butte. On a corner lot near the top of a hill at 219 West Granite Street is the Copper King Mansion: Clark's grand thirty-four-room redbrick Victorian completed in 1888 for the then-astonishing sum of $250,000, more than $6 million today. The Clark mansion remained in the family until the 1934 death of the senator's son William Clark Jr. Now listed on the National Register of Historic Places, the home is open for tours and operated as a bed-and-breakfast.

The house is imposing from the street, but it's the elaborate craftsmanship inside that shouts *robber baron*. Sunlight streaks through colorful stained-glass windows, illuminating an ornately carved wooden staircase featuring flowers and birds from many nations,

ceilings with painted frescoes, parquet floors, and European chandeliers. The house was designed for entertaining with a sixty-two-foot
ballroom.

Clark built this showplace with his first wife, Katherine, relocating from the town of Deer Lodge, thirty-seven miles away. The
Clark family then included five children: Mary (born 1870), Charles
(1871), Katherine (1875), William Jr. (1877), and Paul (1880). (A sixth
child—Katherine's twin sister, Jessie—had died at age three, and
another child died at birth.) The Clarks ventured far afield, sailing off
for lengthy travels in Europe and establishing a second residence in
Garden City, Long Island. After his wife passed away in 1893, Clark
was mostly on his own in Butte, his children either grown or off in
boarding schools, when he became involved with the plucky teenage
girl, Anna La Chapelle, who would become his second wife and the
mother of two more daughters.

Those girls, Huguette Clark and her older sister Andrée, never
lived full-time in the house on Granite Street—they grew up in Paris
and then Manhattan—but visited Butte well into their teenage years.
Compared to the family's treasure-filled 121-room Fifth Avenue mansion, the Butte house was informal and relaxed, a place where children
could be seen and heard. Later in life, Huguette always cast a honey-
colored glow on her reminiscences as she paged through scrapbooks
of family photos. She often told Irving Kamsler about "how much she
loved her father, how he took good care of her, how close she was to
her mother."

Still, Butte was an odd place for a wealthy child: there were no
trees, bushes, or flowers in the Clark backyard, although the copper
king could certainly afford a gardener. The reason? The fumes from
William Clark's mining operations had killed all the vegetation in
the city. "There is a hell on earth; it is Butte, Mont.," declared the
Philadelphia Record in 1904. "Why do they call Butte the early realm
of Satan? Chiefly because roasting ores give off fumes of sulphur. This
smoke—the color of watered milk—sometimes gets as thick as a London fog. Not one green leaf ever flutters in Butte; nor does a sprig of
grass grow there."

Mines dotted residential neighborhoods in Butte. Just a few blocks from the Clark mansion, the remnants of a mine have been preserved as a historic structure, a distinctive huge black metal frame resembling an oil derrick. Miners called them by the evocative name "hanging gallows," since the mechanism lowered them hundreds of feet into the dark earth. Death came quickly in mines, via an explosion or a fire underground, or slowly from damage to miners' lungs, silicosis.

Small children are innocents, but as she grew up, Huguette could not help but become aware that her parents occupied a rarified world. The grimy miners coming off a shift passed right by the house where Huguette, in a frilly white dress and oversized white hat, smiled shyly as she posed for a photograph on the front porch with her dolls, the most reliable companions in her life. She lined up her dolls in a row as if giving them their marching orders and arranged them in mother-and-children scenes. Like a theatre director orchestrating the onstage action, Huguette took joy in the imaginary world of her dolls and her ability to control their inanimate lives. Just as other children invent make-believe friends, she gave her dolls names, a habit she would continue into her adult life.

Huguette had enough pride in her family heritage and fond memories of her time in Butte that many years later—in 1964— Huguette and an older half sister, Katherine Clark Morris, unsuccessfully tried to buy back their father's Granite Street home from a new owner, Anna Cote, who had turned it into a boardinghouse. They hoped to transform it into a historic monument, but Cote declined to sell.

Just two blocks from the Copper King Mansion is the second most famous house in Butte: a French-style château that William Clark built for his oldest son, Charles; it is now a museum. After graduating in 1893 from Yale—where he was notorious for "spending more money in one year at Yale than any man who had ever attended," according to the *Washington Post*—Charles Clark went to work for his father, holding well-paid positions in the mining conglomerate. But he was always best known as a rich man's spoiled son. A gambler who was fond of women and liquor, Charlie lost $20,000 in one night at roulette in Los Angeles in 1908, complaining to the police when gangsters harassed him to pay. He built a racetrack at his California estate, buying thoroughbreds (splurging $125,000 for Harry Payne Whitney's colt Whiskaway) and racing the horses under copper-colored silks. No matter how much money he had, it was never enough; he was sued repeatedly for nonpayment of bills. Even his indulgent father joked about his son's free-spending ways: William Andrews Clark once gave a shoeshine man a quarter tip. The ungrateful man complained that was a meager sum compared to the $5 tip left by Charlie Clark. According to oft-repeated Butte lore, William Clark replied, "Well, that's all right for Charlie. You see, Charlie has a rich father and I haven't."

William Andrews Clark was a regular presence in Butte until his death in 1925. His family then severed business ties to the city, selling Clark's holdings in 1928 to the Anaconda Copper Company (the company later responsible for the Berkeley Pit catastrophe). *Montana American* reporter Byron Cooney once asked Clark why he did not build a monument to himself in Butte. "Columbia Gardens is my monument," Clark replied. "Of the many business enterprises, it is the one I love best and it is practically the only one on which I lose money." The amusement park could have been donated to the city by William Clark's children in his memory, but they included it in the sale. Despite civic protests, Anaconda Copper later shut down Columbia Gardens, and a mysterious fire destroyed the remains.

Visitors to the Copper King Mansion in Butte are treated to an expurgated version of the family history. The owners, Anna Cote's children Erin Sigl and her brother John Thompson, have created a script for the tour guides. A recent version recites Clark's accomplishments and his "reputation as one of the hundred men who owned America." There is no mention of the darker elements of Clark's life. An unapologetic racist, as a senator he opposed efforts to allow more Chinese immigrants into this country, stating, "We should not allow what we call coolie labor to come into this country unrestricted."

The master of political backroom deals, a man willing to engage in bruising industrial battles, Clark was envied for his riches and reviled for his tactics. There are corrupt moguls who are charming enough to be forgiven, but Clark built a reputation for being just plain unlikable. "If the element of failure or near-failure ever touched him, it was in human relationships," wrote Mary Montana Farrell in her 1933 University of Washington master's thesis. (Her mother, a Butte native, was well versed in Clark lore.) "He seemed unable to make and keep friends, due to an innate penuriousness which characterized all his contacts with the public. If men admired his keen mentality, they hated his tight-fistedness."

———

For William Andrews Clark, the ultimate self-made man, his millions were the tangible symbol of his intelligence and cunning, and how he kept score. He relished recounting early tales describing how hard he worked to earn each copper penny. The grandson of Scots-Irish immigrants, Clark was born, literally, in a log cabin on January 8, 1839, near the town of Connellsville, Pennsylvania. His father, John, was a thirty-nine-year-old second-generation Presbyterian farmer, while his mother, Mary Andrews, twenty-three, was the daughter of a member of the Pennsylvania State Legislature.

As the second-born of eleven children, William Clark watched his family suffer when three younger siblings died, two as infants and then three-year-old George from whooping cough. As an adult, Clark was often described as cold and uncaring, but he learned at an early age the survival skills of stoicism and carrying on.

Like many children of nineteenth-century farmers, William Clark attended school for three months during the winter and spent the rest of the year helping out on the farm. Once he showed academic promise, his ambitious parents were willing to invest in his future, sending him and his older sister Sarah to the local Laurel Hill Academy.

In 1856, John Clark bought a larger farm near Bentonsport, Iowa, more than seven hundred miles away. As a seventeen-year-old, William helped his father till the new land and found paid work teaching at a local school. He used his savings to study law for two years at Iowa Wesleyan University in Mount Pleasant. His next stop was teaching school in rural Missouri. The Civil War erupted in 1861, but Clark did not feel obligated to join the Union cause. Instead he fled to Colorado in 1862 to join the gold rush.

He learned the rudiments of mining by working on another man's claim in the countryside near Denver. Rumors of lucrative spots in Montana led Clark and several companions to buy two yokes of cattle, a wagon, picks, shovels, and gold pans and set off for a sixty-day trip through the wilds. Shoshone Indians had recently attacked settlers in Wyoming. "Quite a number of emigrants had been killed," he later recalled in a speech to the Society of Montana Pioneers in 1917, "and afterwards, passing through that country we saw the newly-made graves of a number."

In Bannack, Montana, Clark and his partner, Lloyd Selby, ran into a saloon keeper who offered to pay them to trek alcohol to a new camp where gold had just been discovered. This request had profound repercussions for William Andrews Clark. As he watched the thirsty miners grab the marked-up booze, he realized just how much money could be made by selling supplies to men living miles from what passed as civilization. He filed away that observation as he and Selby purchased a claim in a small gulch and began prospecting, excavating dirt and hauling it to the Colorado Creek to wash in sluice boxes for the gold residue.

Clark later painted a romantic picture of that gritty time, highlighting the virtuous Sundays when he would contemplate nature and read poetry. "My partner, who was very fond of cards, usually passed the day and sometimes the night at the Dorsett camp, a mile below," he told the Montana Pioneers. "I usually spent Sunday mornings sauntering in the hills or mountains, looking for gold-bearing quartz ledges... frequently taking a book to amuse myself while reposing on some grassy plot under the shade of the majestic pine trees." His reading matter, or so he claimed, was the *Elements of Geology* plus a book on contract law and *The Poems of Robert Burns*. In telling the story of his life, William Andrews Clark always stressed that he was never a common workingman and had an educated sensibility.

Prospecting was backbreaking labor, and once the snows came, Clark took his stake of $2,000 in gold dust and began his career as a merchant. He went to Salt Lake City to buy supplies and spent twelve days on the road hauling those groceries back to the mining camp in

Bannack. As he told the Pioneers, "I had taken the risk of shipping quite a lot of eggs, well knowing they would freeze, yet they were admirably adapted for the making of 'Tom and Jerry,' which was a favorite beverage in Bannack, and I disposed of them at a price of $3.00 per dozen." (The British eggnog and brandy drink had been popularized in America by the noted bartender Jerry Thomas.) Clark's price was quite a markup, since eggs then cost roughly twenty-five cents per dozen.

He found moneymaking opportunities everywhere. Clark and a friend opened a store in a mining area near Helena, selling everything from New York butter to California lemons. Clark and his brother Joseph landed a contract to bring the U.S. mail from Missoula, Montana, to Walla Walla, Washington, making the nearly four-hundred-mile trip themselves by horseback and even snowshoe. He continued delivering marked-up goods to remote mining camps. His price gouging was resented by the miners, but Clark could set his own rates given the minimal competition. With profits rolling in, he came up with another gambit: making loans at the rate of 2 percent a month.

By 1869, at the age of thirty, Clark was a well-to-do man in search of a bride. Taking a trip with his mother to his childhood home in Pennsylvania, he courted a former classmate, Kate Stauffer. She came from a prominent local family; her father owned a manufacturing company. Her sister had married a man who would become the chief clerk of the U.S. Senate.

Clark and his bride took a meandering honeymoon train and stagecoach journey, stopping off in Chicago and St. Louis, eventually settling in the small Montana town of Deer Lodge. Their first child, Mary, was born in 1870, and Charles would follow a year later. Clark was known as ruthless, but his wife softened his image; she was appreciated for her "generous hospitality and sunny sociability," according to a newspaper account.

Clark joined with partners to establish a bank that bought up gold dust and shipped it to an assay office in New York at a sizable profit. Clark later spun that off into yet another banking venture,

W. A. Clark and Bro., bringing in his brother, James Ross Clark. Eleven years younger, Ross proved to be a valuable partner, willing to run the operations that his sibling amassed. William Andrews Clark realized that loan terms could be structured in ways that made it virtually impossible for a miner to repay on time. A default allowed his bank to snap up valuable property for pennies on the dollar.

In 1872, Clark ventured from Deer Lodge to Butte to examine shallow quartz mines reputed to be worthless. Taking an astute gamble, he bought the claims to four Butte mines. But before investing in expensive equipment, he decided that he needed to learn more about geology and the science of mining.

Taking a leave of absence from his bank, Clark moved to Manhattan to attend Columbia College's mining school, founded in 1864. Clark was so eager for knowledge that he was willing to take classes with undergraduates nearly half his age. The couple left their young children with family members in Pennsylvania so they could experience New York unencumbered.

The Clarks arrived in Manhattan, then a metropolis with nearly a million residents, during the post–Civil War boom when the city was rife with newly minted millionaires and served as a destination for those who had made their fortunes elsewhere. The 1872 guidebook *Lights and Shadows of New York Life*, by James McCabe, depicts the social-climbing follies of the nouveau riche, terming them the "Shoddyites." "They are ridiculed by every satirist, yet they increase," McCabe wrote. "They occupy the majority of the mansions in the fashionable streets, crowd the public thoroughfares and the Park with their costly and showy equipages, and flaunt their wealth so coarsely and offensively in the faces of their neighbors, that many good people have come to believe that riches and vulgarity are inseparable."

The Clarks, with their shiny new Montana fortune, fit right in with the Shoddyites. The couple had a hunger for culture, satisfied by the proximity of the newly opened Metropolitan Museum at Fifth Avenue and Fifty-Third Street. The new Grand Opera House featured the top talents of Europe, and the Knoedler Gallery's art exhibitions drew the monied social set. Clark would purchase many works at the

Knoedler in the years to come. During his studies at Columbia, he and his professors examined mineral samples from his newly purchased Butte mines, and the results confirmed his instincts: he had tapped into major copper veins.

Once back in Montana, Clark developed those mines, relying on modern technology to maximize their potential. He built a mill in Butte that used machinery to break down raw ore into metal residue, a process previously done by hand with a hammer. The environmental desecration accelerated when Clark built the first smelter in Butte to process raw ore. The smelter sent plumes of chemicals into the skies. The process of roasting ore in open pits made things worse. The miners, with their lungs damaged from their time underground, were especially vulnerable to deadly pneumonia. Vegetation dwindled down to only four trees in the entire city.

William Andrews Clark would later sing the praises of the pollution that his mining operations created. "I must say that the ladies are fond of this smoky city, as it is sometimes called," Clark told the Montana Constitutional Convention in a speech in the late 1890s, "because there is just enough arsenic there to give them a good complexion, and that is the reason that the ladies of Butte are renowned wherever they go for their good complexions." He added that Butte's physicians perceived the smoke as a "disinfectant" that destroys "the germs of disease."

Eager to provide his family with a sophisticated social milieu and probably cleaner air, Clark embarked on a European sojourn in 1878 and moved his wife and children to Paris. The City of Lights, a fashionable destination for the American upper class, had an expatriate community that included the Boston Brahmin Henry James and painters John Singer Sargent and Mary Cassatt. Kate and the children, who became fluent in French and German, spent three years in Paris (another son, Paul, was born in 1880), followed by two years in Dresden. Clark learned French and a smattering of other languages and began avidly collecting art. An absentee but indulgent father, Clark spent winters in Europe and the rest of his time in Montana or visiting his increasingly far-flung enterprises.

His parents never had the wherewithal to give him the Grand Tour of Europe, that British tradition embraced by wealthy Americans who sent their aristocratic young heirs on cultural tours to Roman ruins. So he belatedly gave it to himself. Clark took his family to Italy (Pompeii), Greece (Athens), and Turkey (Ephesis), and even took a steamer to Algeria. When the Clarks returned to America, Kate and the children settled on Long Island, while her husband went back to Butte to supervise construction of their mansion on Granite Street.

A trip to the 1884 New Orleans World Exposition led Clark to his next bonanza. Intrigued by a display of ore by Arizona's mineral department, he asked where the rocks were from. The source was the United Verde Copper Mine in Jerome, which the owners had been unable to make profitable after digging down one hundred feet. Clark purchased the mine for a pittance. Under his auspices, United Verde produced eight million pounds of high-quality copper per month at a time when demand for the metal was surging due to the newly invented telephone.

Clark was set on a collision course with another Montana mining titan: Marcus Daly, an upstart Irish immigrant with an even better eye for undervalued assets. Daly scored with a silver mine in Butte and then purchased an even richer copper mine, the Anaconda. He was backed by a syndicate that included George Hearst, the California mining magnate who was elected to the U.S. Senate and bankrolled the newspaper aspirations of his son William Randolph Hearst. Just as Clark put his money into developing Butte, Daly turned the tiny town of Anaconda, twenty-four miles from Butte, into his company town, building a courthouse and library and starting his own newspaper, the *Anaconda Standard*.

The two Montana moguls were opposites in appearance and personality. "William Andrews Clark is a little man with a big head," wrote the *San Francisco Call*. "He is as dapper as a fashion plate from his feet to his glossy hat. His tailor works wonders with his frock coats. Clark's fingers are manicured and not a hair lies awry on the bushy red thatch which covers his head." The newspaper wrote of his opponent: "Marcus Daly is big, broad-shouldered, deep chested and powerful. He is of mercurial and choleric Irish temperament, genial to friends, vindictive to an enemy, quick of speech and given to a lusty swear word on occasions."

William Andrews Clark and Marcus Daly hated each other so much that they were willing to spend millions of dollars to blacken each other's names and corrupt their fellow citizens. The origin of this feud has mystified historians, who cite possible causes ranging from insulting remarks the men made about each other to business deals gone awry. The feud went viciously public when William Andrews Clark was unanimously nominated in 1888 by Montana's Democrats as the territory's delegate to Congress. Daly was a Democrat but bolted his party to block Clark from winning. In this era before the secret ballot, Daly arranged for his Anaconda shift bosses to view and change miners' ballots in favor of Clark's Republican opponent.

Clark lost but he was undeterred in his effort to seek national office. In 1889, when Montana became a state, Clark made a bid to become one of its first senators. He lost again, this time amid charges that he and Daly both flagrantly bribed state legislators. Clark eked out revenge by orchestrating a vote by the state legislature to defeat Daly's efforts to shift the state capital from Helena to Anaconda.

As Clark schemed in Butte and plotted his political future, he and his wife, Kate, were living separate lives. She visited Montana but spent more time in Garden City or their suite in the luxurious Navarro Flats apartments on West Fifty-Eighth Street in Manhattan. In October 1893, Kate Stauffer Clark traveled to Chicago for the Columbian Exhibition in honor of the four hundredth anniversary of Christopher Columbus's arrival in America. The fair featured two hundred temporary pavilions designed by famous architects, the very first Ferris wheel, and gardens by Central Park designer Frederick Law Olmsted.

For Kate Clark, Chicago was a city with sentimental memories. On her honeymoon in 1869, she and her husband had stopped off in Chicago so he could purchase merchandise to sell to miners in Montana. Now twenty-four years later, she could see the sweeping changes in the city and in herself, transformed from a provincial single woman to the sophisticated wife of a multimillionaire and the mother of five children aged thirteen to twenty-three. Just two years earlier, she had presided over the Manhattan wedding of her oldest child, Mary, to Dr. Everett Mallory, with a guest list that included two senators (Delaware, New Jersey) plus financier Cyrus Field, a society-page testament to the family's upward mobility. Kate's mother, back home in Pennsylvania, was still alive, and Kate had every reason to anticipate watching the rest of her children walk down the aisle. The Butte friends who saw her at the Chicago exhibition would later report that she "looked the picture of health."

But after she returned to New York, Kate became feverish. William Clark was in Butte when he received a telegram announcing that his wife was ill but appeared to be rallying. He and his son Charles got on a train to New York, but they were delayed in Chicago. Clark learned by telegram that his wife was sinking rapidly. Before he could reach Manhattan, Kate died of typhoid fever at their Navarro Flats apartment at 10:30 a.m. on October 19, 1893.

William Clark shut down his Butte mines and banking office for a day. Clark's newspaper nemesis, Marcus Daly's *Anaconda Standard*, ran an obituary: "Of strong intellectual traits and of marked elegance in manner, cordial towards all yet entirely without affection toward people of whatever station in life, tactful yet always sincere, a delightful hostess, a faithful wife, a devoted mother and the gracious matron of a cultured home which found in her its chief adornment—such was Mrs. Clark." (The words "without affection" may have been a typo, meant to be "without affectation," but it is possible the writer, the typesetters, or even Marcus Daly subtly inserted the dig.)

Clark buried his wife in Woodlawn Cemetery in the Bronx, a four-hundred-acre spot with rolling hills known as New York's most prestigious final address. The large plot was in a serene central location, perched on a rise with a view. He hired the noted architecture firm of Lord, Hewlett and Hull to construct a $150,000 family-sized stately white mausoleum. Fluted Ionic columns support the soaring portico and stained-glass windows permit colored light to flow in, but the most distinctive element is a Beaux Arts bronze door designed in 1897 by Rodin disciple Paul Wayland Bartlett. Entitled *The Vision*, it features the mysterious likeness of a woman with long flowing hair and a windswept gown. Her head is slightly tilted and she gazes out at the world with sad, thoughtful eyes.

More than a century later, Clark's last surviving child, Huguette, continued to pay for a standing weekly order of fresh flowers to be delivered by a Bronx floral shop to the mausoleum, including holly wreaths for Christmas, lilies for Easter, pots of cheerful chrysanthemums, and special arrangements to honor the birthdays of family members.

Chapter Five

The Reinvention of Anna

In New York society, an upper-class British or French accent has long added cachet, conveying Old World elegance and culture. When Anna Evangelina La Chapelle Clark, the mother of Huguette Clark, entertained in her Fifth Avenue apartment in the 1930s and 1940s, guests came away convinced that she was originally from Paris. The impeccable widow of Sen. William Andrews Clark served French food, and her décor included Louis XIV antiques and Impressionist paintings. The guests at her chamber music concerts or dinners were often from France—such as harpist Marcel Grandjany—or conversed with her in French, like Polish portrait painter Tadé Styka.

"I always assumed that she was French," says Leontine "Tina" Lyle Harrower, now in her late eighties, who spent childhood Sundays wearing white gloves to attend four-course lunches at the home of her godmother Anna, known by the nickname "Lani." "It never occurred to me that Lani was born in the States," says Harrower, now based in British Columbia. "She had a very marked French accent when she spoke English. I was totally shocked when I learned just recently about her past."

Harrower's older brother, Gordon Lyle Jr., was also under the impression that Anna was foreign-born, asking even now—"Was she French?"—and expressing surprise at the answer. Dr. William Gordon Lyle, the father of Tina and Gordon, had been the chief physician to Senator Clark and his family. "Lani was an absolutely wonderful woman, poised and charming," says Lyle Jr. His imagination was sparked by Anna's description of her husband's Wild West past. As Lyle Jr. recalls, "She told me that when the senator used to go to bed for the night, he always put a pistol under the pillow."

Anna Clark was more than a turn-of-the-century adornment for a business magnate; she was a master of reinvention. The patina of money plus a Parisian education smoothed over the rough edges of her frontier Montana upbringing. As a result, she was the shimmering picture of refined glamour in middle age, adorned with diamonds, emeralds, and rubies that were compared favorably in the press to the jewels worn by Astors and Vanderbilts.

Anna was not pretentious but she was proper, impressing on the children of her friends the importance of etiquette as if to train them as she had been trained. "Lunch there was always such an ordeal because I had to have such good manners," says an octogenarian who was a child when her parents socialized with Anna. "I can see the dining room, where Lani sat, where I sat. She had so much silver and gold cutlery and I was absorbed with that. She spoke French fluently, which I had to do when I was with her. But she was sweet and real and loving."

Anna never tried to hide her Montana girlhood. But as the years went by it had become ancient history—unknown to most New Yorkers—so this sophisticated woman with a mischievous sense of humor could enjoy the hard-won status that she had achieved in upper-crust Manhattan. If exquisite manners and a French accent gave people the illusion that she was wellborn, so be it.

In truth, Anna's accent had a less glamorous origin than the boulevards of Gay Paree—her parents were French-Canadian Catholics from Montreal. Her father, Pierre (who often used the Americanized version, Peter) La Chapelle, claimed to have trained as a physician at a medical school in Montreal, at least according to a bio in *Progressive Men of the State of Montana*. After he married the farmer's daughter Philomene Rock de Dubie, the couple moved to Calumet, Michigan, where Anna was born in 1878. She had two younger siblings: sister Amelia, born in 1881, and brother Arthur, born in 1883.

When Anna was ten years old, the family moved to Butte and Peter set up a practice as a physician. Two years later he got into trouble with local authorities for practicing medicine without a license. ONE OF BUTTE'S FAKIRS FOUND GUILTY BY A JURY, trumpeted a headline in the November 14, 1890, *Anaconda Standard*. At the trial, an engineer testified that La Chapelle had professed to be a doctor and treated his wife for an illness; a pharmacist showed prescriptions written by La Chapelle. A member of the board of medical examiners stated that La Chapelle had never applied for a license. If Peter La Chapelle did indeed have Canadian medical training, this would have been the moment to present his documentation. But he did not testify, and his lawyer offered no defense witnesses. The jury returned a guilty verdict in fifteen minutes: the defendant was fined $100 and told to find another profession. La Chapelle hung out a shingle as an eye specialist, listing his profession as "oculist."

Anna's mother, Philomene, ran a boardinghouse in the seedier part of town on East Park Avenue, close to Butte's bars and brothels. The wide-open city was infamous for its whorehouses on "Venus Alley" servicing the miners and the well-to-do. The La Chapelle family was on the downhill slide. Anna was a pretty teenager with long, lustrous hair, blue eyes, a high forehead, and a serene smile, and her performances in school plays had been favorably received. Her practical sister, Amelia, enrolled in secretarial school and her brother, Arthur, worked as an elevator operator in an office building. And then— suddenly—everything changed.

What brought Anna La Chapelle and William Andrews Clark together? Historians have relied on a spitefully entertaining 1904 account in the *Anaconda Standard*. Anna is portrayed in this article as a brazenly ambitious fifteen-year-old who went searching for a sugar daddy in the early 1890s.

"About nine or ten years ago," the *Standard* wrote, "a little golden haired girl of prepossessing appearance walked into the banking house of James A. Murray in this city, and without much ceremony, asked Mr. Murray to bear the expense of her education, adding that he was wealthy...At that time, she possessed an ambition to become an actress...Mr. Murray did not know the girl and had never heard of her, so he declined to accept the girl's invitation to help her."

According to the article, the altruistic banker suggested that she contact William Andrews Clark, telling Anna, "Mr. Clark was unmarried, had plenty of money and would undoubtedly help her along the road she desired to travel. Miss La Chapelle then asked Mr. Murray if he would introduce her to Mr. Clark and he declined..."

The problem with this tantalizing account is that it ignores the classic tenet of journalism: consider the source. The owner of the *Anaconda Standard* was Marcus Daly, who despised William Clark. The newspaper staff delighted in running stories aimed to embarrass the Butte copper mogul. James Murray, a gambler turned millionaire mine owner, was one of Marcus Daly's close friends, and he ran a bank that competed for business with Clark's bank. Murray was a Republican, and his name was floated as a potential rival to William Andrews Clark for a Montana Senate seat.

Yes, maybe Anna La Chapelle strolled into a rich banker's office and tried to insinuate herself into his good graces. But the article is equally likely to reflect the yellow journalism efforts of William Clark's enemies to tarnish the reputation of his beloved.

William Clark's version also strains credulity. Clark claimed that he first spied Anna La Chapelle at a July Fourth parade in 1893, a few months after the death of his wife. Anna, an appealing beauty, was dressed in a toga to portray the Goddess of Liberty. The age gap between them was thirty-nine years—she was young enough to be his grandchild. After the parade, Clark made inquiries and met her parents. "Anna La Chapelle early displayed an unusual musical talent," he later told reporters. "She was bright and studious. I encouraged her inclination for study by placing her in the young ladies' seminary at Deer Lodge, of which institution I was a member of the executive board."

Clark became an enthusiastic backer of not just Anna but her entire family. The copper king paid for her father's tuition at a genuine medical school in Chicago and her sister Amelia's education at St. Mary's Academy in Salt Lake City, followed by a stint at the National Park Seminary in Forest Glen, Maryland. The youngest member of the family, Arthur La Chapelle, became a timekeeper at one of Clark's mines.

In August 1895, all three La Chapelle siblings performed at Maguire's Opera House in Butte at a well-attended show called "Dream of Fairyland." Anna displayed her graceful physique with a Spanish dance. Amelia played an orphan in a skit, and Arthur sang the aptly named song, "I Am Not Old Enough to Know."

After Anna graduated from high school, Clark offered her a trip to Paris to study the harp under the auspices of Alphonse Hasselmans, a professor of harp at the National Conservatoire of Music. To reassure Anna's parents of his virtuous intentions, Clark came up with a chaperone—his sister, Lizzie Clark Abascal.

Lizzie was married to one of William Clark's closest friends, Joaquin Abascal, an older, well-to-do Spaniard who ran mining and mercantile businesses in the small town of Bear Gulch, Montana. The parents of two daughters, Lizzie and her husband split their time between Montana and Los Angeles. As William Clark would later tell reporters, "Anna had shown such disposition for the study of music and languages that I sent her abroad with my sister, Mrs. Abascal, who was going to Paris to educate her daughters."

Paris was such a de rigeur destination that the *Chicago Daily Tribune* chronicled the goings-on of expatriates in an 1893 feature, AMERICANS IN PARIS: BRILLIANT WOMEN WHO LIVE IN THE FRENCH CAPITAL. The article described the opulent homes occupied by the likes of Mrs. Joseph Pulitzer and the competitive social circuit revolving around literary salons, art exhibitions, and "tender philanthropies." "Many old and well-known American families have been or are represented in Paris," the newspaper noted, reeling off a list including Vanderbilts, Winthrops, and Morgans. Anna's trip to France was planned as a short-term educational tour to enhance her musical abilities and give her language skills an upper-class polish. Instead, Paris would end up becoming Anna's home for more than fifteen years.

Clark visited Paris in March 1896 to see his protégée, but their happy reunion was cut short when Clark received devastating news: his sixteen-year-old son, Paul, had died of a strep infection while at boarding school in Andover, Massachusetts. Paul was his father's favorite, a rugged, manly boy who planned to study law. Clark sailed back to New York, burying his son at Woodlawn Cemetery in the family mausoleum. In Butte, he underwrote the Paul Clark home, a refuge for orphans. The robber baron would often stop by around Christmas bearing gifts for the orphans, according to newspaper accounts, and tear up at the memory of his son.

Clark had mercurial relationships with his two surviving sons from his first marriage. Like so many self-made men, he had high expectations for his progeny. His well-educated oldest son, Charles, dabbled in the family enterprises but his second son, Will Jr., made more of an effort to live up to his father's name as a lawyer and businessman. Despite their sophisticated upbringing in Europe and at elite boarding schools and colleges, both of Clark's sons fell for small-town Butte girls from undistinguished backgrounds. William Clark showed his paternal disdain by skipping the wedding in July 1896 of his son Charles to legal stenographer Katherine Roberts. The copper mogul sent his regrets along with a $100,000 check. He always publicized his gifts to his children, flaunting his wealth.

Rather than attend his son's wedding, William Clark chartered a private train in Butte to take him to Chicago in July 1896, as a delegate to the Democratic Convention. The events of the next few days would have embarrassing repercussions for him. At the raucous convention, William Jennings Bryan, a young Nebraska congressman, gave his "Cross of Gold" speech championing silver coinage. On the fifth ballot, Bryan won the Democratic nomination. (He would lose to William McKinley.) Clark was a Bryan man for a simple reason: the potential boost in the value of silver mines.

At the hotel housing the Montana delegation, Clark noticed a pretty young New Yorker, Mary McNellis, who identified herself as a newspaper correspondent. They struck up a conversation and discussed having dinner. Clark was favorably impressed, later describing her as "rather agreeable and highly intelligent."

A few weeks later, Clark checked into the Waldorf Hotel in Manhattan, a fact mentioned in the *New York Times* (HOME NEWS: PROMINENT ARRIVALS IN HOTELS, July 26, 1896). The enterprising McNellis dropped by and sent up her card. Clark came right down and took her for drinks in the hotel's Turkish room, a romantic setting with plush banquettes. Dinner, gifts, and other assignations followed.

An ocean away in Paris, Anna La Chapelle was in mourning for her father, who had died unexpectedly of a stroke at age forty-nine in the spring of 1896. But despite her grief, she had no desire to return to Butte and her old life. Now accustomed to living in luxury, Anna had taken to the harp as a serious student and had a circle of talented and noteworthy friends. Her entrée was eased by William Andrews Clark's generosity as a patron of the arts. He gave large sums to the American Art Association of Paris to support exhibitions and prizes; the judges included sculptor Augustus Saint-Gaudens and painter Jean Charles Cazin. Clark purchased two nude sculptures directly from Auguste Rodin and a striking painting by Edwin Austin Abbey, *Who Is Sylvia? What Is She, That All the Swains Commend Her?*

Anna was soon accompanied by a new live-in chaperone, Madame de Cervellon, whose expenses were paid by William Clark. Clark would later pointedly praise Madame de Cervellon's respectable credentials, referring to her as "a woman of education and means, the widow of an officer of the French Army." The widow played the delicate role of intermediary, a confidant to Anna and a spy for her benefactor, reporting back to Clark when other men expressed interest. Madame de Cervellon was worldly enough to look the other way at the sexual overtones between the visiting Clark and his young protégée.

As a widower, Clark was free to remarry. But he found it preferable to have a young paramour stashed away in Paris, keeping his private life private, while he once again pursued what he saw as his manifest destiny—a seat in the United States Senate.

The 1899 Montana Senate race cemented Clark's reputation as a man willing to do anything—bribe, threaten, risk public ridicule—to get what he wanted. This race was one of several turn-of-the-century election scandals that led to the country's ratification of the Seventeenth Amendment in 1913, taking away the power of state legislatures to elect senators and mandating a popular vote.

To influence political coverage, Clark bought Montana newspapers (the *Great Falls Tribune*, the *Helena Herald*), gained leverage over others by making investments or purchasing their debts, and sent emissaries around the state to directly grease the palms of key editors and writers. "The spree of bribery and newspaper buying that accompanied William A. Clark's push for the Senate made most charges of journalistic prostitution seem plausible," wrote historian Dennis Swibold in *Copper Chorus: Mining, Politics, and the Montana Press, 1889–1959.*

When the Montana State Legislature convened in January 1899, Clark set up his headquarters at the Helena Hotel. Since he did not want to be seen making questionable deals, he brought in his twenty-six-year-old son Charles as a bagman. Charles Clark took on the job with filial enthusiasm, declaring in an oft-repeated but perhaps apocryphal quote, "We'll send the old man to the Senate or the poor house." State Senator Fred Whiteside promptly threw a grenade into the race when he plausibly claimed that Clark's allies had given him $30,000 for his vote and that of two other legislators. Clark claimed that this charge was a setup by Daly.

A Helena grand jury launched an inquiry (finding that the evidence was inconclusive) even as the balloting continued. During the eighteen days that the Montana legislature wavered, Clark's son and his other allies reputedly offered enticements to Democrats and Republicans for their votes—deeds to valuable real estate, new jobs, debt repayment, and good, old-fashioned bundles of cash.

After Clark finally won the election, he celebrated by giving the citizens of Helena free unlimited champagne at the bars. The newly anointed senator was not scheduled to take office until January 1900, which gave Marcus Daly nearly a year to regroup. Daly filed charges of corruption with the Senate Committee on Elections, which began an investigation.

Witnesses trooped from Montana to Washington to testify in the winter of 1900. With the capital mesmerized by the corruption charges, there was tremendous interest in this eligible widower poised to be the richest man in the Senate. A syndicated story hit the wires on March 19 announcing that Clark would soon be married. "Gossips say Miss Ada La Chappelle, Protegee of Copper King, Will Probably Become His Bride," trumpeted the *Chicago Daily Tribune.* The femme fatale was described as "tall, dark and slender, with a typical French face and the great soulful eyes which are associated with artistic temperament."

The story was rife with errors, including the name of the supposed bride: not only was there no "Ada," but the background description and accompanying sketch fit Anna La Chapelle's sister, Amelia, now attending finishing school in Forest Glen, Maryland, and training as a vocalist.

Clark indignantly denied the marital rumor and stressed that he was a father figure to both La Chapelle sisters, insisting, "I would as soon think of marrying one of my own daughters." But stories about the romance kept appearing with salacious variations. The *Pharos-Tribune* of Logansport, Indiana, wrote, "There has been much gossip about Miss La Chappelle, most of it to the effect that she once began a breach of promise suit against her benefactor." The newspaper delicately added, "Somewhat different rumors, which are not so flattering to the copper king, are persistently circulated." The *Davenport Daily Republican* insisted that Clark's children vehemently disapproved: "Mr. Clark's daughters have been opposed to his marriage to so young a wife."

Amelia La Chapelle was so upset that she fled the Washington suburbs to return to Butte. A second round of articles followed, claiming that the feisty Amelia was going to marry former Montana senator Lee Mantle. "This is the first I have heard of it," Mantle responded, diplomatically adding, "and unfortunately for me there is not a word of truth in it."

While gossip columnists feasted on this family drama, Clark was on Capitol Hill, facing his accusers. He was so confident that he would prevail that he purchased "Stewart's Castle" on Massachusetts Avenue near Dupont Circle, a four-story mansion built by Nevada senator William Stewart. But Clark's election trophy was snatched away when he was unable to convince the Senate that he had won the election legitimately. SENATE COMMITTEE AGAINST MR. CLARK, blared the *New York Times* on April 24, 1900. DECISION BASED ON BRIBERY. REPORT SAYS CLARK IN HIS TESTIMONY ADMITTED CORRUPT PRACTICES BY HIS AGENTS.

Clark resigned before he could be thrown out. Then the crafty mogul tried to make an end run. Montana governor Robert Smith was lured to California on a business trip, and Lt. Gov. A. E. Spriggs used his temporary power as Montana's highest official to appoint Clark to the empty Senate seat. Crying fraud, the outraged governor named his own candidate. The Senate adjourned without acting on either appointment, leaving the Montana Senate seat vacant.

Some humiliated office seekers might have opted for a low profile after such a searing defeat. But William Andrews Clark threw an extravaganza of a wedding in Manhattan on May 28, 1900, for his daughter Katherine to Dr. Lewis Rutherfurd Morris, the scion of a family who traced its lineage back to a Founding Father. Clark invited four thousand guests including President McKinley, Cabinet members, generals, and fellow robber barons J. Pierpont Morgan and E. H. Harriman. (The La Chapelle sisters did not make the cut.) Crowds thronged St. Thomas Church on Fifth Avenue to see the dignitaries. The reception was held at Clark's apartment at the Navarro Flats on West Fifty-Eighth Street, where the lines for the elevators were so long that many people walked up seven flights. As a Hungarian orchestra played, guests could scarcely make it through the melee to reach the sumptuous buffet tables.

Clark had already decided that his residence at one of New York's premier buildings—featuring seven-bedroom duplexes with extra-high ceilings and Gothic and Queen Anne architectural details—was not sufficient to display his burgeoning art collection. After purchasing land on Fifth Avenue at Seventy-Seventh Street, he began planning a French-style mansion that would rival the palaces of the Astors and Vanderbilts.

Returning to Butte, Clark plotted another zigzag route to take him back to Washington and a Senate seat. He teamed up with mining mogul Augustus Heinze, and the duo came up with a plan to stack the Montana legislature with like-minded Democrats. They courted the labor vote by announcing that they would grant their miners an eight-hour day. Then Clark went off to Europe to spend two months with Anna. In the November 1900 election, the Clark-Heinze slate of Democrats won the statehouse by a landslide. In January 1901, the new Montana legislature elected Clark to the Senate seat he had long craved.

The most widely quoted description of the robber baron's political career came from Mark Twain, a friend of Marcus Daly, and therefore not an entirely objective source. Twain excoriated Clark in 1907 as the epitome of corruption: "He is said to have bought legislatures and judges as other men buy food and raiment... he is as rotten a human being as can ever be found anywhere under the flag; he is a shame to the American nation and no one has helped to send him to the Senate who did not know that his proper place was the penitentiary, with a ball and chain on his legs."

Rumors spread that the Montana senator would be arriving in the capital with a bride. A new name emerged: Hattie Rose Laube, of Huron, South Dakota, announced that she was engaged to Senator Clark, claiming that they had kissed and that he had written her a letter proposing matrimony. Clark issued a public denial. Even the *Anaconda Standard*, which gleefully trumpeted Clark's every peccadillo, sided with him, stating that the stunt appeared designed to advertise "her pa's spiritualism racket..."

Other tales of Clark's romantic entanglements circulated. The copper mogul had taken under his wing a new Montana protégée, Kathlyn Williams, an acting student at Montana Wesleyan College who had appeared in Butte productions. Another hard-pressed teenager (her father had died), Kathlyn had approached the senator and asked him to pay for her tuition at the Sargent School, now known as the American Academy of Dramatic Arts in New York. Kathlyn was later described as the senator's "ward" by the *Washington Post*. She publicly credited Clark for his financial support but was discreet about their relationship. The blonde ingenue would go on to become a silent film star, appearing in dozens of serials and movies such as *Rendezvous at Midnight*, *Everything for Sale*, and *The Politician's Love Story*.

In the fall of 1901, Anna La Chapelle was seen in Washington, staying at the Arlington Hotel and being entertained by the senator's friends, including the sister of his first wife. Then Anna moved to Butte temporarily, sharing an apartment with her sister, Amelia, within easy walking distance of Clark's Granite Street mansion.

Anna had now been involved with the copper mogul in some fashion for eight years. Whether on purpose or by accident she became pregnant. On February 6, 1902, she was accompanied by Amelia on a ship to France, and then she headed south to a villa near the Bay of Algiers with the ever-loyal Madame de Cervellon. In August 1902, Anna gave birth to Louise Amelia Andrée Clark, known as Andrée. The news was kept so quiet that not even a hint of a new Clark descendant was heard back in America. In fact, the *San Francisco Chronicle* ran an article that month announcing: "Rumor is persistent that Senator W. A. Clark of Montana will marry during the coming autumn or winter either the widow of a well-known New Yorker of distinguished lineage or the recently divorced wife of a Missouri Congressman." The story drily commented that the senator had a "partiality" for the ladies and "is constantly credited with being about to marry this or that prominent woman in whose company he may have been seen."

His fortune made him attractive, and the senator knew how to charm women. He was able to knowledgeably discuss art and literature—he collected rare books—as well as business. But he was deeply in love with Anna, a bond that would only become stronger through the years. Two decades later, he would still be writing impassioned letters to his "Darling Wife" and "Sweetheart Cherie" and "Ma Chere Anna," signing them "fondest love."

Even as Anna was giving birth to her first child, Andrée, Clark's children from his first marriage were preparing their own engraved birth announcements. (These children were the grandparents and great-grandparents of the Clark relations who, a century later, would express interest in Tante Huguette.) Clark's oldest daughter, Mary, had given birth several years earlier to a daughter. Now his second daughter, Katherine Clark Morris, was pregnant; plus his son and namesake Will Jr., a University of Virginia law school graduate, and his new wife, Mabel Foster, were also expecting.

Senator Clark took sibling rivalry to new heights by promising $1 million to his first male grandchild. Katherine gave birth to a girl, but a month later, Mabel produced William Andrews Clark III, nicknamed Tertius. Will Jr. jubilantly wired his father: "I claim the million!" But the celebration was short-lived. Mabel became ill with blood poisoning and died a month later.

Although William Andrews Clark had been obsessed with winning entry to the world's most exclusive club, as the Senate was known, once the prize was attained he was more interested in enlarging his financial empire than bothering with the details of crafting legislation. Constantly traveling, he went to Russia to look at potential mining acquisitions; visited Paris to see Anna and purchase paintings, tapestries, and antique lace; headed to Los Angeles to check on his widowed mother and meet with his brother Ross to inspect their new sugar beet farms; and traveled to Arizona and Montana to look in on his mining operations. He spent many hours hammering out the settlement of a long-running fight with E. H. Harriman over constructing a railroad from Salt Lake City to Los Angeles. Clark chose a dusty Nevada outpost as a railroad refueling stop, which was incorporated as Las Vegas. Grateful Nevada citizens christened the area Clark County. The *Los Angeles Times* gushed in a headline: W.A. CLARK THE BUSIEST MAN IN THE SWIM.

His triumphant march through the business pages hit a snag, however, with the eruption in April 1903 of a long-brewing scandal. Mary McNellis, the New Yorker whom he had wined and dined back in 1896 at the Chicago convention, went public with the details of her $150,000 breach-of-promise lawsuit against him. McNellis complained that her lawsuit, filed many years earlier, had been unfairly dismissed in secret proceedings and demanded a new trial. An irate Clark announced, "I would rather stand publicity than give up money when I am innocent." In McNellis's version, Clark had been a frequent caller at her Forty-Second Street apartment, helped her with her German lessons, and sent her notes signed "Votre ami." Clark admitted that he'd met McNellis four times and had been fond of her but was offended when he began receiving letters from her lawyer "trying to induce me to pay money. I would not submit to the demands and I will not do so now." Clark prevailed and the lawsuit was thrown out.

At the end of 1903, William Andrews Clark was in a reflective mood. Anna La Chapelle had become pregnant again earlier that year but this time the baby—a boy—died within an hour of his birth in France. Anna's place in the senator's life remained a secret, so his children and colleagues were unaware of the loss of the child.

Sitting in his Wall Street office, the senator gave an unusually candid interview to the *Dallas Morning News* (SENATOR W. A. CLARK, CROESUS, TELLS ABOUT HIMSELF). Clark came across as a lonely and self-important man consumed by work yet eager to be admired for his good taste as a patron of the arts. "His shoulders are spare, his frame is lean, his features are sharply cast. He has the eyes of an eagle," the writer noted. "It was his quiet demeanor, his soberness, his seriousness which can, if necessary, give way to dramatic and forceful denunciation, which impressed me."

Clark described himself as an early riser, up for an energetic stroll around his Central Park neighborhood at dawn and finished with breakfast by 8 a.m. He often walked from his Fifty-Eighth Street apartment down to Wall Street for the exercise and at night avoided rich meals, limiting himself to one cigar and poring over business until late at night. "So what if I do work twelve, fourteen and sixteen hours a day?" the sixty-four-year-old Clark said, emphasizing that he still felt like a young man. "I can do good by working. Thousands of men and women are depending upon my energies for their bread and butter."

He cited two great passions: fine European wines that he took with him by the case when traveling, and splurging on art. "I was born with the innate love of the beautiful in nature and in the arts," he said, bragging that he had sixty-four masterpieces in storage in Vienna awaiting the completion of his Fifth Avenue mansion. He stressed that he had rarely relied on art advisers and instead relied on his own taste and judgment. (Which may explain why the Corcoran Gallery later identified numerous fakes in his collection.) Reciting the countries where he had toured galleries and museums—England, France, Germany, Belgium, Spain, Italy, and Holland—Clark said, "I acquired a distinctive perception and correct notions and taste in painting, sculpture, architecture and other beautiful arts."

With a nod to his children, he mentioned that in his rare time off, he took pleasure in the Sunday afternoon musicales given by his two Manhattan-based daughters, Katherine and Mary, as well as attending the opera.

Asked about his philanthropic plans, Clark gave a surprisingly honest answer, noting that he especially liked to help young women. "I find that a direct application of aid to young people—especially girls without means—to prepare themselves for the unequal struggle in life is fruitful in gratifying results," Clark said. Gratifying indeed, judging by the devotion expressed toward him by Anna La Chapelle.

The journalist ended the interview by asking Clark whether he would follow in the footsteps of three other senators who, "in the autumn of their lives," had recently wed. Clark laughed at the question, replying, "I can not tell you how happy I was with my beautiful wife, who died in 1893. I believe in marriage when one can afford that luxury, but I am not seriously considering it." Then he added, with another chuckle, "I am quite too young to think of it yet."

————

A few weeks later, Clark was reminded of his own mortality when he developed mastoiditis, an acute ear infection that spread into his skull. With a high fever and intense pain, Clark underwent two operations and was confined to bed for several weeks at his New York apartment. Even as he was recovering, tragedy struck the family yet again. The wife of his son Charles, who was visiting friends and staying at the Algonquin Hotel in New York, became ill and died suddenly in January 1904. Both of Clark's sons had now become widowers, within just two years of each other.

In April, word spread that Clark was on his deathbed. MODERN CROESUS A VERY SICK MAN. CLARK MAY NOT LIVE TO RETURN TO BUTTE. HIS WEALTH, ESTIMATED FROM $50,000,000 TO $200,000,000, LIKELY TO GO TO HIS SONS AND DAUGHTERS AND HIS GRANDSON, W.A. CLARK III was the headline of the April 22, 1904, story in the *Minneapolis Journal*. The article noted that the senator had recently had a falling-out with his namesake lawyer son. "It has been reported in Butte for a year or more that W. A. Clark Junior has become estranged from his father and the rest of the family and certain things have happened to lend color to this report." (The reason for the estrangement never became public, but years later a Clark family retainer went public with a vivid description of Junior's energetic sexual pursuit of attractive young men.)

The deathbed reports were exaggerated, but Clark's health remained poor. Clark sailed to Europe on the American liner *Princess* with plans to cruise the Mediterranean, announcing that he was taking a trip that might last seven weeks to "put the finishing touch" on his convalescence. Anna joined him.

By now, William Andrews Clark had painted himself into a corner in terms of his relationship with Anna La Chapelle. He had repeatedly insisted publicly that the relationship was platonic. He had lied to his four older children, neglecting to mention his bouncing new baby, Andrée. He told the Dallas newspaper that he had no plans to remarry.

But Clark had decided that he was ready to officially acknowledge Anna in his life as his wife. He was sixty-five years old, and there was never going to be a good time to explain their tangled past. But before he went public, he needed to break the news to his children. Clark's dilemma: finding a palatable way to explain the existence of his and Anna's nearly two-year-old daughter. There was only one quasi-respectable solution: backdate the year of a supposed wedding and claim it occurred prior to Andrée's birth.

On June 30, the senator returned from Europe and met with his two daughters, Katherine and May, to apologetically break the news of their new stepmother and half sister. Katherine described her reaction to this painful revelation in a letter to her younger brother Will Jr., writing: "A line only, dearest Will, as of course you know by now of our father's marriage—while May and I are greatly grieved and disappointed we must all stand by our dear father and try to make it as easy for him as possible because he realizes his mistake—your heart would have ached could you have seen him the night he left us for St. Louis, and I can't get over the way he looked so badly. Don't let anyone know that I have written you..."

While attending the St. Louis Democratic Convention, the senator remained discreet about his personal life as his party nominated New York justice Alton Parker for president. (Parker would be trounced by incumbent Teddy Roosevelt in the fall.) Then on July 12, 1904, Clark issued a terse announcement, stating that he had married Anna La Chapelle three years earlier, on May 25, 1901, in Marseille and that they had a two-year-old daughter.

The secret to getting away with a big lie is making sure that all the minor facts are straight. The senator should have checked his calendar before choosing a date and place for the alleged ceremony. It turned out that his own newspaper, the *Butte Miner*, had interviewed Clark on June 1, 1901, and published a detailed account of his recent European trip in which Marseille was not on the itinerary or even close to the cities named.

Newspapers went wild over the news of Clark's marriage to his former ward. The *New York Times* reported that Anna's mother, Philomene La Chapelle, was "dumbfounded" to hear of the secret wedding. In a story with a Washington, D.C., dateline, the *Minneapolis Journal* noted that the tale of Clark's not-so-new bride had created "feverish interest" in the capital: "Official society is particularly concerned. Indeed, it is viewing the situation with anxiety, not to say alarm. It is wondering, for instance, whether or not the senator will attempt to secure social recognition for the wife. The consensus of opinion seems to be that if he is a wise man he will not."

Behind the scenes, Clark's friends tried to sanitize the tale, insisting that the couple had indeed wed back in 1901 but that it was a religious ceremony, explaining the lack of an official license. These statements, from anonymous sources, were treated with skepticism.

This was such a delicious melodrama that no angle went unexplored, most notably the concerns of William Clark's four older children that their inheritance would shrink due to his new marriage and child. "The whole family of Senator Clark resent his last matrimonial alliance and it is doubted if they will ever become reconciled to receiving Audree [*sic*], the little interloper, into the bosom of their confidence," wrote the *Seattle Star*, in words that proved prophetic. To ameliorate his children's concerns, Clark had quietly transferred assets to them; Will Jr., for example, received title to Clark's Butte home plus an interest in several mines. Meanwhile, Charles Clark was embarking on a new chapter of his life and had just become engaged to the polo-playing California banking heiress Celia Tobin.

William Andrews Clark was forced to defend the virtue of his bride. He issued a carefully worded statement that appeared in the one newspaper that would not challenge his account: the *Butte Miner*. He explained the supposed two years of secrecy by saying, "Mrs. Clark did not care for social distinction nor the obligations that would entail upon my public life. She was anxious to remain in Europe for a time to continue her studies and felt she could do with more freedom." Then he added the busy-man excuse, saying, "Personally, I would have preferred to have her with me at all times, but my extensive interests compelled me to spend a great deal of time traveling through the United States…"

He attempted to address the reports that his children were mortified by his marriage. "It has been stated that my family objected to this union. Whatever apprehension, if any, may have existed in this respect on my part was entirely dissipated when the facts were disclosed by the cordial reception of the information and their approval of these relations which were so essential to my happiness. Then again, I wanted my child to be educated in America and brought up as a resolute and patriotic American."

His older children found it impossible to remain simultaneously honest and diplomatic. His eldest daughter, Mary Clark Culver, made grudgingly supportive comments to reporters, making it clear that she and her siblings had been caught off-guard. "My father's happiness is the first consideration of his children," Mary said. "All talk of opposition to my father's marriage is ridiculous. He literally gave us no time for opposition. It came as a complete surprise." She admitted that the family was not entirely clueless about her father's romance. "Oh, yes, we had heard rumors of it before but never considered them seriously at all…we gave them no credence whatever. When we learned the fact here from my father's lips, it was completely unexpected." Mary acknowledged that she had been startled to learn that she now had a new half sister. Mary and her siblings were wary of Clark's new wife due to her youth, her undistinguished background, and her religion—Anna was a practicing Catholic, while they had been brought up Presbyterian.

Anna La Chapelle Clark remained in Paris with Andrée during her trial by press. After spending so many years in a country tolerant toward affairs of the heart, Anna felt the judgmental reaction of post-Victorian America as a brisk slap. She was in no rush to join her newly announced husband at his homes in New York, Washington, or Butte. Anna delayed her return to the United States for nearly six months, which gave her plenty of time to plan her revenge on the naysayers.

Chapter Six

A Parisian Girlhood

When the German ocean liner *Kronprinz Wilhelm* docked in New York City on January 11, 1905, reporters jostled on the pier, awaiting the arrival of Senator Clark and his newly unveiled bride. Anna had stayed in her stateroom for much of the crossing complaining of seasickness, although nerves may have accentuated her desire for privacy. But now she appeared by her husband's side, dressed from head to toe in furs and carrying a bunch of purple violets, smiling shyly as she clutched his arm. The usually somber senator was in a jovial mood. "How are we?" Clark said. "Why as happy as sunflowers."

The reporters inquired about the whereabouts of the newest sunflower, the couple's toddler, Andrée, and were told that she had remained in Paris with a governess. "Oh, we hated to leave her," Anna quickly explained. "But we are going back in the spring as soon as the Senator attends to some business here and in Montana." Clark added this update on his youngest daughter: "She has grown so fast that we felt no anxiety over leaving her on the other side. She is in excellent hands."

Six months had passed since the Clarks' wedding announcement, but press curiosity about the unusual circumstances lingered. "Our marriage was not a secret one," Clark insisted to the reporters. "It was known to our friends. I did not take the public into my confidence because I did not have to."

The senator and his bride had returned home just as the New York subway system had opened and the Wright brothers were fine-tuning their flying machine. Later that year Edith Wharton would publish her first best seller about the fault lines in New York City's upper classes and an ambitious young woman's efforts to land a socially acceptable rich husband, *The House of Mirth*.

For the senator and his wife, this trip had been carefully orchestrated to introduce Anna to society at events such as President Teddy Roosevelt's 1905 inauguration in Washington and the intimate second wedding of Senator Clark's divorced daughter Mary, followed by a Butte homecoming. But three weeks after arriving in New York, Anna was rushed into surgery for an unspecified ailment. Since Clark's four children had scarcely welcomed their new stepmother into the family, Anna was probably relieved to miss the wedding at the Navarro Flats, where her husband gave away his daughter, Mary Clark Culver, to lawyer Charles Potter Kling, a Harvard graduate and native of Maine.

After a few weeks in the hospital, Anna telegraphed to her brother, Arthur La Chapelle, announcing that reports of her illness had been exaggerated: "Don't pay attention to the papers, I am perfectly well." When the senator and his wife arrived in Butte on April 16, a large crowd greeted them at the Northern Pacific depot. In the years since Anna had first met William Clark, she had been in and out of Butte, quietly visiting her mother and siblings, aware of the gossip that swirled around her. Now, she was back in triumph as Clark's wife, and Butte society was eager to witness her transformation into the spouse of the richest and most powerful man in Montana.

This was the moment that Anna had been waiting for, her chance to step out of the shadows onto center stage. Her cue came with a knock on the front door. Three of the most prominent women in Butte showed up together at the redbrick mansion on West Granite Street to call on the new Mrs. Clark. A butler ushered them into the grand entry hall and took their cards. They waited. The women could hear the servant, in an adjourning room, announcing their arrival, and arranged their faces in friendly anticipation. But instead of coming out to greet them, Anna told the butler, in a voice meant to be overheard, to inform the visitors that Mrs. Clark was not at home.

Not home? This was a social slap heard from coast to coast. Everyone gasped over the cleverness of the new Mrs. Clark, especially since she was welcoming old friends who knew her when she lived near the red-light district. Newspapers lapped up the story. SENATOR CLARK'S WIFE GETS EVEN, blared the headline in a Rhode Island newspaper. SOCIAL WAR IN BUTTE, announced the *Philadelphia Inquirer*. The *Boston Herald* urged readers to learn from her etiquette lesson: "Treat kindly every poor and good-looking girl, shop girl, telephone girl, stenographer, for at any moment she may become the wife of a multi-millionaire and society queen."

Anna gave an interview elaborating on her feelings, which was quoted in the *Chicago Daily Tribune*. "As far as society is concerned, I know nothing about it and care nothing about it," she said. "It has absolutely no charms for me. I am domestic in my habits. I love family life. I like to read, study and above all, to look after the interests of my little girl. I have been told that society people rarely mean what they say or say what they mean. As for me, I always wish to say what I think and I believe I do so." Anna, always an independent woman, would mellow over time in deference to her husband's desire to entertain. But this was a coming-out party that Butte would never forget.

The senator's twenty-eight-year-old wife headed to Paris to join her daughter Andrée, but her aging husband then had a health scare that sent Anna racing back to Manhattan. In mid-July, an abscess began pressing down on the senator's brain, which if untreated might have left him paralyzed. A radical two-hour operation was performed in which part of his skull was removed. Once he was able to travel, the couple sailed for Paris on August 23 and then went on to Italy, bringing three-year-old Andrée. Clark lingered in Paris, since in those slow-moving times the Senate was not in session until December.

This was one of the longest stretches of uninterrupted time the couple had spent together. Celebrating Clark's return to health, they did the most life-affirming thing possible: conceive a new child. Their daughter Huguette would be born June 9, 1906. Rumors later spread that Huguette was the product of an affair between Anna and her doctor. While nothing is certain without a DNA test, all accounts indicate that the Clarks were together during the relevant time.

———

As he approached fatherhood at age sixty-seven, following two frightening health crises, William Andrews Clark was ready to change his life. The month before the birth of his new child, he sent a telegram to the *Butte Miner* to announce that he was retiring from the Senate at the end of his six-year term in early 1907 and would not run again. His departure was not treated as a major loss for the Senate, where he had served on eight committees, including foreign affairs, Indians, and mining, but had not been influential on any of them. With a Republican majority in Congress, as a Democrat, Clark was in the minority during his entire Senate career. Political observers suggested that the aging Clark had fallen under the sway of his young spouse, or as one headline put it, WIFE RULES THE SENATOR: MRS. W. A. CLARK'S LIKING FOR PARIS AT THE BOTTOM OF HIS RETIREMENT. He flatly denied it, insisting that Montana would always be his true home.

Anna had retreated into the background in Paris, keeping her pregnancy secret while caring for her ailing former chaperone. She probably either heard about or saw the sensation in the art world that spring: two new paintings by prodigy Tadé Styka were exhibited at the prestigious Salon of the Société des Artistes Français. Born in 1889 to the aristocratic Polish painter Jan Styka, Tadé had been the youngest artist ever chosen to show his work at the 1904 salon. Now he was back with two sophisticated offerings: a scene of Tolstoy on his deathbed, surrounded by sad-eyed peasants and greedy family members, and a portrait of prominent American lawyer Donald Harper and his hunting dog. His father was known for florid religious works and creating what was then the largest painting in the world, *Golgotha*, while Tadé specialized in refined lifelike portraits. His striking painting of Donald Harper brought in many new commissions from Americans in Paris.

As Anna's pregnancy bloomed, she explained to Andrée that she was going to have a sibling. The precocious four-year-old Andrée's reply: "Let me think that over." It became a family joke. Once

Huguette was old enough to understand it, she thought the comment was funny and adopted that phrase for herself. "She thought it was a clever remark and she had a great relationship with her sister," recalls Huguette's night nurse, Geraldine Coffey, who recalls that whenever she'd ask her patient to do anything, "She would raise her finger and say, 'Let me think it over.'"

Once again, William Clark was not in the vicinity brandishing cigars when Anna gave birth in Paris to Huguette Marcelle. Instead, the senator had chosen this moment to visit his son Charles in San Mateo, California, and see his newest grandchild, a six-month-old girl. William Clark waited six weeks before turning up in Paris to admire his new daughter.

The occasion was commemorated by a formally posed family photograph. Anna is seated, looking elegant in a floor-length dark skirt, matching jacket, and lacy white blouse, with her hair carefully put up and crowned with an enormous hat with a feather. On her lap, she is holding the baby. Tiny Huguette, with her wispy blonde hair, looks doll-like in a white lace christening dress that trails several feet to the floor. Andrée, now nearly four, has been posed by the photographer on a chair, her expression sulky, her brunette hair flowing to her shoulders, clad in a short white dress, white knee socks, and a straw hat. The senator, with a full head of hair, bushy mustache, and beard, is dressed like a dandy in a summer white suit, white shirt, and tie. Looking directly into the camera with a formal but proud expression, he has one arm protectively around his wife and another encircling Andrée.

The photo previewed the family's dynamics: Andrée's closeness to her father, Huguette's tie to her mother. William Clark affectionately described Andrée as "a little charmer," and he was so indulgent with her that his wife was forced to play the disciplinarian. Huguette would develop into a shy child, eager to please, quietly hungry for the affection dispensed so freely by her father toward her sister, seeking warmth instead in the arms of her doting mother.

Two months later, in September 1906, the parents left their children at home with the servants, taking a jaunt together in their new Mercedes touring car. The chauffeur was speeding up a hill on a country road outside Marseille when a tire blew. The car flipped over, and the Clarks were thrown out. "I had quite a knackering on account of [a] busted tire and the chauffeur I think lost his head," wrote Clark, in a handwritten letter to his Montana lawyer, Walter Bickford, on September 17. "I had a rib broken…Mrs. Clark is with me. Fortunately she was not hurt, only bruised a little."

In the spring of 1907, they brought Andrée with them to America while Huguette was left behind in Paris with nannies. The Clarks gave Andrée a party at their Butte home in June, complete with performances by trained dogs and singing and dancing in the ballroom. In honor of the absent Huguette's first birthday, they put her picture on the table next to a small cake. This was an era when wealthy parents considered long absences to be acceptable, and before the existence of such phrases as "attachment disorder." But for a baby to be without her mother and the rest of her family for several months— unable to see and hear familiar faces and voices—is frightening, creating inchoate fears of being abandoned that can linger beyond a reunion.

Even though he had retired from the Senate, Clark remained in the headlines because of the grandiosity of his nine-story Fifth Avenue mansion, which had been under construction for six years with no end in sight. The Beaux Arts structure, complete with an enormous tower topped with a cupola, had been nicknamed the "Fifth Avenue Horror" and "Clark's Folly." The senator had hired a French architect, Henri Deglane, to design the house and the New York architectural firm of Lord, Hewlett and Hull to build the hotel-sized 121-room dwelling. The supervising New York architect, Washington Hull, had taken to pointing to his gray head of hair and joking, "They were brown when we broke ground for the Clark mansion." The mansion was known as the most expensive private home in America: the original cost had been estimated at $3 million, but as the years passed that number grew to more than $7 million. Fifth Avenue was known as Millionaire's Row, dotted with the Vanderbilt Petit Chateau, the Carnegie Mansion, and the Astor palace, but Clark sought to outdo them all.

Clark's oldest daughter, Mary, had originally been involved in planning the Fifth Avenue palace, since she had expected to live there with her family and serve as her father's hostess. Mary liked amateur theatricals and had customized the design to include a large theatre with a hydraulic lift for scenery and changing rooms for the actors. But Mary had lost her hoped-for social position now that her father had remarried; Anna would now be hosting parties at the senator's side. The theatre plans were scrapped, and the mansion was reconfigured to accommodate the Clarks' two young children and eliminate living quarters for Mary and her family.

Clark instructed workmen to create a magical nursery for his young daughters including hand-painted tiles illustrating nursery rhymes and fairy tales. (LUXURY FOR THAT CLARK BABY, announced the *Syracuse Journal*.) Concerned about pandemics and the health of his children, Clark had even created a secure room in a turret if they needed to be quarantined.

Clark demanded every modern convenience: a swimming pool, dressing rooms fitted with Carrara glass, a Turkish bath, a wine cellar, safe deposit vaults for Anna's impressive jewelry, an air filtration system, three boilers, and an eighty-ton coal storage room, all in the basement. An elevator large enough for twenty people had been installed, as well as a spectacular white marble staircase suitable for a grand entrance, with balustrades of gold and bronze. Clark built four large art galleries to showcase his paintings, sculpture, tapestries, Egyptian antiquities, and majolica. The banquet hall, paneled in English oak, was carved in the style of Henry IV. Now that every robber baron was installing an organ in his home—including John D. Rockefeller, J. P. Morgan, and Andrew Carnegie—Clark had trumped them all with a massive instrument that cost $120,000.

The copper mogul commissioned sculptors such as Augustus Saint-Gaudens, Paul Bartlett, and George Grey Barnard to create bronze decorations for the house. Raphaël Collin, a painter and professor at the École des Beaux-Arts in Paris who had painted panels used in the Opéra-Comique and Hôtel de Ville, advised on the décor. An Oriental art expert honored by the Japanese government with the medal of the Order of the Rising Sun, Collin created an Oriental room with hand-painted panels. This room would fascinate the young Huguette, sparking her lifelong interest in all things Japanese, from geisha-clad women to kabuki theatre to the royal family.

The showstopper in the Clark mansion was the Salon Doré. The widowed Count d'Orsay, renovating his Parisian mansion in 1770 in honor of his second marriage to a princess, had commissioned a profusion of gold leaf panels for the walls depicting love, music, victory, and the arts. On the third floor, Clark imported a library from a Normandy château with carved woodwork dating from 1523. That floor included his-and-hers suites. Anna's opulent living quarters overlooked Central Park: the parlor was paneled in yellowish white satinwood from Ceylon and carved with flowers, and the boudoir was made of bird's-eye maple. Her bathroom featured onyx and alabaster set with precious stones, and tiny faucets to dispense perfume so she could scent her bath with roses or violets.

Frustrated with cost overruns, Clark decided to seize the means of production after a granite quarry owner tried to triple the contractual price to $650,000, claiming that design changes had pushed up the price. He bought the Bangor, Maine, quarry and five other industrial facilities for the sole purpose of completing his dream mansion: a stone finishing plant, the Henry-Bonnard bronze foundry in Manhattan, a New Jersey marble woodworking plant, a woodworking factory, and a Long Island decorative plaster plant.

Against this backdrop of conspicuous consumption, Clark practiced ludicrous frugality. He took the subway in New York and caused a scene one day when he lost a penny in a chewing gum machine at the Fourteenth Street station. One of the richest men in America, he was sufficiently annoyed that he complained to the station manager, missing two uptown trains until he got his money's worth, much to the merriment of his fellow passengers.

Clark was consumed with the idea that people were trying to cheat him, which had some basis in reality. Art dealers frequently tried to sell him fakes and sometimes succeeded. Clark's architects sued one another over charges involving misappropriation of funds. In his business dealings, Clark repeatedly sued other companies—and was sued by them—and hated to give in. "This man who is said to have one of the largest incomes in the world is a born fighter for the sake of winning, no matter what the cause," wrote the *Washington Post*, in a story about Clark's efforts to avoid being fleeced on home building costs.

"He would slash when driven into the last ditch to accomplish his goals."

While waiting for the house to be completed, Clark loaned eighty paintings to the Corcoran Gallery in Washington and had the pleasure of taking President Roosevelt there on a private tour to see his treasures. As word spread about Clark's prodigious spending on art, the Metropolitan Museum's curatorial staff began to send him solicitous letters. Clark was not considered socially eminent enough to be invited to join the Metropolitan's board, one of the most desired honors in the city, but presumably his Corots and Gainsboroughs might be welcome. He invited the Met's curators to an exhibit of his artworks at the Lotos Club.

The construction of his colossal mansion at 927 Fifth Avenue dragged on in comic fashion. Clark kept announcing that it was almost done and he and his new family would be moving in soon. Then that deadline would pass. Anna saw no need to uproot herself and her daughters from Paris until the Fifth Avenue palace was finished.

———

The painting pulses with life. The brightly colored scene depicts children playing at a park in Paris, young girls in their pinafores playing with friends, well-dressed indulgent mothers watching nearby and knitting or gossiping to pass the time. There is energy and exuberance and carefree joy captured in the brushstrokes. Painted in 1906 by American Impressionist William Glackens, purchased courtesy of William Clark's copper fortune, the painting *Luxembourg Gardens* hangs in the Corcoran Gallery, as if providing a window into the early life of Clark's two youngest daughters.

Huguette and Andrée lived with their mother and the servants in a magnificent home on the Avenue Victor Hugo in the 16th arrondissement, close to the Bois de Boulogne. Sheltered in a cocoon of luxury, the girls had a pampered existence that was radically different from their parents' hardscrabble childhoods. Even the girls' miniature jewelry was exquisite, tiny gold trinkets crafted with care. Both of their parents had worked with their hands—William Clark doing chores on his father's farm, Anna helping at her mother's boardinghouse—but the two girls would never have to set a table or make a bed, much less earn their keep.

Huguette was fey and otherworldly, a sunny child who in family photos often looks like she is skipping along by herself, content with her own company. Andrée was the adventurous one, more likely to rebel and get into trouble. Huguette would remember their mother exploding with anger when Andrée began to whine one day about being bored. "Look at all that you have compared to people who have so little," Anna lectured her eldest daughter. "You have the nerve to complain when you live in a palace." Huguette idolized her mother and never wanted that furious tone directed at her. That maternal outburst was so unforgettable for Huguette that even as a centenarian, she remembered her mother's comments word for word, recounting them to her assistant, Christopher Sattler.

Andrée and Huguette spoke French as their primary language. "Huguette giggled when she talked about her father's French accent," says Huguette's goddaughter Wanda Styka, the daughter of painter Tadé Styka. "Everyone around her was speaking Parisian French, but he spoke with an American accent." The girls were tutored in English, Spanish, Italian, and German. Anna, consumed by the harp, was eager for her children to embrace music lessons. Huguette took up the violin and Andrée studied the piano. In the summer Anna took her daughters to a villa in Cabourg on the coast of Normandy—the favorite watering spot of Marcel Proust—or to the Château de Petit-Bourg. That majestic property had belonged to a Bourbon duchess before the French Revolution. Huguette would talk about these carefree days as among the happiest of her life.

William Clark spent long stretches in Butte and Manhattan, occasionally summoning his family back to the United States. When the White Star liner *Teutonic* landed in New York in July 1910, an enterprising photographer snapped the senator alighting with his daughters, and the photo was sent around the country as newsworthy: "Former Senator Clark and his daughters: First photograph taken in the United States of the little girls, both of whom were born abroad." Huguette, four years old, is staring shyly at the ground and trying to avoid the camera as the senator adjusts her straw hat; Andrée smiles, enjoying the attention.

From then on, these two young heiresses were treated as American royalty. The two pretty Clark girls were frequently photographed by the newspapers, and even the smallest revelation about their privileged lives was devoured by the public. Huguette hated being on display. When her mother took family photographs, Huguette would fetchingly pose and smile, but when photographed by strangers in public, she would usually look away from the camera.

They were well-traveled children, covering thousands of miles in any given year in a Paris-Manhattan-Butte circuit, traveling first-class on luxury liners across the Atlantic and in their father's private railcar in America (extra-large car No. 2001, paneled in oak from Sherwood Forest, seating twelve at dinner, sleeping compartments finished in vermillion, buttons to summon servants). The Clark family stayed in Butte long enough on this visit that the girls were listed as residents in the 1910 local census. These trips allowed Huguette and Andrée to become close to their grandmother—Anna's mother, Philomene La Chapelle—who lived in Butte. Clark's children from his first family, however, had long since scattered to the coasts: his two daughters were in New York City, his son William Jr. had remarried and moved to Los Angeles, and son Charlie was in San Mateo.

Huguette enjoyed Butte and described those trips fondly in later years. "She mentioned that house many times, the steps where she used to line up her dolls, the pansies that they planted just below it, she really liked it," recalls her assistant, Chris Sattler. Clark took his wife and two young daughters to William Jr.'s fishing camp near Missoula; Anna was so enamored of the natural beauty that Clark wrote to his lawyer inquiring about renting a similar spot for future vacations.

At the end of 1910, the Clarks returned to Paris for Christmas, and then began preparing for the moment that William Clark had been anticipating for a decade: taking up residence in his much-ridiculed Fifth Avenue mansion. "There may be uglier structures, but none come to mind," harrumphed the *Boston Journal*, calling the Clark house "towering and massive in its arrogant hideousness." Shortly before William Clark and his family moved in, the *Chicago Daily News* joked that the copper mogul had actually shown restraint: "In the description of the residence, we find no hint that he has incorporated a game reserve, a section of Adirondack mountains, a slice of Mediterranean shore, a volcano for heating purposes, a glacier for refrigeration, or a geyser for hot water."

The public be damned—William Clark was happy with his new home. He expressed his good cheer on January 29 in a letter to his Montana-based lawyer, Walter Bickford. "Mrs. Clark and the rest are all well and we are gradually getting settled down," Clark wrote. "We have been on the fourth floor for some time but soon expect to be 'promoted' to the third. I am engaged in hanging pictures, and you may be sure I am somewhat busy."

In public, Clark conveyed a dour and pompous persona, presenting himself as a world-weary, self-important captain of industry. Yet in his letters to Walter Bickford, the mogul comes across as a man with a sense of humor, engaged and curious about politics and business. He writes fondly of his late-blooming sons and their prowess in business, but he is truly effusive when it comes to Anna. He sings her praises in chatty postscripts like a man very much in love, and often adds affectionate words about his two youngest daughters. (Even jaded journalists had noted the success of the marriage. The *Chicago Tribune*, in a story headlined WOULD YOU LET YOUR DAUGHTER MARRY A MAN OLD ENOUGH TO BE HER FATHER, wrote that "the senator appears to be devoted to his one time ward and she to him.")

For Huguette and Andrée, moving into the mansion on Fifth Avenue was an adventure—the vast house was great fun to explore. There were shrieks of childish laughter in this forbidding palace. William Clark urged them to be careful about colliding with the art, or as Huguette would later tell Christopher Sattler, "Her father didn't like her to run around in the gallery, the Salon Doré."

The girls shared a room in the vast quarters. Huguette would later describe Andrée to her nurse, Geraldine Coffey. "Her sister was a wonderful writer and reader and she would tell her stories at night. She would not finish them," says Coffey. Inspired by Scheherazade of the Arabian Nights, Andrée would keep Huguette in suspense and pick up the tale the following evening.

These happy scenes were marred by two scares during the family's first few weeks in the Manhattan mansion. Anna was rushed to Roosevelt Hospital on a Sunday night in terrible pain. The doctors pronounced her condition critical. The senator spent most of the night by her side. The next morning she was successfully operated on for appendicitis. For her two young daughters, their mother's near-death experience was terrifying. Then just a few days later, while Anna was still recuperating at the hospital, and Andrée and Huguette were at home with their father and the servants, thieves tried to break into their Fifth Avenue mansion via the roof.

It happened late at night. After hearing reports from neighbors about an attempted robbery nearby, Clark's watchman went up to the fourth floor of the house and spotted a flashlight shining on the roof of one of the art galleries. He called the local precinct, and thirty policemen responded to the call, a massive show of force, but the would-be burglars escaped. Clark sat in his library calmly reading a book as the search took place.

The family headed for England in late May on the *Adriatic* to attend the coronation of King George V. Once again photographers snapped shots of Huguette and Andrée, accompanied by William Clark's young grandchild, Katherine Morris. The family spent a leisurely summer at the French seaside. In late August, William Clark wrote to Walter Bickford, "Mrs. Clark and the children are still at Trouville where we have a beautiful villa. We have had a six weeks period of unceasing heat in Paris but out there it has been very pleasant." At Trouville, the Clarks befriended a French couple, Andre and Noemie de Villermont, artists with two sons, Etienne—two years older than Huguette—and Henri, two years younger. The childhood playmates would remain close for decades.

William Clark had been listed in *Who's Who in New York* as a member of numerous well-known private clubs (Manhattan, New York Yacht, Downtown, City Ardsley, National Arts), but he had never been fully included in the life of New York's 400, the top echelon of society. He and his wife frequently stated that they had no interest in clubs that would not have them. When Clark was in Los Angeles in late October that year on a business trip (Anna and the girls were still in France), reporters asked whether he planned to entertain society in his new Fifth Avenue palace. "That depends on what you call society," replied Clark, giving a windy and defensive answer. "If you mean giving big parties, these will be very few; if you mean meeting our friends and the people of the artistic and professional world, I hope these occasions will be many."

In this interview, the senator was eager to boost the artistic credentials of his wife. "Mrs. Clark is a woman who enjoys the beautiful side of life, which means that side which includes artistic expression and effort," Clark said. "She is a brilliant harpist herself and is intensely fond of music and the kindred arts, as I am, and we both like the sort of people of similar tastes and inclinations. Formal society, that which devotes itself to formal society affairs, has little attraction for either of us."

Noble sentiments to be sure, but in truth, Clark was hungry to be recognized as a sophisticated art collector. He had scoured Europe and the auction houses of New York for treasures, outbidding his fellow robber barons to amass a cornucopia of art. He told the reporters that he felt a civic obligation to allow others to see his masterpieces, saying that he did not think he had "a right to be selfish with the objects of art that I have collected." So he and Anna, who returned to New York with the girls in mid-December, decided they would give a grand party to showcase their collections.

The evening was a disaster. Anna was mortified by what occurred. Huguette was quite young, but she undoubtedly heard about the night. As one newspaper account put it, "When the new house was completed, Senator Clark gave a huge party. Hundreds of invitations were sent out to all the best people in New York but all the best people did not come for these were many in high society who always spurned the advances of the aspiring senator and to whom he was always just an 'upstart' from the wild west."

Many years later, when Anna was a widow living several blocks away, she would confide her memories of that humiliating experience to Robert Samuels, an elite decorator. The story became part of the mythology surrounding Anna and Huguette, and their two-against-the-world, mother-daughter relationship. Samuels passed the story on to Neal Sattler, Chris Sattler's older brother and the contractor who renovated Huguette's apartment. "Bob told us about the debacle when the father had the big party and they were shunned by society," Neal Sattler recalled. "The senator did not have a great reputation and none of the important people showed up. They were very hurt by this." The Clarks would entertain again, but not for a while and not on this kind of scale.

Anna remained close to her mother, who had been able to relocate to a much larger home in Butte thanks to the generosity of her son-in-law. Philomene La Chapelle was sixty years old, nearly thirteen years younger than William Clark, and had always been the picture of good health. In January 1912, Philomene was on the phone with her son Arthur's wife and complained of feeling ill. Eight hours later, she was dead from pneumonia. "The death of Mrs. La Chapelle was a very sad affair and it was so sudden and unexpected, and Mrs. Clark was all worked up about it," wrote William Clark to Walter Bickford. "However, she is very brave about it and started yesterday for Butte." Rather than accompany his wife to the funeral, Clark left instead on a business trip to Chicago, Arizona, and Los Angeles. Once again, their daughters were on their own on Fifth Avenue with the servants.

The death of their grandmother was a shock to Huguette and Andrée. But another untimely death, just a few months later, would haunt Huguette for the rest of her life. She would obsess about what happened, read about it, talk about it, and conflate the events in her mind until she imagined that she could have been among the dead, too. The unlucky family member who passed away: her first cousin Walter Miller Clark, the twenty-eight-year-old son of William Clark's younger brother and business partner James Ross Clark. Walter Clark had spent his early years in Butte, then moved with his parents to Los Angeles. A graduate of the University of California, he had joined the Clark family sugar beet operation and become the supervisor of the Los Alamitos Sugar Factory. He had married a Butte woman, Virginia McDowell, in January 1909, and the couple had a baby boy,

James Ross II. The couple decided in 1912 to take a belated honeymoon to Europe, leaving their two-year-old son with his maternal grandmother. When it was time to return home, Walter Clark and his wife boarded a luxury ship in Southampton destined for New York: the *Titanic*.

"All the way over, we had such beautiful calm weather, in fact up to the accident, the sea had been like glass," Virginia Clark later told reporters. She had retired to their first-class stateroom when she felt a jolt at 11:30 p.m. She got dressed and went to find her husband, who was in the smoking room playing cards with friends. Alerted that the ship had struck an iceberg, the couple went to their room to change their clothes. "We took with us our heavy overcoats, I my furs, two life preservers, and what valuables we could pick up. My husband also saw that I was provided with money in case we should be separated." On deck with John Jacob Astor and his pregnant wife, Madeleine, Virginia and the other women were helped by officers into lifeboats, but the men were not allowed to board. "I know from the way he bade me good-bye that he felt no apprehension and fully expected to join me later. There was room for fifteen others in our boat and three men could have been taken as well." Walter Clark perished at sea.

William Andrews Clark, who had been fond of his nephew, wrote to Walter Bickford, "We have been shocked by the disaster to the *Titanic* and filled with the deepest regret at the drowning of Walter Clark. We had hoped for a day or two that he had been saved but now it seems as if all the saved have been accounted for."

Huguette was only five years old, but as a veteran of several ocean crossings, the news left her terrified. Later in life, she would frequently inform people that her father had purchased tickets on what was meant to be the next voyage of the *Titanic*, from New York back to Europe. The story became convoluted in the telling, as if Huguette imagined that she had nearly been in danger herself. Her physician, Dr. Henry Singman, recalled, "She told me about somebody who died on the *Titanic*, who went down, and that she was supposed to be going back to the States but her father had changed the time of the departure from Europe." She told the same story to her best friend, Suzanne Pierre, who passed it to her granddaughter, Kati Despretz

Cruz. "Huguette and her mother were supposed to be on the *Titanic* but changed their plans at the last minute," Cruz says. Huguette fixated on her cousin's death and the near miss for herself for decades, going obsessively over all the might-have-beens. Her night nurse, Geraldine Coffey, recalled that she often talked about this disaster that befell "a young person, newly married man, a relative."

Judging by William Clark's letters, his family was never in danger. They spent the winter of 1912 in the United States: he noted that Anna was in Chicago in February, and mentioned her plans to return to Europe in May. Clark wrote to Walter Bickford on May 25 that he was en route to Jerome, Arizona: "Before I left my wife and the children sailed on the good ship *George Washington*, which I hope will not get Titaniced before its arrival at the French port."

Children are often resilient on the surface—frightening moments can be held at bay, reemerging later in life—and Huguette did not seem unduly troubled to her parents. On July 15, 1912, Clark reported, "I have just heard from Mrs. Clark and they are all very well. She has taken a place at Fontainebleau for the summer." Five weeks later, Clark was in France himself, noting approvingly that son William and his second wife, Alice, had come to visit, and adding, "Mrs. Clark never looked better in her life than now, and the children are growing fast and are having the time of their lives."

For the next two years, the Clark family continued their transatlantic commute. Huguette would later mention her father's frequent absences. The mining mogul had founded a new town—Clarksville, Arizona—for the employees of his booming United Verde Copper company in nearby Jerome. This was one of the first planned communities in the United States, and Clark had built six hundred homes, a school, a library, a church, and the entire infrastructure of water, sewage, and power lines.

Anna's sister, Amelia, who did not have children of her own, often joined the family in Europe for months at a time. Amelia's first marriage in 1901 to Edward Hoyt, a Minneapolis securities dealer, had unraveled within a few years, and she had begun listing the Clark's Fifth Avenue mansion as her home address on shipboard immigration forms. Amelia played the role of second mother to Andrée and

Huguette, and Huguette would later talk about her with love. "She was very close to Aunt Amelia," says Hadassah Peri, Huguette's nurse for two decades. "Amelia was married to a guy and he walk out. The first husband is no good."

For Anna La Chapelle Clark, her musical skills were an asset in her New York life, perceived as an admirably genteel hobby. She won a favorable mention in *Town & Country* for her proficiency in playing the harp, a sign that she was starting to win acceptance among the members of the *Social Register*. "A pretty woman playing the harp makes a very delightful picture and stirs the memory with scenes from Jane Austen and suggests dainty little watercolors in gilt frame," stated the magazine story about the newly fashionable artistic pursuit. "The society women who are taking the harp seriously include Mrs. William A. Clark, wife of the ex-senator, who makes the instrument a feature of her beautiful new music room."

The spring of 1914 found Anna once again headed for France and the Château de Petit-Bourg. But Clark was preoccupied over labor unrest at his Missoula operations, and concern about socialists running for office in Montana. He could not get away until mid-July, writing to a friend that he was eager to see his family and "get a little rest."

Clark crossed the Atlantic just as war was about to erupt in Europe. On June 28, Archduke Franz Ferdinand and his wife were assassinated in Sarajevo. As Clark was arriving on the continent, on July 28 Austria declared war on Serbia, and within days Russia and Germany mobilized their troops. When Germany declared war on France on August 3, the Americans in Paris began scrambling to get out.

American ambassador to France Myron Herrick was deluged with cries for help, as his assistant and biographer, T. Bentley Mott, later recounted. "It was the height of the tourist season, and upon the declaration of war, from every quarter of Europe whence they could escape, travelers poured into Paris on their way to the channel ports of France and England…They expected that their troubles would be over when they reached Paris, when in fact they had often only begun. Train service was everywhere disorganized by the requirements of mobilization, busses and private automobiles had been requisitioned, taxis became scarce, hotels began to close, the whole mechanism of modern life was topsy-turvy. And they had no money and could get none."

The French banks refused to cash checks from foreigners. Even William Clark, who was now with his family and Anna's sister, Amelia, at the Château de Petit-Bourg outside Paris, was unable to secure the money to pay their way out of town. William Clark's name was on a list released by the State Department of well-known Americans in Europe whose safety was at risk. The United States government announced it was sending a battleship, the USS *Tennessee*, to bring in a supply of gold to France and then transport Americans to England.

Huguette vividly remembered what happened next, because she had been the little heroine. As her assistant Chris recalled, "They had to get to Le Havre, the port, but they had no cash. Millionaires don't walk around with cash. The senator had given her a gold coin every week, and she never spent it." The eight-year-old and her sister volunteered their savings; their parents used the contents of Huguette's and Andrée's piggy banks to pay for their escape. According to Sattler, "They took these gold coins, hired a carriage, and it took them to Le Havre." Even the hardened William Clark was sobered by the journey, later telling reporters, "Every road from the city is choked with fleeing refugees. From what we heard in Paris, a great battle will soon be fought in the region of Marne." Huguette cherished a photo taken on the deck of the USS *Tennessee*. Her father looks up from his newspaper at the camera; Anna and Andrée are smiling while Huguette gazes shyly at the ground.

William Clark had asked the American embassy to keep an eye on his Paris home, but after a few weeks in England, he and Anna decided it was safe for them to cross the English Channel again. "Mrs. Clark and I have just returned from Paris where we went to get a lot of things that we left there when Paris was supposed to be almost within the grasp of the enemy and we had a pleasant time," he wrote to his lawyer in Butte.

When the Clarks arrived in New York in late October, they were photographed yet again disembarking from the boat, with Huguette clutching one of her constant companions, a doll. "When she traveled in the early years with her family, she always took her dolls," says Geraldine Coffey, Huguette's night nurse. "She knew everything about dolls."

Now that the family planned to live in Manhattan full-time, the two girls were enrolled in private school. Huguette did not last long at her first placement. Since she was the only blonde in her class, the teacher asked her to play a German girl in a skit. Since Huguette and her family had just fled the Germans, she refused to take the part. She was so proud of her protest that she still spoke about it years later. Her supportive parents moved Huguette to Miss Spence's school instead. Their youngest daughter was showing some spunk.

Chapter Seven

The Fractured Fairy Tale

The life of a typical eight-year-old does not involve hours spent practicing on a Stradivarius or posing patiently for a renowned artist. But now that Huguette Clark was living full-time on Fifth Avenue, her day-to-day existence required a full-scale immersion in the dual passions of her parents, art and music. They were force-feeding her culture. Not only was Huguette living in a vast art museum, walking past paintings by Titian and Turner, but strains of music were ever present, from her mother playing her harp to chamber music groups giving private concerts.

Huguette strived to improve her musical skills—she had once cheerfully serenaded passersby from the balcony of their Paris apartment—although rarely has there been such a mismatch between the rudimentary skills of a struggling pupil and a concert-worthy instrument created by the world's greatest violin maker. To give her every opportunity to excel, her parents arranged for Huguette to take lessons with Anna's friend André Tourret, a celebrated Parisian violinist who was performing with the New York Chamber Music Society and shared concert billing with Enrico Caruso at a Biltmore Hotel musicale.

The artist chosen in the fall of 1914 to capture the likenesses of Huguette and Andrée was another Parisian émigré. Pierre Tartoue charged up to $20,000 per portrait and would go on to paint King Gustav of Sweden and President Calvin Coolidge. In his portraits of the Clark girls, the artist highlighted their age difference. At twelve, Andrée looks like a worldly teenager, somberly holding a large basket of flowers, wearing a dancing school costume—a red blouse and white skirt—with her dark hair carefully coifed and legs demurely crossed. The eight-year-old Huguette is a sprite, her short blonde hair in a pixie cut, wearing a short-sleeved frilly white dress and perched on a table with her feet akimbo as if she's ready to jump off, holding onto her favorite prop, a doll. Tartoue prided himself on capturing the personality of his subjects, and he conveyed Andrée's bookish seriousness and Huguette's I-won't-grow-up charm.

Clark allowed Tartoue to display the paintings at the Henry Reinhardt Gallery, a Fifth Avenue showplace that sold masterpieces by Corot, Rubens, and Van Dyck. The portraits of the Clark girls were favorably reviewed in the *New York Herald*: MR. TARTOUE LIMNS SOCIETY DELICATELY. But the copper mogul may have had second thoughts after the *New York World* used a mashed-up photo of the portraits with the misspelled caption: "Miss Andre and Miss Hugette Clark and their six million dollar home on Fifth Avenue." Public interest in the Clark heiresses, two of the richest girls in America, remained intense even as gossip columnists feasted on morsels about the extended Clark family. Every birth, death, divorce, custody fight, and society antic was covered by newspapers coast-to-coast as entertainment for the masses, a vicarious glimpse at how the other half lived. The fascination was so strong that even a California con man who pretended to be a Clark scion—shades of twenty-first-century "Clark" Rockefeller—received ample ink.

Three of the senator's children from his first marriage were portrayed as caricatures: divorcée Mary Clark Culver Kling with her flamboyant Manhattan parties and busy love life; spendthrift Charlie's splurges on his racing stable and battles against his creditors; and culture maven Will Jr., who collected rare books and manuscripts with a special interest in the works of Oscar Wilde, and launched the Los Angeles Philharmonic Orchestra. Clark's fourth child, Katherine Clark Morris, married to a physician, was the lone respectable pillar of New York society, and unlike her siblings, she did not ostentatiously display her wealth. "She was frugal, she wore mended gloves to the

Philharmonic," says Erika Hall, who was married to John Hall, the grandson of Katherine Morris. "She had wonderful jewelry but she only wore it for the family, not to impress people. She was immensely private, she hated publicity." Katherine Morris looked askance at her siblings' antics, or as Hall says, "She was distant from her brothers. She laughed about her sister, but she loved her."

The age gap between William Clark's two families was sufficiently large that Huguette and Andrée were virtually the same age as their nieces and nephews. Now that the girls were based in New York, they saw more of their similarly named Manhattan contemporaries, Katherine Clark Culver and Katherine Elizabeth Morris, developing childhood friendships. The young Katherine Morris attended Spence with the Clark girls. Huguette and Andrée occasionally spent weekends with their relatives at Morris Manor, a large farm estate near Oneonta.

In Manhattan, rich arrivistes have long turned to philanthropy as a route to move up in society. William and Anna Clark put their much-vaunted residence on display to raise money for World War I relief in France. More than two hundred guests paid $5 each for a concert of French music featuring violinist Tourret at the Clarks' home on February 24, 1915, with proceeds going to the Villa Molière, the French military hospital in Paris. As the *New York Tribune* quipped, "This is the first time that the would-be visitor to the art treasures collected by the millionaire Senator did not have to present a certificate of character before a pass to the house would be issued." The Clarks' next charitable event was a $3-per-person fund-raiser on April 7 for the American Artists Committee of 100, aiding destitute families of French artist-soldiers. The party featured an organ recital and lecture by James Barnes, who spoke about his recent time overseas, "Back of the German Lines in the First Weeks of the War."

The Clarks may have been motivated by their love for France, but they were rewarded with prominent mentions in the staid *Sun* (SOCIETY GOES CHARITY MAD AND FINDS ITS REWARD) and, most important, the *New York Times* (WILL SOCIETY KEEP LENT? MRS. JOHN JACOB ASTOR, MRS. ANDREW CARNEGIE AND MRS. WILLIAM A. CLARK TO OPEN THEIR HOUSES FOR LENTEN BENEFITS).

That headline might just as well have read: "Anna La Chapelle

Clark has arrived." Now that she had been given equal status with the wives of other robber barons, her social standing was now secure. Anna had been listed in the *Social Register* as of 1904, when William Clark first announced their marriage. But now newspaper articles no longer dredged up questions about the couple's peculiar backdated nuptials and instead simply stated that their marriage occurred in 1901. The past had been airbrushed.

At the Spence School for girls, then located in a gray stone building at 30 West Fifty-Fifth Street, Huguette and Andrée took classes with other young heiresses such as Margaret Carnegie. After a Parisian upbringing with private tutors, Huguette, whose first language was French, initially had a hard time adjusting to an American school and all-English classes. Her studious and outgoing older sister, Andrée, had an easier time fitting in. A letter from William Andrews Clark to his wife indicates that Huguette was initially placed in a class with students a year younger, with the promise that once she caught up, she could jump a grade.

The Spence School day started promptly at 8:55 a.m., and the dress code required the well-bred girls to wear skirts at least three inches below the knee. They took classes in literature and Latin, art history and geography, chemistry and physics, penmanship and elocution. Huguette developed exquisite handwriting resembling calligraphy and memorized poetry that she could still recite as a centenarian. Deportment and manners were emphasized at the school; Huguette always wrote gracious thank-you notes and never raised her voice in anger.

Clara B. Spence, the progressive educator who founded the school in 1892, gave weekly dramatic readings from Shakespeare at Wednesday morning assemblies. "Miss Spence was very strict," says an East Side woman in her eighties whose mother attended school with Huguette but requested anonymity. "My mother was a boarder, and she was homesick and crying one night. Miss Spence said to her, 'How can you cry when you are lucky enough to be in my school?'" To expose her students to the interesting minds of the era, Miss Spence arranged for such speakers as Edith Wharton, Helen Keller, and George Washington Carver. Huguette later recalled taking a dance class with Isadora Duncan.

Conservative in matters of decorum but liberal in championing the rights of women, Miss Spence tried to imprint her values on her students. In an undated commencement address probably given while Huguette was at the school, Miss Spence urged students to cultivate their imagination, saying, "Sympathy, that great bond between human beings, is largely dependent on imagination—that is, upon the power of realizing the feelings and the circumstances of others so as to enable us to feel with and for them." Huguette Clark lived in her imagination, and she would grow up to be so sensitive to the plight of others that she would send anonymous checks to strangers after reading hard-luck stories in the newspapers.

Her elitist classmates did not know what to make of the daughter of the showy copper mogul. "My mother remembered going to the house and the gold-plated faucets," says the Upper East Side octogenarian. "It was really garish." Huguette apparently felt that her early school problems could have been handled with more sensitivity. Later in life, she would often ask her night nurse, Geraldine Coffey, if her children were being mistreated by teachers. "She would reminisce about old times and the schools she went to and how they varied," Coffey says. "How teachers were nice in one school and not so nice in the other and the fact that they didn't do good psychology." But Coffey recalls that Huguette always praised her headmistress. "She loved Miss Spence. Miss Spence was a kind and generous woman."

The workaholic William Clark and his upwardly mobile wife believed that their daughters' education should be a twelve-month-a-year experience, hiring tutors to travel with the family as well as provide after-school lessons. Anna Clark's sister, Amelia, recommended her Spanish teacher, Margarita Vidal, an Argentine artist who was supporting herself by giving language lessons. Margarita and her sister Jaquita Vidal, a violinist, became a regular part of the Clark family entourage, accompanying them on summer travels and amusing the adults while keeping Huguette and Andrée company.

William Clark did not normally socialize with his staff, but he grew fond of these two attractive young women who could converse knowledgeably about art and music. Anna Clark took Spanish lessons with Margarita, sending a car to pick her up. Margarita Vidal's son,

Roberto Socas, a retired political science professor, says, "My mother and my aunt traveled with them. They were like tutors, elder sisters to Huguette. [My aunt] Jaqui was very social, a live wire. My mother was more introverted, very involved with her art." Margarita encouraged Huguette's interest in painting and later told her son that the young heiress was "energetic and social."

———

Even in his late seventies, William Clark put in long hours at his Wall Street office and traveled frequently to Chicago, Salt Lake City, Los Angeles, and, of course, Butte. Clark kept up-to-date on even his smallest operations, writing to his lawyer, Walter Bickford, that his Butte streetcars had become unprofitable due to the popularity of the automobile, and it was time to shut down the trolleys. Although Clark had voluntarily left the Senate, he wanted to be perceived as politically relevant. On a 1916 trip to Washington, D.C., Clark was miffed that President Woodrow Wilson did not invite him to the White House, writing to Bickford: "The President did not call around to see me. It is too bad!"

While he relied primarily on family members to run his operations, Clark had a few trusted managers such as his controller, William B. Gower, a British accountant who worked for him for thirty-five years, keeping the books at twenty of Clark's companies. Gower was the resident problem solver, called upon to deal with Clark family issues. One of Charles Clark's creditors sued the senator for $37,000, but the case was dropped after Gower gave an affidavit saying that there was nothing in the company books indicating that the father owed any money to his son. The copper titan perceived the controller as indispensable. "Mr. Gower left for a little visit to Montana, but I expect him back here within a few days," Clark wrote to his lawyer. The Clarks and the Gowers, who lived in Westchester with a son and daughter close in age to Huguette and Andrée, occasionally socialized together.

Vain about his appearance and proud of his good health, Clark practiced a physically abstemious and athletic lifestyle that he imparted to his children. In 1917, when the *Anaconda Standard* asked him about the secret of his longevity, Clark replied, "I find what is termed 'the simple life' very conducive to the maintenance of good health—that is, temperance in eating, observance of full quota of sleep particularly up to eight hours, plenty of exercise in the open air and freedom of mind from disturbances and annoyances. This can often be secured by exercise of the volition and mental control."

But it was Anna—thirty-nine years younger than her husband—whose life was marked by a disability. She began losing her hearing in her twenties. By the time Anna reached her thirties, she relied on a hearing aid, an unwieldy box with an earpiece. For a woman who loved performing and listening to music, this was demoralizing, although she seldom complained. "Her hearing was a great impediment to her," recalls Gordon Lyle Jr., whose father was the Clark family physician. "She carried this little box around. An electronic box about the size of a purse. When you wanted to talk, she held it up to you." Anna's condition took a toll on her children, since crying out for "Maman" did not always produce the desired response. Huguette suffered from frequent ear infections as a child and, aware of her mother's struggles, feared that she would go deaf, too.

With Europe off-limits due to the war, the Clarks sought domestic vacation spots: a summer at Greenwich, Connecticut (where William Clark and Andrée humored Huguette by posing for pictures on the lawn with her and her dolls), a trip to Yosemite, and frequent summer vacations in Montana. It was important to Clark that his first and second families get along, and Anna acquiesced, agreeing to spend time with his older children and grandchildren. They often joined Will Clark Jr., his second wife, Alice, and son William Andrews Clark III (Tertius) at the family fishing camp in Salmon Lake, Montana. The senator enjoyed watching the athletic exploits of his grandson Tertius while Anna and the girls, used to the cloistered environs of Paris and Manhattan, reveled in hiking, biking, swimming, and the great outdoors.

Unlike her dreamy and obedient younger sister, Huguette, Andrée had become rebellious as a teenager, battling with their mother. A family Montana summer vacation in 1918 ended with a mother-daughter spat and a painful parting. Andrée left to accompany her father to Butte but wrote a conciliatory letter to her mother. Anna cherished her daughter's words so much that she saved the note.

August 27, 1918

My Dearest Little Mother,

I know that you will not answer me nor do I think that you will read this letter, but if you do, you will know that you are the best friend that I have ever had, or ever will have.

We all had a most beautiful, wonderful time at the Lake and we regret so much that it is all over!!! And we are all indebted (especially me), to you for this lovely summer we have had.

We had a very sunny, windy incidental trip to Butte and we arrived here at quarter to seven. We had dinner at the house and then separated. This afternoon Daddy is going to take me to the gardens to see his marvelous begonias . . .

I am ever so sorry to have made you unhappy yesterday for I was heartbroken to see you cry and send me away without one of your smiles and fond kisses which are worth more to me than a world. I hope you will forgive me. Whether you write to me or not or do not open my letters. I am going to write to you every week or so and it may prove to you, or it may not, that I love you above anybody else in this earth and though I am selfish, I'd die first, before anything could happen to you. Good-by, dearest little Mother, and please forgive me.

Your loving daughter, Andrée

In the spring of 1918, reports began to spread from overseas about a deadly strain of Spanish influenza. The epidemic hit America with a vengeance that fall, setting off panic as it spread from city to city. Public events were canceled, people were urged to wear face masks, and the sick were quarantined. More than 20 million people worldwide would perish from the flu. The Spence School delayed the start of the school year in September 1918 to protect the students. Huguette and Andrée stayed safely at home. But their father continued to travel the country in his private train car, sending reports to his lawyer. "We are quarantined here, which I hope may have good results," he wrote from Butte in early October. A few days later, Clark worried about his Arizona mine, writing, "In Jerome, Arizona, the town is quarantined and no trains are allowed to run and the disease is very malignant; about thirty persons have already died, including several nurses."

Clark was en route to California to spend time with his son Will Jr., whose second wife, Alice, was seriously ill from an unspecified ailment. Shortly after William Clark's visit, his daughter-in-law died, in December 1918. For Huguette and Andrée, who had gotten to know their aunt Alice on Montana vacations, this was a loss and a reminder of the fragility of life. Even though their elderly father was vigorous, they knew that he would not be around forever. This fear shadowed their adolescence.

On January 1, 1918, Andrée began keeping a diary that displayed her interest in current events. "Here in this little book I open my diary in the first year of peace, after four long years of horrible war. How thankful we all must be that at last Alsace-Lorraine is liberated...I begin, then, this little memorandum of my daily life and I wonder what feelings will prompt my pen...the mission of a young girl in this world is to render everybody around her happy and fill the home with love and peace...and so, New Year, I do not dread you."

In precise and thoughtful prose, Andrée chronicled her daily life with such entries as "a walk with Daddy Dear on Fifth Avenue" and "We are preparing a surprise for Mother's Birthday—Huguette is learning a piece on the violin." Their concerned parents wanted to insure their continued health, and Andrée noted, using her sister's nickname, that "Hugo and I were vaccinated for typhoid."

The sisters usually got along well but Andrée would occasionally confide in her diary about her preteen sister's pranks. "Huguette played a mean trick on me," she wrote on January 5. "Miss Vidal was coming for her Spanish lesson and I asked Hugo if I could go out with them. She promised to wait for me and ran away!!! But I read a book and played with Tommy." Tommy was the family dog.

Andrée described how Huguette had rebelled against her lessons. "Huguette was rude, stubborn and disagreeable with Miss Vidal yesterday. She was worse today. The poor little Spanish teacher was nearly driven to tears!" Yet Andrée also conveyed affection and concern for her sister ("Huguette had a little cold, she did not go to school.") and mentioned that she wished Huguette had come along on an outing to see an art exhibit at Columbia.

Anna Clark had hired yet another well-qualified specialist to work with Andrée, who suffered from a bad back. Alma Guy, the niece of a prominent New York judge, had trained as a dance instructor but lost her sight as a young woman. She had become a pioneering gym teacher at the Lighthouse for the Blind, an inspiring figure who encouraged blind children to test their limits. Guy had become a darling of the New York social set for organizing play groups for "poor little rich girls," as one newspaper feature put it. This was the Suffragette era, with the country on the verge of opening up new opportunities for women; President Wilson gave a speech to Congress on September 30, 1918, supporting the right of women to vote, although the Nineteenth Amendment would not be ratified for two more years. Anna Clark brought the free-thinking Alma Guy into her home to help Andrée with back exercises. The teacher would wake Andrée up at 6:45 a.m. on school days for the stretching routine—much to Andrée's dismay according to her diary, since the teenager preferred to sleep in. But Alma Guy quickly developed bigger ideas after spending time in the gargantuan Fifth Avenue mansion.

As Guy later told an interviewer for the Girl Scouts, she found Andrée Clark to be "shy, timid and afraid to call her soul her own. Her parents were so occupied with other things that they really did not know what was happening to their daughter in the hands of maids and governesses." Guy encouraged Andrée to join the Scouts. Founded in 1912 by Juliette Gordon Low, a wealthy and artistically inclined widow, the Scouts encouraged girls to be self-reliant and consider careers outside the home, then a revolutionary notion. "Her mother was not sure that she wanted Andrée to be a Girl Scout, because it was too democratic for the daughter of a senator," Guy said in an interview with a representative of the Girl Scouts. But Anna ultimately gave her blessing, allowing Andrée to join the Sun Flower Troop and thus break out of her rich-child bubble.

Andrée learned Morse code, how to build a fire in the woods, and bandage rolling for the Red Cross, during the Tuesday meetings at 99 Park Avenue, a town house built by a railroad mogul. Andrée wrote a triumphant letter to a friend on February 22, 1919, announcing, "I have now attended ten meetings of the Girl Scouts and I love it!! I am a Tenderfoot. I was 'Sworn In' last week. It is the most impressive ceremony you ever beheld!" She confided to her diary: "Thanks to scouting, I have become what I am. I have changed from a moody and somewhat careless child to a scout who tries her best to be worthwhile, to follow the great noble and deep ideals. It is very hard sometimes…Scouting has been like a hand in the dark, has taught me how to climb, how to 'be prepared.' Scouting has been my guide."

Huguette was not interested in trailing along in her sister's wake. In fact, the athletic Miss Guy had been unimpressed with Huguette, saying in her Girl Scout interview that the thirteen-year-old "was always inclined towards social things and was quite a different type. She was bored with school and Scouting." The gym teacher was apparently unaware that Huguette was pursuing a passion that consumed her free time: she had become serious about the violin. Her teacher, André Tourret, had returned to France during the war to volunteer his services and had remained in his native country after the World War I armistice. On the eve of heading off on summer vacation, Huguette wrote to him, in French, about her musical dreams.

June 11, 1919

Dear Good Great Friend,

Tomorrow evening I leave for Maine…You said yourself that you would like to see me again. But the only way is to come back. But great friend I am quite proud of you…

You know that it is my dream to go to the conservatory in Paris. I know it is very hard…one has to work 4 hours a day so that you make much progress every week. But I would do it well to learn my violin. Do not mock me for thinking of such a thing for as inattentive as I was back then is as attentive as I will be now. Alas being big we always regret what we did when we were small…write to me and I will work hard. I send you a big, big kiss.

Your little friend who loves you, Huguette.

That summer, Huguette accompanied her parents to the rural resort town of Rangeley Lake, Maine. The usual Clark entourage came along: Anna's sister-in-law, Hanna La Chapelle, and daughter, Anna; Anna's social secretary, Adele Marié; plus tutors Margarita and Jaquita

Vidal. Anna had been ill that winter, and the senator arranged to take a longer vacation than usual to spend time with her.

Separate arrangements had been made for sixteen-year-old Andrée, who went off early in the summer to Morris Manor in Oneonta to spend a month with her aunt and uncle, Katherine Clark Morris and husband Dr. Lewis Morris, and their teenage daughter, Katherine. Their large working farm estate had sheep, cows, chickens, and horses, but Katherine Clark Morris ran a formal household. ("She had finger bowls at the farm," recalls Erika Hall, who married into the family and visited many years later. "She wanted everyone to behave.")

Andrée wrote in her diary that she was sorry to miss Huguette's birthday: "It is too bad I cannot be near her today." It was a busy time for the Clark family: Andrée was scheduled to take a houseboat trip to Canada with her relatives and then join her mother and Huguette in Maine. William Clark was slated to spend August in Butte, joining his two sons for a civil trial over a business dispute.

This was a family built on independent relationships: Andrée wrote chatty letters that summer to "Dearest Daddy," although her parents were together. The senator sent back affectionate replies, while Anna often sent brief but loving telegrams to her daughters. Andrée rhapsodized to her father on June 7 about the rural life at the Morris estate, writing, "The farm is just the same as when I left it, in the stalls, the dear old horses, Diek, Major Niger, Ethel and many others. The dogs recognized us and jumped up and barked wildly when we went to see them. How is New York? Just as hot and dusty as ever?" Once his vacation began, the senator wrote Andrée to tell her that all was well.

June 18, 1919

My dear Andrée,

We arrived the day before yesterday and found everything very satisfactory... Huguette of course misses you but when Anna E. gets here she will get along all right. I feel sure that our dear mama will be much better here.

A week later, the ever-indulgent father wrote to tell Andrée that he was mailing her comic strips—*Bringing Up Father* and *Mutt and Jeff*—and that he was spending his days playing golf "none too brilliantly" and croquet. He rhapsodized about the unspoiled landscape. "The evenings are calm and lovely and the declining sun casts a narrow streak of golden light…and this narrow streak extends for miles across the lake. I am sure that you will enjoy your visit later on…"

The senator stopped off in New York on July 13, en route to Butte, writing to Andrée, "The house seems very lonely with only me." He wanted to reassure his daughter that "I left all in excellent health. I do believe your dear mother has improved quite a good deal…Huguette is growing very fast…Altogether it is a fine place and I am sure you will like it."

Huguette was eager for her sister to turn up, anticipating her arrival in a letter that she wrote to her traveling father.

Dear Father,

I hope you are having a nice trip. It is quite warm here and the lake is very calm and we have just been in swimming. Yesterday night there was the most beautiful sunset the mountains were blue and the sky was a beautiful pink and purple, the water looked like silver, I could not say in words how beautiful it all was. I am sure we will have also a beautiful sunset tonight. Soon Andrée will come back and how glad I will be to see my dear big sister again, never have I missed her so much. And so I will be glad to see you again my dear little father. I send you a big kiss, your little daughter, Huguette.

Andrée's arrival in Maine was uneventful and she was delighted to be reunited with her mother and her sister. She wrote to her father on July 30:

My dear Father,

We are now at Rangeley and I love it! It is so pretty and wild! I had been told so much about it that I was very anxious to see it and I am not disappointed in my expectations…Andrée

Clark, who was now in Butte, missed his family and regretted his departure from Maine. He replied to Andrée: "I spent a most enjoyable month there in which I enjoyed so much *la vie intime* and where I saw more of your dear mother and Huguette than I have in some time. I wish I were there to go with you to the White Mountains as that country is reputed to be interesting and picturesque…"

The senator had promised to return to Maine in time for Andrée's seventeenth birthday on August 13. Andrée had conflicted feelings about turning seventeen and becoming a grown-up, writing in her diary on August 1 about her concerns, plaintively wishing that she could somehow skip the day. But she put those feelings aside to cheerfully describe, in a letter to her father, how much fun she and Huguette were having together, traveling the countryside in a horse-drawn cart.

August 7th

My dear Father,

I am very happy that you will be here next week. I know how to drive quite well and so does Huguette. We go out in the cart every day. We have a great deal of rain here…I am very glad you are going to be here for my birthday. With much love and many many kisses, your little girl Andrée.

What Andrée did not mention in her letter to her father, however, was that she had been feeling wretched for several days. In fact, in her diary on August 1, she had written, "Dinner came and I was not hungry." Andrée became annoyed when her observant mother expressed concern. But Anna, after consulting a local doctor, became so worried about Andrée's health that she summoned Dr. William Gordon Lyle from New York. He diagnosed Andrée with spinal meningitis. "My father tried to save their oldest child," Tina Lyle Harrower says. "He spent day and night. She had not been well handled."

William Clark received an urgent telegram from his wife, informing him that Andrée was severely ill. Frantic with worry, the senator raced to the Butte station for the next train to the East Coast. While en route he received an unimaginable telegram from Anna:

Western Union.
Hon. W.A. Clark. Care conductor, North Coast Limited, Eastern
Bound, Bismarck.

Received your very dear messages our little angel is at rest
now everything was done that was possible for Monday evening she
was singing all her scout songs this gives you an idea how quickly
all took place. Huguette left for New York with Miss Marié...
Huguette does not know of her sister's loss...tomorrow I and the
remaining ones leave with remains for New York and I will be there
Saturday. I am all right don't worry be brave as you know how to
be and as much as the dear little one was during her illness. Love,
Anna.

Desperate to hold on to traces of her eldest, Anna took photographs
of her dead daughter and saved a lock of her hair. Andrée's body was
brought to the Fifth Avenue mansion. William Clark had spent a decade building his fantasy palace, but now the large halls echoed with
loss. He had created a quarantine room, he had hired bodyguards, he
had done everything possible to keep his family safe, all to no avail.
He had never had the chance to say good-bye. Andrée's last letter to
him, written on August 7, arrived after her death, an unbearable final
token. The family ordered black-bordered condolence cards.

"Thank you very much for the kindly expression of sympathy
to Mrs. Clark and myself in this hour of our great distress," wrote
Clark to his lawyer, Walter Bickford. "The funeral service on Monday forenoon, held at the house, and presided over by Dr. Stires of
St. Thomas Church, was most beautiful. We had the entire boy choir
of the church. We laid the precious body away in the mausoleum in
Woodlawn Cemetery. Mrs. Clark is very desirous now of going with
me to Montana...Mrs. Clark has wonderful fortitude, and little
Huguette is also very courageous."

The thirteen-year-old put up a good front for her parents' sake,
but she was traumatized. Andrée had been her closest companion,
her protector, the big sister who told her bedtime stories and com-
forted her in the middle of the night. They had shared a room up

until two years earlier. For the rest of her life, Huguette would talk about how much she missed Andrée and reminisce about their adventures together. There was no one else who understood the rhythms of their privileged family life, or who could share the shorthand of sisterly conversation. This loss was such a central fact of Huguette's existence that she talked about it whenever she met someone new: she needed people to know that she had once had a sister. She did not want Andrée to be forgotten. Andrée's birthday, August 13, was seared in Huguette's memory as a day of mourning.

A few days after Andrée's funeral, the family took their private railcar to Montana. Despite his grief, William Clark went ahead with a planned speech to the Society of Montana Pioneers. His *Who's Who* entry listed many illustrious organizations, but this unheralded group was the one he really cared about, where he felt at home and appreciated by his peers who had tamed the wilderness.

Clark was not a man who expressed his grief in public, but he did confide in Byron Cooney, the editor of the *Montana American*, who had known Clark since 1888. "A bitter blow to him was the death of his daughter Andrée," Cooney later wrote in the newspaper. "He liked to talk of her. He seemed to like to have someone to talk to about her. He emphasized her brilliancy and other admirable qualities... Every time he referred to her his eyes filled up with tears which he did not try to conceal. He was also very devoted to his daughter Huguette..."

That fall, William Clark and Anna decided to keep Huguette with them and stay away from New York for a few extra weeks. From Butte, the family went to Long Beach, California, where they stayed at a beachfront resort, the Virginia Hotel. "Mrs. Clark and the little girl are in excellent health," Clark wrote to Walter Bickford on October 10, noting that they were "now going directly through to New York as Huguette's time of entrance to Miss Spence's school is past due."

Travel can offer a distraction from cares and woes, but there is always an inevitable reckoning upon coming home. The Clark mansion on Fifth Avenue was a different place after the death of Andrée. Andrée had been closer to her father, Huguette to her mother. Three people grieving side by side can be islands of isolation, as each mourns the loss separately. A surviving child is inevitably desperate to make things right at home and comfort her parents but cannot fill the void. Questions like *Why her, why not me?—Should I feel lucky? guilty?—* cast a shadow on a vulnerable adolescent.

Huguette dealt with her feelings by putting them on paper. She began keeping a diary on January 1, 1920, mostly in French, with the entries addressed to "Chere Petite Andrée" or "Chere Grande Soeur." Since she could no longer confide in Andrée about her life, she described to her sister what she was up to every day, from practicing on her Stradivarius to buying a small statue to reluctantly attending the opera ("My, but Hugo is cranky!!!!!!!!!" she wrote in English). Huguette would often draw a heart under her name by way of sending Andrée her love. The diary lasted for only a few months, but it was a release. Modern-day grief therapists sometimes suggest that bereaved patients write a letter to their beloved; Huguette spontaneously figured out for herself a way to ease the pain. She could retreat to her room and privately convey her thoughts to her sister.

During their immediate period of mourning, the Clarks drew inward. When William Clark appeared at the Easter parade in April 1920, this was considered such a notable sighting that a syndicated picture and story went out across the country: "Ex-Copper King Senator Emerges," noting that he is "seen little in public now" but had "promenaded Fifth Avenue with a silk hat and cane."

Fearful for Huguette's safety and their own, the Clarks became phobic about contracting illness. A visitor to their home would later describe an unusual phenomenon: the servants frequently wiped down the doorknobs to protect the family against any germs brought in by visitors. When Huguette went out with a governess, the staffer was instructed to make sure the heiress did not touch surfaces that might have germs.

When summer came around again, Anna took Huguette back to the Virginia Hotel in Long Beach, bringing along tutors so Huguette could continue her studies even during school vacation. Huguette usually took a few dolls with her when she traveled, comforting companions and reminders of home. Huguette wrote her father sweet, descriptive letters once a week, eager to please him by demonstrating how hard she was working on her lessons. At fourteen, she sounded young for her age, as if she had regressed from the trauma but was determined to sound cheerful. All she wanted now was to make her parents happy. She even made a little joke about going to work for her father.

Hotel Virginia, Long Beach, June 17, 1920

Dear Daddy,

...We are waiting for an earthquake because it is so warm today...I must say that I like the Montana climate better than this but I just love the beach, the waves when they come over you are so wonderful. This afternoon the water is so dirty and muddy. I am getting along fine with studies. I like Miss Keeling, my English teacher. She is very sweet, arithmetique is the hardest thing for me to learn the rest is easy, I am getting to like grammar better...I love history it is so interesting and to color maps. I am learning Spanish verbs which I find quite hard. I just learned a Spanish poem.

A week later, she wrote to her father again, stressing that she was practicing the violin so she could perform for him.

Hotel Virginia, Long Beach, July 24, 1920

Dear Daddy,

This morning I have no lessons because it is Saturday and as I am quite lazy I slept until nine o clock. At half past eleven I am going in swimming. I am learning how to float but when I use my arms I forget to move my feet and so it doesn't carry me very far. I am also learning the overarm stroke, which is even harder than floating.

I am learning a pretty piece on my violin and I am sure you will like it, it has lovely notes on it, but I am getting along pretty well with it. I think I will know it all when you will be back...I am also learning two pages of concertos. Tonight mother is going to Los Angeles to study the stars through the telescope.

I know I am getting alone fine in arithmetique and don't despair of some day becoming your auditor. I find it easier because my teacher explains it so well to me. The last earthquake they had in Los Angeles, mother was in, she got an awful scare, and she thought it would be written in the paper in huge black letters and it wasn't even mentioned. The canaries are fine and just now are singing.

With her blonde hair and fair skin, Huguette was in danger from too much sun, but she was so in love with the beach that she paid no attention to that scorched sensation, as she admitted to her father in her next letter.

July 30, 1920

Dear Daddy,

Thank you so much for the check you sent me and also your type-written letter and the paper about Columbia garden, it is nice of you to write to me so often. I am sure that you are fine and I wish you were with us. We are having so much fun. Yesterday I had my violin lesson and the rest of my studies I had done there the day before and afterwards we all went on the beach, after swimming we had a picnic on the sand. And we stayed there all day getting sunburned.

Mother has a big police dog he is lovely and we have lots of fun with him. This afternoon I am going to Los Angeles because my brace is loose on one side and so I must go to a dentist. Sometime next week we are all going to Santa Barbara. I must go in to lunch because mother is waiting for me. I send you lots of kisses and love and mother also, your daughter Huguette

Now that a year had passed since Andrée's death, her parents wanted to establish a suitable memorial. Since she had been enamored of the Girl Scouts, William Clark purchased 135 acres in Briarcliff Manor, about 25 miles from Manhattan, and gave it to the Girl Scouts to create Camp Andrée Clark. He brought Huguette to a ceremony in November 1920 to announce the gift, a scene captured by a photographer. Nearly as tall as her five-foot-seven father, Huguette stands by his side with perfect posture and her head held high, her blonde shoulder-length curls peeking out beneath a fashionable hat. She looked on stoically as her father read out loud portions of Andrée's diary.

Anna had been very involved in the project, visiting often to comment on the construction of the cabins and kitchen. But rather than join her husband and daughter at the dedication, Anna had gone to the one place where she could find peace, Paris. After more than a year of living with her grief and regrets, she needed time away from the gloomy Fifth Avenue mansion. Anna told her husband that she was only planning to be abroad for a few weeks. But once in Paris, she stretched out her stay and arranged to deliberately miss spending Christmas with her husband and Huguette. Clark mentioned Anna's change of plans to his lawyer, but he expressed relief that her spirits seemed to be improving. Anna returned in time for New Year's and spent a few months in Manhattan but then left abruptly for Los Angeles to see her brother, Arthur, who was in poor health.

For Huguette, being left behind on Fifth Avenue, either with her workaholic father or with just the servants, was a way of life. It was lonely, but she was used to keeping herself occupied. She had friends at the Spence School and played violin in what she called "Mrs. Harriman's orchestra." The American Orchestral Society, created by the railroad titan's wife, Mary Harriman, showcased upper-class young talent.

Assigned to write a paper for Spence on "Happy Moments," Huguette chose to describe self-sufficient activities:

> *When one has a thrilling book and in the middle of an exciting story, what could be more delightful on rainy days. I love to read good books.*
>
> *Another happy moment is when I go swimming. We have a swimming pool at home so it makes it very easy for me to go in swimming before school. What fun it is to glide through the water, dive and plunge.*

Another thing I like to do is travel, what fun it is to pack one's things and think that in a few days one will be away from horrid Old or should I say New, New York.

I like to travel on the train just as much as I do on the boat. How delightful it is to fly, almost, over fields and woods and to think that the summer vacation has started.

Most teenagers tire of childhood toys, but Huguette still cherished her French comic books and her growing doll collection, housed in a separate room at the mansion. She treated her dolls with care. These porcelain lifelike objects reminded her of a more innocent time, when her existence was not so solitary.

Chapter Eight

Beginnings and Endings

S unshine and blue skies, palm trees and white beaches, hot days and cooler nights. The summer of 1921 was magical for Huguette Clark, a perfect few months for a fifteen-year-old who was coming of age and discovering that she was attractive. Anna took her to Honolulu to stay at the most luxurious resort on the island, the Moana Hotel, a beachfront property where the Prince of Wales had tarried a year earlier. Jaquita and Margarita Vidal came along as their companions.

Huguette looks radiant in family photos as she and Jaquita frolic in the sand, hugging each other in a pose that borders on sapphic. The Vidal sisters dressed Huguette in imaginative costumes. In one photo, she has gone native in a grass hula skirt with her blonde hair wildly flying; in another, she is grown-up and alluring in a black lace flamenco-style dress, wearing dangling earrings with her hair pinned fashionably up, striking an insouciant pose. The senator was planning to join his family partly through their holiday, and Huguette, looking forward to his arrival, wrote to him about beach life.

July 12, 1921

Dear Daddy,
. . . It is so wonderful here, I will just hate to leave it . . . The other evening we visited the Duke Kahanamoku, the whole family was there, they are charming people. The Duke Kahanamoku is the champion swimmer of the world. He has about six brothers and

three sisters. One of the brothers called Sam plays the guitar beauti-
fully. Every evening after supper he plays out on the pier. The other
night [illegible] and I were serenaded. It is thrilling. I practice my
violin every day. And I am taking lessons on the Yukelele but I like
the guitar much better and would like to take lessons on it. Mother
is taking lessons and she plays well... Well, I will now say goodbye
and hope you are fine.

The six-foot-three Duke Kahanamoku, the 1912 and 1920 Olympic swimming champion and the inventor of modern surfing, towers over Huguette in photographs, giving her an indulgent smile as she gazes at him with total adoration. Duke posed in the ocean with Huguette and a surfboard, and with her and her parents at the Outrigger Club, leaning against a canoe.

The Olympian was a regular at the Moana Hotel, earning extra cash by entertaining the guests, such as the Prince of Wales, whom he'd taught to surf a year earlier. Kahanamoku would paddle out on a long boat a half mile offshore with his pupils, and then show them how to catch a wave back to the beach.

Anna Clark became so fond of the Hawaiian beach boys who entertained the family that she promised to pay for the education of Duke's younger brother, Sam Kahanamoku, as well as two of his friends, Pau Keolahu, who wanted to study the violin, and Joe Bisho, who had been accepted at a St. Louis college but could not afford the tuition. The Clarks sailed with Sam and the rest of their entourage to San Francisco and checked into the St. Francis Hotel. But the Belmont Military Academy, the school they had chosen for Sam, refused to accept the dark-skinned Hawaiian, claiming there were no slots available.

The aging senator stayed out of the resulting furor. "The affair is entirely in Mrs. Clark's hands," the copper mogul told the *San Francisco Call* from his hotel room. "I do not think any attempt will be made to put the boy into another school. We will probably send him back to Hawaii. Mrs. Clark is the only one who can say anything definitely about the case and she has gone to a moving picture show for the evening." Sam Kahanamoku told the *San Francisco Chronicle* that Mrs. Clark "decided I had better start back...but I pleaded with her and she said I might remain for two weeks before returning. She is very gracious and kind."

Anna would later tell friends that she bought Sam Kahanamoku new clothes and a car as a consolation prize. Returning to the beaches of Hawaii worked out for him: Sam won a bronze swimming medal in the 100-meter sprint at the 1924 Olympics swim meet, while his brother Duke took the silver and Johnny Weissmuller won the gold. The Hawaiian surfing brothers continued to enrapture wealthy tourists, and Duke would later become the paramour of tobacco heiress Doris Duke.

The senator's failure to get Sam Kahanamoku into Belmont Military Academy was the least of his worries. Two of Clark's older children were enmeshed in scandals, one hushed up for years and the other about to become embarrassingly public. His namesake, William Clark Jr., twice widowed with a teenage son (Tertius), was now pursuing young men in Los Angeles, and discretion was not his strong point. His older brother, Charles, had written Will Jr. a pained letter in 1920 urging him to break off a relationship with Harrison Post, a San Francisco store clerk.

"Post bears the reputation of being a degenerate of the Oscar Wilde type," Charles Clark wrote to his brother. "When Maizie [their older sister, Mary] was visiting you she received two anonymous letters on the subject, which she destroyed...You can't afford to have your name tainted and in justice to yourself, the boy, your sisters and father." Ignoring his older brother's advice, Will Jr. put Post on his payroll and built him a house across the street from his own mansion in Los Angeles. But Junior's love life remained private for now.

The talk of the town in Manhattan in the spring of 1922 was the divorce of William Clark's oldest daughter, Mary. The convent-school-educated Mary had become known for her romantic misadventures. In the midst of her first divorce, she had been sued for alienation of affection by the wife of a male friend. Now Mary was divorcing her second husband, lawyer Charles Kling, and the details were ugly. In an effort to keep the divorce out of the newspapers, she had filed the legal papers in outlying Rockland County, but the press discovered the story. It was a titillating tale: Mary insisted in court papers that Charles Kling had repeatedly committed adultery. But even though she claimed to be the injured party, she ended up paying her husband a $580,000 settlement.

William Clark was pained by his oldest daughter's multiple trips to the altar, but what really worried him was the fate of his youngest and most naïve heir, Huguette. Realistic about his own age, Clark, then eighty-three, did not know if he would be alive when suitors came to call. To protect Huguette, he began to repeatedly tell her that she needed to be wary of the motives of men and even potential female friends. Huguette would later repeat her father's instructions to her closest friend, Suzanne Pierre, who passed on the stories to her granddaughter, Kati Despretz Cruz. "Her father always said to her, 'No one will really love you, you have to be careful. No one will love you for who you are. They will love you for your money,'" recounted Cruz. William Clark's understandable fatherly concerns were crippling to an insecure young girl.

Huguette was going through the giggly teenage phase of longing for a boyfriend. She entertained a group of girlfriends at the society restaurant Sherry's, just a month before her sixteenth birthday. Huguette was celebrating early because her parents had booked passage for the three of them on a steamer to Europe, with plans to see the Passion Play at Oberammergau and visit France and Italy. What Huguette remembered from this trip was an awakening sense of the possibilities of her future. Nearly eighty years later, at Christmas 2001, she wrote a revealing note to Sheila Lodge, the former mayor of Santa Barbara. After thanking Lodge for sending an account of her recent travels, Huguette added, "The trip that you made to beautiful Venice reminded me of the one I made at the age of sweet sixteen. I greatly enjoyed the gondolas and the singing of the gondoliers. It was all so very romantic."

Huguette's visits to Europe inevitably involved a crash course in art history, joining her parents on visits to painters' salons, art galleries, and museums. Art remained a way that she could connect with her father. Huguette and her mother were drawn to the work of the Impressionists, the graceful dancers of Degas, the hauntingly beautiful water lilies of Monet, and the lush scenes by Renoir, while William Andrews Clark retained a taste for old masters, religious scenes, and the Barbizon school. He could talk knowledgeably for hours to his daughter about painters and their technique and the history of prices at auction. His passion was acquiring art, but Huguette's would become creating it.

———

In 1922, New York State enacted its first residency law, leveling taxes on anyone who spent more than seven months living in the state. William Clark had always claimed Butte, Montana, as his primary residence, and the frugal mogul was determined to avoid high New York State taxes. So he shut down his Fifth Avenue mansion that fall. On September 11 he sent a telegram to Anna, who had lingered on in Paris: "Regrets that we had to keep the house closed and not even allow the pool to be used on account of the law on taxation."

To allow Huguette to continue at the Spence School, the family rented a suite of rooms at the Ambassador Hotel, a luxury building at Park Avenue and Fifty-Second Street that the Clarks favored from then on whenever their residence was closed. At Spence that fall, Huguette welcomed new classmates with familiar faces, the three daughters of her San Francisco–based half brother, Charles Clark, and his wife, Celia. The couple had separated and Celia had decamped to Paris, so they sent their three teenage daughters— the music-loving pianist Agnes, the polo-playing Patricia, and the sweet-natured Mary—to attend school in New York. As William Clark wrote to his wife from Butte on October 3, 1922: "Sweetheart Cherie…I was glad to have a message from Charles of their safe arrival. I suppose the little girls will enter the Spence school. I hope that you are all well."

Huguette became close to her niece Agnes Clark, two years her junior, thanks to their mutual interest in music. When the senator returned to New York and reopened his house, his three granddaughters often came over for Sunday lunch. After witnessing the rocky relationship between her own parents, Agnes was so struck by the evident affection between William Clark and his wife that she mentioned it years later to her son Paul. "Anna would sit on the senator's lap and pull his beard," recalls Paul Albert. "She was so much younger that [it] lent itself to that kind of generational play."

Agnes also noticed that Anna seemed extremely protective of her shy daughter. Huguette's fascination with her doll collection puzzled her nieces, since they had outgrown such childish things. The young women were especially taken aback when Huguette, in madcap heiress fashion, brought a doll dressed up in finery as an accessory to an evening black-tie event. A photo shows Huguette, wearing pearls and a gown with a doll perched in her lap, seated demurely next to an attractive young man in a tuxedo, who appears to be unfazed by his date's prop. Huguette's niece Mary Clark looks stiffly at the camera, as if embarrassed to be there, while Anna Clark smiles serenely. Later on, these nieces would pass along to their own children and grandchildren tales of Huguette's eccentricities.

But the Spence School during that era was used to the quirks of its patrician students. Huguette would later recall that one of her younger classmates was a Bouvier, a cousin of Jacqueline Bouvier Kennedy and Lee Bouvier Radziwill. That Spence classmate was Edie Bouvier Beale, a beauty who was eleven years Huguette's junior. Edie would later become famous with her mother as the reclusive broken-down socialites of *Grey Gardens*, living in a deteriorating estate in East Hampton. Their dependent mother-daughter relationship and sad lives would be the fodder for a documentary, musical, and movie.

———

The acclaimed Polish artist Tadé Styka sailed on the *Majestic* from Paris to New York on January 4, 1923, to attend an exhibit of his work at the prestigious Knoedler Gallery. Deluged with requests for portraits, he set up shop on the gallery's second floor for six months and scheduled sittings. The onetime child prodigy was so much in demand that the *Washington Post* wrote, "The craze that is sweeping New York for Tadé Styka's portraits is most extraordinary...Ain't nature grand when one becomes the fad of the fashionable world." William Clark, who had returned to New York from Montana, ordered eleven portraits of himself in a burst of enthusiasm as well as portraits of Anna, her sister, Amelia, Huguette, and even several versions of Andrée, based on photographs. The family members spent hours posing for the debonair bachelor artist.

So when Huguette later expressed interest in taking painting lessons, there was an obvious candidate. Tadé had not taken on private pupils before, but he could hardly refuse the blandishments of his well-heeled patron. Huguette was ferried by chauffeur to his Central Park South studio, along with a chaperone who remained in the next room. Tadé became fond of the shy and sheltered but artistically inclined teenager. They chatted away happily in French, and he liked to play practical jokes to make her laugh. He would occasionally dash off an impromptu portrait of Huguette while she was working. In one of these paintings, he depicts Huguette standing at her easel with a paintbrush and a palette in hand, a slender young girl with a thoughtful and engaged expression, alive with the pleasure of creating—an artist at work.

————

Anna Clark had discovered that she liked California during her visits to her brother, Arthur, in Los Angeles and her vacations at Long Beach. Now that the family needed to shut down their New York residence for five months a year to avoid taxes, they needed another home. In 1923, Anna and her husband rented a house in Santa Barbara for the summer. The sun-drenched city with its palm trees, ocean vistas, and hilly canyons had become the West Coast version of Newport, dotted with grand estates built by Goulds and Peabodys.

The Clarks took a handsome white oceanfront villa, Bellosguardo, perched on a cliff with views of the mountains and water. Bellosguardo had been built in 1903 by Tulsa oil magnate William Miller Graham and his wife, Lee, whose houseguests included the Duke and Duchess de Richelieu, Pittsburgh banker William Mellon, actress Elinor Glyn, and members of the Vanderbilt family. But the owners had recently divorced, so the sprawling property was available, with its wraparound porch, verdant gardens, football-field-sized lawn, and private white sand beach.

While Anna and Huguette played golf—the athletic Huguette also went horseback riding and tried out her surfing technique—William

Clark continued to crisscross the country on business. He was now eighty-four years old, lonely for his wife during his frequent absences, but he refused to retire.

The teenage girl whom he had taken as his protégée in 1893 had become his great love, and he missed Anna so much that he wrote to her constantly. On July 23, he wrote to his wife from Butte, "I can also see you all in my minds eye around the yard in various games and on the beach and in due course of time I shall be glad to get back again." The family man urged Anna a few weeks later to encourage Huguette to write to him, saying, "My love to Huguette and tell her I have had only two letters from her since I came away. How easy it is to forget. I am so glad that you remember me so often."

He wrote affectionate letters to Huguette, encouraging her to keep up her golf game. "I know you will like golf when you get to playing well. This requires a great deal of practice...I am glad that you are getting along well with your studies." The former Democratic senator lamented to his daughter the sudden death of Republican president Warren Harding on August 2: "It was such a pity as he was one of the greatest and best Presidents we have had for many years."

With Anna, he discussed his business problems in his letters: "The Socialists are trying to induce me to sell the water system to the city at a low price so they can get cheap water. They would not care what I would lose as they would like to have the city buy it at half price the cost." The elderly robber baron felt beleaguered and bitter about his legacy. "I sometimes feel that all that I have done for the betterment of mankind is not worthwhile as there is very little appreciation but one should not encourage that feeling..."

Andrée was always on his mind, and he wrote to his spouse on the fourth anniversary of their daughter's death:

Darling wife,
  My thoughts are with you and our darling girl who passed away and who we loved so dearly...such a great loss to us and our dear Huguette who happily has been spared to us. She had such a mar-velous intellect and such a sweet disposition and such regard for the

*happiness of those whom she knew. I have great confidence that we
will see her again and that we will all be together again. I may be
mistaken but it is a comforting thought and I love to think that our
hopes may be confirmed.*

*With all my fondest love for you and dear Huguette and hoping
that you are both well and happy.*

That August, the headmistress and founder of the Spence School,
Clara Spence, died at the age of sixty-one while on vacation at a cottage in Greenwich, Connecticut. William Clark wrote to his wife on
August 16 that he was sorry to hear the news, adding, "It is such a pity
as she took such an interest personally in my girls. I hope that it will
not interfere with the plans she professed to me to advance Huguette
this year…" In the same letter, he mentioned he was going to the
"Old Timer meeting" of the Montana Pioneers, but joked in a post-
script, "Don't worry about me at all. I am not going to do anything
indiscreet. W.A.C."

His older children were concerned about Clark's health. His son
Will Jr. alerted his sister Katherine Morris that the aging senator did
not look well. Katherine sent a telegram to her stepmother, Anna, urging her to get the senator to take it easy: "Letter from Will says father
doing altogether too much is losing weight and does not get proper
rest and food. Cannot you get him back to Santa Barbara as we are all
much worried about him." Will Jr. followed up himself, alerting Anna
in a telegram on August 29 that he would be accompanying his father
from Butte to California by train and "think it would please him if
you would meet us at Los Angeles."

Once William Andrews Clark arrived in Bellosguardo, he was
delighted to join in the easygoing resort life. "We are all very well and
all enjoying this splendid climate," Clark wrote to his lawyer, Walter Bickford. "Today we had the eclipse to attract our attention…
the effect of it was wonderful." In a photograph of the senator and
his wife, he is sitting in a wooden chair and Anna is perched on the
armrest with her arms around him, a picture of domestic tranquility.
A wire dangles from her ear, attached to her hearing aid on a table

nearby. She was not vain about her disability and was willing to be photographed with the box so that she did not miss a word of conversation. Anna had brought along Huguette's tutors, the Vidal sisters, and the senator also posed with the flirtatious beauty Jaquita Vidal, looking pleased by her attention. The two young women doted on Huguette, and she beamed in their presence.

William Andrews Clark was so taken with the twenty-three-acre Bellosguardo that he bought the estate that fall for a reduced price of $300,000. The Italian-style two-story mansion featured white marble floors, oak ceiling beams, and ample porches, and the private beach included cabanas. The building was secluded on three sides by its location on a bluff at the edge of the ocean; the only neighbor was the adjoining cemetery. He and Anna decided to stay there for the fall, sending Huguette back to New York with chaperones to stay at the Ambassador Hotel. The seventeen-year-old Huguette did not seem to mind, writing a series of upbeat letters to her father as she continued to try to impress him with her dedication to classwork.

> *The Ambassador, New York, October 3, 1923*
>
> *Dearest Daddy,*
>
> *I am so glad to hear that you are well. We are fine here, the rooms are very comfortable . . . I found school of course very sad without Miss Spence. My program is very interesting and I have nice teachers.*
>
> *Here are the subjects: English speech, mythology, geometry, psychology, spelling and reading, French modern history, chemistry, 18th Century literature, history of architecture drawing, Shakespeare. A lady will come every Thursday and read to us Shakespeare to take Miss Spence's place and she acted with John Barrymore and a few other celebrities. Of course I am positive she could not make the class half as interesting as Miss Spence. The Clark girls are here and they are fine . . . The weather here is beautiful and we haven't had a day of rain since we came, which is quite wonderful for New York. Well Daddy I'll keep you posted on what's going on here. I will be delighted when I see you again and I send you a million hugs.*

A week later, Huguette wrote to him again. She wanted to send word that she was spending time with her Clark relatives at Spence as well as John Hall Jr., the husband-to-be of her older niece, Katherine Elizabeth Morris. Huguette had been chosen as a bridesmaid for the couple's upcoming January wedding, with the party to be held at her father's Fifth Avenue mansion.

> *Dear Daddy,*
>
> *I am very busy with my school lessons and that is the reason I don't write to you more often. But I think of you very much and I am looking forward to your arrival in New York. I hear mother is getting along very well with her riding and driving. I am so glad that she takes enjoyment in these excursions as they surely are very beneficial to her health. I see the Clark girls very often and they all look fine. Katherine's fiance paid a call on me. He is very nice, very polite and I am sure will make Katherine very happy... Well, Daddy, it won't be long until you will be on your way home. How glad I shall be to see you and mother again!*
>
> *From your affectionate daughter. Hugs (my nickname. Do you like it?)*

Her father arrived back in Manhattan in time to celebrate his eighty-fifth birthday on January 9. He was still considered such a formidable figure in the business world that the *Wall Street Journal* wrote a tongue-in-cheek article about this momentous birthday, joking that Clark continued to be "a driving personality so prejudiced as to be against the right of such words as 'leisure' and 'vacation' to repose in the dictionary." The article quoted an unnamed business colleague who said Clark's idea of fun is "to drop down to Wall Street and put in the night working." The article closed by saying, "He's months and months older than Mr. Rockefeller; but try to tell him—you try!" John D. Rockefeller was six months younger than his fellow robber baron, born on July 8, 1839.

That year, a new, imported fad swept the country that had a profound impact on Huguette. In London, the renowned architect Sir Edwin Lutyens built an elaborate four-story Palladian dollhouse for

Queen Mary at the behest of her cousin Princess Marie. It included a tiny Rolls-Royce Silver Ghost in the garage, miniature furniture, 750 tiny paintings, and even miniature bottles of Château Lafite. James Barrie, Rudyard Kipling, and Arthur Conan Doyle wrote new stories that were included in miniature books, prompting a *New York Times* feature, QUEEN'S DOLLS HAVE PRICELESS LIBRARY. Prohibitionists in America complained about the display of liquor: WINE CELLAR IN DOLL HOUSE FOR QUEEN IS QUESTIONED was the headline of a *Washington Post* article. The dollhouse was put on public display to raise money for charity.

This much-publicized Lilliputian 1924 dwelling launched a craze among upper-class American women for dollhouses. Mrs. James Ward Thorne of Chicago, who had married into Montgomery Ward's family, was inspired to commission craftsmen to create sixty-eight miniature rooms, with replicas of antique American furniture and European interiors, which would later go on permanent display at the Art Institute of Chicago. "This was a very female hobby," explains Lindsay Mican Morgan, a curator at the Art Institute, explaining that wealthy women seized on the novelty constructions as a form of self-expression. "These women often didn't have full control over their own world and their own lives. Here they were reaching out to create their own little worlds that they completely controlled themselves."

For the already doll-obsessed Huguette, these idealized miniature worlds were a source of wonder. She already owned dollhouses, but this upscale enthusiasm made her passion a respectable hobby. Huguette would go on to commission and collect many dollhouses, paying meticulous attention to getting the period details and proportions just right.

———

Although her father still bragged about having the energy of a robust middle-aged man, William Andrews Clark had begun to look and feel his age. In the summer of 1924, the senator and his wife and daughter decamped for Santa Barbara again, joined by three of his grandchildren: Charles Clark's daughters Mary, Patricia, and Agnes. Local man-about-town Marshall Bond Jr. lovingly described a party that the senator and Anna gave for the young women in his 1974 memoir, *Adventures with Peons, Princes, and Tycoons*. A Los Angeles band played jazz—this was, after all, the Roaring Twenties—and couples danced until twelve, after which they ate a midnight meal that included Lobster Newberg and Chicken à la King. "I later learned that the Clarks had one of the most celebrated French chefs in the world," Bond wrote. But the senator sat out the event. "Mrs. Clark took me into the study to meet the senator, who was slumped in an easy chair, scowling like an ancient bird of prey… We had one of the shortest conversations in history, consisting of the word, 'Hello.'"

The writer noticed that the copper mogul showed up at the local barber shop in the sleepy resort town "in a limousine with a chauffeur and armed bodyguard, followed by another limousine with a chauffeur and another bodyguard." William Clark had survived the boisterous mining camps of Colorado, the outbreak of World War I, dangerous brain surgery, and a car accident, but as an octogenarian he was obsessed about his safety and that of his wife and daughter.

That August, Tadé Styka joined the Clarks in Santa Barbara to complete a series of portraits of the familly. "Eight times I have painted former United States Senator Clark's picture," he told the *Los Angeles Examiner*. "I also have painted Miss Huguette Clark, his beautiful daughter. Now I have been asked to come to California to paint Mrs. Clark."

Tadé, who had developed a handsome physique similar to Charles Atlas, was now making as many headlines for his romantic life as his art. Tadé's sensual portrait of film star Pola Negri, in a nearly backless gown, created a sensation, especially after newspapers reported that the duo had been a couple but the femme fatale had dumped Styka for Charlie Chaplin. The *Los Angeles Times* reporter Antony Anderson interviewed the artist and pronounced himself impressed, writing, "I found him as modest as anybody and quite unspoiled. Which says much for his strength of character… When you're a Polish aristocrat and a genius, at one and the same time, and the haut-monde tries to make a pet of you, look out!"

As a man who loved art, music, and the beach, Tadé fit in well with the Clark household in Santa Barbara, admired by Huguette and her parents. But for Huguette, the idyll had to end with the start of the school year. She returned to Manhattan for her senior year at Spence, traveling home with a chaperone. Anna sent her daughter a telegram on September 24: "Dearest Huguette, We both send our dear love. Without you the house is as gay as a bell without a sound. Styka is at work on your portrait all afternoon. Love to all, Mother." Tadé painted one portrait of Huguette playing the harp, plus another of Huguette wearing a pink dress and pearls.

Anna liked the speed of Western Union, sending Huguette another telegram a few days later: "I wish you all good luck in your senior year. All well here your father the same." She also told Huguette that she was about to have family houseguests: Katherine Clark Morris and her physician husband, Lewis Morris; plus Charles and Celia Clark, who had separated but were showing up together in a temporary display of unity. Aware of Clark's advancing age, his children were especially attentive.

To update her parents on her New York life, Huguette wrote to her father on October 5, 1924, listing her classes—including nineteenth-century literature, Bible literature, botany—and reassuring him that she was seeing a lot of her relatives. "The Clark girls are here in New York and have a nice apartment which I think is much nicer for them than staying at a hotel all winter as they have home cooking," she wrote. Her mother's sister, Amelia, who had recently married the retired mining engineer Bryce Turner, was in Manhattan watching out for Huguette, too. "Tante Amelia took me out to the theatre tonight and I had a lovely time," Huguette wrote to her father. "The rooms here at the hotel are lovely and very comfortable…My bedroom is perfectly lovely. The sun pours in in the morning and I think it is most cheerful."

William and Anna Clark had planned to return to New York by Thanksgiving, but he had unexpected business to attend to in Los Angeles, so Anna sent a telegram apologizing for the delay to "Dearest Hugo." But the Clarks were back in time for Christmas, reopening their showplace of a home.

In early January Tadé Styka, who had lingered in California after a successful exhibit of his paintings at the Cannell and Chaffin gallery in Los Angeles, sent flowers to Huguette along with a teasing and affectionate letter, in French.

Chere Mademoiselle,

Because you love them, I would like to send you all of the red flowers in the world! But I fear that it would be too significant.

Here everything is so superficial that I cannot wait to return to New York.

Ten days and I hope to contemplate the canvasses smeared by your "little paws" that I kiss now.

Avec mes affectueux hommages por vos parents, Tadé Styka

That was quite a flirtatious letter to send to an impressionable eighteen-year-old.

On February 28, 1925, Clark's oldest daughter, Mary, married her handsome third husband, Marius de Brabant, who had worked his way up from a lowly clerk to become a Los Angeles traffic manager for the Union Pacific Railroad. As a wedding gift, Mary gave him $500,000. The wedding was held at a secret location, and family members refused to give the press any information about the guests or last-minute ceremony.

The reason for the secrecy became clear a few days later: William Andrews Clark was dying. He had contracted a cold that had turned into pneumonia and was raging through his body. At his Fifth Avenue mansion, Anna, Huguette, and the copper king's two older daughters gathered at his bedside, holding a vigil during the final few hours as he lay there unconscious. Clark died on the evening of March 2. He was eighty-six years old, and his life had spanned the era from the stagecoach to the invention of the airplane, from a frontier country with only twenty-six states to a star-spangled flag with forty-eight stars. The contents of his wallet included the totems of his life: a copper penny, a newspaper clipping of the hymn "Abide with Me," a photo of himself with Anna, his newly renewed January 9 pistol permit, a ticket to the Metropolitan Museum, membership cards to the National Democratic Club and the Freemasons, and a business card for Tadé Styka.

Huguette had grown up worrying about her elderly father's health, but he had always seemed indomitable. Their four-unit family was now down to her and her mother, and she felt very much alone.

Headlines coast-to-coast marked Clark's death, and thousands of flowery words were typed on deadline to convey his only-in-America ascension from farm boy to copper Croesus. SENATOR CLARK'S VIVID LIFE: HE WON FORTUNE IN WESTERN INDUSTRY, ACHIEVED POWER IN POLITICS AND ROSE TO FAME AS AN ART COLLECTOR, summed up the *New York Times* headline. The most revealing accounts appeared in the Montana newspapers, where the pioneer's passing was treated as the end of an era. In Butte, the city government ordered the flags to fly at half-staff. FROM ALL SIDES COME TRIBUTES TO BELOVED MAN, gushed the *Butte Daily Post.* Byron Cooney of the *Montana American* wrote a personal reminiscence, noting that Clark's favorite song was "The Star Spangled Banner," and that "he would stand on a chair, leading the chorus; at times he even stood on a table."

There was a run on New York florists as more than four hundred arrangements were sent to Clark's Fifth Avenue mansion, including President Coolidge's offering of orchids and lilies of the valley. The service began with the hymn "Abide with Me." Clark had planned his funeral to mimic that of his daughter Andrée, with the same minister presiding, Dr. Ernest Stires of St. Thomas Church, and the reading of his favorite poem, William Cullen Bryant's "Thanatopsis," a comforting paen about recalling the glories of nature on one's deathbed, including such lines as: "The golden sun, the planets, all the infinite host of heaven, are shining on the sad abodes of death." Montana senator Burton Wheeler attended along with the president of the Anaconda Company. But only the immediate family went up to Woodlawn Cemetery in the Bronx for the interment. Clark had put in writing that he wanted to be buried "without undue pomp or ceremony."

What many mourners undoubtedly were wondering was: how would the Clark millions be divided up? The answer came in early April when Clark's will, which he had signed on May 29, 1922, was filed in Butte for probate. The same flinty-eyed instincts that helped William Andrews Clark accumulate his fortune—gouging on the price of eggs, giving miners ruinous terms on bank loans—had returned with a vengeance in his dotage, and he had punctuated his will with hurtful clauses.

Clark's last will and testament bluntly gave Anna and Huguette an eviction notice from the Fifth Avenue mansion and even decreed a precise date for vacating. By June 10, 1928, the day after Huguette's twenty-second birthday, they needed to be out of the home in which they had lived since 1911. Clark then wanted the house to be sold—along with virtually all of the possessions other than the art—with the proceeds divided among his five children. If Anna and Huguette wanted any of the objects that they treasured, they could bid for them at auction just like everyone else. His motivation may have been fairness to both of his families, but the tone and arbitrary date were cruel. The senator had put aside $600,000 to pay for Anna's and Huguette's expenses while they were in the house, but if they did not use all of the money, it was to be parceled out equally to all of his children.

His estate was underestimated for tax purposes in Montana as being worth $48 million, although unverified estimates have put it as high as $250 million, about $3.3 billion today. New York authorities mounted a court challenge to probate the will in New York to impose local taxes but lost, thanks to Clark's meticulous record keeping of his time out of state.

Anna received a bequest of only $2.5 million, although her husband indicated in his will that he had previously provided for her needs. Clark gave her the belongings from their Paris apartment at No. 56 Victor Hugo, which included silverware, rugs, hangings, and furniture. Bellosguardo was not specifically mentioned in Clark's will, but he had made prior arrangements to give the estate to Anna. The senator included one clause in his will that appeared to be designed to protect Anna from any efforts by his older children to seize her extraordinary collection of diamonds, emeralds, pearls, and rubies. Clark pointedly noted that if Anna had anything stored in a safe deposit box, no one could "hamper or hinder" her access.

He named Anna and his older four children as executors, but Anna promptly resigned, unwilling to tangle with her stepchildren. They had all tolerated one another while the senator was alive, but she still remembered their cool reaction when she initially joined the family and their unsubtle hints that she was an adventuress. Even though she would have received a fee as an executor, she preferred not to be in the awkward position of discussing money with her Clark relations. She had the security of a trusted adviser in place: her husband's controller, William B. Gower, was an administrator of the estate.

Since Huguette was under twenty-one years old, her father put in special provisions including a sliding scale allowance: $5,000 per month at age nineteen, rising to $7,500 per month at age twenty. To protect her from fortune hunters, Clark decided to make the rest of her inheritance available in bits and pieces as she grew older. When Huguette reached the age of twenty-six in 1932, she would receive one-third of what she was due, and the remaining one-third portions would be paid when she turned thirty and then thirty-three. If she died before reaching age thirty-three and did not yet have children, the money would go to her half siblings. Anna was named Huguette's guardian, with a backup of Clark's oldest daughter, the serial monogamist Mary Culver Kling de Brabant.

Clark's other four children initially received an estimated $15 million each—inflation adjusted, that's $200 million today—in addition to previous gifts they had been given such as Clark's stock in the Union Pacific Railroad. Clark was penurious in the rest of his bequests. He gave his three surviving sisters $25,000 each. His loyal butler, Frederick Dean, and his Butte housekeeper for more than twenty years, Annie Harrington, each received $2,500.

The surprising twist in Clark's will was his plans for his art collection. Fancying himself a brilliant collector with impeccable taste, he wanted that legacy to be admired by future generations in the most prestigious museum in the country. Executives at the Metropolitan Museum were startled to learn that the copper king had bequeathed the museum more than two hundred paintings plus statues by Donatello and Canova, tapestries, seventeenth-century rugs, antique lace, and Grecian and Etruscan antiquities.

But the gift came with a catch: Clark had insisted on conditions designed to infuriate the Metropolitan's trustees, a group that included financier J. P. Morgan and artist Daniel Chester French, best known for his sculpture of Abraham Lincoln at the Lincoln Memorial. Clark demanded that the museum accept his entire collection and create a special gallery in which to display it. This was an all-or-nothing offer, a display of egomania of the first order and an attempt to impose his will from the grave.

Metropolitan Museum president Robert de Forest, a blue blood who had inherited his board seat from his wealthy father-in-law, acted as if he was offended by the bequest. He immediately announced that the trustees might turn down the art because of the onerous conditions. Telling reporters that he did not want to "tie the hands" of future administrators by forcing them to showcase the entire Clark collection, de Forest added that the museum lacked the gallery space to house the artworks. This contemptuous view was echoed in the newspapers. "Not all of the items are worthy of a place in the Museum," sniffed the *New York Times*, adding that if the museum gave in to Clark's wishes, the Met was in danger of becoming a "mausoleum to enshrine the fame of American collectors."

In a unanimous vote, the Met trustees turned down the Clark bequest. His children were outraged. "Any city in Europe would have accepted it without question," complained Katherine Morris, Clark's daughter. The senator had foreseen this outcome, shrewdly designating the Corcoran Gallery as an alternate recipient. He had a long history with the museum, serving as a trustee, loaning paintings, and donating thousands of dollars for art prizes. After the women in the Clark family—Anna, Huguette, and Clark's daughters from his first marriage, Mary de Brabant and Katherine Morris—eventually agreed to contribute $700,000 to fund a museum expansion, the Corcoran accepted the art.

Shortly after Clark's death, Tadé Styka completed his final portrait of the senator and delivered it to his widow and daughter. Huguette responded with a grateful note, written on a black-bordered condolence card.

Cher Monsieur,
Thank you a thousand times for the portrait of mon cher papa, and please accept the expression of my admiration for your marvelous talent, which makes me so happy at the moment.
Bien sincerement a vous, Huguette Clark

Huguette graduated from the Spence School that May, but it was hardly a moment for celebration. She was in mourning, not just for her father but for the life they had led as a family. On May 27, she received congratulatory telegrams from friends and family members like her aunt Hanna La Chapelle. A few of her academically oriented classmates were going on to college, while some of her school friends were already engaged. In her Spence autograph book, her classmates wrote sweet inscriptions. "Let's hope you have the best luck in the world," scribbled her friend Aileen. "Here's to the time I almost killed myself by slipping on the side of your pool," wrote Frances. Added a friend nicknamed Twinkle, "Let's not make this a real goodbye for we must see each other a lot next year."

For Huguette's half brother Charles, the death of the family patriarch proved liberating. Charles Clark and his wife, Celia, had been at odds for many years. Although tired of his philandering, Celia had nonetheless balked at his request for a divorce. But the prospect of a large settlement made Celia amenable to her husband's wishes. Celia filed for divorce within weeks of her father-in-law's funeral and was granted her marital freedom five months later. As part of the divorce settlement, Charles set up trust funds for their four children, but even though he was now extremely rich he was also punitive—he later sued to get $860,000 in dividends from his children's trusts. As soon as his divorce came through, Charles Clark married his latest paramour, Elizabeth Judge of Louisville. Once he remarried, he not only cut his son and three daughters out of his will but excised them from his life.

William Andrews Clark had spent his life trying to thwart

adversaries from cheating him out of his money. After his death, the battle continued, but now it was his children who were forced to defend their inheritance. The most serious challenge was launched in February 1926 by three middle-aged Missouri sisters, who claimed that Clark was their father, too, and demanded millions from his estate.

Mrs. Effie Clark McWilliams, Mrs. Addie Clark Miller, and Mrs. Alma Clark insisted that their father, druggist William Anderson Clark, was the same person as William Andrews Clark. The women stated that their father had abandoned the family in Stewartsville, Missouri, in 1879, moved to Montana, and struck it rich as a miner. The women had no recollections of their father, just a tintype that they claimed was a likeness.

Despite this flimsy evidence, the sisters won the right to a jury trial in Butte in July 1926. It turned out to be less of a serious legal battle than a two-week vaudeville show with spectators clamoring for seats. A parade of witnesses on both sides came forward to detail the whereabouts of Sen. William Andrews Clark and his purported doppelganger at various dates. There were a few vague similarities: both men had briefly been schoolteachers, both had been members of the Masonic Lodge, and both had lived in Montana.

Anna and Huguette did not attend the trial but hired their own lawyer, unwilling to trust the attorneys brought in by Clark's four oldest children. The senator's entire life was replayed, with Montana pioneers in their seventies and eighties taking the witness stand to recount Clark's early mining days and his honeymoon by wagon train with his first wife. His son Charles Clark testified about his own privileged youth in Paris and Long Island, emphasizing the time he spent with his father. One of Tadé Styka's oil portraits of William Andrews Clark was even propped on an easel as evidence to demonstrate the senator's distinctive patrician appearance.

Anna Clark submitted a document showing that she and William Andrews Clark had registered their marriage on May 5, 1909, in the state of Montana. The piece of paper stated that the couple had been married on May 25, 1901, in the Republic of France.

The decisive evidence was unearthed by the former circulation manager of the *Butte Miner*, Phil Goodwin. Appointed by President Wilson as the postmaster of Butte, Goodwin remembered the names of many city residents and belatedly recalled a man named William Anderson Clark. Goodwin tracked down the man, who was on his deathbed. This other William Clark admitted that he was the father of the three women and had walked out on them in Missouri. Without bothering to get a divorce, in 1880 he had married a woman named Anna Pierce, who then became Anna Clark. Worried about being charged with bigamy, he had not come forward after he read about his daughters' faulty paternity claims. But now with only a short time left to live, William Anderson Clark agreed to give an affidavit admitting, "I left this family down there owning to disagreeable family surroundings and with the intention of never going back."

It took the jury just forty-five minutes to reach a verdict and throw out the fortune hunters. When court officials polled the panel, the questions were framed in disconcerting fashion. The jury was asked to determine whether Anna La Chapelle was indeed Clark's wife and "is the defendant Huguette Marcelle Clark a child of the marriage?" The jury's answer, both times, was yes. News accounts of the verdict cited these questions, which was humiliating for Anna and Huguette.

The pragmatic Anna La Chapelle Clark recoiled at the idea of sitting in her husband's Fifth Avenue mansion and counting the days until she and Huguette would be forced to vacate. She began looking for a new home, settling on an Italian palazzo-style luxury building at 907 Fifth Avenue, which had been built in 1915 and was located just five blocks away from the senator's mansion. The twelve-story limestone residence, with a central courtyard, had been laid out so that each floor featured two large apartments. Advertisements for the building boasted: "The twelfth floor is considered one of the finest apartments that has ever been constructed."

With fourteen rooms, including four bedrooms, the space was a fraction of what Anna and Huguette had grown used to. But as in many luxury buildings of the era, top-floor single-room servants' quarters were available that could be rented by tenants; Anna signed up for several spots. In November 1926, Anna went on a spending spree to decorate the new abode, buying antiques from the London firm Charles including a $3,500 Queen Anne walnut wing chair with needlepoint and a $4,000 William and Mary sofa covered with seventeenth-century tapestry. She also spent $13,500 for a Louis XV sofa and five armchairs, and ordered thirty yards of blue chenille carpet for Huguette's suite of rooms. The soothing color matched Huguette's eyes.

Chapter Nine

Society Girl

Huguette first appeared in the black leather–bound *Social Register* as a twelve-year-old in 1918 but only now, as a young woman ready to enter society and find a husband, did the status-oriented designation truly matter. Even though her family had not arrived on the *Mayflower*, thanks to her late father's fortune, she was perceived as a good catch. Social mores were changing as the Jazz Age and the suffragettes' victories made women more adventurous, but the time-honored rituals for an heiress of Huguette's generation endured. The mating dance officially began with a round of parties culminating in coming out.

Huguette and her mother sailed back from Europe to New York in October 1926 on the *Berengaria*, the most luxurious ship in the Cunard fleet, which featured a palm garden, a ballroom, a tea room, a grill, and large promenade decks for the seven hundred first-class passengers. Other notables included Vincent Astor, his sister Alice, and her husband, the polo-playing Russian prince Serge Obolensky. Within days of her return to her new Fifth Avenue apartment, Huguette was deluged with invitations from friends and former Spence classmates for their debutante parties.

She was eager to reciprocate, giving a luncheon in honor of her friend Carolyn Storrs at Pierre's Park Avenue restaurant, a society haven owned by Monte Carlo émigré Charles Pierre Casalasco, who would later launch the Pierre Hotel. Carolyn Storrs, an outgoing blonde beauty who never missed a chance to perform an undulating dance at a charity gala, was the daughter of advertising entrepreneur Frank Vance Storrs. The self-made Storrs, an Ohio native, had launched the theatre program *Playbill* in 1884 in Manhattan, distributing it to theatres for free and amassing enough advertising revenue to subsequently buy and build two dozen movie theatres in New York and New Jersey.

A show business character known for his block-long black limousine with snow-white doors, he had changed his name from Strauss to Storrs during World War I, claiming that he was concerned about anti-German prejudice. His ties to Anna Clark and her sister, Amelia, were due in part to their mutual love of France. Storrs had been given the French Legion of Honor in 1926 for promoting French culture in the United States. The families had many mutual friends, including Tadé Styka. Storrs's daughter Carolyn had studied in Paris, and she and Huguette could converse in French. Storrs and his wife, Amanda, gave opulent parties, and Huguette, her mother, and her aunt Amelia were regulars on the guest lists.

William Andrews Clark had celebrated the coming-out festivities of his two New York granddaughters by giving large and lavish parties at his Fifth Avenue palace. The debutantes could descend his marble staircase to the sound of his magnificent organ. But Anna, now a widow for less than two years, opted for a more subdued affair in honor of Huguette, just a simple luncheon. But even without the senator's excess, Huguette was featured in the *New York Times* on December 5, 1926, as one of the debutantes of the season. She looks slender and attractive in the studio photograph. She has bobbed her wavy hair to ear-length and is wearing pearls and a dark short-sleeved dress with a lacy shawl collar. In contrast to her joyous and relaxed appearance in family snapshots, she has a vulnerable and dreamy expression in this photo, as if gazing into the future for clues about the next stage of her life.

Architectural critics had once attacked her father's palace as a vulgar eyesore. But now the mansion was a hulking ghost presence, a vestige of bygone times, and on the verge of being dismantled. After more than a year on the market, no buyer had emerged who had the money and the moxie to become the new lord of the nine-story manor. By now the grandiose Fifth Avenue residences built by robber barons had fallen out of fashion—the taxes and upkeep were ruinous—and the châteaus of Cornelius Vanderbilt and John Jacob Astor had already succumbed to the wrecking ball, replaced by luxury apartment buildings. Henry Frick saved his Fifth Avenue home for posterity only by turning it into an art museum. The *New York Times* lamented that "the great gargoyle-fronted bronze villas of New York's admitted social set" were being torn down "with magic swiftness" and pronounced the Clark house "doomed." Indeed, developer Anthony Campagna spent less than $3 million for William Clark's "folly," which had cost the senator more than $7 million to build. Campagna planned to replace it with a twelve-story, sixty-eight-unit apartment building.

In February 1927, the doors of the Clark mansion were opened to the public for a final viewing. A crowd lined up to pay the fifty-cent admission charge, with proceeds going to the Travelers Aid Society and the Junior Emergency Relief Society. The curious New Yorkers marched through the marble halls, the billiard room, the music room, and even the once-intimate bedroom suites of Mr. and Mrs. Clark. Charlie Chaplin was among the gawkers, bringing along several friends and admiring the banquet hall. The place had been denuded of most of the furnishings. The Genoese red velvet wall hangings, blue Sèvres porcelain plates, silverware with a fruit pattern for twenty-four, Italian Renaissance lamps, Chinese furniture in black lacquer and teakwood, embroidered screens, and Circassian walnut bedroom furniture had all been sold at auction a year earlier.

Film companies, hotels, and interior decorators came in to bid for the hand-carved paneling and remaining fixtures. William Fox, the founder of the Fox Film Company, bought the Sienna marble dining room fireplace for use in a movie theatre. The decorating firm Maison Cluny of Paris purchased parts of the state dining room. Mary Clark Culver Kling de Brabant proved to be the lone sentimental member of the family. William Clark's oldest daughter hired an artist to sketch the interiors of the house and purchased the wood-paneled library for her eighty-acre estate Plaisance, located on Long Island's northern

Gold Coast at Centerport. Anna Clark would regret that she had not made a similar bid, and later acquired some of the Sherwood Forest paneling from a decorator for use in her renovation of her California estate, Bellosguardo.

On March 27, 1927, a symphony of hammers and wrecking balls could be heard on Fifth Avenue as workmen began reducing the mansion to rubble. With William Andrews Clark's home torn down just sixteen years after its completion and his art collection shipped to Washington, he had left no tangible legacy in New York.

Huguette, now living just a few blocks away, could see her childhood vanish. The rooms where she had played with Andrée, the music room where she had practiced the violin, the pool where she had done laps, would soon be gone. She was experiencing a rarified form of downward mobility, adjusting to fewer servants and apartment living, which required sharing a common elevator with neighbors, albeit mostly of the proper social class.

That spring Huguette's dance card was filled with engagements: luncheon parties at Sherry's, joining fellow Spence alumnae at a theatrical review at Pierre's, helping out with other debutantes at a charity concert at Carnegie Hall. At the April wedding of her friend Grace Cuyler to Count Albert de Mun of Paris, Huguette was treated as quite the catch. "The reception at the Park Lane is said to have set some new marks by bubbling exuberance and enthusiasm," according to a syndicated feature writer. "And two or three of the French count's groomsmen elbowed each other again and again to get closer to fair-haired Huguette Clark whose French is so excellent."

A familiar face from her childhood was also dancing the Charleston on the debutante circuit that season: William MacDonald Gower, the tall, good-looking son of her father's longtime accountant, William B. Gower. The younger Bill Gower had grown up in New Rochelle but attended Manhattan's elite Trinity School (then an all-boys "brother" school to Huguette's Spence), where he was popular enough to be elected class secretary and was a member of the track team and the Dramatic Society. At Princeton, he had roomed with his Trinity classmate Frank Warburton, who was from a socially prominent family. Gower joined the literary and debating society Whig Hall, whose notable recent members had included F. Scott Fitzgerald and Adlai Stevenson. But while his roommate was chosen for the selective Tower Club, Gower did not get into one of the college's prestigious eating clubs and had to settle for the undistinguished Terrace Club. He listed himself as Republican and Presbyterian, like many of his classmates.

After graduating from Princeton in 1925, Gower had spent a year in California, and then returned to Manhattan to take a job at a well-known banking firm, J. and W. Seligman and Company at 54 Wall Street. Unsure whether he was cut out to be a banker, Gower was thinking of attending law school.

Gower was a well-groomed man with a high forehead and deep-set eyes, and his tuxedo was getting a workout that season. Carolyn Storrs invited him to a small dinner with friends at the Ritz-Carlton roof garden as an extra man, the sort of event where he came across the willowy Huguette. He soon began to quietly woo her. Gower had attended the right schools, his prospects appeared bright, and they had an overlapping social circle. There was a comfort in the fact that the young people had known each other for years and their parents were friendly. While Bill Gower had no money of his own, he did not convey any of the warning signs of a fortune hunter.

For Huguette, this romance seemed to be the path of least resistance. The man she had a crush on—Tadé Styka—had returned to Paris. She had continued to paint even without his instruction, and they wrote and saw each other whenever they were both in the same city, Paris or New York. But as much as Tadé had flirted with her, he was an older, sophisticated artist who was linked to movie stars, quoted by newspapers for his opinion of the most beautiful women in the world. Here was William Gower, not only attentive and interested but preapproved by her late father.

Anna had discouraged her daughter's crush on Tadé, and she had complicated feelings about Huguette's romance with Bill Gower. She confided her thoughts to her in-law Celia Tobin Clark, and those tales were later passed down to Celia's granddaughter Karine McCall. "Anna wanted Huguette to get married and she didn't want her to— she was worried that someone would take advantage of Huguette," said Karine. "She thought the artist wasn't the right type of person. She opposed Bill Gower, but Huguette thought she was in love with him."

Anna took Huguette to Paris that June for their usual seasonal trip, and gave her daughter a party in conjunction with the Quai d'Orsay Ball, a Franco-American charity that drew Vanderbilts and other well-known Americans. Anna might have been keeping an eye open for a titled husband. Many of Huguette's friends were either marrying European royalty (Carolyn Storrs would wed the son of the Countess Napoleon Magne of Paris) or at least young American princes of industry.

Following their trip to Paris, the two Clark women spent the summer at Bellosguardo. Santa Barbara was still recovering from a devastating 1925 earthquake, but there was an active summer social scene—polo matches, dances at the Biltmore Hotel, croquet on the lawns of the large estates.

Around this time, Gordon Lyle Jr. recalls that his family visited Huguette and her mother in Santa Barbara. His father, Dr. William Gordon Lyle, was married to the much younger Leontine De Sabla Lyle, who had been one of Huguette's classmates at Spence. This was a close and enduring family friendship: Gordon's younger sister, Tina, was Anna Clark's goddaughter. "We'd stay at the Miramar Hotel for a month, but we went swimming almost every day at their beach. I saw a gay young girl," he recalls. Lyle remembers meeting Bill Gower and being unimpressed. "He was tall and nice looking, and it didn't seem to me that he was in the same social league that the Clarks were in," Lyle says. "We didn't think he belonged in that family."

On December 14, 1927, Anna Clark announced to the world's social editors that her daughter Huguette was engaged to marry William Gower. The two photos that ran in newspapers accompanying the story show Huguette looking surprisingly matronly but laughing and looking happily at the camera, while Gower sports a smug smile of satisfaction.

PRINCETON GRAD TO MARRY HEIRESS read the headline in the *Trenton Times*, as if Gower's Ivy League pedigree made him fit to be her consort. But the *New York Sun* cast a more jaundiced eye, writing of William Gower: "Neither he nor his father are listed in the New York Social Register." The *Sun* pointed out that Huguette could have had her pick among available men, noting, "Miss Clark was one of the popular debutantes of last season." Virtually every article mentioned her eye-popping inheritance. The *Havre-News* of Montana helpfully suggested that Gower's profession as a banker might prove useful: "One of the city's wealthiest debutantes is to have a husband who should know how to help her take care of her money. Huguette M. Clark, who is in her minority, receives an allowance of $7,500 a month and will have control of millions later."

Huguette and Bill Gower made their first appearances as an engaged couple at two December holiday parties at the Ritz-Carlton given by the ubiquitous Frank Storrs. The first party was built around an elegant Southern garden theme but included a miniature airplane hanging from the ceiling, a nod to Charles Lindbergh's historic New York–to–Paris flight earlier that year. Frank Storrs's next extravaganza two weeks later celebrating his younger daughter, Anne, caught the attention of jaded society writers, who termed it "the jungle party." Hearst society editor Maury Paul, who wrote a syndicated column under the pseudonym "Cholly Knickerbocker" and made his nightly rounds wearing a white tie and his signature red carnation, devoted an entire article to the hedonistic event. The man who invented the phrase "café society" explained that Mrs. Storrs had been so captivated by a jungle-themed restaurant in Europe that she purchased the props and had them shipped to the Ritz-Carlton.

The roof of the hotel's ballroom was hung with Southern moss, live monkeys cavorted about, the waiters wore monkey costumes, and the tables were decorated with exotic flowering plants and displays of coconuts and pineapples. As Knickerbocker wrote, "All in all, Mr. and Mrs. Storrs provided the debutante set with the unique party of the season." Professional theatre entertainers amused the crowd, and after dinner, the tables were cleared away and two orchestras played so that the guests could dance until the wee hours. Photos of Bill Gower in his tuxedo and Huguette wearing her ubiquitous pearls and a simple, well-tailored sleeveless gown made the newspapers.

The new year of 1928 entered with a cold snap and brought with it a round of celebrations for Huguette and her fiancé. Carolyn and Anne Storrs were so happy about the engagements in their social set that they gave a dinner for four couples, including Huguette and Bill, at the Ritz-Carlton, then took their guests to a performance of *Rosalie* at the New Amsterdam Theatre. The Gershwin musical featured an airy merengue of a plot about a princess who comes to America and falls in love with a West Point lieutenant, with a score including, "How Long Has This Been Going On?"

Huguette was given a formal engagement party by Lewis Latham Clarke and his wife, the parents of her Spence classmate Florence Kip Clarke. A descendant of Emperor Charlemagne via his father and one of the signers of the Declaration of Independence via his mother, the pedigreed Clarke was the president of the American Exchange National Bank. This was as upper-crust Manhattan as one could get. An orchestra played for eighty guests at the Clarke home at 998 Fifth Avenue. The popular songs that season included "Someone to Watch Over Me." Huguette had never enjoyed being the center of attention, but this was her moment to take a whirl on the dance floor. Despite her father's dire warnings—that no one would love her for herself; her money was the draw—she believed she had found the man of her dreams.

That March, Huguette, her fiancé, and her mother went to Washington for the Corcoran Gallery's official opening ceremony for the newly built William Andrews Clark annex. President Calvin Coolidge, who arrived at 9:10 p.m., gave his arm to Anna Clark, and they led a procession to the entrance of the new wing. Silent Cal cut the cord, and the crowd applauded; news reports noted that Coolidge responded with a broad smile. Designed by architect Charles Platt, known for creating the Freer Gallery in Washington, the pink granite building included seven rooms to display the former senator's artworks, including a special room for the Salon Doré. For Huguette this evening was a chance to show her husband-to-be the treasures that had surrounded her as a child.

The *Washington Post* gushed about Clark's gifts in a grateful editorial, noting, "Some of these rarities are beyond price, notably the Gothic rugs and thirteenth century windows..." But the *New York Times* art critic Elisabeth L. Cary took a more acerbic view of the Corcoran's new offerings. She bluntly stated that as a collector, Clark was the victim of his own taste: "He bought only what pleased him, and if, as not infrequently happened, he was deceived in the quality of his purchases he accepted disclosure philosophically and shouldered the blame."

———

Huguette's engagement had been announced in December, but she and her mother were coy about setting a wedding date. Anna arranged to rent and decorate an eighth-floor apartment in the same building, 907 Fifth Avenue, for herself, so that her daughter and Bill Gower could begin married life on the twelfth floor. Huguette had been a bridesmaid and a guest at the weddings of many friends, and it was expected that Huguette would reciprocate with a large wedding at her family's usual religious locale, St. Thomas Church on Fifth Avenue.

So New York society was taken aback when Huguette opted for a small wedding at Bellosguardo on August 17, 1928. "The wedding will be extremely quiet, with only members of the family present and there will be no attendants," according to an item in the local Santa Barbara newspaper. A wedding photo shows the bride and groom with Anna Clark; William and Helen Gower; Anna's sister, Amelia, and her husband, retired mining engineer Bryce Turner; Anna's brother, Arthur La Chapelle, and his wife, Hanna; and Dr. and Mrs. William Gordon Lyle and their impish, blonde, four-year-old daughter, Tina.

Despite the understated ambience, Huguette wore an elaborate white wedding gown with a veil and a train that stretched out six feet, and she carried an enormous bouquet of flowers. Just a week earlier, she and Bill had happily joined in the annual Santa Barbara fiesta celebration, featuring polo matches and garden parties. But now in the group wedding portrait, Huguette seemed nervous and downcast. In a formal photograph given to the newspapers, the newlyweds look more serious than joyous.

For Bill Gower, marrying Huguette elevated his social status by several notches. In the discussions leading up to the wedding, Anna and Huguette had agreed to give the groom a large dowry estimated at around $1 million. William Andrews Clark had settled money on Anna La Chapelle when they married. Perhaps Anna saw this as a way to try to start off her daughter's marriage on a more equitable foot-ing. But to put it bluntly, William Gower was being paid to marry Huguette. "They were so mismatched," says Gordon Lyle Jr. "I don't know why she married him, whether she got pushed into it or lured into it."

From the groom's perspective, the substantial sum quieted any qualms he might have felt about embarking on matrimony with his sheltered and unworldly bride. He could not lose: he would either be rich and happy with Huguette, or he could move on with his finances assured for life.

The couple honeymooned in San Francisco: their wedding night was a disaster. Huguette could never bring herself to reveal the full details. But later in life, when her friend Suzanne Pierre and her nurses asked why her marriage did not last, Huguette always referred to how unprepared she had been for the shock of sex. She used phrases like, "It hurt, I didn't like it." As Kati Despretz Cruz says, "Huguette told my grandmother [Suzanne Pierre] that the marriage was never consummated."

Many years later, Huguette's assistant, Chris Sattler, was organiz-ing the thousands of books in her apartment when he came across a poignant find: a dozen how-to sex manuals. "They were all from the 1930s, after her marriage," says Chris. "They were very clinical, unhelpful, written by doctors. But she was interested in knowing about it."

Despite their apparent sexual incompatibility, the newlyweds did not immediately separate. A month after their marriage, a syndicated article analyzed the financial inequities in the marriage and concluded that the couple would not last together. A $30-A-WEEK HUSBAND FOR THE $50,000,000 HEIRESS: THE NEWEST MONEY ROMANCE-DOMESTIC PROBLEMS OF THE POOR LITTLE RICH GIRL CLARK AND HER DAILY $333 was the headline of the article in the *Salt Lake Tri-bune*. "The average young man refuses to live on his wife's money," wrote society writer Eleanor Town. "He thinks it is a disgrace. And of course, that is the manly and proper way for him to feel." The author added that for the couple to try to live on Gower's meager income would be equally disastrous: "Who pays the club dues? Is Mr. Gower's income sufficient to enable him to travel with her friends? If not, what happens?"

In keeping with the national obsession with Huguette, on October 28, 1928, an item appeared in the *Salt Lake Tribune* reporting that she and her husband would be passing through Salt Lake on the Union Pacific at 9:30 p.m. "The young couple are returning from a honeymoon spent in Los Angeles," the newspaper said. "Gower is to enter Columbia upon his return and begin the study of law."

William Gower moved into Huguette's apartment at 907 Fifth Avenue. The overly blushing bride marked her return to Manhattan by treating herself to jewelry. On October 31, 1928, the new Mrs. William MacDonald Gower went to Cartier and splurged on $15,500 earrings combining emeralds, pearls, and diamonds, a $2,640 diamond wristwatch, and a $3,125 diamond bracelet. In January, she returned to the store to purchase a $320 gold cigarette case. The Gowers continued to appear in public as a couple with their whereabouts charted in the society columns, such as attending a wedding anniversary party for friends at the ever popular Sherry's. On April 8, Mrs. Gower bought herself a Steinway piano, but as always she remained more passionate about painting than music.

That dedication was rewarded in a way not normally available to fledgling artists—with a show in a major museum. The Corcoran Gallery freed up wall space from April 28 to May 19 for a showing of seven paintings by Huguette Clark, who used her maiden name for the exhibit. The museum's gratitude to the Clarks shone through the catalogue, yet the curator went beyond boilerplate politeness, announcing that the twenty-two-year-old heiress was creating impressive work:

"From the day of her birth Huguette Clark has lived in an artistic atmosphere. She has been surrounded by many treasures of various Schools and Periods, contained in the notable art collection bequeathed to this gallery by her father, the late William Andrews Clark. She has had the benefit of extensive European travel; and added to these advantages, she is endowed with unusual natural talent."

Huguette included two scenes of Central Park as viewed from her Fifth Avenue home, one of the sparkling oasis at night and the other a pristine wintry scene after a snowstorm. The show also included two intricate portraits of her dolls, a party scene, a study of hydrangeas, and a work entitled "Portrait of Myself."

A self-portrait by Huguette, included many years later in a Christie's catalogue, might have been the one shown at the Corcoran. In the painting, the artist is standing in front of a canvas holding a brightly-hued palette of paint, and turning to look over her shoulder. She wears a flowing rose-colored painting jacket, her wavy, blonde hair shines, and her mouth is a lipsticked red bow. She looks serene, an artist deeply involved with her work, taking a momentary break. The painting is striking and well-executed.

The Corcoran exhibit was a triumph for Huguette. Her painting teacher, Tadé Styka, was in Paris but returned to the United States to see the show. A few weeks later, Huguette, her husband, and her mother attended a dinner and concert on May 9 at the home of Huguette's half sister Mary de Brabant. The guests that night included Huguette's other half sister, Katherine Morris, and her husband, Lewis Morris, plus Dr. William Gordon Lyle and his wife, Leontine. The grand de Brabant stone mansion at 7 East Fifty-First Street, on a block then known as Millionaire's Row, would later be occupied by the jewelry store Harry Winston. This was a festive family evening, with no apparent sign that trouble was bubbling just below the surface.

The bombshell dropped five days later in the Cholly Knickerbocker column in the *New York American*. "The distressing task of reporting, exclusively, that Huguette after nine short months of married life is about to divorce 'Bill' Gower comes to my lot," Knickerbocker wrote. "The possession of untold wealth, all the luxuries vast wealth will provide and enviable social position failed to make the union a success and about a week hence, Mrs. Clark and Huguette will start westward to spend the summer at their palatial estate in Santa Barbara, formerly the home of Mrs. William Miller Graham. From Santa Barbara, Huguette will go to Reno to establish residence and seek a divorce. The above is certain to cause a sensation in society for the Gowers were supposed to be happy and there have been no rumors of an estrangement."

Even though her marriage was over, Huguette did not actually go to Reno for another year. But she did immediately sign a new will, leaving everything to her mother. As Christie Merrill, a San Franciscan whose mother, Aileen Tobin, attended Spence with Huguette, recalls, "My mother told me that the family paid him a million to marry Huguette, and after he got the money, he ran off." Cholly Knickerbocker would later write in a follow-up column about Huguette that at the time of her marriage, she had given "her none-too-well dowered bridesgroom a cool million dollars so he would 'feel free.' He felt so 'free' Huguette had to divorce him and resume use of her maiden name."

That was an inside reference to Gower's romantic life. Within months of separating from Huguette, William Gower began squiring around a new woman who would never have wedding-night jitters: Constance Baxter Tevis McKee Toulmin.

Gower's new love collected wealthy husbands the way some women add charms to their bracelets. The daughter of rancher George Baxter, who served as the territorial governor of Wyoming, and his Southern belle wife, Constance (sometimes known as Cornelia) had been shipped to convent school in Paris. It didn't take. At age eighteen, she jilted her wealthy Denver fiancé to wed forty-year-old San Francisco widower Hugh Tevis. On their honeymoon to Japan in 1901, Hugh Tevis died suddenly in Yokohoma. Constance returned a pregnant widow and claimed her husband's million-dollar fortune.

But a million dollars only goes so far. Four years later, she befriended Pittsburgh playboy Hart McKee Jr., whose deceased father had made $20 million as a glass manufacturer. McKee was in the middle of divorcing his wife for a married woman. But as soon as his divorce came through, he dumped his paramour and married Constance in a quickie ceremony in 1905. The couple moved to Paris and she gave birth to a second son, but the marriage dissolved in spectacular fashion. The couple's 1908 divorce was a publicly covered brawl. She claimed that he stole her jewels and beat her, and that thirty-five maids quit one after another, fleeing McKee's sexual advances. McKee charged that Constance had conducted a flagrant affair with an Italian marquis. The scorching testimony produced such headlines as BEAUTY WILL TELL STORY OF GROSS CRUELTY followed by NOT SO INNOCENT AS SHE PRETENDS. She won custody of her son with McKee, but the French judge issued an order excoriating both parties for bad behavior.

Constance's saucy past would have been well-known to Huguette's mother, since they moved in the same social circles in Paris, prior to 1914. Constance was more than twenty years older than Bill Gower, and in fact, two of her three children were older than Gower. Newly divorced from her third husband, Evelyn Toulmin, Constance split her time between Paris and America.

Had Gower been a junior bank clerk, she would not have seen him as a serious suitor. But thanks to Huguette's dowry, he was a wealthy man. While some of Constance's luster had dimmed with age, she more than compensated by offering social entrée. Her well-connected parents entertained in style at their Southampton estate, and the family boasted new publishing connections, since her twenty-year-old niece, Leslie, had just become the second wife of fifty-five-year-old Condé Nast.

Huguette appeared to be sad and subdued after her marriage ended, pained by feelings of rejection. Gordon Lyle Jr. says, "I'm guessing it had a very negative effect on Huguette." The carefree, naïve young woman had learned a sobering lesson about the ways of the world.

Since Anna believed in the healing balm of a change of scenery, mother and daughter headed west for several months, spending time in Santa Barbara followed by Hawaii (where Huguette was listed on the *Malolo*'s ship manifest as Huguette Gower) and then back to Santa Barbara for the remainder of the summer. The vacation seems to have lifted Huguette's spirits, and she found solace in painting, judging by her letter to Tadé Styka, written in French on August 8 from Bellosguardo.

Cher Maitre,

I found your letter upon our return from Honolulu. What to tell you about my work? You will certainly be disappointed in your pupil. The heat was so strong that it stripped me of a little of my energy.

I only did five paintings, having only stayed five weeks and I have two in progress that I can finish here.

Really, you would create wonders if you spent a few months on this enchanting island. The color of the water is jade, sapphire, mauve and varies every day. The streets were lined with trees garnished with fiery red flowers, other flowers formed pink, yellow or mauve clusters.

The prettiest are the rainbow trees. I painted a branch, also a marvel of a white flower that lives but one night and dies with the sunrise.

One night we saw a moonlit rain shower followed by a magnificent rainbow, very visible. I so would have liked to paint this beautiful scene.

The departure is very moving, the Hawaiian music plays Aloha and they cover you with flower garlands and wish you a good trip.

The hotel is so trendy, they even clean the change. For my personal taste I would have liked it better at a more primitive time.

Maman joins me in sending you our
kindest regards, Huguette

In October, Tadé Styka moved from Paris to live in Manhattan full-time, renting an apartment with a studio on Central Park South. Huguette wrote a note to him from Santa Barbara, expressing her enthusiasm.

Cher Maitre,
I would like to welcome you to New York and am sending you five brushes so that you will quickly get to work.
I hope that they will please you.
We send you our best regards; your studious pupil, Huguette.

In December 1929, Walter Winchell mentioned the artist in his newspaper column, writing, "Tadé Styka, who charges them 10 G's for their portraits, is here from Paree looking for chumps." That was a plug since the chumps, of course, were the rich and famous regularly featured in Winchell's column. Tadé had shown his work at a

Chicago gallery in January and the Clarks sent him a telegram from California: "With all of our best wishes for a huge success in Chicago, Anna and Huguette Clark."

The Chicago art critics ran out of adjectives in enthusing about his work at the branch of the Knoedler Gallery. "It is a very rare exhibit that leaves you wordless," wrote Eleanor Jewett of the *Chicago Daily Tribune*. "It is astonishingly and astoundingly fine. The sweep of it rushes you from your feet...if there is genius in the world today, Styka is possessed of it."

But with the onset of the Great Depression, fewer wealthy patrons could afford to splurge on a portrait, even by a "genius." So Tadé had the free time and financial motive to resume his two-hour, four-times-per-week painting lessons with Huguette once she returned to Manhattan. (The market crash did not daunt Huguette, who dropped $2,700 in January 1930 at Cartier on a diamond, onyx, and emerald brooch, and also bought Monet's painting *Nympheas* from the Durand-Ruel Galleries.)

Bill Gower had been fond of his mother-in-law, and a year after he and Huguette separated, he wrote an apologetic note to Anna on March 19, 1930.

> *Dear Mrs. Clark,*
>
> *I have wanted for some time to write to you, but have hesitated because it seems quite impossible to convey with words what I want to say.*
>
> *I am very sorry that there had to be parting. I am sorry that the end came as it did in anger. I wish that there could have been the success we hoped for but were unable to attain.*
>
> *Your friendship and esteem always meant more to me than I can ever express. Your tireless efforts in every possible way to make things turn out for the best I shall always remember. There has been a loss greater than I have ever had. Sincerely, Bill.*

A month later, Huguette and her mother made the trip to Reno for the required three-month residency to get a divorce. In 1930, divorce was still a novelty: census records show that 196,000 divorced that year. New York State's unforgiving laws required proof of infidelity and a yearlong wait, but in wide-open Nevada, a spouse could list such grounds as desertion, neglect, or habitual drunkenness. Reno had become the nation's divorce capital, with dude ranches opening up to accommodate the flow of soon-to-be single women, a world chronicled in Clare Boothe Luce's 1936 catfight of a play, *The Women*. In petitioning for divorce, Huguette claimed that Gower had deserted her. The *New York Times* tried unsuccessfully to reach William Gower for comment, stating "he is understood to be in New York."

Huguette's arrival in Reno created a stir. She had brought along a large entourage including her dogs, a cook, a butler, several maids, a chauffeur, and a social secretary. Her uncle Arthur La Chapelle had arranged for Huguette to lease an entire floor at the Riverside Hotel, a redbrick luxury property, at the cost of $2,000 per month. In a syndicated feature that ran on June 28, 1930—WHY AMERICA'S $50,000,000 HEIRESS CAST OFF HER $30-A-WEEK PRINCE CHARMING—Huguette was criticized for violating the social mores of divorce land. "Extravagance and exclusiveness may be all right for Park Avenue, but they're out of place in Reno," the article huffed. "The majority of even the wealthiest divorce hunters have been satisfied with a suite at the most. It was recalled that Cornelius Vanderbilt was content with a single room...while even Mary Pickford selected an unostentatious home."

Avoiding other would-be divorcées, Huguette remained cloistered with her mother and the servants. Her vulnerability is palpable in a poignant letter that she wrote in French on hotel stationery on July 4, 1930, to Tadé, in which she expresses the desperate hope that she can count on him:

Cher Maitre,

I intend to return to New York by October 1rst and I hope to be able to get to my work on the fifteenth by the latest. Would you write to me as soon as possible, if I can count on you, as I would like to seriously work with you this winter?

It is still very hot here but fortunately we do not have New York's humidity.

The small dogs are fine and Shan is getting so fat he looks like a ball.

I hope your health leaves nothing to be desired.

Maman would like me to extend her greetings, to which I add my own, Huguette

When she did not hear back from him, Huguette was so upset that she sent him a needy telegram on July 26, 1930, which was uncharacteristically written in English.

DEAR MR. STYKA,

How are you standing the terrific heat. Did you receive my letter? Please wire.

All Good Wishes from us, Huguette Clark Gower.

She received her decree on August 11, which stated that she had been "granted an absolute divorce on the ground that the defendant has willfully deserted plaintiff for a period of more than one year, and the bonds of matrimony now and heretofore...dissolved." Given legal permission to return to her maiden name, Huguette nonetheless held on to the honorific "Mrs.," identifying herself for the rest of her life as Mrs. Clark.

Within hours of receiving her decree, Huguette and her mother left for Santa Barbara. Five days later, they sailed from San Francisco to Hawaii. Some newspapers used an unflattering photo of Huguette that had been taken by the Associated Press while she was on her honeymoon. She is wearing a fur coat, cloche hat, pearls, and two diamond Cartier Art Deco bracelets. She looks much older than her age and her expression is unbearably sad. This was the last public photograph of Huguette.

Chapter Ten

Alone Again

At the end of January 1931, Edward FitzGerald, the seventh Duke of Leinster, sailed for America on the ocean liner *Europa*. His fellow passengers included movie producer Samuel Goldwyn and heavyweight boxing champ Max Schmeling. The duke had a dinner date scheduled with Huguette's mother, Anna, and her aunt Amelia for the day after he arrived in New York.

Long on pedigree but short on funds, the duke was what wags of that era would call a "no-account count." Dating back to the fourteenth century, the FitzGeralds had been among Ireland's wealthiest dynasties, amassing multiple glossy titles—the Dukedom of Leinster, Marquess of Kildare, Earl of Kildare, Baron of Offaly, Viscount Leinster—and building massive castles and Georgian mansions. Edward's older brother Maurice FitzGerald, the sixth Duke of Leinster, came into his title in 1893 as a six-year-old after both of his parents died. As the eldest of three sons, Maurice inherited a huge family fortune plus the 1,100-acre family estate, Carton.

Edward FitzGerald grew up with all the affectations of great wealth, but as the third son in a country built on primogeniture, he was entitled to a mere fraction of his family's riches. At age twenty-one, this ne'er-do-well fell in love with showgirl May Etheridge, known as the "sweet little pajama girl" for her preferred onstage attire (presumably, offstage she wore less). To break up the match, the FitzGerald family kidnapped Edward and spirited him out of London. Promising to end the romance, he was set free—and promptly returned to England and married the actress in 1913. The couple had a baby boy but separated in 1923 and finally divorced in 1930.

During World War I, Edward's middle brother, Desmond, a major in the Irish Guards, accidentally set off a bomb in his tent in France that killed him. Edward had a good war and came away physically unscathed. But unaccustomed to living within his means, he gambled and racked up huge debts, filing for bankruptcy in 1918. Described by the British newspapers as a "daredevil sportsman" who liked fast cars and fast yachts, Edward was in constant need of cash.

Assuming that he would never inherit, Edward sold his life interest in the family's $50 million estate to Harry Mallaby-Deeley, a financier and Conservative member of Parliament. Edward FitzGerald received approximately $365,000 and the guarantee of a $5,000 yearly payment for life. It was a decision that Edward would quickly regret.

In 1922, his oldest brother Maurice FitzGerald died suddenly while locked up in what the newspapers called a "lunatic asylum." Edward assumed the title of the Duke of Leinster, but Mallaby-Deeley continued to live in the family's historic homes and receive the income from the duke's estates. The profligate duke filed for bankruptcy again in 1922, with creditors claiming that he owed more than $1.5 million. The following year, the duke was briefly jailed in London for borrowing money without alerting gullible lenders that he was bankrupt.

Even before his 1930 divorce, the Duke of Leinster had begun prospecting for an American heiress to save him from his creditors. It was a transatlantic tradition: riches in exchange for a title. A handsome man with a raffish charm, Edward began his search during trips to New York in the late 1920s. The duke would later admit that he lived "at an extravagant rate," entertaining lavishly to give the right aristocratic impression as he attempted to "marry somebody rich." Edward FitzGerald set his sights on two women who could afford to keep him in style: the name of the first heiress remains shrouded in mystery, but his second prospect was Huguette Clark. As he later described it in distinctly unromantic terms, he then began negotiations.

While he was en route to New York on the *Europa* to close the deal, the duke's plans became public in a series of front-page stories in America. "His Grace, the Duke of Leinster, first Duke of Ireland, whose arrival in New York City is said to portend wedding bells with himself and Mrs. Huguette Clark Gower, as principal figures," reported the syndicated item. "Mrs. Gower is a daughter of the late Senator William A. Clark." Huguette's debutante photo and a picture of the duke looking dapper in his fedora ran side by side.

Besieged by reporters when the *Europa* docked in New York, the panicked duke denied any talk of an engagement to Huguette. Edward insisted that he was "not going to be married to anyone" during his American holiday. DUKE DENIES PLANS TO WED was the *New York Times* headline, stressing that he was refuting rumors that he had marital intentions toward Huguette. The duke still attended the scheduled dinner with Huguette's mother and aunt at the Fifth Avenue home of mutual friends Mr. and Mrs. Irving Hogue. It must have been an awkward evening.

Was Huguette ever interested in this Irish bounder? Perhaps fleetingly. She was enough of a woman of her era to be flattered by the notion of a European title. And with his wild Irish hair and daredevil smile, the Duke of Leinster was undeniably handsome. But the European fortune hunter was not artistic, he did not share any of Huguette's interests, and he was nakedly avaricious.

For Huguette, still recovering from the humiliation of being forced to state that she had been deserted by William Gower, it was an unpleasant jolt to see her name dragged through the press with the implication that she had been rejected by a man yet again. Five years later, the duke would admit that Huguette and her mother had walked away from his marriage proposal. But that was not the impression that he fostered at the time. Later in life, Huguette acted as if this embarrassing chapter of her life had never occurred. She would often discuss the men who had mattered to her, but she never mentioned the Duke of Leinster.

Nonetheless, the tale dogged her for years. In 1932, when the duke married an American, Agnes Raffaela Kennedy Van Neck, the ex-wife of a bandleader, articles stressed his near miss with Huguette. In 1936 when the duke filed for bankruptcy for the third time, he told a courtroom of creditors about his search for a rich American bride. Huguette was portrayed as a savvy woman who had broken off the ill-suited romance. As the *Boston Globe* put it, "Mrs. Gower, as wise as her father the late Senator Clark, scoffed as ridiculous all rumors and reports that she was to enter into any matrimonial alliance with the Premier Duke of Ireland. Indeed, the Clark millions were not to be exchanged for a title and a lot of debt-burdened castles." Those Clark millions were an inescapable part of Huguette's public identity. A woman who prided herself on being an artist, time and again she was portrayed as a walking dollar sign.

————

As a newly minted divorcée, Huguette developed a distinct rhythm to her life: winters in her twelfth-floor New York apartment with her mother four floors below, summers with Anna in Santa Barbara, with an occasional side trip to Hawaii. Huguette's days in Manhattan revolved around her painting lessons four days a week with Tadé Styka. Even though she was a divorced woman, she still brought along her mother's overbearing and protective social secretary, Adele Marié, known as Missy, who would sit in another room and wait for her twenty-five-year-old charge.

Seventeen years older than Huguette, Styka was a courtly man, Old World in his ways, a man who painted while wearing a suit. As his daughter Wanda says, "My father was used to traveling in rarified circles and his family was of nobility. In Europe, he had many friends who were counts and baronesses. In his manner, he was very reserved with people he didn't know well. If he knew someone well, he was vivacious and warm."

The art magazine *Apollo*, in a lengthy feature on the artist, wrote, "On personal contact with Tadé Styka, one was bound, sooner or later, to experience the feeling that he was the spiritual exile of another and a greater age. Beneath his large, warm kindness, which was of the heart, there was a melancholy of the spirit, a shade of impatient, unresigned indignation—never expressed—as of a banished monarch or a caged lion."

Each year, Huguette and her painting teacher, who spent his summers in Europe, were separated for several months either by a continent or by an ocean. For all her girlish warmth and enthusiasm, in Huguette's many letters to Tadé there is a sense that the watchful Anna Clark or her social secretary was monitoring the correspondence. Her chatty letters have an undertone of unrequited passion, but she seems reluctant to express herself for fear of rejection. Huguette comes across as cheerful and independent, with bubbly descriptions of her activities. On July 18, 1931, she sent him a four-page missive, in French, on monogrammed stationery from Bellosguardo.

> Cher Maitre,
>
> I thank you very much for your nice letters. My intention was to respond immediately, but the lizard life that we are leading here at the beach makes one very lazy.
>
> I have begun to daub a canvas. You are going to tell yourself, "It was about time!" We have greatly regretted not being able to call you in accordance with our promise. Maman's amplifier was not working well.
>
> Our trip to Honolulu is not quite yet decided upon. The weather here is superb and the small dogs are fine. Maman and Madame Bellet thank you for your kind greetings and send their fond regards, to which I add my own.
>
> Your pupil, Huguette

Painting gave her a sense of purpose. An Associated Press story on September 6, 1931, updated readers on Huguette's postdivorce life with a favorable mention of her talent. "Huguette Clark, who inherited millions from her father, William A. Clark, copper magnate and senator, has won considerable recognition as an artist. Her paintings received high praise at the Corcoran Galleries in Washington last year and now she's planning an exhibition in Paris. She is an accomplished musician." Huguette's lush painting of a blue night-blooming flower was featured in the prestigious 1932 Winter Exhibit of the National Academy of Design in Manhattan. She was beginning to make a name for herself.

Tadé was also making news. A syndicated item noted: "The talk of Paris being 'gay' is rot and drivel, so far as Tadé Styka, Polish portrait painter, has been able to observe. New York is more wicked than Paris and Harlem is much 'hotter' than anything gay Paree has to apologize for." Tadé presumably had gone up to the Cotton Club in Harlem to see the uninhibited scene—jazz greats, gangsters, movie stars, ample alcohol despite Prohibition—but there is no evidence that he ever brought his devoted pupil along.

As the nation plunged deeper into the Depression, Anna and Huguette felt the stirrings of philanthropy. They helped friends: Dr. William Gordon Lyle's finances had taken a hit from the market crash; the Clarks underwrote tuition for his son Gordon at St. Paul's School in New Hampshire. Anna sent a $250 check to the Fund for Relief of the Unemployed in the fall of 1931. Huguette, who read the *New York Times* religiously, was touched by the heartrending stories featured in the Christmas fund-raising effort for New York's Neediest Cases. For two years in a row—1930 and 1931—Huguette wrote the largest checks received by the newspaper charity, $2,500 each year, the equivalent of more than $34,000 in current dollars. Throughout her life, Huguette was moved by individual appeals rather than organized charity.

———

The crime broke the nation's heart: on March 1, 1932, Charles Lindbergh's two-year-old son was snatched from the second-floor nursery of his parents' New Jersey home. The police fielded thousands of tips as they hunted for the baby, and the aviator eventually paid a $50,000 ransom. Two months later, the baby's body was found less than a mile from his home. After a marked bill from the ransom turned up in the possession of German immigrant Bruno Hauptmann, he was charged and convicted of the crime. Still protesting his innocence, he died in the electric chair in 1936.

At the time of the kidnapping, Huguette Clark was an adult, but the crime obsessed her and panicked Anna. Beyond imagining the agony of the Lindbergh parents, mother and daughter worried that the extensive publicity about Huguette's inheritance might make her a ransom target. If an innocent baby's life could be bartered for a $50,000 ransom, what were the odds of threats to an heiress said by the newspapers to be worth $50 million?

Mother and daughter knew that they were not immune to crime. Robbers had attempted to break into the Clarks' Fifth Avenue mansion many years earlier. William Andrews Clark was so worried about his family's safety that he kept a pistol under his pillow and traveled with bodyguards. Anna now employed a chauffeur who doubled as the protector for both women. After the Lindbergh kidnapping, Anna and Huguette continued to go out in New York but were more careful about their travels. "They never came to our house," says Gordon Lyle Jr., although his family lived a few blocks away from the Clarks. "We always went there. I guess they felt safer there. They were on their own turf."

The Lindbergh tragedy was imprinted on Huguette's consciousness, an event that increased her sense of vulnerability and reminded her yet again that her fortune singled her out for uncomfortable attention. Beyond the symbolism, the fear of kidnapping stayed with her. In 2000, when Huguette was ninety-four years old, she offered to buy a Manhattan apartment for the granddaughter of her friend Suzanne Pierre. Huguette became agitated when she learned that the young woman, Kati Despretz Cruz, had chosen a second-floor unit, insisting that she move to a higher floor. Cruz had a two-year-old son, Julian, the same age as the Lindbergh toddler. "I was only there a year because Mrs. Clark thought it was too dangerous," Cruz recalls. "She thought that someone could get access to Julian through a window."

Even as the Lindbergh kidnapping was fading from the headlines, Huguette suddenly lost a family member only four years her senior, who had been constantly around during her childhood. William Andrews Clark III, known in the family as Tertius, had become an amateur pilot and hired as his full-time instructor Jack Lynch, the pilot who taught Charles Lindbergh how to fly. The twenty-nine-year-old Clark was in Arizona taking a flying lesson from Lynch on May 15, 1932, when their plane went into a spin and plunged two thousand feet into foothills near Clemenceau. Both men were killed. The senator had doted on his clever grandson and namesake; Tertius was a frequent visitor to the family's Fifth Avenue home and a big-brother figure to Huguette.

In the seven years since William Andrews Clark's death, the copper mogul had vanished from public consciousness. The death of Tertius sparked the *Boston Globe* to publish an editorial noting how quickly the family patriarch had been forgotten. "Traditionally, the American cycle is from shirt sleeves to shirt sleeves in three generations. Though William Andrews Clark Third was not exactly in his shirt sleeves when he was killed in an aviation accident the other day, the Clark family fairly illustrates the proverb. Today, the name is hardly known and the once vast fortune of its founder has been divided up and diminished till it has almost disappeared."

The following year, Huguette's half brother Charles Clark, the big spender known for his love of horse racing, died at age sixty-one of pneumonia at Mount Sinai Hospital in New York. Charles Clark was buried in Woodlawn Cemetery in his father's mausoleum. He had disapproved of his father's marriage to Anna and had minimal contact with his stepmother after the death of the senator. Charles had ended contact with his own four children after divorcing their mother, Celia, in 1925. He had skipped the 1929 Paris wedding of his daughter Mary to French baron James Baeyens, so her uncle gave her away. The newspaper obituaries conveyed that Charles had been more enthusiastic about the running times at the racetrack than running his father's enterprises.

The ties binding the Clark relatives were fraying. Mary de Brabant, William Clark's oldest daughter, had separated from her third husband, Marius; he had returned to Riverside, California, and moved in with his older sister. Mary was nonetheless still giving parties at her Manhattan mansion and her Long Island estate, a twenty-five-room waterfront mansion with a farm building, greenhouses, and kennels, right next door to the residence of William K. Vanderbilt. But when her guest lists made the society columns, Anna and Huguette were no longer mentioned. Katherine Clark Morris, William Clark's second daughter, spent time at her three properties—a Fifth Avenue apartment, a large estate near Oneonta, and a plantation in Savannah—but did not see much of Anna and Huguette, who lived only twelve blocks south on Fifth Avenue.

During her marriage, Anna had worked to nurture her relationships with her stepchildren, and she resented being cast aside. Huguette would later say that her mother felt abandoned by her stepchildren. As Huguette's assistant, Chris Sattler, recalls, "She told me that they did not treat her mother well. They ignored her. There was very little interaction between the first family and her mother." Huguette confided in her nurse Hadassah Peri about the estrangement between Anna Clark and her stepchildren. Peri recalls hearing that William Clark's first family "didn't have much communication with her mom."

There was one exception: Anna remained close to Celia Tobin Clark, Charles Clark's ex-wife. Banking heiress Celia had become a patron of the arts, hiring George Bellows to paint a portrait of her son, Paul, and supporting San Francisco music groups. Celia and her children—Mary, Patricia, Agnes, and Paul—visited Anna and Huguette at Bellosguardo and eventually brought the next generation along, too. Anna had a special fondness for Agnes Clark, who trained as a pianist and debuted with the San Francisco Orchestra in 1932. In 1933, Agnes married Alexander Albert, the son of a German industrialist and an American socialite, and began to split her time between Europe and California. When Agnes came through New York, she often stopped by 907 Fifth Avenue to visit Anna and Huguette.

———

For a divorcée, there is one piece of information that is inevitably jarring: learning that your spouse has remarried. On the morning of June 4, 1932, if Huguette had picked up the *Sun* at the breakfast table, she could have read all about it: her ex-husband, William Gower, was getting married that very day to Constance Baxter Tevis McKee Toulmin. A follow-up *New York Times* article a day later mentioned that "Mr. Gower's marriage to Huguette Clark, youngest daughter of the late ex-Senator William A. Clark, ended in divorce in August 1930."

Constance had been living in a château in the French countryside but spent the winter at the Waldorf Astoria, the site of the couple's wedding. The newspapers tracked her comings and goings: the newlyweds honeymooned in Italy at her summer home, the Palazzo Brandolini on the Grand Canal in Venice, then moved into an apartment at 1 Sutton Place on the East River, a luxurious 1926 co-op designed by Rosario Candela.

Huguette harbored complicated feelings toward her ex-husband. Her initial bitterness was wearing off, and in the years ahead, she allowed herself to remember what she had liked about him in the first place. She did not sound angry when she talked about Bill, simply telling friends that it was not meant to be.

The heiress was now developing her own alternate life, taking pleasure in Tadé Styka's companionship. Tadé appreciated and encouraged her creativity. No one knew better the extent of her artistic talent. After arriving in Santa Barbara for her annual vacation, Huguette was giddy with joy when she received an artist's palette that Tadé had crafted for her. Not only did she send him a grateful telegram but she followed up immediately with a letter in French, on July 20, 1932.

> *Cher Maitre,*
>
> *What an enjoyable surprise you have given me. I am delighted by my palette. It's amazing! So light and so balanced. Thank you very much for the great pleasure I felt in receiving this beautiful gift!*
>
> *I am still on vacation, which means that I have yet to pick up a paintbrush since we have been here, as all of my mornings are busy with Italian lessons and swimming in the afternoon, golf.*
>
> *But this palette is so tempting that I will be starting another painting. I hope that you are spending an enjoyable summer and that you are still in good health.*
>
> *Maman's eye is still the same but she looks healthy and plays three to four hours of golf a day. We both send you our best regards, hoping to hear from you soon.*
>
> *Huguette.*

Huguette cherished this gift so much that when she managed to break it, she was distraught. Anna sent an urgent telegram to Tadé: "An accident has befallen the superb palette that you gave to Huguette. A painting fell on it, split and flattened it. Would it be possible for you to send her a new one? Huguette is disconsolate and heartbroken by this accident. Kind regards, Anna Clark."

Of course, the artist complied.

That summer in Santa Barbara, Huguette stopped into the G. T. Marsh shop, a branch of the San Francisco emporium of Japanese antiques, and became enthralled by the items on display. The original store was founded in California in 1876 by Australian George Marsh, who ran away from home as a boy, jumped ship, and landed in Japan, where he began collecting jade and porcelain. Renowned for his expertise in all things Japanese, Marsh designed the Japanese garden at Golden Gate Park. When he died in 1932, the business was taken over by his son Lucien.

During her childhood, Huguette had been fascinated by the Oriental room in her father's Fifth Avenue mansion, and she owned several Japanese dolls, depicting them in a painting for her Corcoran show. Now the Marsh shop, with its antique screens, kimonos, and intricate fans, reawakened her interest in the Land of the Rising Sun.

Huguette began purchasing Japanese artifacts in 1932—the Marsh family still has the invoices—but then had an idea far more artistic. She began to commission miniature castles based on Edo-era Japanese structures, as well as tiny furniture, painted screens, doll-sized Japanese food, doll-sized kabuki theatres, and the costumed characters to go with them. These were her own versions of Queen Mary's dollhouse but with an Oriental flair. The Marsh family tracked down Japanese artisans to do the work. Huguette was so pleased with the first miniatures that this enthusiasm became a lifelong passion.

She turned herself into a scholar on Japanese architecture and culture: her collection of books about Japan would eventually fill three large bookcases in her Fifth Avenue apartment. "She was a great teacher for me," says Caterina Marsh, an Italian who married into the Marsh family and became Huguette's contact at the firm. "She was very knowledgeable." Huguette would look at blueprints before agreeing to the work and ask for extensive revisions, fixated on getting the tiny details right. As Marsh puts it, "The pleasure for her was in creating something."

In her own way, Huguette was mimicking her father's passion when he built his fantasy Fifth Avenue mansion and looted Europe to stock it with art and antiques. The understated Huguette was re-creating history on a smaller but no less artistic scale. William Andrews Clark had been a perfectionist, focusing on such details as the color of the marble, while his daughter fretted over the precise proportions of doll-sized rooms. With fond memories of her girlhood in France, Huguette commissioned a Parisian toy store, Au Nain Bleu, to arrange for the construction of miniature French châteaus.

After growing up in a haunted hotel-sized home—with a mother who could not always hear her, a preoccupied elderly father, and a beloved sister who died young—here was a kingdom that Huguette could control. This artistic enterprise was time-consuming and intellectually challenging, requiring historic research and imagination.

Even as Huguette was embarking on her new artistic venture, Anna had a much larger project in mind: improving her California real estate. Huguette had previously donated $50,000 to turn a wetland across the street from her property into the Andrée Clark Bird Refuge. Now Anna decided to tear down Bellosguardo and put up an entirely new and grander mansion on this cliffside property with unobstructed ocean and mountain views. She told her daughter and friends that she felt inspired to offer employment to the struggling local workmen ravaged by the Depression. Anna hired Pasadena architect Reginald Davis Johnson, whose Mediterranean and Spanish Revivalism helped define the look of that community just as Addison Mizner's designs did for Palm Beach. Johnson, who had designed the Santa Barbara Country Club and the Santa Barbara Biltmore Hotel, created the new house with a budget of $1 million, the equivalent of more than $17 million today.

The original Bellosguardo, an Italianate country villa, was replaced with a twenty-three-thousand-square-foot eighteenth-century French-style formal gray reinforced concrete mansion. Unlike the over-the-top excess of Mar-a-Lago, the Palm Beach mansion built a few years earlier by heiress Marjorie Merriweather Post, Bellosguardo has an austere elegance. The airy house, with six large bedrooms plus servants' quarters, features parquet floors, richly colored marble fireplaces (gold, green, rose), antique chandeliers sporting crystal and amethyst glass, as well as fanciful gold-plated bathroom fixtures in the shapes of dolphins' and swans' heads. The building is U shaped, with a reflecting pool and orange trees tucked into the outdoor middle space between the two wings. The formal driveway features a mosaic made of black and white stones.

Upon entering the building at the center of the U, a small reception area leads to a long central hallway. Down the hallway to the left is the magnificent dining room with antique Sherwood Forest woodwork from the senator's Fifth Avenue mansion, 167 distinctive panels, each carved with images including dragons, peacocks, oak leaves, fish, and horns of plenty. At the other end of the grand hallway—past the powder room and an Oriental-style carved-wood-paneled reception room with Chinese-themed paintings on the ceiling—is the right wing of the house and the large corner music room, with two Steinway pianos and Anna's harp. An avid bridge player, Anna chose chairs and a table that could be used for a game, as well as plush couches and armchairs to accommodate guests listening to musicales. Portraits by Tadé Styka of a girlish Huguette in a pink dress and pearls, and a thoughtful-looking Andrée, grace the walls, as does a charcoal sketch by Italian artist Edmondo Pizzella of the serene Anna in an evening gown.

Next to the music room is the library, featuring ornate wood paneling from the senator's home and stocked with leather-bound volumes by Voltaire, Molière, and Goethe. Anna commissioned what she called the "bureau room" next door, another wood-paneled room with Fragonard-style cherubs painted on the ceiling. She used this study to conduct correspondence and handle the estate's business.

Huguette had the equivalent of a private duplex wing situated at the very end of that hall, the right-hand top of the U, with a small ground-floor kitchenette, a bathroom with a silver leaf ceiling, and a large closet to store her easels and canvases. Her large painting studio featured sixteen-foot-high ceilings and views of the ocean and the gardens. The room was austere compared to the rest of the house, without elaborate molding and with an oak-pegged floor rather than parquet. A staircase tucked into the studio led to the second floor and her bedroom, directly above the studio.

Her single bed, with an upholstered wood frame, was angled so that her first sight in the morning was the lawn and the rose garden, although if she looked out the window to the right she could see the

Pacific. Huguette ordered a dozen half-size Empire-style chairs to display her antique doll collection; she could line the chairs up against the walls of her bedroom, or put them in her adjoining dressing area. She rotated her selection; when the dolls were not in use they were stored in numbered boxes. Her bathroom included a gold-colored marble tub and a scale built into the floor, with the dial at eye level on the wall.

Anna had spared no expense for her own second-floor master bedroom, an enormous sea-green room with unusual curved molding, furnished with a bed with a carved wooden headboard, a velvet daybed, an antique desk and bureau, and a large standing mirror. A large balcony overlooked the ocean. Her bathroom included a marble bathtub large enough for two people. The suite included a dressing area as well as a second music room. In the built-in bookcases tucked into two closets, Anna stored her bridge books and medical literature, including volumes on surgery and eye diseases.

In the family quarters, one large bedroom was dedicated for the use of a family retainer (likely Anna's social secretary Adele Marié). The three ample-sized guest rooms included a gold-painted luxurious haven with a spectacular chandelier made of porcelain flowers, as well as a masculine wood-paneled suite. Anna decorated the upstairs hallway with riotously colorful Hawaiian paintings with an Impressionist-style flair by Anna Woodward, a Pittsburgh painter who studied in Paris in the 1860s and then made her home in Hawaii.

The property boasted a tennis court, a thatched-roof play cottage named after Andrée, and a plant nursery. An Italian fountain with a marble nymph was installed, and Anna hired landscapers to create the largest rose garden in Santa Barbara, featuring every possible shade of pink. Concerned about privacy, Anna decided to sacrifice part of the view, planting one thousand trees directly in front of the house to block beachgoers below from peering up. A private beach below included wooden cabanas.

Huguette admired her mother's vision. More than fifty years later, she would reminisce about the construction of the new Bellosguardo in a June 10, 1988, handwritten letter to Santa Barbara mayor Sheila

Lodge. "My dear Mother put so much of herself into its charm and had the satisfaction of knowing that during the great depression she was a bit helpful in giving much needed employment." Once the rebuilt Bellosguardo was complete, the Clarks employed a large year-round staff: twenty-five gardeners, two full-time painters, a plumber, an English butler, a chauffeur, and a complement of housekeepers, maids, and chefs.

Anna began a practice that her daughter would emulate: loyal employees were taken care of for life. Most of the Clark staff continued to receive salaries after they retired, and even after they died, checks kept going to their spouses and children. Huguette was so grateful to a childhood nanny that she supported the woman's daughter, Ninta Sandre, for decades, buying her a New York apartment, paying for nursing home bills and, finally, burial expenses. Although Anna was a long way from her impoverished adolescence in Butte, she still remembered what it was like to worry about money. Treating employees like extended family, she and her daughter were strong believers in rewarding devotion.

———

When Huguette returned to New York and her painting lessons in 1933, Tadé Styka began work on a haunting portrait that shows her seated in front of the easel, intent on her artwork. He was painting her to amuse himself; this was not a commission. Wearing lace-up leather shoes, a skirt well below the knee, and a blouse and jacket, she is totally focused on her work, with her brush on the canvas as she tries to capture an image. The back of the canvas faces the viewer so that one cannot see what she is painting. But off to the right is a well-proportioned, naked male model, posing with his back to Huguette.

Explaining his efforts to psychoanalyze his subjects, Tadé once told a journalist, "I do not paint the mask, I paint the character beneath." This painting is simultaneously serious and humorous as Tadé reveals Huguette's earnest schoolgirl determination to appear blase against the backdrop of the glorious sexuality of the male model. Tadé understood Huguette's quirky mixture of shyness and adventurousness in a way that no one else ever had or would.

The artist was a quick study, giving his undivided attention to his subjects. As *Apollo* later wrote in its obituary, "It was a memorable experience to watch Tadé Styka at work during these short seances that left him exhausted, as after a fencing match, so rapid and violent were his lunges and strokes—while the sitter was hardly aware that the tediousness of posing was over almost before it had begun..."

Those hours at Tadé's studio on Central Park South were what Huguette lived for—the fulfillment of her own creativity plus the chance to bask in the teasing and supportive friendship of her teacher. They had an ongoing game: making silly bets for a dime. Tadé saved a drawerful of Huguette's dimes as an amusing symbol of how often he won. Tadé was still resolutely single, and Huguette fantasized that one day the relationship could turn to requited love. For her, it already was love.

One day in 1933, a visitor arrived at Tadé's studio during Huguette's lesson, a young woman who had heard about the famous Polish artist and wanted to see his work. A twenty-one-year-old model with high cheekbones, porcelain skin, and long wavy brunette hair, Doris Ford had posed for magazine fashion spreads and illustrations. A New Jersey native, her father was a naval architect and her mother was a pianist and painter. An art student herself, Doris had called Tadé in advance to ask permission to visit, and he invited her to come by at 1 p.m. Huguette took morning lessons and was usually gone by then, but today she was caught up in her work and her art teacher and lingered on.

When the elevator door opened and Doris walked into the room, she and Tadé took one look at each other—and it was a *coup de foudre*. Huguette saw the way they reacted to each other, and she knew at that moment that the spinning globe of her life had just tilted off its axis. She put down her brush, politely excused herself, and left for the day. Tadé then invited Doris to show her painting technique by taking a brush to his current work-in-progress, his portrait of Huguette at her easel. Doris was nervous but began to touch up his version of the heiress. It was a symbolic moment that Doris never forgot. "She was so astounded that he would do that," says Wanda Styka, the couple's daughter, who heard the courtship tale from her parents. "She was so beautiful and he enjoyed it." When Huguette decided to buy the completed painting several years later, Doris was dismayed to lose the artwork that held so much meaning for her, too. She propped it on a chair and snapped a final photograph, right before Huguette took possession.

Now Huguette had a rival for the painter's affections. She and Doris would circle around each other in the coming years, the blonde heiress and the younger brunette fashion model, waiting for this sophisticated older European artist to make up his mind.

Chapter Eleven

Facts, Fiction, and Betrayal

The screwball comedies of the 1930s buoyed the spirits of Americans during the Depression by featuring the foibles of the fortunate and the harebrained schemes of heirs and heiresses. A social butterfly escapes from a gold digger (*It Happened One Night*) only to fall for an out-of-work reporter, or a wealthy Boston Brahmin moonlights as a butler (*My Man Godfrey*). This escapist fare was a tonic against breadlines and the daily struggle of surviving.

The Clark family's riches and romances continued to provide newspapers with similar grist for entertaining the masses. Everyone wanted William Andrews Clark's money, accumulated over sixty years, and some were willing to go to court to pry away a piece of the copper fortune. The public had the fun of watching the financial hijinks play out as modern-day morality plays.

The pattern began before the stock market crash, when William Andrews Clark's eldest daughter, Mary Clark Culver Kling de Brabant, was sued in January 1929 by her social secretary for $123,000 allegedly owed for "personal care in public and in private." Mrs. Vernon Howe Bailey, Mary's assistant and the wife of an artist, promised to deliver racy evidence and even call a psychic. But she suddenly dropped the lawsuit, and her lawyer issued an apologetic statement saying that "her fancied grievances were due to unfortunate misstatements and gossip by acquaintances." The *Los Angeles Times* noted with disappointment, SOCIETY TONGUES CEASE WAGGING AS SUIT FIZZLES.

But nothing roused the newsroom symphony of chattering typewriters like the death of music lover William Andrews Clark Jr. On June 14, 1934, he had a heart attack at age fifty-seven, a day after arriving at his fishing camp at Salmon Lake, Montana. By the time the closest doctor, forty-five minutes away, arrived, it was too late. Clark Jr.'s last will and testament contained a startling bequest: the founder of the Los Angeles Philharmonic and rare book collector left a large share of his $9 million estate to a seventeen-year-old boy, George John Pale, the son of his housekeeper. News stories implied that Clark's affection for the teen had sexual overtones. The *Los Angeles Times* stated that George Pale had been Clark's ward and "has been reared and educated by him"—an unfortunate word choice—with the expectation of a legal adoption. The Associated Press said that Pale had been Clark's "constant companion" and had been with him when he died.

George Pale submitted personal letters from his benefactor to the probate court. Most were tame but in one memorable note, William Andrews Clark Jr. wrote: "My Dear Baby, You promised to write me…Do not forget. Anyway, I have a whip here and your fanny will be well spanked and you will have to eat off the mantel piece… I love you and I kiss you with all my heart, Sincerely yours, Daddy." George Pale received $1.135 million. William Andrews Clark Jr. also left $125,000 and a Santa Monica home to the "Oscar Wilde type"— Harrison Post—who had been a source of concern to his older brother, Charles Clark.

In 1936, the family name was back in the headlines when Thelma Clark, the widow of William Andrews Clark III (aka Tertius) was sued for $150,000 for committing "love theft." The lawsuit claimed that Thelma had seduced ship's purser Michael Fitzpatrick on a boat traveling from Los Angeles to the Panama Canal and convinced him to abandon his marriage. Hot-and-heavy telegrams and a private detective's report were produced during the trial. Thelma Clark lost and was ordered to hand over $30,000 to the aggrieved wife, Christine Fitzgerald, for a "love balm."

Every tidbit about the Clarks and their money was treated as good copy. Huguette's finances remained a semi-open book: newspapers reported that she received $500,000 from her trust fund in 1935. The devoted daughter gave half of the money to her mother. This was an unimaginably large sum in the year that President Franklin Delano Roosevelt created the WPA to boost national employment, hiring workers for $41.57 per month for construction jobs fixing roads and bridges.

Although Anna and Huguette were maintaining a low profile in Manhattan, they adopted a decidedly more public one in Santa Barbara. Anna took a box at the polo matches, subscribed to concerts, and opened her home to out-of-town guests during Fiesta Week. Mother and daughter were listed in the California society pages as a matched pair, Mmes. William Clark.

In the summer of 1934, while Huguette luxuriated at Bellosguardo, her painting teacher headed for Europe, sailing into an art world controversy. Tadé Styka's sensual portrait of actress Marion Davies had mysteriously turned up in the American Pavilion at the Venice Biennial Exhibit, although it had not been one of the artworks officially selected for the show. Whitney Museum director Juliana Force angrily demanded that the painting be removed, arguing that since Styka was Polish, not American, his work should not be displayed. The mastermind who concocted this stunt was unmasked as William Randolph Hearst. The newspaper publisher was so eager for the painting of his mistress, Davies, to receive acclaim that he had secretly cut a deal with Count Volpi di Misurata, the biennial's director, to sneak the Styka painting into the exhibit.

For Tadé Styka, the publicity only burnished his reputation. He was already flourishing; his portrait of President Roosevelt's mother, Sara, had received glowing reviews. He and his younger brother Adam, an artist, were planning a joint American exhibit. The *New York Daily Mirror*'s society column ran a flattering item: "Teas given by Tadé Styka, the noted Polish artist, are among the most interesting in New York. The walls of his studio are hung with the portraits of beautiful women. His Japanese bartender makes excellent cocktails which vanish speedily down fashionable throats. One meets only worthwhile people beneath his roof."

Perennial bachelor Tadé sent his new muse Doris Ford a telegram inviting her to join him in Italy, with the reassuring promise that his sister and family members would be there to chaperone. "The person who delivered the telegram said, 'It requires a response,'" says Wanda Styka, repeating oft-told family history. Her mother replied, "Yes, I would be delighted." A newspaper item noted that Tadé Styka had taken Doris Ford to Rome to pose for murals that he was creating for the Vatican.

An ocean and a continent away, Huguette wrote to Tadé that July. In lyrical language, she described a vacation with her mother in Colorado, scribbling on the back of three postcards about her love of nature and rigorous traveling. Huguette had visited the home of Ganna Walska, an oft-married Polish opera star believed to have been the model for the screeching and untalented singer in *Citizen Kane*.

Cher Maitre,

I do not want to leave Colorado without sending you these few photos taken of an uninhabited chateau that we visited around the Garden of the Gods, which is one of the curiosities of the country. The chateau is called Glen-Eyrie, because of a nest of perched eagles on the park's boulder. It belonged to one of Ganna Walska's husbands. She got a divorce before living in it. Now it is for sale. This castle is like a dream it's so picturesque and a fairy-like and fantastic landscape that surrounds it.

The Royal Gorge is also very beautiful and the suspended bridge is the highest in the world. We went down in an elevator to admire the view at the bottom, which is as grandiose but far from as beautiful as that of the Grand Canyon or Yellowstone...

Tomorrow we are going to visit Pike's Peak, the highest mountain in Colorado. Hoping to soon hear of your good news and I send you my fondest regards,

Huguette

Although the artist had taken Doris with him to Europe, once he was back in New York in the winter of 1935, he began to squire Huguette around town at night, in addition to giving her painting lessons four times a week. His appointment calendar is dotted with their frequent outings: taking Huguette to the theatre and a Fifth Avenue fashion show; a dinner at Brooklyn's ornate 1909 Hotel Bossert on Montague Street with its romantic roof terrace and sweeping views of Manhattan; a movie date followed by dinner and music at the new popular French nightclub Versailles on East Fiftieth Street. "The management of the Versailles Restaurant continues to shoot at the moon," the *New York Times* reported earlier that week, "…and on Monday, the trophy room will celebrate the addition of Libby Holman, the singer of sad, sad songs…a proper adornment for the luxurious spot." Tadé also joined Huguette and her mother for dinner and a bridge game at 907 Fifth Avenue. He jotted down notes in his appointment calendar about her artwork, noting that on April 15 she had started work on a painting of a Japanese courtesan. Tadé hired Japanese female models so that Huguette could work from real inspiration. (He could not resist noting in his calendar that one had "beautiful breasts.")

For Huguette, this was the life that she had dreamed of, painting the town with the man she had adored for years. Yet as fond as Tadé was of the heiress, his feelings were platonic. She had an appealing innocence compared to the sophisticated society ladies he was commissioned to paint. The lines between his work and his friendships blurred: he was often included in the dinner parties and social lives of his clients, the perfect continental extra man. He was the frequent escort of Mrs. Amanda Storrs, the widow of *Playbill* founder and theatre owner Frank Vance Storrs, and one of Anna Clark's closest friends. He did not intend to lead Huguette on, but his flirtatious nature could not help but continue to give her hope.

Anna Clark was not a shut-in, either; she showed no inclination to remarry, but the wealthy widow had a new admirer: the radio personality Major Bowes. The pioneering entertainer's *Original Amateur Hour* show on NBC had recently become a national sensation. Each week, more than ten thousand people applied to perform on his show in the hope of being discovered. Recently widowed and a Catholic like Anna, Bowes came from an impoverished background. This grammar school dropout had reinvented himself as a theatre owner and an on-air performer. (His name was Edward Bowes, but he assumed "Major" as a showbiz moniker.) Bowes was known for using a gong to cut off performers, and his on-air catchphrase was: "The wheel of fortune goes 'round and 'round, where she stops, nobody knows." An aspiring young Frank Sinatra appeared on the show with the quartet the Hoboken Four.

An art collector with paintings by Renoir, Van Gogh, and Rembrandt, Bowes became so fond of Anna Clark that he gave her a large, square canary diamond that she had mounted as a ring. He was four years her senior, much more of a contemporary than her husband had been. Bowes also presented her with the requisite autographed photo, which she displayed prominently in her music room along with signed photographs of celebrities she had known, such as the opera star Enrico Caruso. Anna also cherished a photo of Bowes in a more relaxed setting: playing cards while clad in an elegant smoking jacket and slacks.

Mother and daughter entertained together: on April 28, Tadé Styka went to the Clarks' Fifth Avenue apartment to listen to a Major Bowes broadcast and then have dinner afterward with the radio host. The artist spent Thanksgiving with Huguette and Anna at the home of Anna's sister, Amelia. The evening ended abruptly when Tadé made an emergency trip to the hospital for appendicitis. Anna sent her chauffeur to the hospital to bring him home several days later. On Christmas Day 1935, Anna and Huguette celebrated the holiday by hosting an intimate dinner for Major Bowes, Tadé Styka, and Amelia and her husband, Bryce Turner.

Huguette's dance à deux with Tadé continued into 1936, with regular outings in addition to her lessons. On January 25, the couple went to see the opera *Carmen*; on February 15, he took Huguette to the Ziegfeld Follies to see Josephine Baker sing and dance and the Nicholas Brothers tap dance on stage. "Miss Baker cannot sing but sure can wear clothes. And roll those eyes," pronounced *Variety* in a review of the show that appeared that very morning. "She looks best in an exotic scene called '5 a.m.' in which she sings and dances with four shadowy black-masked men. It is a Balanchine ballet." After seeing the Follies, the painter and Huguette dined at Maisonette Russe at the St. Regis Hotel.

Three days later, Tadé accompanied Huguette, her mother, and

her aunt to an art exhibit. On February 22, he took Huguette dancing at the St. Regis; on Sunday, March 22, he and Huguette went to
hear a violin concert. On April 27, they dined at the Hotel Sherry-
Netherland with her aunt; on May 6, he took Huguette to the French
Casino to see the extravaganza *Folies de Femmes* show of dancing
girls. (This risqué performance had become a must-see after a mag-
istrate acquitted the theatre owners in late February—CABARET MEN
CLEARED, announced the *New York Times*—of charges of "conducting indecent shows.") When his brother Adam and his sister-in-law
Wanda visited from Poland, the artist took them out to dinner with
Huguette.

Throughout the 1930s, Huguette continued her summer pilgrimages to Bellosguardo. When she was leaving New York by train for
Santa Barbara, the gentlemanly Tadé escorted her to Pennsylvania
Station and gave her a corsage. She sent him a playful telegram en
route: "Cher Maitre. Infinite thanks for your magnificent corsage
which still keeps all of its freshness. I am tending to it in order to wear
it while disembarking the train in Los Angeles. It was a hit in Chicago. Again, I wish you a good vacation. Regards, Huguette."

———

The best-seller lists for 1937 included Margaret Mitchell's *Gone with
the Wind*, Dale Carnegie's *How to Win Friends and Influence People*,
volumes by Virginia Woolf and Somerset Maugham, plus a novel by
newcomer Myron Brinig, *The Sisters*. The *Atlanta Constitution* labeled
the Brinig novel "one of the better books of the season," and the *New
York Times* promised readers that they would be "engrossed" by *The
Sisters* since it "has something of the sweep of *Gone with the Wind*."
When the movie version came out a year later starring Bette Davis
and Errol Flynn, the *Boston Globe* described it as a "sentimental,
heart-warming story of three beautiful girls which is sure to please
every woman patron..."

Not every woman. Not Anna La Chapelle Clark. Set in Montana
in 1904, *The Sisters* stole liberally from her life story and that of her sister, Amelia. Brinig, who lived in Butte and is believed to have known
the La Chapelle sisters, used many identifying details. The fictional
Elliott family is originally from Michigan (where the La Chapelle

family had lived) and the fictional Elliott patriarch is a pharmacist (Peter La Chapelle was convicted of practicing medicine without a license after writing prescriptions to Butte pharmacists). The fictional Elliotts live on West Granite Street, the location of William Andrews Clark's Butte mansion.

One of the three intertwined plots centers on the rebellious, beautiful, and amoral youngest sister, Helen Elliott. She weds a widowed copper titan more than twice her age—a man who was originally from Pennsylvania and took a metallurgy course at an eastern college. (In case the reader doesn't get the heavy-handed message, William Andrews Clark makes a cameo in the novel, stopping into a shop in Silver Bow to buy the New York newspapers.)

In the movie version of *The Sisters*, Helen's mother announces in abject horror that her daughter does not love the mogul and is marrying for money. The copper titan's daughter from his first marriage bitterly resents Helen and tries to undermine her. In the book, Helen cheats on her elderly husband, and he dies while she is in bed with another man.

Anna's name was never mentioned in either the novel or the book. But the portrayal of her doppelganger as a heartless gold digger and adulteress was inescapable and infuriating. It was made worse by the fact that during a two-year period, the book and the movie embedded themselves into late 1930s popular culture.

————

Even as Tadé Styka was spending ample time with Huguette, he was also seeing model Doris Ford. Curious about the artist's relationship with Huguette, Doris began to make notes in her journal about their activities. Rather than feel threatened, Doris tried to ingratiate herself with the painter's wealthy pupil. On January 17, 1937, Doris wrote that Tadé was taking Huguette to see a Hindu dancer, bringing his brother and sister-in-law along. On April 30, Doris tried to be helpful by looking for Japanese models to hire for Huguette's lessons. Doris occasionally lingered in the background at Tadé's studio during Huguette's sessions, trying to avoid disrupting the heiress's concentration. She described the scene in her notes: "She liked quietly to paint, a pin could be heard if dropped." Much to Doris's frustration, when Huguette and Tadé did converse they spoke in French, which the model did not understand.

Doris kept track of Tadé's dates with Huguette, noting that he took the heiress out for her birthday, June 9, to a movie and then dancing at the Rainbow Room atop Rockefeller Center. Tadé spent the summer in France, but as soon as he returned, the artist began spending time with both women yet again. Using his initials, Doris jotted such notes as "TS went to a movie with HC in the afternoon to the Clarks for dinner" on October 15, and "TS to florist where he made an arrangement for HC."

But word was starting to circulate about the artist's romance with Doris. On November 30, Tadé went to the Clarks' home for dinner and then to the opera. Anna's sister, Amelia, took him aside that night to say that her dear friend Amanda Storrs had seen Tadé out for the evening with a "tall dark girl." Then Anna cornered him (presumably out of Huguette's earshot) to ask if he planned to marry that girl. When Tadé recounted the story to Doris the next day, he did not tell her what he replied, but she wrote in her journal: "He's not much for words, he silently hugged me."

Huguette's dance card, however, included another attentive man. Her childhood summer playmate from France, Etienne de Villermont, had turned up in New York and was now frequently featured in the gossip columns. Etienne, his younger brother, Henri, and their artist parents had been befriended by Anna and William Andrews Clark at the beach resort of Trouville in the pre–World War I era. Now Etienne, known as the Marquis de Villermont, was making headlines for his amorous American adventures. The handsome bachelor was linked in the columns to several eligible women. On March 3, 1936, he was reported to be engaged to the widow of a coffee magnate, Mrs. Claire Eugenia Smith, who had inherited $6 million. But that turned out to be a joke. Villermont and one of his closest friends, Russian prince Alexis Droutzkoy, at a nightclub with Mrs. Smith, had quipped to the *Daily News* that they had been rivals for her affections (MARQUIS IS WINNER OF HEIRESS WIDOW), but the emerald-draped Mrs. Smith later denied the engagement. Etienne was described as a perfume importer, but he would not hold that job for long.

In February 1938, Huguette attended a lunch with Etienne de Villermont at the St. Regis Hotel. The event honored Lady Decies, the American wife of a British aristocrat, who was due to sail on the *Normandie* for her home in Paris. It was the first time Huguette was seen in public with the marquis. But Etienne, two years older than Huguette, was playing the field. On November 25, 1938, Walter Winchell wrote that the marquis, now working at the French consulate, "is lavishing most of his diplomacy on Jayne Gayle, the modelulu."

Huguette continued to go out with Tadé that spring: they attended the opera, a Japanese-themed dinner, and the Rodgers and Hart musical *I Married an Angel* at the Shubert Theatre. In honor of Tadé's birthday on April 13, Huguette and her mother gave a dinner party for him.

During that summer in Santa Barbara, she wrote to Tadé as always. Even after so many mornings in Tadé's painting studio and evenings by his side, her letters to him are chaste, as if the thirty-two-year-old's emotions are so repressed that she cannot express deeper feelings. She plays it light and girlish, the younger pupil to older mentor. On August 14, 1938, she wrote to Tadé on stationery monogrammed with an elaborate "H." By then it was likely that she knew Tadé was involved with Doris Ford.

Cher Maitre,

What a good and enjoyable surprise you gave me by calling from New York. I who had believed you to be in South America. Imagine my astonishment! Thank you for offering to have me resume my lessons on September 15th. This will not be possible for me, but I am delighted at the thought of picking my paintbrush up again on the 25th of next month.

I can't wait to resume my lessons. It is such a privilege to work with you.

There was recently a horse show here which was very interesting for me, as my niece Patsy took part in it.

We are spending a lot of time at the beach. The ocean air is so good and invigorating but I find the water quite cold.

*Included here are a few photos of the house...and of your little
rose bush which has grown nicely and faces my studio, as well as
some newspaper clippings about the earthquake in New York that I
think must be very exaggerated.*

*Write me a note, dear Maitre. I will be happy to hear from you.
I hope these few lines will have found you in good health. Maman
joins me in sending our best regards, Huguette.*

(New York City did indeed experience a minor earthquake at 3 a.m.
on July 29, 1938. Huguette's horse-mad niece was Patsy Clark, the
daughter of Charles Clark and Celia Tobin.)

In this letter to Tadé, Huguette sent along photos of the newly
rebuilt Bellosguardo and a fetching photo of herself, standing by the
trees on the cliff overlooking the ocean. She is wearing a white skirted
suit with a cheerful polka dot blouse and matching belt. Plumper than
her previous slender self, more curvaceous and womanly, Huguette
looks at the camera with a wistful expression.

Huguette's artistic love affair with Japan had intensified. Concerned about the verisimilitude of her Japanese-themed paintings,
she had begun an ongoing correspondence with a Japanese woman
based in California, Mrs. Sajiri. Huguette inquired about everything
from the appropriate names for female figures to what kinds of insects
she should portray. Mrs. Sajiri wrote to Huguette in January 1939
that there were more than one hundred known species of cicadas in
Japan but "for your parasol study, however, I think that a dragonfly
or a butterfly would be more appropriate." That April, Mrs. Sajiri gave
Huguette detailed instructions on where a geisha might place a coral
pin on her kimono and obi.

Huguette's and Tadé's paths diverged that spring, although they
remained close. On May 11, 1939, Tadé Styka presented a large diamond solitaire surrounded by twenty pigeon red blood rubies to
Doris, whose modeling career had blossomed with magazine covers.
But he did not propose. Only months later, when a friend asked Doris
whether this was an engagement ring—and she repeated the conversation to Tadé—did he admit that was what he had in mind. But the
perennial bachelor was in no rush to set a wedding date.

Just a few days after giving Doris the ring, Tadé took Huguette to an art exhibit; then on May 21, he and the heiress attended a concert by harpist Marcel Grandjany, Anna Clark's harp teacher. Huguette and Tadé ventured out to Queens—likely courtesy of her chauffeur— to see the wonders of the 1939 World's Fair. Tadé and Huguette marveled at Broadway showman Billy Rose's spectacular Aquacade, a ten-thousand-seat amphitheater featuring an enormous pool and cascades of water. Ornately costumed glamour girls performed dance routines and then stripped down to bathing suits to show off synchronized swimming feats. Olympic champion and actor Johnny Weissmuller was featured in the act. After the show, Tadé and Huguette dined at the Italian Pavilion's second-floor restaurant, where imported chefs concocted dishes dotted with white truffles.

Huguette, however, had romantic news of her own. She had warmed up to the idea of the Marquis de Villermont as a suitor. Her mother's social secretary, Adéle Marié, told family friends that she had helped broker the match. The society columns heralded another upcoming walk down the aisle. Walter Winchell declared on May 31, 1939, that "The Marquis de Villermont and Huguette Clark will probably wed this summer. He's due for a post with the French diplomatic Service."

Winchell prided himself on getting his facts right, and was saved in this case by the word *probably*. There was no wedding that summer, much less a formal engagement. The relationship between Huguette and Etienne never did progress to marriage. But they would continue to see each other periodically over the next few decades.

On Christmas Day 1939, Tadé Styka spent the holiday at dinner with Anna and Huguette at 907 Fifth Avenue, but he did not bring along his fiancée. However, he did repeat to Doris a conversation that he had that evening with Huguette. The heiress teased Tadé about his engagement. As Doris wrote in her notes, "She was joshing him about me—saying for him not to fool her as she could find out a lot but did not want to." Huguette was trying to graciously accept the news that he was now committed to someone else, but this transition troubled her.

Ever since the newspapers had feasted on the tale of her 1930 divorce, Huguette had loathed publicity. But she could not avoid it. As one of the wealthiest women in Manhattan, she remained a figure of interest. Less than a year after her purported engagement to the Marquis de Villermont was mentioned in the newspapers, syndicated columnist Cholly Knickerbocker wrote an item on March 16, 1940, stating that Huguette had given up on romance.

"When lists of American heiresses are compiled, ink-slingers usually overlook popular Huguette Clark, whose father the late bewhiskered Senator William A. Clark amassed a fortune in Montana's copper and Alaska's gold." After mentioning her failed marriage to William Gower, the columnist continued, "She's been disillusioned ever since, most of her time is given over to art work, and on Fifth Avenue in the winter and at Santa Barbara in the summer. She prevues [sic] oils and watercolors that win high praise from art critics. If she didn't have $15,000,000, she could amass a fortune as an artist."

Gossip columnists could not resist pointing out that her ex-husband, William Gower, and his second wife were tripping through Europe, highballs in hand. Gower's niece Jan Perry recalls, "He led a fast life. We all adored him. He was a name-dropper who knew everyone." When Perry visited her uncle in London and he honored her with a cocktail party, Lady Astor was among the guests. Gower was nominally affiliated with a law firm but, as Perry adds, "He sure acted as if he didn't have to work." His wife remained a social climber par excellence. As the New York Sun wrote, "Mrs. Gower is one of the most popular hostesses in the American colony in London."

———

Anna and Huguette employed a large retinue of servants at 907 Fifth Avenue: cooks, maids, housekeepers, and a chauffeur. One day, a staffer delivered an unexpected, and unwanted, package to the two women—an eye-opening tell-all manuscript about William Andrews Clark and his family, written by a former family employee from Butte, William Daniel Mangam. The loose-leaf pages were in dark green three-punch binders, with copies of photos and excerpts of personal letters.

Every family has its secrets: the cruelties and shameful moments, the sibling rivalries, the forbidden romantic entanglements and hidden financial finagling. But only rarely is the dirty linen hung on the clothesline for public ridicule. Nothing ever written about the Clarks—even *The Sisters*—exuded vitriol like this little book entitled *The Clarks of Montana*.

Mangam had been the confidant of William Andrews Clark Jr. and had spent decades on the Clark payroll. In 1902, Mangam got into such a bloody bare-knuckles brawl in Butte defending Senator Clark's reputation that the fight made the national newspapers, in which he was described as "the protege of Senator Clark." Mangam worked his way up to become the secretary-treasurer of the Clarks' Timber Butte Mining Company. Mangam read and kept copies of letters between family members and collected damaging internal financial documents. Even after the Clark estate sold the senator's Montana enterprises in 1928 to the Anaconda Mining Company, he remained close to William Clark Jr. But once Junior died in the company of a teenage boy, Mangam decided to cash in.

Mangam's lacerating book portrayed the senator as a reprobate who fathered illegitimate children with Indian women and favored "aberrant" (albeit unspecified) sexual practices. The author went after the entire Clark family, including Anna and Huguette, with vicious portraits exposing embarrassing moments. Mangam filed for a copyright in 1939, but the book got wider circulation when it was issued in 1941 by a New York publisher, Silver Bow Press, with an introduction by University of Wisconsin sociology professor Edward Alsworth Ross, who pronounced it a "priceless social document." Ross added, "The author makes charges which would undoubtedly lay him open to ruin by many successful libel suits were he not in a position to substantiate them." Mangam wrote an expose of Will Clark Jr.'s activities as a sexual predator, attacked Charles as an alcoholic and a philanderer, and portrayed Mary Clark de Brabant, who had died in December 1939, as a snob with terrible taste in men. Katherine Clark Morris, the only surviving child from Clark's first marriage, is described as a stingy social climber.

Anna La Chapelle is depicted as an ambitious teenage fortune hunter who became pregnant out of wedlock and manipulatively reeled in her man, negotiating a large prenuptial settlement. Mangam quotes letters that convey the distress of Clark's older children over the relationship. The senator's oldest daughter, Mary, thought that her father should have married someone elevated in society, and Mangam says that she "resented it deeply" that he chose Anna La Chapelle.

The portrait of Huguette was even more cruel. Mangam flatly stated, without a shred of evidence, that she might not be Clark's daughter but instead the product of an affair by Anna. He says that William Andrews Clark did not love Huguette. The expose described Huguette as a spoiled child with a "mother complex." Mangam wrote with clotted syntax: "Huguette Marcelle never occupied the place in the affections of the Senator that the winsome Andrée did. His feelings toward Huguette at times seemed almost to approach indifference. It is not believed that the Senator's attitude was dictated or influenced by the tale that Huguette was not his offspring but that of a New York doctor, a story, incidentally, in the truth of which his sons and one grandson expressed their belief."

Those sons and grandson—Charles Clark, William Clark Jr., and William Clark III—were all dead now. But the possibility that they had not only believed but spread this sleazy story hardened Huguette and Anna against their relatives. Twisting the knife, Mangam announced the reason for the short-lived nuptials of Clark's youngest daughter: "Huguette refused to consummate the marriage."

Many of Mangam's stories were probably embellished or even invented. But his description of Huguette and Anna's bond rings true: "They seem now to live largely for each other." The author sent the unpublished manuscript to Anna and Huguette to purportedly protect himself from a lawsuit. In his foreword, Mangam writes: "To guard against the possibility of error in the presentation of factual statements, the chapters of this narrative were submitted to all the characters who are still alive and to their legal representatives."

Unlike *The Sisters*, the Mangam book was not a best seller. Rumor had it that family members tried to buy up all the copies and pulp them, although the slim volume was periodically reprinted and made its way into libraries. If anyone wanted to learn about the history of William Andrews Clark, his wife, Anna, and daughter Huguette, this was the standard volume to consult from now on. And it was merciless to Clark's youngest daughter.

———

For Huguette, the seacliff estate in Santa Barbara remained her refuge, a place to escape from New York and societal expectations. She could paint, play golf with friends, swim in the ocean, and relax away from prying eyes. In 1941, she spent more time than usual in Santa Barbara. Early that year, she began writing to Tadé to ask him to save dates for painting lessons, but postponed her return to New York four times, finally returning on June 11.

In her notes to her teacher, she mentioned how tan she was becoming, so he decided to play a practical joke: a tan-a-thon. In the weeks before her scheduled arrival, he began sunning himself on the roof at lunch. Huguette swanned into his studio on June 12 and discovered that Tadé was darker than she was. He wrote a letter to his brother later that day about the prank: "She stayed in California because she wanted to astound me, astonish me with her own tan. In the meantime, I stupified her when she saw me. She did nothing else but tan."

Huguette had always come for morning lessons, but she abruptly announced that she wanted to switch to afternoons, from 1 p.m. to 3 p.m. This upset Tadé's own painting schedule. But much to the annoyance of his fiancée, Doris, he accepted Huguette's demand without complaint. As his daughter, Wanda, says, "My mother mentioned that this made it difficult for my father, since he'd have to schedule a sitting in the morning or after 3 p.m., and if it was the winter the light would be going. My father was very delicate, he would never have said, 'Gosh, this is a problem in life.' He thought, noblesse oblige, I have to be chivalrous."

Huguette had temporarily put aside Japanese themes to work on a new series about envelopes, some with white flaps fetchingly open, a hint of the mysteries of the letters inside. "She has been so fanatical about the little envelopes she has been painting for months, if not for all of last year," wrote Doris in her notes. "Studying abstract perspectives to finish them."

The heiress did not spend much time in New York that year, heading back to Bellosguardo for the month of August. Etienne de Villermont was a houseguest at Bellosguardo during the annual fiesta, which included a pageant, a parade, street dancing, and parties at the Montecito Country Club and the Biltmore's waterfront Coral Casino. Huguette met Etienne at the train station, and a photograph caught the happy moment as she gave him a hug.

Huguette's and the Frenchman's social circles overlapped: when he returned to New York that fall, Etienne was a guest at a dinner given by the ubiquitous Amanda Storrs, the widow of the theatre producer. The marquis benefited financially from his friendship with the Clarks. He was named to the board of a newly formed Vermont copper company chaired by George Ellis, a lawyer who had worked for William Andrews Clark. His Manhattan firm handled legal affairs for Anna and Huguette.

Huguette returned briefly to New York that fall, but then turned around and headed back to California to spend December 1941 and the Christmas holidays with her mother at Bellosguardo. The weather was balmy, perfect for tennis or golf, a pleasant seventy-eight degrees on December 7, 1941, the day of the Japanese attack on Pearl Harbor.

Ever since the Clarks had fled France at the outbreak of World War I, Anna and Huguette had a tendency to panic. But trapped on the West Coast in the harrowing days after Pearl Harbor, they had genuine reason to be fearful. Air sirens went off in major cities, antiaircraft guns were fired into the sky over Los Angeles, and fear was rampant that Japanese troops were about to invade by air or by sea. Beaches were laced with barbed wire.

Huguette and her mother desperately wanted to flee California after the Japanese attack, but they were competing with thousands of terrified residents. She sent a telegram to Tadé Styka, explaining that they were having difficulty obtaining tickets and would be arriving in New York later than she had hoped.

The location of the Santa Barbara Cemetery—high above on the ocean with a sweeping view of the horizon, right next to Bellosguardo— offered an ideal observation post. The Army established a presence in the cemetery, stationing troops with artillery and searchlights there as sentries patrolled the beaches below. Bellosguardo was now part of a war zone.

Huguette and Anna had left Santa Barbara by the time the city was traumatized on February 22, 1942, when a Japanese submarine surfaced a half mile from the coast and fired at the Ellwood Oil Field. Just twelve miles from Santa Barbara, the oil facility sustained minimal damage and no one was injured, but the attack ratcheted up concerns about the region's vulnerability.

Back in New York, Huguette and Anna began to ludicrously worry about money despite their ample means. Huguette announced that she needed to economize and cut back her painting lessons from four times a week to two visits, although it hardly dented her budget. "Her manager of financial affairs said she must cut down on expenses since the government is taking too much from her," wrote Doris in her notes.

For Huguette, the outbreak of war was emotionally shattering. She loved Japanese culture and had been collecting Japanese artifacts for a decade, but now Japan was the enemy. She had befriended Japanese Americans and immersed herself in learning about the country. Lucien Marsh, the proprietor of the Japanese importer Marsh and Company, wrote to Huguette on January 29, 1942, to convey the obvious: "When we succeed in abolishing the war lords of Japan I believe we will be able to accomplish your unfilled orders." He added, hopefully, "And any future orders..."

But now any American with close ties to Japan was considered a potential subversive. Until Pearl Harbor, Huguette had been receiving regular shipments from Japan of dolls, castles, and antiques. At her Fifth Avenue apartment, she received a series of unsettling visits from the FBI. She talked about the experience many years later with her assistant, Chris Sattler. As he recounts, "There was so much correspondence between Japan and Mrs. Clark, she was actually interviewed on a number of occasions by the FBI."

The government paranoia was not as far-fetched as it seems. Velvalee Dickinson, the proprietor of a New York doll store, was later convicted of spying for Japan and sentenced to ten years in prison.

She sent coded letters about American ship movements that were disguised as routine correspondence about doll shipments and repairs.

When California began rounding up Japanese residents and shipping them to internment camps in February 1942, Huguette had first-hand knowledge of a few of those taken away. Her uncle Arthur La Chapelle's Japanese cook, Taka Muto, and his wife, Saburo Muto, were forced to leave his Beverly Hills estate and sent to a barbed-wire enclave in barren Cody, Wyoming. Huguette knew the couple well and stayed in touch with them for many decades following their release.

All of it—the specter of attack right after Pearl Harbor, the FBI interrogation, the demonization of Japan—sent Huguette into a tailspin. Already relatively slender, she began to lose weight. She even stopped turning up for her painting lessons. Tadé and Doris bought orchids for her birthday on June 9, sending them to her apartment. Ten days later, Tadé was so worried that he spoke to Adele Marié to see how Huguette was doing. As Doris wrote, "She said Miss Clark is so terribly worried over war conditions, Miss Marié worried her health will break." Those fears proved true.

Huguette spent the next few months under the care of doctors, suffering from a psychological breakdown. She cut off contact with the outside world. On September 24, she finally emerged to tentatively make her way to Tadé's studio. Doris described in her notes what happened: "Miss Clark came today for the first time in over two months. TS had amazingly divined her reason for staying away... She called the other day to confirm the words that TS had told me weeks ago—that she had been taking a rest cure to gain weight. She was not even allowed to talk because this wasted energy." Where Huguette spent these months recovering from her breakdown was not spelled out, but her inability to make phone calls suggests an institutional setting.

Huguette remained in fragile shape for the remainder of the year. On December 3, Doris wrote, "Miss Clark has been staying home trying to gain weight." To cheer her up, Tadé sent Huguette a dozen long-stemmed red roses and a new artist's palette that he had spent months meticulously carving and sanding, with wood specially chosen from the Steinway factory to match the color of Huguette's blonde hair. It was a Christmas gift, meant to remind Huguette of her identity as an artist and to entice her to pick up a brush again. Tadé had finally married Doris in August with a simple City Hall ceremony, but he remained attached to his favorite pupil.

Anna worried about her daughter's emotional health. "Lani would sometimes make little semicritical comments about Huguette," recalls Gordon Lyle Jr. "That Huguette wanted to be sheltered from all the problems of the world. For which I don't blame her." From then on, Anna appeared to family and friends to be especially protective of Huguette, concerned about keeping her sensitive daughter on an even psychological keel. At the end of the year, the family suffered another loss when Amelia La Chapelle Turner's husband, Bryce, died of a heart attack on December 26. The former mining engineer had been a constant presence at family events, and the three women had now lost their final male anchor.

————

Once Huguette recovered enough to reengage with the world, she did her small part to aid in the war effort. She donated money to the YWCA for hospitality for the troops, loaned a painting to the Museum of Modern Art for a fund-raising exhibit for Navy relief, and appeared at a morale-boosting USO party to cheer up soldiers headed to war. She kept a photo from the event as a souvenir, which she showed to Chris Sattler. "She is sitting with three other society women, with a sailor, a Marine, and a couple Army guys, young roughhousing guys," he says. "She looked incredibly uncomfortable." Making small talk with homesick soldiers was not in her repertoire.

She returned to painting Japanese scenes again, although she bought a zipped case to carry her paintings out of Tadé's studio, to avoid arousing hostility from strangers on the street.

Huguette's disappearance from public life had the inadvertent and undesired effect of making her even more of a figure of public curiosity. In May 1943, Cholly Knickerbocker devoted an entire column to Huguette, noting that she was keen to keep her "activities out of the news." As the columnist wrote:

Although Huguette makes her home in a luxurious apartment on upper Fifth Avenue, you seldom encounter her about the haunts of "cafe society" and you NEVER see accounts of her comings and goings in the "sassiety" columns...

Huguette inherited great wealth—but she never had any desire to go in for a big social splash and her simplicity and directness, going hand in hand with a certain shyness are in contrast to the chi-chi and splurge affected by other Mayfairites blessed with far less coin of the realm... Huguette has continued to devote her time to her art work...

Her former husband now is married to the one-time Constance Baxter Tevis Toulmin, and, as an executive to the Red Cross, was appointed to a post with the Civilian Relief mission in London.

Huguette goes her quiet way, occupied with her art and her music, attending concerts, the theatre, the opera, various art exhibits, etc.—wartime exigencies permitted. She will have none of "cafe society."

Huguette and Anna finally returned to California that August. Worried about possible food shortages, Anna bought a 218-acre ranch nearby with grazing cows and vegetable gardens. Anna and Huguette never lived at Rancho Alegre but relied on its produce. For Anna, the ranch was a psychological safety net, a place where she and Huguette and the staff could flee if the coast of California came under attack. Anna held on to it even after the war when the previous owner, publisher Thomas Storke, tried to buy it back.

———

Infants were not a regular part of Huguette's life. But when Tadé Styka's wife, Doris, gave birth to a daughter, Wanda, on August 19, 1943, the Clark women were besotted. Huguette was on her own in California at the time, but her mother and aunt paid an immediate visit. Tadé wrote to Huguette: "Votre dear Mother and your Aunt came to see Wanda and true to her sex, she seems to have been born with the art of winning hearts."

Huguette accepted the mantle of godmother with joy, showering baby Wanda with affection and gifts including musical dolls, French illustrated children's books, and $1,000 bonds. Encouraging Tadé and Doris to take home movies, she sent them an early projector. She wrote frequent notes to Doris in English conveying how much she reveled in watching Wanda grow up. Proud father Tadé painted numerous portraits of his enchanting daughter and crafted busts of her likeness, sending a bronze sculpture of Wanda to Huguette as a gift.

In a handwritten note from Santa Barbara dated June 16, 1944, a week after her own thirty-eighth birthday, Huguette wrote,

Dear Doris,

It was sweet of you and "the maestre" to remember my birthday. I am still getting much enjoyment from the delicious candy and I want to thank you both many many times. The ivy poisoning is better which makes me glad as it will be so nice seeing you again and you can imagine how I can hardly wait to see my godchild. Mother and my aunt and Uncle Arthur just rave about her... with much love, Huguette.

Six months later, Huguette sent another note gushing about Wanda. She uses a surprisingly formal address for her painting teacher, as if still trying to get used to their changed relationship.

Dear Doris,

Thank you and Mr. Styka so much for the delicious box of chocolates you so sweetly sent me for Christmas and for your thoughts of me. I so enjoyed seeing you and Wanda the other day. Wanda looked so well and has grown considerably since I last saw her. She is adorable and so intelligent. I thought it was so by the way she handed me my photograph. I just have her photographs and will have one of the larger ones framed. With much love and wishing you all three a most Happy New Year, Huguette.

Huguette frequently requested visits. "I love my little godchild," she wrote. "Wanda has to spend the afternoon with us when you and Mr. Styka go to the movies or are otherwise engaged. Will call up very soon as I should also like you both to come to dinner one of these days."

Once Wanda learned to talk, Huguette asked to be called "Marraine," the French word for "godmother." Huguette liked coming up with ways to amuse Wanda, such as demonstrating her new Polaroid camera. She wrote to Doris Styka: "I have a new camera which in minutes develop its photos. You can play a joke on Wanda. Snap her and then show it to her a minute later."

When Huguette came to the Styka family's duplex complex of apartments—living quarters and studio—at 222 Central Park South, Wanda would often be kept company by Anna and Huguette's social secretary, Adele Marié. "I had to be very quiet," Wanda recalls. "It seems to me that the lessons were two hours, but of course a child thinks that everything is very long." Bizarre as it seems, even after Huguette reached her late thirties and was visiting a full household, she still brought along a companion.

Looking back on her early years when she was a young observer in her father's studio, Wanda recalls being struck by how her father and Huguette expressed their very different personalities in their art. "My father was a virtuoso—he painted fast, he had an unerring touch. He liked to let the viewer finish some of the lines, to leave something unsaid in the paintings. Marraine liked everything very precise, finely delineated. She was very careful. I don't think she was a fast worker." For Huguette, it was all about control. She labored to show every ripple in the fabric of a gown and every flower petal unfolding, creating lifelike images.

As avidly as Huguette pursued painting, her mother remained devoted to music. Undaunted by her diminished hearing, Anna still played the harp and often invited chamber music groups to perform at her Fifth Avenue music room. In 1945, she played host to her visiting California relative, pianist Agnes Clark Albert, the daughter of Celia Tobin and Charles Clark. Agnes had proposed a musical afternoon and brought along Robert Maas, the former cellist of the Pro Arte Quartet, a Belgian group that had been stranded in America by the war. Maas had parted company with the quartet and told Anna that he was unsure of his musical future. As Agnes Clark Albert later told her daughter Karine, Anna responded with a wildly extravagant gesture. Pointing to a Cézanne painting of his wife, Anna announced,

"My daughter Huguette won't come into this room because she hates this painting so much." Then she took the Cézanne portrait of his wife off the wall and left with it.

When she returned a few hours later, Anna announced that she had just sold the painting at the Wildenstein Gallery and spent the proceeds at the finest music store in New York. She then produced four Stradivarius violins that had belonged to the nineteenth-century Italian violinist Niccolò Paganini. Anna offered to lend them to Robert Maas if he would launch a new string quartet. (The exact details of the story may have been exaggerated through frequent retellings but Anna Clark definitely purchased the instruments and inspired the formation of the Paganini Quartet.)

After the debut performance of the chamber music group at Manhattan's Town Hall in November 1946, the *New York Times* praised the Bartók and Schumann selections and expressed gratitude toward "Mrs. William A. Clark" for supplying the historic instruments. As the quartet performed across the country, Anna was credited time and again for making this heavenly music possible, an artistic legacy of her own.

The quartet performed at Bellosguardo, where Anna and Huguette continued to hold court. "The Clarks sponsored the Paganini Quartet and held concerts in the music room with its back-to-back Steinway concert grand pianos and harps," wrote Barbara Hoelscher Doran in an essay for the *Santa Barbara Independent*. Born in 1944, Doran grew up on the estate, where her father, Albert Hoelscher, was the caretaker. In her essay, she described "lawn parties at the tennis court, with a quartet playing in a tree-house platform, and plays in the outdoor setting." The Clarks were democratic enough to socialize with favored retainers and their children. "When Huguette and Anna E. Clark came out to the estate, Huguette would phone our house and invite me over for afternoon tea," Doran wrote. "I would walk over with our dogs and sit with Huguette and Anna E. on the terrace under big umbrellas overlooking the great lawns and ocean."

Huguette led a quieter life when she was in Manhattan, continuing to take her painting lessons. She had begun to correspond frequently with longtime family friends based in the South of France—not only man-about-town Etienne de Villermont but his younger brother, Henri. Their letters back and forth were always in French. Ever generous, she sent them checks, and they wrote back with family news. "I thank you endlessly and with eternal gratitude for all you have done and are still doing for us," wrote Henri.

In April 1951, Huguette became weak and ill, ending up at St. Luke's Hospital on Manhattan's Upper West Side for several weeks. The hospital, which had a specialty in respiratory diseases, had an upscale clientele, treating bankers, politicians, and actresses. Tadé made note of Huguette's illness in his appointment calendar but did not specify the problem. Henri de Villermont wrote to her on June 5: "We were so sorry in learning that you had suffered and worried about it." On November 23, Henri reiterated his concerns, saying, "I hope, dear Huguette, that your health is definitively back to normal and that you don't feel anything anymore. You have suffered so much for several months."

That year, Huguette purchased a new country refuge close to Manhattan, a sprawling twelve-thousand-square-foot French-style château in New Canaan, Connecticut. Built in 1938 with parquet floors and marble fireplaces, the twenty-two-room mansion was located on a private twenty-three-acre wooded lot with a meandering stream and waterfall. But the bucolic setting was not the primary draw: amid the nuclear panic of the early years of the Cold War era, this estate offered a ready escape from New York. "They had a place in Connecticut because people were scared about the atomic bomb," explains Gordon Lyle Jr.

The terrified atmosphere of the era rings through in a 1951 letter that Doris Styka wrote but ultimately did not send to Huguette, in which the artist's wife stresses "the fears that have become so much part of life in New York":

> It seems that just as one starts to relax and forgets about any wars or bombing along comes other dread news over the television reviving again the thoughts of escape I have thought to smother... With an atom bomb, survival would be few. I am confiding these fears to you, Huguette, in hope you could help me to know what to do. It

isn't for myself that I fear, but the survival of our little Wanda...as well as her father whose loss to us and to the world would be irreplaceable. When I constantly hear these words of possible bombing and what to do in case of an attack, I feel I don't want to risk the possibility of it. This fear is making me actually ill...

Huguette had similar worries, which her new refuge helped alleviate. She began renovations on her Connecticut estate, importing marble fireplaces and adding a painting studio above the master bedroom with a staircase featuring fanciful balustrades shaped like paintbrushes. She would now have a place in the country to use for weekends or if anything frightening happened in Manhattan.

———

On June 28, 1952, Tadé and his wife and daughter went to Long Beach on Long Island for the afternoon. On this extremely hot day, he suddenly felt quite ill and was taken by ambulance to the hospital. At sixty-three, he had experienced a stroke. Worried about her dearest friend, Huguette sent him joking get-well cards at New York Hospital, with such scenes as a patient trying to lasso a nurse and gift certificates to be claimed upon leaving the hospital for a Scotch'n Soda, six Easy Rhumba lessons, or a Ride in a Roller Coaster. She reverted to writing notes in French to him on cards imprinted with colorful flowers, rather than writing in English to his wife.

Tadé spent months recuperating in warmer climes and at his country house in Ashley Falls, Massachusetts. On January 23, 1953, Huguette scribbled, "Am so glad you are getting better and better. I hope that in Cuba you will find some nice hot water that will quicken your full recovery." A month later, she followed up with another note:

Cher Maitre,

I am rejoicing at the idea of seeing all three of you again soon. I found the photos of Wanda very good. She is gorgeous. I hope the water in Miami has decided to become hotter so that you can finally enjoy it. With all of my most affectionate thoughts to all three of you and see you soon, Huguette.

P.S. I am laying down one of the dancer in a yellow kimono.

Five months later, she wrote to him in Ashley Falls to say, "I was so glad to have had this little chat on the phone with you today." Her notes are meant to cheer him up, but her own anxiety is what comes through. Whenever Tadé left Manhattan, Huguette dropped him a line—in July, October, November—stressing how much she missed him and his family and asking to send Wanda a "big kiss."

Tadé Styka died on September 11, 1954, at New York Hospital. The *New York Times* obituary of the sixty-four-year-old artist recalled his precocious exhibit at the Paris salon and a portrait that he had painted in 1948 of Harry Truman, presented to the president at a White House ceremony.

Shortly after the funeral, Huguette paid a condolence call to Doris and Wanda at their Central Park South apartment, the scene of decades of memories. Aware of how much Huguette had loved her painting lessons, Doris mentioned that Tadé's artist brother, Adam, might be available to work with her. But Huguette declined. Her precious hours with Tadé could not be replicated with anyone, even his brother. A second-best consolation could not heal the hole in her heart.

When Huguette left Doris and Wanda Styka after the condolence call, they assumed that they would see her again. Huguette loved Wanda, savoring their time together and eagerly anticipating visits. Huguette remained a major part of their lives for the next half century. The heiress who blossomed as a painter under Tadé's tutelage would engage in long, affectionate phone conversations with both Wanda and Doris. She paid for Wanda's private-school education at the Convent of the Sacred Heart and sent frequent checks and gifts. But the visits mysteriously halted. "We were always in communication by telephone," says Wanda. "That was her medium. We were never out of touch." But after Tadé Styka died, Wanda would never lay eyes on Huguette again.

Chapter Twelve

The Lady Vanishes

When two people who have already been keeping a low profile decide to withdraw even further from the world, it can take years for anyone to notice. Later on, puzzled friends and acquaintances of Anna and Huguette would rack their memories for clues to explain the women's behavior and try to recall the *last* sightings.

The first sign that something was amiss came when mother and daughter abruptly stopped going to Bellosguardo, ending a thirty-year tradition. Santa Barbara was their sunny sanctuary, and in the past, Huguette would not give it up even if it meant forgoing lessons with Tadé Styka. Barbara Hoelscher Doran, the caretaker's daughter, believes their last trip to Santa Barbara was in 1953. Huguette was then forty-seven and her mother was seventy-five years old. They never explained why they halted their California vacations. But reflecting their free-spending heritage, Anna and Huguette continued to keep the estate well tended and fully staffed.

In 1958, the staff at Bellosguardo got the welcome news that Huguette intended to return. Sherry Howard Stockwell, then an art history student at the University of California at Santa Barbara, went to Bellosguardo with a professor who was supervising repairs to the estate's Louis XV tapestries. Seamstresses imported from Holland were doing the work. "Huguette was supposed to be coming soon," Stockwell recalls. "The staff was all excited and getting ready."

Stockwell toured the art-filled house, including the library stocked with first editions, Anna's bedroom ("She had a bust of the daughter who had died, a harp, and grand piano"), and Huguette's painting studio ("the best oils and watercolors an artist could want"). Piled high on a wall of shelves in the studio were numbered boxes containing exquisite antique Japanese and Chinese dolls. But Huguette canceled her visit and never ventured west again. Maintaining the fantasy that she might reappear, she continued to pay her dues to her golf club, the Valley Club of Montecito, for the next half century.

A caretaker at Bellosguardo, Harry Pepper, who had worked there since 1942, wrote Huguette a heartfelt letter in 1961 to say that he needed to quit because he was suffering from "isolation fatigue." Pepper wrote, "I do not believe it is good for one to work too many years alone...Would never have thought of leaving if Bellosguardo was open every 4 of 5 years." The estate on the cliff had become a lonely, haunted place.

Huguette's lawyer, Charles Bannerman, was under the impression that she and her mother were using their new Connecticut house as an alternate weekend retreat. But as the attorney's widow, Jane Bannerman, now 102 years old, recalled in an interview at her Park Avenue apartment in 2012, "It was the funniest thing. My husband took me up to Connecticut where the Clarks had this large house. My husband had been insuring the contents for a long time, and when we went in, there was not a stick in the house." Huguette had never bothered to furnish the place. She hired a full-time caretaker but did not visit, even for a quick day trip. Even though she was a woman passionate about nature and had hiked the Grand Canyon, splashed in the ocean in Hawaii, and endured railroad cross-country trips to Santa Barbara, Huguette was no longer leaving the concrete canyons of Manhattan.

There were, to be sure, a final few nods to society. Fondly recalling her many years in Paris, Anna Clark bought a table for an October 1954 fund-raising dinner for the American Friends of Versailles at the Waldorf Astoria. French cuisine and wine were served, and the Starlight Roof was decorated with faux Versailles-style statuary. Her patronage was noted in the *New York Times*—and that was the last appearance in the society columns for a woman who had graced the *Social Register* since 1904.

Rumors began to circulate that the two women had become germphobic. Anna's chauffeur passed along tales, mentioning to a friend that when the two women attended the opera, Anna bought up all the seats around them.

For Anna, her harp remained a life-sustaining pleasure and she continued studying with her longtime teacher, Marcel Grandjany, a Frenchman who headed the harp department at Juilliard and had given private lessons to Harpo Marx. Thirteen years younger than Anna, Grandjany had been taught to play the harp by Alphonse Hasselmans, who had been Anna's teacher in Paris. Students usually came to Grandjany's Upper West Side home for lessons, but he had always made house calls to Anna Clark. "My father was a regular visitor to her at 907 Fifth Avenue at Seventy-Second Street, going about once a week. This went on for nearly twenty years," says Bernard Grandjany, who often drove his father there and picked him up afterward. "My father was a great listener. He would take time to listen to a person's problems like he was a father confessor."

In a quiet life with few daily markers, Anna's lessons were an event to savor. Kathleen Bride, now a harp professor at the Eastman School of Music, began studying with Grandjany in 1958, and recalls that each week, "His wife would say to him, 'Don't forget that at four o'clock, you have to go see Mrs. Clark.'" Anna also made occasional pilgrimages out of the house to the salon of her hairdresser, Roger Vergnes, on East Fifty-Seventh Street, who had an elite clientele including the Duchess of Windsor.

As Anna aged, her circle of intimates had inevitably become smaller. Her brother, Arthur La Chapelle, and her suitor, Major Bowes, both died in 1946, and Anna's close friend Amanda Storrs died in 1954. Anna's widowed sister, Amelia, had remarried a socially prominent lawyer, Thomas Darrington Semple, a widower with two grown children. The sisters still saw each other frequently, and Huguette doted on her aunt, sending Amelia yellow roses and cakes for her birthdays. Amelia called her "Dearest Huguette" and "Darling Huguette" in her affectionate thank-you notes.

Two family confidants, who had been close to William Andrews Clark, died within months of each other. Dr. William Gordon Lyle, the physician who had tried to save Andrée's life, died in November 1955 at the age of eighty-four. The physician had retired years earlier but had still made himself available to the Clarks. His much younger wife, Leontine—Huguette's former Spence classmate—had a bond with both mother and daughter. "Right to the end, Lani didn't want anyone else but Dr. Lyle and he would be there," says his daughter, Tina Lyle Harrower. The Clarks switched their medical care to a French physician, Dr. Jules Pierre. That same year, their longtime attorney George Ellis died. While Ellis had handed over the Clarks' legal matters to his partners, Charles Bannerman and Frederick Stokes, several years earlier, this was yet another loss. Ellis had worked for William Andrews Clark for decades; Anna Clark was the godmother to the lawyer's daughter, Ann.

Anna and Huguette remained in touch with a few California Clark relatives, the family of Huguette's deceased half brother Charles Clark. Celia Tobin Clark; her daughter, Agnes Clark Albert; and Agnes's three teenage children (Karine, Paul, and Clare) would come to New York at least once a year and take a suite of rooms at the Savoy Plaza on Fifth Avenue. The grand Art Deco hotel, which was torn down in 1964 and replaced by the General Motors skyscraper, was opposite the Plaza Hotel.

Karine McCall remembered visiting her relatives at Anna's grand apartment at 907 Fifth Avenue in 1955. Huguette was fashionably dressed in an outfit that the then teenager had never seen before, orange culottes, recalling, "I was quite fascinated by them." Her brother Paul Albert recalls chatting with Anna and Huguette at his grandmother's cocktail parties at the Savoy. "Anna was very outgoing and kind of vivacious," said Paul Albert, who as a teenager in the 1950s was fascinated by Anna's hearing aid. "She had this box with a wire to her ear and she let me play with it."

His memories of Huguette are hazy, but he can date them. "The last time I saw her was in 1957," he said, recalling a visit to her Fifth Avenue apartment. He was in boarding school at the time and went to see Huguette and Anna for tea; he found it odd that most of the furniture was under dustcovers, as if the rooms were not in use. Many years later, when he and his younger sister Karine tried to retrace the family history, that date was a milestone. It was the last time that they could recall for certain that anyone from their branch of the Clark family had actually seen Anna or Huguette.

Now that Huguette was spending all of her time in Manhattan, she indulged in an upscale version of nesting, enjoying the perks of her inheritance. She purchased musical instruments, art, and jewelry— nothing but the best, of course. On May 3, 1955, she bought a 1709 Stradivarius, known as La Pucelle, from the Rembert Wurlitzer store, dispatching her mother's social secretary, Adele Marié, to negotiate a 5 percent cash discount for a total of $50,985. Three years later, she dropped $125,750 at the Knoedler Gallery on a Renoir painting, *Girls Playing Battledore and Shuttlecock*, depicting young French women indulging in an early version of badminton. The next year, she bought a harp from a Paris dealer for $1,750. She ordered couture clothes from Jean Patou in Paris. At both Cartier and Van Cleef and Arpels, Huguette was an honored customer, treating herself, her mother, and friends to sparkling baubles: a $13,750 gold bracelet with diamonds and rubies; a $6,000 Van Cleef platinum ring with nine carats' worth of 110 diamonds; and an array of earrings and bracelets adorned with emeralds and sapphires.

She bought a new set of Limoges china in order to entertain elegantly at home. Huguette held on to reminder notes that she scribbled to herself during this period, as well as dinner menus and grocery shopping lists for her maids. For one dinner, Huguette served thick carrot soup, shad roe, sliced tomatoes (no dressing), potato balls, string beans, peas, caramel custard, and after-dinner coffee; at another meal, guests were fed carrot soup again, lamb chops, mashed potatoes, beets, and peas. Huguette liked French treats such as brioche, petit fours, and Gaufrette biscuits, with the occasional lowbrow weakness for Twinkies.

Her long-ago admirer, Etienne de Villermont, had married in 1953, and he and his wife, Elisabeth, lived part-time in Normandy, in the village of Bonneville-sur-Touques. But he and Huguette carried on a long-running flirtatious correspondence. When Etienne came to New

York, he made a point of seeing Huguette. In several of her address books, she lists Etienne as staying at the Beekman Tower Hotel, a hotel on a quiet block near the East River with soaring views from the rooftop bar. The marquis sent her very affectionate letters in French, thanking her for financial gifts. After one long-distance France–New York phone call, Etienne wrote to Huguette on January 30, 1956, to say, "I felt an infinite joy conversing with you. It was as if I was seeing you. I don't know how to tell you of our eternal gratitude, since I don't know another person on earth motivated by such heavenly spirit who has done so much for others."

From the way that Huguette spoke about Etienne in her later years, her assistant, Chris Sattler, came to believe that "he was her soul mate." Yet Etienne was also the perfect romantic object for a woman who was scarcely leaving her apartment anymore. He sent her pink roses on her birthdays along with loving telegrams and letters, including such sentiments as "You can guess how much my thoughts and heart are with you" and "I kiss you wholeheartedly." She could have the illusion of romance without the day-to-day and face-to-face realities of actually living with a man. He was three thousand miles away, a disembodied voice on the phone, an occasional friendly face in person. His wife, who suffered from numerous debilitating ailments, wrote to Huguette, too, treating her as a family friend.

The hobbies that Huguette had embraced as a young woman endured: she was still collecting dolls, and she even ordered doll-sized couture clothes from Maison Christian Dior in Paris. The Marsh family in California knew they could count on Huguette's annual outlay for Japanese castles. And now she expanded her reach. As a girl, Huguette had fallen in love with the work of French illustrators who published in children's magazines and books, notably Felix Lorioux, whose work appeared in a French weekly, *La Semaine de Suzette*, and who had briefly done work for Walt Disney. She began to commission work from Lorioux and a handful of other French illustrators such as Manon Iessel and Jean Mercier.

Huguette had developed her own new artistic passion that she could pursue right at home: photography. She had an account at the

Willoughby-Peerless camera store and constantly ordered the latest equipment. When her regular salesman lost his job, she told Wanda Styka that she felt sorry for him. "She was worried that because he was in his midfifties he would have trouble finding a job," Wanda recalls. "I thought it was so thoughtful of her." Huguette took photos from her apartment windows of street scenes below. At Christmastime, she would dress up in an elegant cocktail dress and pose for a self-portrait, often in front of her Steinway or near one of her Impressionist paintings. A well-dressed woman in her midfifties, she usually exuded a sense of good cheer, but in some of the photographs, she looks pensive, as if longing for something more in life.

When her mother's health began to fail, Huguette turned to Etienne for a sympathetic ear. On September 18, 1962, he wrote to Huguette: "Have you at least managed to have your mother take some beneficial vitamins? I put myself in your shoes and it's all very difficult." The following year, he worried that Huguette was not taking care of herself due to her concern over her mother: "Make sure you aren't tiring yourself too much and that you're eating enough."

Although frail and ill, Anna was determined to stay at home where she could see the seasons change from her windows overlooking Central Park. She was surrounded by mementoes of her life, from Andrée's diary to the Impressionist paintings that she had fallen in love with in Paris as a young woman. Anna was tended round the clock by nurses in her eighth-floor apartment, and Huguette could look in several times a day. But one darker incident etched itself indelibly into Huguette's memory. "One day she came in and saw that the nurse was not treating her mother well," recalls Wanda Styka. Huguette did not describe what she saw, but it was upsetting enough that Wanda recalls, "She let go of the nurse."

Anna Evangelina La Chapelle Clark, the self-invented Montana beauty who rose from the brothel-filled streets of Butte to become the wife of one of the richest men in America, died on October 11, 1963, at the age of eighty-five. Although her death was considered noteworthy enough to make the newspapers, most of the obituaries primarily recited her husband's accomplishments. MRS. ANNA CLARK, SENATOR'S

WIDOW; ART PATRON, WHOSE HUSBAND LEFT $250 MILLION, DIES was the headline of the *New York Times* article, which noted that Mrs. Clark had subsidized the Paganini Quartet plus the Loewenguth Quartet of Brussels. The *Washington Post* emphasized the local angle: ANNA CLARK, PATRON OF THE CORCORAN GALLERY—describing the artworks that her husband had given to the museum.

Anna Clark's will, which she had signed on May 9, 1960, left the bulk of her estate to her daughter. Huguette received her mother's jewelry, her museum-worthy paintings, antique French furniture, and real estate, which included Bellosguardo, Rancho Alegre, and Anna's Fifth Avenue co-op. Anna put $500,000 (the equivalent of $3.8 million in current dollars) in trust for her sister, Amelia, with the income and profits flowing to Amelia during her lifetime and the principal reverting upon her death to Huguette. Anna made an identical arrangement for her brother Arthur's widow, Hanna La Chapelle. Outside of her immediate family, Anna gave the largest bequest to her confidant and social secretary, Adele Marié, who received $100,000 plus the income from another $100,000 trust. Anna's two goddaughters, Tina Lyle Harrower and Ann Ellis Raynolds, each received $10,000.

Once again, the Corcoran Gallery benefited from the Clark generosity: Anna gave $100,000 to the museum in her husband's memory as well as her Stradivarius violins and other valuable cellos and violas. But she did not want the historic instruments to sit silently in cases. To keep the music alive, Anna asked the museum to loan the instruments to string quartets and even left $50,000 for the instruments' upkeep. In other philanthropic bequests, Anna gave $100,000 each to the Girl Scouts (a tribute to her daughter Andrée), the Juilliard School of Music, the American Red Cross, and the United Hospital Fund.

Even though Huguette had known for several years that Anna was seriously ill, losing her mother was wrenching. Huguette had made several painful trips out to the Bronx to Woodlawn Cemetery—her sister and father were buried in the family's white mausoleum—but now at age fifty-seven, she was the only one left. She clipped and carefully saved her mother's obituaries in a folder. Etienne wrote Huguette a comforting condolence letter on October 14 to say, "Your news of your mother passing filled me with sadness, but she left us only temporarily, and she is in a better place now with the angels, Andrée, her parents and God. She is probably happier since her last years were difficult. She will be with you forever, though there is emptiness for you now..." A month later, he wrote again to say, "I hope this note will still find you well, despite the great change that must seem quite sad at times..."

Huguette's life had always revolved around Anna; as an adult, she had rarely been apart from her mother. Even during the brief nine months when the newlywed Huguette lived with William Gower, her mother was only four floors away. They were unusually close, two women who had lived through two world wars plus the Depression, protected and isolated by their millions. Now aside from her household employees—a housekeeper, maids, a chauffeur—Huguette was on her own.

Time stopped.

Huguette had rarely seen her Clark relatives in recent years. But shortly after Anna Clark died, Huguette's half sister Katherine Morris invited her to lunch at her home at 1030 Fifth Avenue followed by a Friday concert at Lincoln Center. They were joined by a handful of female family members including Gemma Hall, who was married to Katherine Morris's grandson Lewis Hall. Gemma Hall later said she came away with the distinct impression that Huguette was unused to modern life. When the women arrived at Lincoln Center, Gemma recalled, "What always came to mind was of someone who had never seen an escalator before, so she [Huguette] was hesitating, shall I take that step...Eventually, courageously, she did...She had a beautiful chiffon dress which was perhaps something that would have been used many years before."

As far as Huguette was concerned, this was a social outing that she had no desire to repeat. From then on, she turned down invitations from these New York Clark relatives. As Katherine Morris's great-granddaughter Carla Hall, born in 1952, recalls, "I sat every Sunday with my grandmother and great-grandmother at their table for lunch. My perception as a child growing up about my aunt Huguette is that she was invited to lunch very often for holidays and for a couple of these Sunday lunches. She would call up prior to the lunch and say that she had a little cold, and that she would be indisposed, and she sends the family greetings."

Alone now at 907 Fifth Avenue, rambling around the spacious apartments, Huguette had to deal with the business of death—handling her mother's estate—and find a way to fill the hours that she had previously spent tending to Anna. Huguette gave Rancho Alegre, the Santa Barbara ranch that Anna had purchased during World War II, to the Boy Scouts. She commissioned music in her mother's honor from her mother's harp teacher, Marcel Grandjany. As a way to move forward in life, Huguette decided to renovate Anna's eighth-floor apartment, using the decorating firm French and Company, which her mother had employed for various jobs since 1926. The family firm was now run by Robert Samuels Jr.

But Huguette insisted on one provision that reflected her reclusive state of mind: she refused to meet with him. Samuels orchestrated work on her apartment periodically for the next thirty years, but Huguette would never see him face-to-face. "He'd tell us stories at the dinner table, how she'd hide behind a door and slip him notes," says Ann Fabrizio, the decorator's oldest daughter. Her younger sister, Margaret Hoag, recalls, "My father talked to her through the door. She would never open the door. After her mother died, she started to stay hidden."

Huguette never explained her behavior.

She spent more than $78,000 in 1964 fixing up her mother's co-op, replacing the floor with reproduction parquet de Versailles and renovating the new kitchen with a black Garland gas stove and a Kelvinator refrigerator. "Everything is proceeding nicely although the apartment is in shambles at the moment," Robert Samuels wrote to Huguette on September 4, 1964. The eighth floor had two apartments, and her mother had lived in 8W, facing Central Park. When the unit next door, 8E, became available, Huguette bought it to insure her privacy, although she never furnished it. Now she had forty-two rooms at 907 Fifth Avenue. But she was a voracious reader who constantly ordered new books, her doll collection kept increasing, and she never threw out any piece of paper that entered the house. Consequently, some rooms became cluttered with stuff. Radiator leaks in the aging building were a constant problem. Huguette primarily lived on the twelfth floor for at least fifteen more years before switching to sleeping downstairs in 8W.

For Huguette, her daily mail deliveries provided an infusion of life from the outside world. One of her frequent correspondents during the 1960s was a man who had once been dear to her: her ex-husband, William Gower. He had retired from his Paris-based job as the European head of the American publishing firm Cowles Media and was now splitting his time between a villa in Antibes and vacation lodging on the island of Antigua. His second wife, Constance, had died in 1951. He had been very discreet about his first marriage. Gower's niece Jan Perry, now eighty-three, was unaware that he had previously been married to Huguette Clark, saying, "He never talked about her."

But the former spouses were now frequently in touch, sending each other telegraphs and letters. Huguette mailed him checks as well as her photographs with witty captions, and he replied with amused sentiments.

> *Dear Huguette,*
> *I can't honestly say that I detect much quality between your 800 and 1000 lenses because they are both excellent... Your picture stories were cute and the Japanese house and doll were charming. It won't be long before you have enough confidence to tackle the rooftop blonde sunbather. When you do, use the 1000 lens, follow her around and be careful not to make the pictures blurry! Love, Bill*

The former magazine publisher followed up with another letter commending her pictures.

> *Dear Huguette,*
> *I have difficulty keeping track of all of your photographic exploits! Your sequence pictures have the same effect as movies and I enjoy your amusing titles. I still like the larger close-ups better but they are all excellent. Why don't you try some shots up or down Fifth Avenue?...Affectionately, Bill*

The old flames made plans to meet when Bill Gower came to Manhattan in 1964. Huguette sent him a telegram on February 15, asking: "When are you thinking of coming to the states STOP Be sure to let me know in advance so I will be in New York. STOP. With affection, Huguette." After she received his reply, she wrote again on February 21 to confirm their plans: "Will call Union Club on 3rd or 4th of March STOP Bon Voyage, Affectionately, Huguette." Her ex-husband sent her a telegram on Feb. 28: "Will telephone you on arrival scheduled Sunday afternoon. Affectionately, Bill."

Judging by the available correspondence, that may have been the only time the two former spouses saw each other during this period. Whatever had gone wrong in their brief marriage, they had nonetheless become friends again. But friends separated by an ocean, content in their separate worlds. Huguette sent Bill a telegraph in April, conveying her sympathies over the death of his dog, Snoopy. "Having had dogs I know what the heartbreak is. STOP. All my best wishes for a good Easter under the circumstances."

In August, Huguette wrote a wistful telegram to her ex-husband.

Cher Bill,
Wondering what you are doing today. STOP we are having marvelous weather STOP how is it over there did you ever replace snoopy not in your heart but in your household. Bien Affectueusement, Huguette

She often wrote chatty notes to him about current events and her extended family including her aunt Amelia, and Amelia's third husband, lawyer Thomas Darrington Semple. On September 26, 1968, Huguette wrote a draft of a letter that she planned to send to Bill, talking about the political unrest in France and the bitter New York City school strike. "From what I hear, France is back to normal again and there is no more talk of strikes for which I am thankful. Here there seems to be no hint of a settlement for the teacher's strike. During my school days such happenings were unheard of (no such luck). Although I am a very poor correspondent you are very often in my thoughts dearest Bill. Do write me soon and in the meantime, all my love."

In the first few years after her mother's death, Huguette still cared about her appearance, sending her maids out to buy false eyelashes, nail polish, and copies of *Vogue*. She had yet another gentleman caller who split his time between New York and California: novelist and screenwriter Polan Banks. Born in 1906, the same year as Huguette, the well-born Virginia native published his first historical novel at the age of twenty and parlayed that into a successful career as a novelist and Hollywood writer. (One of his novels became the 1941 hit *The Great Lie* starring Bette Davis and Mary Astor; another was turned into *My Forbidden Past* in 1951, starring Ava Gardner and Robert Mitchum.) His first wife, Amalie, was the niece of financier Bernard Baruch.

The novelist and Huguette had friends in common, which was likely how they met. Polan Banks and Etienne de Villermont were both close to Russian prince Alexis Droutzkoy, serving as usher and best man at the prince's 1944 New York wedding party and joining him at other society watering spots such as Saratoga Springs.

Polan Banks sent Huguette a jaunty note in March 1966 from his Wilshire Boulevard office in Los Angeles, written as if in the voice of his dog.

> *Chere Mademoiselle,*
>
> *Your gracious telegram so delighted me that I ran around barking until mon oncle Polan cuffed my ear (he is really a brute!) but I didn't mind as it was the first telegram I have ever received.*
>
> *In any event, I am looking forward to sharing a fine bone and some dog biscuits dipped in Pouilly fuisse with us, very soon. It is only too bad that we have to have him along, non?*

But as much as Huguette wanted to trust people, she inevitably worried about being used. Her friendship with Banks unraveled years later when the writer mentioned that he might want to base a character on Huguette in one of his novels. She was so upset that she responded by having her lawyer warn him off. Remembering her mother, whose life had been fictionalized in *The Sisters*, Huguette did not want to be an unwitting star on best-seller lists. Banks wrote back to apologize. His letter indicates that Huguette may have helped him out financially.

> *I just received your attorney's letter. As I told you during our recent conversation, I would not dream of ignoring your wishes about including your name in any way in the current book in work. Please rest assured that you can rely on my word. You do know however that I am and always have been deeply grateful to you for what you have done for me in the past. I shall never forget it. You are a very unique lady.*

With so much time on her hands, Huguette became addicted to watching television. She had eclectic viewing habits: she favored *The Dick Cavett Show* and *The Forsyte Saga* but also had a deep fondness for cartoon shows such as *The Flintstones* and *The Adventures of Rocky and Bullwinkle*. Once early television recorders were developed, she taped shows for her ex-husband, shipping thirty-seven boxes of tapes to Bill in the South of France; he sent a grateful but startled note requesting a valuation for customs.

Throughout this period, the calls and letters kept coming from Huguette's married Frenchman, Etienne de Villermont. The tone of his letters varied markedly. Sometimes he wrote deeply romantic letters: "I join you through my thoughts and neither distance nor time alters the bond of love of half a life, which will never disappear." He often thanked her for innumerable gifts. But he frequently devoted page after page to complaining about his wife Elisabeth's ailments—a lump in her breast, lumbago, eczema—and the difficulties of caring for her and their adopted daughter, Marie-Christine. Etienne's notes often exude a world-weary companionship, rather than sensuality. "I do more food shopping, I change Elisabeth's bandages, empty Marie-Christine's pot, she is still having accidents often," he wrote in one long letter. "If I enumerate all this, it is to show you that I'm not 'twiddling my thumbs' and that genuinely, dear Huguette, the sincere desire to write to you is, alas, often interrupted. I am often tired." Etienne sent Huguette photos of his house and mentioned the sleeping arrangements—"Elisabeth has her room on the side, for I don't sleep well in the same room"—but this was done in matter-of-fact rather than suggestive fashion.

But Etienne did make a point of remembering important dates, writing to Huguette in February 1968: "It's Valentine's Day and my thoughts are on you today, especially and affectionately. I would like to write to you everyday [*sic*] but with this bad weather, we all caught colds and I go out as little as possible." He added that he and his wife and daughter would see her soon in New York.

If Etienne did not hear from Huguette for a few weeks, he wrote her letters with an undertone of panic: "I am very very worried about not having heard from you. I wouldn't be if you tell me you are doing well." Undoubtedly, Etienne cared about Huguette, but losing her as the family's financial patroness would have made his life much less comfortable.

For Huguette, her inheritance was forever an undercurrent in her relationships. She was insecure, worrying about how others perceived her. She often wrote drafts of letters in pencil, tinkering with minor word choices before taking the bold step of putting pen to paper. She fretted: should she thank Bill "many times" or "a million times," wish him a "joyous" birthday or a "very happy one." Writing to a vendor to complain about a bill, Huguette initially planned to say that she was "very much surprised" but then upped the ante to "amazed." This was a woman afraid of spontaneity.

———

Once Huguette passed her sixtieth birthday, her losses began to mount up. Her half sister Katherine Morris, now eighty-nine, remained a living link to her past, but Katherine's daughter, Katherine Morris Hall, who had been Huguette's childhood playmate and a Spence classmate, died in March 1968. Huguette made a rare appearance at the funeral, held at Saint Patrick's Cathedral. She chatted pleasantly with her relatives and then left. They would never see her again.

Huguette was now preoccupied with the lingering illness of her aunt Amelia, confined to her home at 575 Park Avenue, just a dozen blocks from Huguette's Fifth Avenue home. The childless Amelia had been the equivalent of a second mother to Huguette, a calming and loving presence. Huguette worried constantly about her aunt, and both Etienne and Bill Gower sent supportive notes trying to buck up her spirits. On September 24, 1969, Etienne wrote to say that he would be coming to Manhattan in November. "I apologize for not having written earlier," he said in his letter. "It's not that I am not thinking of you, as you suspect, but like you, I have family members with health problems and it has shaken me...I will soon be in New York and I am eager to see you again, and knowing you are worried bothers me very much."

Amelia La Chapelle Hoyt Turner Semple died on October 18, 1969. As Huguette poignantly wrote in an affidavit filed with Amelia's will, "I knew her all of my life." Amelia bequeathed the bulk of her $757,000 estate to her third husband, lawyer Thomas Darrington Semple. He soon moved to Alabama to join relatives.

Huguette was so devastated by Amelia's illness that she once again virtually stopped eating. Just as in 1942 when she began to waste away from stress, her weight plummeted. She kept track of her weight, weighing herself every three weeks and writing down the number. In 1967, the five-foot-six heiress weighed 131 pounds, but she had dropped to a too-slender 114 pounds by April 1969. (She made a note to herself: "120 pounds is good weight.") Huguette often jotted thoughts on scratch paper. One day she made a note to herself: "My get up and go got up and went."

———

Wanda and Doris Styka had been the first people to feel the cool breeze of Huguette's physical absence in their daily lives, but now Huguette's retreat turned into full-scale isolation. In her grief over the deaths, six years apart, of her mother and now her aunt, Huguette turned visitors away, an emotional reaction that became an entrenched habit. She limited her contact to the telephone.

Leontine Lyle, the wife of physician William Gordon Lyle, had been a family friend for forty years, yet Huguette declined repeated invitations to get together. As Leontine Lyle's granddaughter Lucy Tower recalls, "My grandmother tried to see Huguette, but she wouldn't see her. And they were close—they talked by phone two or three times a day. My grandmother would say, 'It's such a pretty day, I think I'll take a walk downtown, why don't I drop in and see you and we could chat over tea?' Huguette would say something like, 'No, I have to take a nap this afternoon.'" As Tower puts it, "There was always an excuse."

Huguette had been friendly with her aunt Amelia's husband. His son, T. Darrington Semple Jr., a lawyer who lived in Manhattan, made numerous efforts to visit Huguette. She had sent the younger Semple numerous gifts—her antique Pierce-Arrow automobile, an apartment's worth of air conditioners—as a tribute to his devotion to Amelia. (Semple Jr. even chose "La Chapelle" as the middle name for his daughter Sarah.) "My father said he felt obligated to try to meet Huguette, as a family member, and he tried," recalls Sarah La Chapelle Thompson. "But after the sixteenth time she had to wash her hair, he gave up. But he talked to her on the phone. He stopped saying 'Let me come visit,' because that made her upset."

Since Huguette was chatty and engaging on the telephone, friends and acquaintances tried artful wiles to see her. Jane Bannerman, whose husband, Charles, was Huguette's lawyer, recalls. "At my husband's firm, they sort of passed her along down the line. None of them ever met her, but they talked to her on the telephone. I talked to her many times on the telephone." Huguette enjoyed reminiscing about her childhood ocean crossings and sent vintage ship menus with unusual artwork to Jane. "When we went out to Bellosguardo with the partners," Jane Bannerman says, "I said to Mrs. Clark, 'Why don't you show us the place yourself, that would be really nice.' She said, 'Oh, no, I couldn't do that because it would make me sad.'"

There may have been a final event that pushed her into solitude—a traumatic incident with her chauffeur. Many years later, her accountant, Irving Kamsler, recalls being told that "she had been in the car with her chauffeur and he had a heart attack. She got scared of people coming around the car." Several other people referred to their own versions of this story. Huguette had often dispatched her chauffeur on errands or to take her staff home, but by 1975 she had an account with Carey Car Service to handle those chores.

During the formative years of her life, Huguette and her family had been subjected to relentless scrutiny by the newspapers. She could not put up a moat around her castle, but in a white-glove Fifth

Avenue doorman building she could now do the next best thing: keep the world out. Huguette refused to see virtually anyone face-to-face other than a housekeeper; her mother's former social secretary, Adele Marié; and a few maids.

It was as if every frightening moment, every heartbreaking event, that had happened in her life had now come back to haunt her—Andrée's sudden death, the illness that caused her mother to go deaf, her parents' phobia about germs. There was nothing wrong with Huguette's own appearance, no ugly scars to make her ashamed of showing herself to others. She had never been particularly vain, so a few wrinkles and other signs of aging would not have been enough to matter. But Huguette did not want to look people in the eye or allow them to get physically close to her. She acted as if most human contact was dangerous.

She was wealthy enough to be able to delegate tasks that might otherwise have required her to leave the house. If she needed money, she would fill out a check and send Adele Marié to cash it at the nearest branch of the First National City Bank (which would eventually become Citibank). Huguette had accounts at nearby Winters Market on Lexington Avenue, and her maids could pick up anything that local stores would not deliver. If she wanted to go from her twelfth-floor apartment down to her eighth-floor apartment, she could use the back stairs and avoid the elevator and her neighbors.

Even though she had ample space, Huguette appeared to live within narrow parameters. The decorator Robert Samuels Jr. took his daughter Margaret to see one of Huguette's apartments, after insuring that the heiress was in the other one. "She lived down at the end, in the maid's quarters," recalls Margaret Hoag, who joined her father's firm in 1968. "They had put in a little kitchenette so she could heat up food. The thing that struck me about the apartment was the paintings on the walls—all Impressionist paintings." Hoag was stunned by the sight of Huguette's carefully organized shoe collection. "The shoes were in boxes all marked with dates. When she had worn them, descriptions of what they were—100 boxes of shoes all stacked up, probably every one she ever had. I was amazed." Huguette's debutante dancing high heels, the sensible lace-up leather shoes she wore to

Tadé's studio, the hiking footwear from her Colorado vacation—all these tangible reminders of the socially active life that she had once led, now all irrelevant.

Yet Huguette remained engaged enough in the world to continue to follow current cultural trends, reading the newspapers and the latest books. She scribbled down the names of two books published in 1969 that she wanted to read: *The Kingdom and the Power: Behind the Scenes at the New York Times* by Gay Talese, as well as the explicit sex manual *The Sensuous Woman* by J. At age sixty-three, she remained curious about the mechanics of sex.

As the years passed, Huguette continued to lose other precious relationships. On December 21, 1976, a telegram arrived: "Bill died at 10 p.m. on December 21rst, please phone to Gerard." She mattered enough to Bill Gower that he had told his valet to alert her when the moment came. They had lived together in her apartment on the twelfth floor. She could remember what it was like to see him coming through the door, what he looked like when he slept, how he smelled after a shower and a shave, the warmth of his smile.

In her isolation, Huguette chose to become the curator of her own life and that of her parents. She wanted to preserve every remnant of family history, turning Bellosguardo and her Fifth Avenue apartments into her personal equivalent of Colonial Williamsburg, a shrine to her own past. She relied on Robert Samuels to track down vintage fixtures and fabrics. If furniture needed to be reupholstered, she demanded the same material that had been used when she moved into the apartment in the late 1920s or when her mother decorated Bellosguardo in the 1930s. Even the lightbulbs had to be antiques. "Anything related to her mother, she wanted to preserve," recalls Ann Fabrizio, Robert Samuels's older daughter. "She would tell my father, 'I want it just like Mommy.'"

But to preserve life as Mommy had created it required allowing strangers into her apartments. In 1973, Neal Sattler, whose family ran a high-end apartment renovation firm, was hired by Robert Samuels to make repairs in Huguette's three apartments, from installing a new bathroom to replacing a parquet floor that had buckled from a leak. "We would have meetings with her, and we would be in the kitchen, and she'd be in the hallway, on the other side of the door," says Neal Sattler. Huguette, simultaneously absent and ever present, was a very involved client to the point of fussing over every detail. "She wanted drawings made to scale—she was very precise," Neal Sattler says. "She asked me to get an architectural ruler for her. She would come down at night after the workmen had left, look at the tiles."

But Huguette abruptly stopped using the firm after an unexpected encounter with the workmen. As Neal's younger brother, Chris Sattler, tells the tale: "The men had worked overtime and they were in the middle of changing, putting on their clothes when she came in. She was a little stunned. She turned around and left." That night, Robert Samuels received a call from Huguette, who said, "Please have the Sattlers figure out their bill and send it to me. I don't want them around anymore." It would be many years before the Sattlers were asked to return.

Her behavior was strange but, in its own way, signified her desire to live forever. Huguette frequently spoke by phone to her California cousin, Anna La Chapelle, who complained of bronchitis and other ailments, underlining that going out in the world was fraught with germs and peril. By staying away from people, talking to them from the other side of doors, Huguette hoped that she would be safe, protected from harm. As a teenager after her sister Andrée's death, Huguette had learned to be self-sufficient and keep herself company. Her list of "Happy Moments" back then had included the thrill of traveling by boat or train away from New York, but now her biggest voyage was the four-floor trip between her apartments.

There was a rare exception to her no-visitors rule: Helen Garrett, the daughter of Huguette's Irish maid, Delia Healey, was permitted an audience. "My mom loved her," recalled Garrett in an e-mail to me. "They talked a lot. Mrs. Clark had never worked a day in her life, and she was fascinated with my mom's life—always working, having five kids." In 1973, Huguette had her heart set on acquiring a special doll, and her maid spent a day unsuccessfully searching Manhattan for the prized object. Helen Garrett, then working at the discount store Alexander's, saw one on display and bought it, and then stopped by 907 Fifth Avenue to drop it off. "My mom brought the doll to Mrs. Clark and she came into the kitchen to thank me in person," said Garrett, who remembered that Huguette was wearing a lovely vintage 1940s designer dress. "My mom said I should feel special, 'cause she didn't come out of her room very often. My mom was preparing her lunch, crackers and sardines still in the can, placed on a silver tray. Mom said she had that for lunch every day."

But this was a brief interlude before Delia Healey disappeared from Huguette's life. By 1978, Healey had developed Alzheimer's and stopped working; she died in January 1980. As Huguette's household employees—primarily hired by her mother—retired or died, she did not replace most of them and did not want to engage directly with newcomers. One maid later confided to decorator Robert Samuels that she had worked for Huguette for several years but had never met her, cleaning rooms after Madame vacated. Once Delia Healey retired, an employee left meals on a tray in a pass-through where Huguette could retrieve them. In a pinch, Huguette could call down and ask a favorite doorman to pick up food and supplies and leave them by her service door.

She kept paying the expenses of her staff even after they retired. In 1980, Huguette confided to Doris Styka about the ailments of a former employee, as well as annoying leaks from the ninth floor into her eighth-floor apartment. Doris jotted down some notes afterward:

> *Dearest Huguette telephoned and told of all the problems she has had in her living room. Had a leak come down wall just behind Pekinese painting. [Tadé Styka had painted Anna's Pekinese dog.] She worries so much about the paintings [of] her mother, father and sister, especially in California with earthquakes and fires. She said the building—907—is old and the plumbing should be changed but the people don't want to go through that disruption.*
>
> *For so long, she was busy with the maid who was ill and fainted constantly and for whom she had nurses... The family of the maid sent her a prospectus for a nursing home when they know she doesn't believe in them...*

She said she would like to move down to her mother's apartment
but there was a leak there too, someone let their bathtub overflow . . .
She spoke for a half hour but was sorry to tell me all her troubles—
dear soul.

For Huguette, the telephone remained her lifeline, and she even managed to make a new friend by telephone: Suzanne Pierre, the wife of Dr. Jules Pierre. The couple lived on Park Avenue, just a few blocks from Huguette. Born in 1893, the physician was thirteen years older than Huguette. After he retired, Dr. Pierre had a heart attack and was unable to leave his home. Calling frequently to check on his welfare, Huguette wound up having lengthy and intimate conversations in French with his second wife, Suzanne. But the heiress declined repeated invitations over more than two decades to get together in person. "They were phone friends for years," says Kati Despretz Cruz, Suzanne Pierre's granddaughter. "They talked every day. She wouldn't receive anyone. My grandmother was always worried about her."

Proud of her friendship with the heiress, Suzanne was instrumental in connecting Huguette with one of her French Clark relatives. Huguette had attended Spence with Mary Clark, the daughter of Huguette's half brother Charles Clark. Mary subsequently married a French baron and diplomat, James Baeyens. When their son André Baeyens became the chief press attaché at the French Consulate in New York in 1977, Suzanne introduced herself to him at a lecture, and then arranged for André to speak to Huguette by phone. Huguette would not see him and declined to hear from him directly, but Suzanne would pass along his messages and Huguette would contact André. Then seventy-one years old, she insisted on a buffer separating herself from her family.

"Our calls were usually brief," André recalled. "We would discuss my duties at the Press office, about which she appeared very interested, as she was pleased that a Clark had what she considered to be such an important position." He dropped off French magazines with her doorman and sent her flowers, adding, "She was sorry when my mother died and expressed her condolences." But their contact ended when Baeyens left Manhattan in January 1982 to become the French ambassador to Korea.

That spring, Huguette lost yet another tie to the outside world: Etienne de Villermont died in France at age seventy-seven. There would be no more pink roses delivered on Huguette's birthday or affectionate letters from her married Frenchman. Huguette graciously continued to send checks to Etienne's wife and daughter, just as she had done after Tadé Styka died by helping Wanda and Doris. But now the heiress had lost all three men who had mattered to her during the past half century.

———

A woman who inherited a cavalier attitude toward money from her mother, Huguette recoiled from the idea of estate planning almost as much as she recoiled from seeing strangers in her apartment. But the death of Anna Clark created a legal conundrum. When Huguette had written a new will in 1929, she made her mother her sole beneficiary. Now with her mother gone, her assets would go by default to descendants from her father's first marriage, relatives whom she shied away from seeing in person. Without the tax avoidance schemes favored by the wealthy, the federal and state governments would seize a sizable portion of her inheritance.

And so began an effort by several generations of lawyers to convince Huguette to write a new will. She consistently refused to do so, but would never explain her reasoning. Huguette turned down the entreaties of Charles Bannerman, the Harvard-educated lawyer of the firm Clark, Kerr and Ellis, who had drafted her mother's will and her aunt Amelia's will. "My husband enjoyed working with her," recalls Jane Bannerman. "He liked her. He was interested in her peculiarities, but in a nice way. I said to my husband, 'Why don't you just walk in and see her?' He wasn't that kind of person." Huguette also worked closely with Frederick Stokes, another partner at Clark, Kerr and Ellis who handled Anna's estate; he, too, struck out in his efforts to get the heiress to consider the future of her fortune.

After Bannerman's death in 1976, his patrician partner, Donald Wallace, took over Huguette's legal affairs. Wallace then spent more than two decades trying to convince Huguette to put her final wishes on paper. She would not see him, either, or countenance writing a new will. He wrote a series of letters to her through the years conveying his growing irritation at her irrational behavior.

On June 15, 1978, Wallace wrote:

> *To my personal knowledge at least since 1955, Mr. Bannerman discussed with you the need to write a new will... Even now, more than twenty-two years after the subject was first brought up to my personal knowledge, nothing has been accomplished. My perhaps annoying and persistent efforts since 1976 have met with complete failure.*

Seven years later, Wallace was losing his patience, writing to Huguette on March 7, 1985, that dealing with her on this topic was "one of the most frustrating experiences I have ever had." He pleaded with her to take action, writing, "You have received and ignored or avoided advice given to you almost every year from 1942 to date outlining all of the reasons why it is essential that you have a current up-to-date will." He sent her a list of Clark family members who would inherit if she did nothing, and even estimated how much money they might receive. Huguette kept his letters but declined to respond to his requests.

But she did rely on Donald Wallace for tasks that, to her, were infinitely more important than writing a new will. He was her proxy in bidding at auctions for antique dolls, many from France. "Don Wallace was a very nice man, very old school," says Ted Poretz, a lawyer who was briefly affiliated with the same firm. "He was Mrs. Clark's go-fer. The standing joke around the office was that anytime you walked past his office, you could hear him saying, 'Yes, Mrs. Clark. Yes, Mrs. Clark.' He had unlimited authority to spend money to get the dolls. The one time she was upset was when he didn't get one— maybe he was unaware that the bid had gone up. She couldn't understand how he missed."

Huguette's free-spending attitude gave her broad latitude with her employees. Tradesmen who accommodated her incessant demands were rewarded with large checks. She called Robert Samuels at home on nights and weekends, but he kept doing her bidding, as did others.

"My father thought she was nuts," says Linda Kasakyan, whose father, Rudolph Jaklitsch, built and repaired Huguette's dollhouses. "He didn't understand why she didn't want to see him, why she had all this privacy and secrecy. She drove my father crazy, because she lived in a fantasy world with the dolls and the dollhouses. The measurements had to be just so, or the people in the dollhouses were going to bump their heads." The carpenter stopped sending bills because Huguette wrote generous checks without requesting an invoice or a time sheet. "Sometimes after my father delivered things to her house, he'd get four or five phone calls back and forth," Kasakyan recalls. "She'd be examining things and seeing little things that had to be changed."

The joy for Huguette was in the act of creation, but once the work was done, she lost interest. "One year, after one dollhouse had gone back and forth a lot with a lot of work, she told my father to keep the dollhouse," Kasakyan recalls. "I had it for many years."

As a lonely adult, Huguette was drawn back on a river of memory to her childhood, that innocent period before her sister Andrée died. This before-and-after dividing line in her life took on more emotional resonance every year. Her dolls loomed large as objects of beauty and totems of the past. "She never lost the magic of childhood," says Wanda Styka. "She kept that all of her life. When we grow up, we say we've lost that, but she preserved it."

Huguette did not want to be seen but she did want to be heard. Hungry for human contact, she spent hours each day on the phone. Her artistic projects gave her a reason to call suppliers such as Caterina Marsh, of the California import firm Marsh and Company. "I talked to her sometimes three times a day," says Marsh, who dealt with Huguette for nearly four decades, dating back to 1971. "I wouldn't call myself her friend, but we had a very nice relationship. She was such a gracious woman, she was of an era that doesn't exist anymore." Marsh was touched by Huguette's ongoing enthusiasm for the Japanese miniatures, adding, "She was an amazing artist in a way to envision creating these projects. It had to be done properly. There were no shortcuts that she would allow."

Though she could be imperious at times, Huguette usually took an interest in her retainers, quizzing them about their families, especially their children. "She sent us presents, she lived vicariously," recalls Ann Fabrizio, the older daughter of decorator Robert Samuels. Adds carpenter's daughter Linda Kasakyan, "She was very pleasant. She had a timid voice, nervous high-pitched voice. When I got married and had children, she'd ask about the kids, she'd ask about me and my husband. She'd ask for pictures and I'd send them every year." Huguette gave elaborate dolls and dollhouses to little girls, and forts equipped with toy soldiers to little boys. When these children became teenagers, she still sent them the same gifts, as if oblivious to the fact that children outgrow these interests.

Huguette managed to simultaneously come across as an introvert and an extrovert. While her father the copper baron had been parsimonious with his employees, Huguette reveled in giving away his money to total strangers. She acted as if inspired by the 1950s television series *The Millionaire*, in which the mysterious John Beresford Tipton Jr.—never seen, only heard—played benefactor to random Americans. "She used to direct Don Wallace to make anonymous charitable gifts," says Wallace's former law colleague, who recalled outgoing checks of up to $50,000. "People she saw on TV, or read about in the paper, who had problems. She liked to take care of people in trouble. She would see some story, and tell him to get money to those people."

Each Christmas, Huguette would outdo herself, devoting months to planning her gift giving, spending tens of thousands of dollars. She ordered hundreds of dolls and toys from the Parisian children's specialty shop, Au Nain Bleu. Decorator Robert Samuels would send his company van and two employees to pick up the precious cargo at JFK, charging $486 on December 29, 1978, for that service alone. Huguette would hand-wrap the packages and send them to a French orphanage in Manhattan. She was enchanted by cutting-edge technologies, and employees and friends would receive the latest electronic gadgets—tape recorders, home video cameras, new television models.

———

Artists often try their hands at different media in search of a new way of expressing themselves. Huguette's artistic impulses and talents gravitated in unexpected directions. She began designing and making gold jewelry, and tried to teach herself cartoon animation. Her self-taught approach to animation was revealing of how her mind worked. As she later explained it to Chris Sattler, she would tape cartoons on her VCR (or have the maids tape them) and then watch them very slowly, constantly stopping the tape in order to photograph the scenes. "She'd take quick-lapse photos," Chris says. "She would have hundreds of photos. Then she would practice by drawing them herself, and then flipping the pictures to see how the animation worked. She did that for a few years in the 1980s and then stopped doing it. There were hundreds of thousands of single-shot frames of cartoons in her apartment."

What began as an artistic project turned into an obsession that filled Huguette's empty days with calming activity. She made list upon list of programs that she planned to tape. She could then spend hours with her camera in front of the television screen, filing away hundreds of snapshots of the NBC peacock, along with other Polaroid photographs.

Was Huguette, with her quirky behavior, a psychiatric case study? On the one hand, it is easy to pile up the symptoms—refusing to see people or leave her apartment, eating the same sardine lunches every day, obsessing about tiny imperfections in dollhouses, mesmerized by cartoons. This is so at odds with the adventurous and outgoing persona she displayed as a young woman, those light spirits conveyed in her letters to Tadé. Yet those who spoke to Huguette during her two decades of exile from the world insist that they never got the sense that she was depressed or longed for a different existence. "She was happy," says Wanda Styka. "She was always upbeat."

Wanda conveyed her love to Huguette one year by taking a four-hour round-trip from the Berkshires, where she worked as an archivist at the historic estate Chesterwood, to Manhattan to drop off a birthday gift at 907 Fifth Avenue. Wanda wanted to make sure the present arrived on June 9, the actual date. But it never occurred to Wanda to ask the doorman to ring upstairs to Huguette, whom she had not laid eyes on for nearly three decades. "I was merely delivering it, I didn't ask to see her. I didn't think she'd say, 'Oh, come up right now,'" Wanda says. "I didn't want to put her in a position where she was uncomfortable."

Huguette had created her own alternate universe based on disembodied connections, and other people humored her, giving her
as much human contact as she could tolerate. Everyone knew that
the way Huguette conducted herself was not normal. Yet she never
came across as a danger to herself or others, because she appeared to
be functional despite her phobias. No one in her life felt they had a
right—or an obligation—to intrude.

Her wispy voice masked a demanding personality. "People make
her out to be crazy, but she wasn't like that," says Neal Sattler. "She
was discerning, she had the money and wanted things perfect, and so
you did it." Adds Caterina Marsh, "She was always in the same mood,
steady. I'm Italian, my moods go up and down like a firecracker. She
never ever sounded unhappy."

The years passed: Lyndon Johnson had been president when
Huguette had last been seen out of her apartment by her Clark relatives; Gerald Ford, Jimmy Carter, and Ronald Reagan had rotated
through 1600 Pennsylvania Avenue while Huguette remained in
self-imposed exile as a phantom, sequestered eight stories above Fifth
Avenue. Every now and then, someone from Huguette's past would
try to break through to her. Frustrated and desperate to connect,
Agnes Clark Albert, her California-based niece, concocted a plan to
see Huguette during a 1982 visit to spend Thanksgiving in Manhattan
with her granddaughter Geraldine McCall, a student at Barnard.

Agnes invited Huguette to lunch with them at the Plaza Hotel. When
Huguette declined yet again with a flimsy excuse, the exasperated Agnes
told Huguette that they would stand in front of her building at 3 p.m.
and wave up at her eighth-floor apartment. And that is what they did,
standing on the sidewalk at Central Park and Seventy-Second Street,
squinting and trying to glimpse a face hidden behind the glass. Over the
next several years, this was Agnes and Geraldine's annual ritual.

"I come from an eccentric family," says Geraldine. "It didn't seem
unusual." One of those years, a doorman at 907 Fifth saw them
waving, and crossed the street to ask what they were doing. Agnes
explained that they were waving at a relative who lived in the building.
Perhaps he knew her—Huguette Clark? His reply: "I have worked in
this building for a dozen years and I've never laid eyes on her."

Chapter Thirteen

A Change of Address

As an athletic young woman, Huguette delighted in luxuriating in the sun for hours on end, bragging to her father about her Hawaiian tan in 1921 and showing off her sun-kissed skin to Tadé in 1941. But by 1991, Huguette had not felt the sun on her face, the breeze on her cheeks, or the snow on her tongue for nearly two decades. Deprived of any firsthand encounter with nature, she could at least convince herself that she was protected from disease in her Fifth Avenue aerie.

But, of course, the nature of human life is that no one—no matter how rich or hermetic—is truly safe. Huguette's carefree sunbathing had occurred prior to the invention of SPF creams, and now she was experiencing the delayed repercussions: she had skin cancer.

When the red blotches appeared, the heiress assumed that they would eventually go away. Then she tried Band-Aids to speed the healing. Instead, the skin cancer spread: a lesion by her right eye became unsightly, and a sore near her mouth made it difficult to eat. Her doormen, who dropped off food deliveries by her entrance, noticed that she had begun ordering ice cream, buttermilk, and bananas, and little else. Huguette knew that she needed a doctor but she no longer had a personal physician: Dr. Gordon Lyle was long dead; Dr. Jules Pierre, now ninety-eight, was confined to a wheelchair; and another physician whom she had relied on had also recently died. The idea of leaving her apartment to see a new doctor was unimaginable to this eighty-four-year-old woman. As the cancer ravaged her skin for several years, Huguette agonized alone for a long time, too paralyzed to act.

On February 13, 1991, she called Doris Styka to apologize for neglecting to send a Christmas gift, behavior that was very much out of character. "Dearest Huguette telephoned, saying that she had not forgotten us but that she had caught a cold. So very thoughtful of her," wrote Doris in her notes, accepting the excuse. Three weeks later, Huguette sent Wanda a check for $10,000 but could not bring herself to tell her goddaughter that anything was wrong.

Huguette would later credit Suzanne Pierre, the wife of her former physician, with saving her life. But in a real sense, Huguette saved herself by picking up the phone and asking for help. After listening to Huguette describe her symptoms, Suzanne insisted that her friend see a doctor. Suzanne even found a doctor willing to make a house call: Henry Singman, who had purchased her husband's practice. A red-headed graduate of New York University's medical school, Singman was an internist whose East Seventy-Second Street office was just two blocks from Huguette's apartment.

When Huguette allowed Dr. Singman to enter her home on March 28, 1991, he was the first stranger she had seen in more than a decade. The physician was shocked by the appearance of this home-bound octogenarian. In a two-page memo that he wrote five years later, Dr. Singman described his disturbing initial encounter with Huguette: a frail and frightened woman, disfigured by illness, materializing out of an unkempt room lit by a single candle.

"She weighed all of seventy-five pounds and appeared to be at death's door," wrote Dr. Singman. "The initial meeting was most strange because I was admitted to her apartment by the elevator operator of the posh building and came face-to-face with an 'apparition' in an old soiled bathrobe and a towel wrapped around her lower face. She was very thin, to the point of emaciation, and when she exposed her face, she resembled an advanced leper patient. She was missing her lower lip laterally and was unable to contain food or fluid in her mouth..."

Huguette insisted on being taken to a hospital by private ambulance, according to Dr. Singman, "because she wanted to be carried up on a stretcher when she left the building, in order to avoid being seen by the building's staff or other residents." At the suggestion of Suzanne Pierre, Huguette asked to go to Doctors Hospital, a storied establishment known for catering to members of the *Social Register* and the cultural elite. F. Scott Fitzgerald and Spencer Tracy had both dried out there after alcoholic binges; Georgia O'Keeffe sought help for depression; Marilyn Monroe was treated for a miscarriage during her marriage to Arthur Miller; lyricist Lorenz Hart, who wrote "You Took Advantage of Me," died on the premises. Dr. Jules Pierre had been affiliated with the hospital, where the staff was used to cosseting well-to-do patients.

The trip from Huguette's apartment by ambulance was short, less than a mile. The genteel Upper East Side, with its handsome 1890s brownstones and 1930s Rosario Candela–designed apartment buildings, is a landmarked historic district, and little had visibly changed in the decades since Huguette had last walked the neighborhood. But this journey through the monied streets of Manhattan to Eighty-Seventh Street and East End Avenue abruptly thrust Huguette into a jarring and alien environment—with bright lights, sickly strangers in the corridors, hordes of white-coated doctors and nurses bustling about, and a complete lack of privacy.

Nurse Marie Pompei, a motherly veteran with an outgoing manner, was standing by after receiving a call that an ambulance was en route with a woman who appeared to be a "recluse." That word struck a chord. Pompei had spent vacations at the Brittannia Hotel in the Bahamas, where the staff told tales about their famous reclusive resident Howard Hughes. The nurse was eager to put Huguette at ease. "When she got off the elevator and she had her face covered, it didn't strike me as being odd. I was familiar, just like anybody, with Howard Hughes," recalls Pompei. "She didn't want anyone to see her, so she had a shawl. But she made sure it was cashmere."

Memories differ on how dire Huguette's condition was at the time. Pompei recalls that Huguette had a serious case of skin cancer but disagrees with Dr. Singman's description of the heiress as a malnourished wraith. "She looked like a leper? No!" exclaims Pompei, recalling that Huguette weighed more than seventy-five pounds. "Her hand was like a man's hand. She was a tall, big-boned woman, but not a fat woman. Did she come in looking like she was well-groomed and everything? No. But it didn't take her very long until she had a bath and washed her hair, she was fine."

For Huguette to disrobe in front of another person was a huge step—the first time that anyone had seen her naked in many years—but that simple act created an emotional bond. During the next few days, the overwhelmed Huguette was hostile to most of the staffers who entered her room, urging the nurses and orderlies to leave her alone. But Huguette was comfortable with Pompei. "I could then go into her room at any time because she had exposed herself to me," says Pompei. "As time went on, if no one was there, I would go in—'Are you okay, do you need anything?' We would talk and get to know each other. She trusted me." Huguette had made new friends by phone in the past, but now the strange world of the hospital provided a new venue to do so in person. Marie Pompei was assigned by the hospital to care for Huguette for only a short period of time, but the nurse paid her social visits for the next two decades. As Pompei says now, "I loved her dearly."

Huguette did not have health insurance and had not signed up for Medicare, so her lawyer, Donald Wallace, rushed over a certified cashier's check for $10,000 to cover her initial costs at Doctors Hospital. (The facility had recently been purchased by the much larger Beth Israel Medical Center and three years later was renamed Beth Israel North.) Three days after she entered the hospital Huguette had surgery; the lesions were sufficiently advanced that she needed additional plastic surgery to repair the damage. Dr. Jack Rudick, the South African–trained chief of surgery, took the lead in handling her problems and ingratiated himself with Huguette by virtue of his diplomatic bedside manner.

Word traveled quickly through Doctors Hospital about this reclusive patient who had arrived under mysterious circumstances from an enormous Fifth Avenue apartment. Dr. Singman informed the

hospital's development office that she was a VIP patient worth cultivating. He treated her like a pet project, making a special effort
to befriend her. "I taught her to play Solitaire and she learned every
game in the book, improving and inventing new games," Dr. Singman wrote in his memo. "She has a 'steel trap' mind but remains shy
and reticent, avoiding most people."

Suzanne Pierre, however, was not most people—she now felt
responsible for Huguette. The two friends had never met before, but
Suzanne came to the hospital to visit regularly. Although Huguette's
medical condition was never serious enough to require around-the-
clock private nurses in addition to the hospital staff, Suzanne thought
that Huguette should never have to ring a bell and wait for assistance.
After consulting with Huguette's lawyer, Suzanne concluded that private nurses would give Huguette the control she wanted over who
could enter her room.

After asking the Hilaire Nursing Registry for job candidates,
Suzanne interviewed and hired private nurse Hadassah Peri, a petite
Filipino immigrant in her early forties. Hadassah had lived in the
United States for nearly two decades—she had moved to Arkansas
in 1972 to work in a small county hospital—but her English was still
stiltled. Hadassah, whose maiden name was Gicela Oloroso, had
a melting-pot marriage. Her husband, Daniel Peri, was a native of
Israel, a tenth-grade dropout who had fought in the Yom Kippur War
and now drove a yellow cab.

Just as Huguette's wispy voice belied her strong-willed persona,
Hadassah's manner was unassuming and deferential, but at her core
the nurse could be fiercely determined, with a quick-witted ability to think three moves ahead on life's chessboard. When her husband, Daniel, later described the dynamics of their marriage in a
legal deposition, he portrayed Hadassah as the family decision maker,
while his role was to obediently handle the daily minutiae of their
lives.

In those early weeks, the $30-per-hour job appeared to be a brief
assignment since Huguette needed minimal medical care. With little
to do but talk, the two women hit it off despite Hadassah's linguistic
difficulties. A sympathetic listener, Hadassah was treated to stories

about Huguette's childhood and "her dear father, her dear mother, her dear sister, Aunt Amelia." Relieved to have someone around who put her at ease, Huguette asked Hadassah to work seven days a week, twelve hours a day.

The idea of working an eighty-four-hour week is daunting, exhausting even to contemplate. Add in commuting time and the situation can be summarized by two words: no life. With three children under the age of eight, Hadassah would be sacrificing her time with her family. No more weekends together, no time to supervise play dates, help with homework, or attend school events. Nonetheless, aware of Huguette's wealth and its potential, the nurse agreed to put her patient first.

Within a month after starting her new post, Hadassah brought her husband and children to the hospital to meet Huguette, who had previously shied away from contact with new people. It is unusual for a nurse to become so personally involved with a patient, especially at such an early stage. But sensing Huguette's loneliness, Hadassah stepped in to fill the void. Daniel Peri described his wife's work life as the equivalent of being on call twenty-four hours a day: "Madame can call anytime if she need anything, miss anything."

Now that Huguette was ensconced at the hospital, her three apartments at 907 Fifth Avenue were receiving a steady stream of curious visitors. Huguette dispatched Suzanne Pierre and her granddaughter, Kati Despretz Cruz, to retrieve dolls to brighten up her antiseptic hospital room. Their walk-through offered a sad glimpse at how Huguette had been living. "It was a mess," recalls Kati. "It was beautiful but it looked like someone went away on vacation a hundred years ago and never came back. The telephones and intercoms were so old. There were cabinets full of beautiful dishes and silver but it wasn't polished. She just lived in her room."

Anticipating her return home, Huguette decided to renovate and soon she was happily looking at parquet floor samples and paint color displays. Although in the hospital she was encountering many new people, she still refused to meet with her decorator, Robert Samuels, or the two Sattler brothers charged with making the improvements, insisting instead on phone consultations. Neal Sattler spoke to Huguette frequently, recalling, "She amazingly knew where every-thing was, like a lawyer who has paper all over his desk but knows exactly where his case is." His younger brother, Chris, built display cases to store her doll collection. "There was so much stuff, but it was piled up in her neat way," Chris says. "There was a method to her madness. One type of doll would be piled up in the bedroom door-way, six feet high." This was a rush job so that the work could be done by the time she was ready to leave the hospital.

Within the cozy confines of her hospital room, Huguette was becoming a mini-celebrity among the solicitous staff. Outside her eleventh-floor window, Huguette had a view of historic Gracie Man-sion and the boats plying the East River. But she usually kept the shades closed during the day, mindful that sunlight was believed to have caused her skin cancer. After avoiding doctors for decades, she was now seeing them daily. The plastic surgery on her face had left minimal scarring ("Her complexion was peaches and cream," says Marie Pompei), but her right eyelid drooped and that eye remained sensitive to light.

After spending so many years on her own, Huguette was initially reticent with strangers, but she came to enjoy the attention, pleased that people seemed concerned and interested. When surgeon Dr. Jack Rudick came by to visit, Huguette kept the conversation going by offering up tidbits about her life. "Early on, she told me about her father, who had apparently been a senator," recalled Rudick. The phy-sician chatted with Huguette about her childhood and discovered that they had shared a common pastime: "We both played the violin."

After two months at Doctors Hospital, Huguette was pronounced well enough to leave. A hospital social worker spoke to her about a discharge plan to return home attended by private nurses or go to a longer-term care facility. But Huguette was in no rush to depart. First she announced that her renovation was not finished and asked to stay a few more weeks. The weeks passed and the hospital staff began pressing her about her plans. Huguette finally became explicit: she did *not* want to go home. In fact, she liked her new life so much that she had decided to stay at Doctors Hospital indefinitely. She announced her plans as if it was a fait accompli. "She refused to leave," says Ted

Poretz, an attorney who worked with Donald Wallace at the time. "She asked to speak to the director of planned giving and made a deal to stay." Huguette made it clear that she would be generous if she got her way.

Why would a woman with three magnificent Fifth Avenue apartments, forty-two rooms decorated with Impressionist paintings and antiques, want to remain in a claustrophobic hospital room? Huguette would be asked this question repeatedly for the next twenty years. She would never spell out her feelings and usually dodged the issue entirely. Yet there are clues to her state of mind.

A woman who had long clung to routines, Huguette was forced by her health to adjust to new surroundings. Once she got over the loss of her precious privacy, the experience had been a revelation. She had come to appreciate the very thing that she had avoided for so long—being with other people. Emotionally, she was turning toward the light, the warmth of human company. After growing up in a 121-room mansion, rattling around those lonely corridors after her sister died, there was something primal and satisfying about a one-room life in which she was the center of attention. Her staff at home had dwindled, but at the hospital there were many people to take care of her needs. It struck her as the ideal solution.

Her doctors were flabbergasted by her stubborn insistence on living in the drab hospital quarters. "She never gave me a reason; she just refused to leave," Dr. Singman said. "I told her she should go home, she had an apartment. I said I would visit her subsequently as often as she wanted, also that the nurses would probably stay with her if she wanted...and she still wouldn't go home." Dr. Rudick came away with the distinct impression that Huguette had been lonely on Fifth Avenue, although she never explicitly used that word. "She felt that in the hospital, at least she had people who would visit her," said Dr. Rudick. "She had developed what she considered friends. Whereas in the apartment, she had nobody."

Huguette acted as if her survival depended on remaining at the hospital. She confided to Hadassah Peri that she feared returning home due to a terrifying experience years earlier: a would-be burglar had gained access to her apartment by pretending to deliver bottled water. "He locked the maid in the bathroom, but Madame says she was lucky she was not there," recounted Hadassah. Huguette was in another one of her three apartments at the time; when she returned, the man was gone. If anything was stolen, Huguette did not mention it. Hadassah said that Huguette described the undated incident as "spooky."

If safety was one of Huguette's reasons for shying away from Fifth Avenue, those concerns may have been exacerbated by a brazen theft from her apartment during the renovations. A valuable Degas pastel of a dancing ballerina in a yellow tutu, *Danseuse Faisant des Pointes*, inexplicably disappeared. Suzanne Pierre stopped by the apartment to pick up some things for Huguette and discovered the painting was gone. Contractor Neal Sattler recalls being summoned to 907 Fifth Avenue by Donald Wallace. Sattler remembers asking the lawyer, "Do you think we had something to do with it? Everything in this apartment goes in and out of the elevators, it wasn't any of my people." His firm was quickly cleared of suspicion as the search continued.

The FBI investigated the theft, and a female agent went to Doctors Hospital to interview Huguette. But investigators ultimately put the case aside as unsolved. Distressed by the loss, Huguette did not file an insurance claim, likely due to her hope that the art would eventually be found.

Meanwhile, the heiress's insistence on remaining at the hospital raised an obvious question that was only briefly debated by the medical staff: was this the choice of a sane and rational person? Dr. Singman was concerned enough about what he called Huguette's "insecurity" that he suggested that she see a psychiatrist. Upset that her mental health was being questioned, Huguette adamantly refused. He chose not to force the issue.

"The woman was an eccentric of the first order, but as far as that, her cognition was excellent, she had perfect knowledge of her surroundings, she had excellent memory," Dr. Singman insisted in a 2012 deposition. "At that point she was perfectly happy with the situation she was in. We tried to get her to go home, we made several attempts, many attempts, and she refused." He believed that at Huguette's age, therapy would not be worthwhile, saying, "I didn't think that there was going to be any great help from a psychiatrist to change her attitude about what she was doing, so when she refused to see one, I went along with her." His was the final word on this subject; other doctors did not challenge his decision.

Was it the right thing to do? Huguette was never evaluated by a clinician, so it is difficult to project how things might have turned out if the hospital had tried to insist on a psych test or attempted treatment. She exhibited symptoms of an obsessive-compulsive personality disorder. Huguette's fear of germs, her rigidity about keeping her homes as unchanging museums of the past, her obsessive collecting and labeling of possessions, her perfectionism with her miniatures that drove the patient craftsmen crazy, her desire to eat the same thing every day to avoid making decisions—it all falls under that diagnostic rubric.

But even if this is an accurate description of Huguette's mental state, there is no simple fix. This disorder is considered incurable and is typically treated with talk therapy and a Prozac-like drug regimen. But Huguette kept telling people that she was already content. She liked her life, even if it was an existence that most people found incomprehensible. Huguette's inheritance had always allowed her to do whatever she wanted: this safe bubble with constant human interaction was now her heart's desire. Given her previous isolation, Huguette appeared to be making a psychologically healthy choice.

———

Huguette's insistence on playing a geriatric Eloise-at-Doctors-Hospital raised another quandary for the administrators. Insurance companies dictate the length of a hospital stay, but since Huguette was paying her own way—the top rate rather than a negotiated insurance discount—money was not at issue. She had already been flagged by the development office as a multimillionaire capable of making a significant donation. Now that Huguette had expressed an interest in becoming a permanent resident, the hospital expected a quid pro quo: help us and we'll indulge you. That attitude was evident in a series of memos written by Cynthia Cromer, a member of the development staff.

On June 7, 1991, Cromer wrote to her colleagues about the "strange" circumstances of Huguette's admission to the hospital, noting that Dr. Singman had described her as "quite wealthy." "Recently, Ms. Clark was told she could be discharged," Cromer wrote. "She asked if she might stay in the hospital longer: she feels comfortable and safe her [sic] and her apartment is being renovated. Since she is a self-pay patient, the Hospital has agreed as long as we do not need the bed." Three days later, Cromer excitedly wrote a memo noting that Huguette Clark "is reported to be worth $70 million" and "has no immediate family." She added that Dr. Singman described Huguette as "extremely eccentric. She has a mind for detail and directs her own affairs...She has an extensive collection of Japanese model palaces and is a Japan-ophile. Dr. Singman suggested finding someone who could speak to her about Japan."

Although Hadassah Peri had been working for Huguette for only a brief time, she had assumed the role of protector. When Cynthia Cromer made a get-acquainted visit to Huguette, the nurse followed the hospital fund-raiser into the hallway afterward for a private conversation. Hadassah seized the opportunity to convey her clout with Huguette. In a July 21, 1991, memo, Cromer wrote that the nurse confronted her to say that Huguette "had asked who I was and why I was visiting. She was concerned that I was trying to get her to leave the Hospital."

Offering to play intermediary, Hadassah said she had already told Huguette that the hospital "needed money" and had even taken the liberty of suggesting to Suzanne Pierre that a donation from Huguette would be appreciated. The nurse assured Cromer that Huguette "has a good heart." For a private nurse with a supposedly temporary assignment, Hadassah was unabashed in her efforts to simultaneously make herself indispensable to Huguette and curry favor with the hospital. The ploy worked: from then on, the hospital fund-raisers frequently consulted Hadassah on how best to ask Huguette for money.

Following up on the suggestion that Huguette was interested in Japan, hospital CEO Dr. Robert Newman stopped by to play his Japan card. He had worked in Japan as an Air Force physician and his wife was Japanese, so he could converse knowledgeably with Huguette about Japanese culture and history. "She had a particular interest in and concern for the well-being of the emperor and the family of the emperor," Dr. Newman later recalled. CEOs rarely make hospital rounds but Dr. Newman became a regular gentleman caller.

The wealth accumulated by William Andrews Clark had always attracted supplicants, but the hospital's executives, doctors, and nurses would mount a full-scale twenty-year campaign to convince Huguette to hand over large chunks of her copper inheritance. Even as administrators maneuvered for hospital donations, several doctors and nurses sought—and received—hundreds of thousands of dollars in gifts for themselves, ignoring hospital rules prohibiting medical personnel from taking cash from patients. Huguette became a personal ATM for a few hospital staffers, yet she did not appear to begrudge it.

The cash crusade started off slowly. In July 1991, Dr. Singman invited Huguette to leave her sickbed to attend a fund-raiser, the President's Luncheon, but his shy patient declined the honor. She expressed her gratitude to Beth Israel North instead by writing a check for $80,000 later that month to the hospital in honor of both Dr. Singman and Dr. Jack Rudick. Dr. Morton Hyman, the hospital's chairman, came by her room especially to thank her. Not since her years as a wealthy debutante had she been courted by so many men. They even sent gifts—a CD player and music by Bach, Beethoven, Ravel, and Debussy—but she could not figure out how to use the machine and had it sent to her apartment.

———

As the next act of Huguette's life unfolded, ushers could have passed out programs highlighting the new cast members. Since even the indefatigable Hadassah drew the line at working more than twelve hours a day, Huguette hired another private nurse for the 9 p.m. to 8 a.m. night shift. (Huguette insisted on an hour off a day between nurses, just to have a little time alone.) Geraldine Lehane Coffey, an Irish immigrant married to a software engineer, had graduated from nursing school just three years earlier. She landed the night job after Huguette fired another nurse who was badgering her to leave the hospital. Geraldine agreed to work seven days a week but insisted on monthlong summer vacations to return to Ireland to visit her family.

During an idyllic part of her childhood, Huguette had shared a room with her older sister, Andrée, who would entertain her with late-night stories. Now if Huguette could not sleep, she could rely on the comforting Irish brogue of Geraldine. They would chat about their lives or sit for hours in companionable silence. For Geraldine, who had a one-year-old son, this was undemanding work. "We did not do routine temperature because Mrs. Clark was very well," recalled Geraldine, adding that her new patient was good company. "She was smart, she was strong, she was intelligent, well traveled, she was a very nice lady... She was joyful. I really never saw anger. She was even tempered."

Outside of the hospital, new personnel were also joining Huguette's circle. After retiring from his law firm in 1987, Donald Wallace had rented office space from another partnership so that he could continue to serve his few remaining clients, including Huguette Clark and Jane Bannerman, the widow of his former partner. Now he was beginning to hand off some legal matters to an understudy, a lawyer down the hall named Wallace Bock. A real estate lawyer with expertise in an obscure tax specialty, Bock was initially taken aback by Huguette's approach to most problems—heedlessly spending money to avoid confrontations.

Although his new client was living in a situation that appeared infantilizing, Bock found her to be very strong willed. "She was very positive, she knew what she wanted, and she brooked no interference," he says, adding, "I can't say we became friends, but I became very attached to her. I saw what she was, and I felt that this was a mission I had, to protect her and to make her life as comfortable as possible." Wallace Bock would become one of the few people in Huguette's life to say the word *no*—insisting in writing that there were things she should or could not do—although she nonetheless often blithely ignored his legal advice.

At 907 Fifth Avenue, the renovation had been finished but Chris Sattler remained on the premises, taking inventory of Huguette's possessions at the request of her insurance company. This was Herculean labor, since each room was stuffed with pedigreed objects: antique furniture (an eighteenth-century Dutch game table, a Chippendale bookcase, a Queen Anne side chair); paintings by Monet, Renoir, Degas, and Cézanne; eighteenth-century chinoiserie; first editions in English and French (Walt Whitman's *Leaves of Grass*, Charles Baudelaire's *Les Fleurs du Mal*); Cartier silverware; and hundreds of antique dolls and toys.

For the newly married Chris, this was a pleasant change from his usual responsibilities at the upscale painting and renovation business launched by his great-grandfather in 1891. Fascinated by Huguette's family, he felt he was finally using his college history degree, learning about the senator and tracking down the provenance of objects. Huguette began to call the affable Chris with requests, asking him to repair a damaged Japanese castle, drive Suzanne Pierre to and from the hospital twice a week, and ferry items to the hospital. Aware of Huguette's reclusive reputation, he was startled one day when she asked to meet him, on a day when he was at the hospital waiting to take Suzanne home. As he recalls, "I thought, *Holy mackerel*, and went in. She's in her gown, a little old lady, but her voice was strong and her hearing was much better in those days. She wanted to thank me. She said, 'Why don't you come back and we'll start some projects.'" Those projects involved historical research for her miniature castles and châteaus. From then on, Chris would talk to her five days a week and make frequent hospital visits, becoming the closest man in her life. "She would call me as late as ten o'clock at night if she had an idea for a project," says Chris, insisting that he did not mind. "It wasn't a problem."

He was befriended by Suzanne Pierre, more than twenty years his senior, as they searched together at the apartment for items that Huguette wanted. "My grandmother adored Chris," recalls Kati Despretz Cruz. "He would drive my grandmother around; they'd go out to lunch. Chris was the one who turned her on to cosmopolitans. He's just a lovely person."

Huguette imported many elements of her old life to her new one. She still perused auction catalogues, instructing her lawyers Donald Wallace and Wallace Bock to buy antique dolls on her behalf. She kept ordering Japanese castles from Caterina Marsh and miniature French châteaus from Au Nain Bleu. A Francophile, she read *Paris*

Match and other French magazines but also kept up on current events by consuming the *New York Times* and listening to all-news radio. After watching cartoons for so many years to master the techniques of animation, she had become fond of the characters and continued to watch *The Smurfs*, *The Flintstones*, *The Jetsons*, and *Scooby-Doo*. But now she had companions who could laugh with her at the antics. "She would show me different cartoons like the Hanna-Barbera series," recalls Geraldine Coffey.

Generous, as always, to loyal friends and her new employees, Huguette gave away $692,510 in 1991, according to her gift tax return. The lucky recipients: Dr. Jules Pierre and his wife, Suzanne, received $114,000; Elisabeth de Villermont, the widow of Etienne, got $29,000 with another $10,000 to their daughter, Marie-Christine; Huguette's childhood Spanish tutor Margarita (Vidal) Socas received $13,000; Doris Styka got $12,000; and the heiress spent $223,510 to pay the nursing-home costs for Ninta Sandre, the child of her former nanny. Huguette also gave her nurses generous gifts: Hadassah received $32,000, and night nurse Geraldine got an $18,000 check.

Secretive about her life, Huguette did not want outsiders to know that she was now residing in the hospital. Even her doormen were instructed not to give out any information about her whereabouts. No one answered her home phone, leaving friends and family members concerned. "I tried to reach her but the phone just rang and rang," recalls Wanda Styka. "I knew she had several apartments, so I kept thinking she was in one of the other ones or out of earshot. I finally wrote to her to say, 'I've been trying to reach you.' She called me." But Huguette did not tell Wanda where she was living. From then on, Huguette would call Wanda regularly, but if Wanda wanted to get in touch, she learned that her best bet was to write, which would then prompt a call. Wanda was puzzled, but by now she had not seen her godmother for nearly forty years, so she did not push for an explanation.

The silence at 907 Fifth Avenue was worrisome to others accustomed to reaching Huguette by phone. Her childhood friend Gordon Lyle Jr. stopped by her building after his calls went unanswered. "I tried to find out where she had gone, but they kept stonewalling me at the apartment," he recalls. Her niece Agnes Albert became so frustrated by her inability to reach Huguette that she called Donald Wallace, and the lawyer passed on the message. Huguette spent hours happily chatting on the phone with friends and longtime associates, but she never gave anyone a callback number.

Huguette wanted to blend in at the medical facility, insisting on wearing a hospital gown although there was no medical reason to do so. "I buy her a nice gown," says Hadassah. "She never wear the gown that I bought her. She prefer the hospital gown, she very down-to-earth."

Yet in this peculiar hospital environment, she was blossoming. Huguette regaled her new companions with tales of her adventures in Montana, Paris, Hawaii, and Manhattan. Huguette told Hadassah and Geraldine about surfing with Duke Kahanamoku and described to Chris taking her first plane ride in 1919, an unauthorized trip courtesy of the pilot boyfriend of her nanny. "They flew over the house, over Central Park, in an open cockpit," says Sattler. "The senator was very, very, very, very angry."

Chris and the others were baffled by the conflicting images of Huguette's fearless childhood and her homebound adult years. "She was an outgoing person, brave, try anything. Nothing like the kind of person she became," he says. "She never talked as if anything had gone wrong with her life, you got the impression that nothing was wrong with it. Obviously, something did." Her life was an enigma to her new circle of intimates. Huguette never discussed why she had retreated into solitude, but she appeared to be at peace in the hospital, able to finally let down her guard.

Sixteen-year-old Huguette Marcelle Clark in 1922—the same year New York society was scandalized by her half sister Mary's second divorce. Huguette's eighty-three-year-old father worried he wouldn't be around to protect his daughter when suitors came to call, so he told her, "No one will love you for who you are. They will love you for your money." *(Reproduced with the permission of the Estate of Huguette Clark)*

Sen. William Andrews Clark with his second wife and Huguette's mother, Anna La Chapelle Clark. The senator met the former Miss La Chapelle when she was just fifteen and he was a widower thirty-nine years her senior. Anna, prematurely deaf, used a boxy hearing aid, seen here. *(Courtesy of Roberto E. Socas)*

Huguette playing with her dolls on the porch of her family's home in Butte, Montana. *(Courtesy of Christopher Sattler)*

Huguette with her father and her elder sister, Andrée (left), at Columbia Gardens, an amusement park that her father built in Butte. *(Courtesy of Montana Historical Society)*

Huguette in a grass skirt in Hawaii with a friend circa 1920. The Clark family made numerous visits to the island, where Huguette befriended and learned to surf from Olympic champion Duke Kahanamoku. *(Courtesy of Roberto E. Socas)*

Huguette, in the background, frolicking on the beach with her violin teacher, Jaquita Vidal. The Clarks hired Vidal and her sister Margarita as tutors and traveling companions for their daughters. *(Courtesy of Roberto E. Socas)*

Huguette on the day of her wedding to William MacDonald Gower, a Princeton man and the son of her father's longtime accountant. It was a very small wedding at her family's Santa Barbara estate. *(Courtesy of Tina Harrower, the flower girl)*

The marriage was brief and the press chronicled the details. (A $30-A-WEEK HUSBAND FOR THE $50,000,000 HEIRESS was a 1928 headline in the *Salt Lake Tribune*.) From the time she was a child Huguette's life was tabloid fodder. *(Courtesy of newspaperarchive.com and the* Salt Lake Tribune*)*

Tadé Styka, who was one of the most sought-after painters of his day—his works included a portrait of Teddy Roosevelt that hangs in the White House. He was also Huguette's painting teacher and confidant. She called him "Cher Maitre," and for twenty-four years after her divorce Huguette came for weekly painting lessons at his Central Park South studio. She eventually became godmother to his daughter, Wanda. *(Courtesy of Wanda Styka)*

A photograph of a Styka portrait of Huguette painting a male nude. She showed her work at both Washington, D.C.'s Corcoran Gallery and New York's National Academy of Design. *(Courtesy of Wanda Styka)*

Bellosguardo, the twenty-three-acre Clark family compound in Santa Barbara overlooking the Pacific Ocean. Huguette spent several months a year there for three decades but ceased visiting the estate in the early fifties, even though she continued to pay for its upkeep until her death in 2011. Bellosguardo became a key asset in the battle over her estate. *(Photograph by @JohnWiley/flickr.com/jw4pix)*

Irving Kamsler (above) was Huguette's accountant (seen here with his wife, Judi), and Wallace Bock (right) was her attorney. In her later years the two men acted as gatekeepers. *(Kamsler photograph by Martha FitzSimon; Bock photograph by Christopher Sadowski)*

Hadassah Peri became Huguette's private duty nurse in 1991 and was eventually given $31 million in gifts, which included real estate, cash, a Bentley, and antique Cartier jewelry. *(Photograph by J. C. Rice)*

Chris Sattler, a high-end Manhattan contractor originally hired by Huguette to renovate her Fifth Avenue apartment, became one of her lifelines to the outside world during her twenty years in the hospital.

(Left to right) Karine McCall, Ian Devine, and Carla Hall—three of the Clark relatives who grew concerned about Tante Huguette's whereabouts. *(Photograph by Angela Jimenez)*

Huguette's painting of the view from her Fifth Avenue apartment, where she lived until 1991. The last time she was seen by her relatives was in 1968. *(Reproduced with the permission of the Estate of Huguette Clark)*

Chapter Fourteen

The Constant Companion

Hadassah Peri was becoming much more than Huguette's nurse. She was her gatekeeper, her confidant, and her new best friend. As the bond between caregiver and patient grew, Hadassah and her husband, Daniel, found that they had stumbled into a fairy-tale existence in which a benevolent and otherworldly figure was willing to fulfill their every materialistic desire. But as with all fables, there was a price to be paid, a price that the couple likely did not anticipate as they began to insinuate themselves in Huguette's life—and she insinuated herself in theirs. The couple's bargain, swapping a normal family life for immense riches, was only made possible by the quiet yet indomitable nature of their patroness.

In marked and perhaps conscious contrast to her penny-pinching father, Huguette enjoyed her identity as a kind and generous woman who liked making other people happy. She received a tsunami of grateful thank-you notes for the cash gifts that she granted to loyal friends and retainers. She saved and treasured these cards as tangible evidence of how much she was appreciated. But Huguette lived in a world of willful obliviousness. Rooted in her lifetime of privilege, it never occurred to her to consider her impact on other people's lives—their needs were irrelevant when compared to her own desires. She wanted what she wanted whenever she wanted it. Surrounded during her childhood by live-in nannies who were there for her round the clock, Huguette now had a desire to replicate that constant intimacy.

Huguette's adult relationships never involved compromise, at least not on her part. Many of them had a transactional undercurrent. She had abruptly changed her painting lessons with Tadé Styka from mornings to afternoons without asking whether it would interfere with his artistic routine. In recent years, she frequently called decorator Robert Samuels and carpenter Rudolph Jaklitsch at home on nights and weekends; it did not dawn on her that such interruptions were rude. Her money gave her the license to be inconsiderate, and no one dared rebuke her. To be rich is to be narcissistic. To be old is to be narcissistic. Huguette had become narcissism squared. And now what she wanted was Hadassah Peri's undivided attention. There was something about Hadassah's radiant smile, eagerness to please, and fierce willingness to protect her patient that proved irresistible to Huguette.

After enduring years of struggle with an unpredictable income based on private nursing assignments and tips from the backseats of cabs, Hadassah and Daniel Peri reveled in her new job with its six-figure income and promise of long-term security. To accommodate Huguette's demand for daily twelve-hour companionship, the couple obediently rearranged their lives. In 1992, Daniel quit driving a cab to become "Mr. Mom," as the Peris' three children came to call him. "I told him to stay home and watch the kids," Hadassah bluntly explained. The couple believed that Daniel's transformation to househusband made more economic sense than hiring a nanny. "I stop working because of the tax bracket," recalled Daniel Peri in fractured English. "Whatever I making is going to pay taxes." This decision meant that all five members of the Peri family were now utterly dependent on Huguette's goodwill.

Huguette quickly became the sun around which the Peri family's daily existence revolved. Not only did Hadassah work eighty-four hours per week (seven days of twelve-hour shifts) at the hospital, but when she arrived home at the family bungalow in Manhattan Beach, Brooklyn, after an hour commute, she spent her evenings doing chores for Huguette, such as washing her hospital gowns and making vegetable soup to replace unappetizing hospital food. In ways that only prisoners can imagine, Hadassah's free time was never free. She could not put her job out of mind for even a few hours. The lonely

Huguette called the nurse every night to make sure that she had gotten home safely and to wish her good night. Hadassah's children often answered the phone. The sound track of their childhood was Huguette's high-pitched voice, asking for their mother.

For Huguette, this was the closest and most intense relationship that she had experienced in three decades. Hadassah was caring and comforting, interested in hearing about the tiniest minutia of Huguette's pampered life. Huguette frequently told Hadassah that she loved her and left messages saying so on Hadassah's answering machine. But for Huguette, love was frightening. Love carried with it the possibility of loss. To be out of eyesight or earshot of her beloved made her anxious, so Huguette kept Hadassah close by. Hadassah's family inevitably became part of the package. This was a mutually beneficial—and mutually manipulative—pas de deux. Huguette craved loyalty; Hadassah coveted financial security. The balance of power began with everything tilted Huguette's way, but it shifted over the years as the nurse realized just how dependent Huguette had become—and that those feelings could be used as leverage.

Daniel Peri began to do errands for Huguette, taking on an expanding series of tasks that had him stopping by the hospital several days a week. At Huguette's request, he purchased a television and VCR and installed them in her room. He shopped for Huguette's Christian Dior stockings, Daniel Green slippers, cashmere sweaters imported from Scotland, new Barbie dolls, doll accessories, and other toys. He steamed artichokes for Huguette plus bought and dropped off her favorite brioche at the hospital.

Still intrigued by animation, Huguette asked Daniel Peri to take over the responsibility for taping cartoons, photographing the videos, and putting the pictures into albums. She wanted the former cabdriver to capture every frame of each video, and in exasperating fashion, she would often make him redo the work. "Sometimes I take twenty [photos] and if she want thirty I go back and take thirty," Daniel Peri said. Huguette bought Hadassah's husband a used car so that he could transport objects for her. She would later give the family enough money to upgrade to a Lincoln Navigator Luxury Sedan, a Hummer, and a $210,000 Bentley. Daniel Peri never kept a time sheet but was rewarded by Huguette with checks for as much as $60,000, often several times a year.

Huguette's every whim was treated as a command by Hadassah and Daniel Peri—and that extended to their children, too. Huguette decided to share her love of cartoons with Hadassah's children: Abraham, born in 1982 and known as Avi; David, born in 1985; and daughter Geula, born in 1987. The kids were required by their parents to watch cartoons that Huguette had taped, and then tell her, by phone or in person, what they thought. As Daniel Peri described the situation, "She make video, she give to the kids . . . Hadassah come home, okay, the kids have to watch *The Flintstones*." This was not hardship duty for three children, but it was an impingement on the children's time and yet another reminder of who ruled their household.

The Peri children were brought to the hospital frequently to entertain Huguette. "They visit in holidays, Jewish holidays, American holidays, sometimes in midweek," recalled Daniel Peri. At least going to the hospital allowed the children a chance to see their mother during the day. Some of their school artwork hung on Huguette's hospital walls rather than in their own home. Middle child David recalled bringing his violin to the hospital and performing for his mother's employer. Huguette promised to give the six-year-old a relevant gift when he grew up. David said he would prefer to get Barbies now, just like his sister, but Huguette smiled and told him to be patient.

When Hadassah began working for Huguette in 1991, the nurse and her family lived in a modest 1,300-square-foot bungalow, all five of them crammed into two bedrooms. The residence was located in the middle-class enclave of Manhattan Beach, home to a mixture of Ashkenazi Jews and Italians. In 1993, their basement was damaged. "We have a big flood in our first house, and Madame told us to take a picture and I show it to her, and that's how it started," Hadassah explained. Huguette offered to buy the family a new home. Hadassah sent her husband house hunting, but Daniel Peri was baffled about how to proceed since "she didn't give us a price range."

He was not sure how high to aim or if he needed to sell their old place for a down payment. After looking at a handful of houses in their neighborhood, the couple chose a spacious $525,000 home, at 3,676 square feet more than double the size of their old property but only three blocks away. Daniel Peri says he did not know that Huguette was willing to pay for the entire purchase until the closing. The couple held on to their bungalow and turned it into a rental.

That home purchase began Hadassah's transition into one of the highest-paid nurses in human history. "I knew that Hadassah was devoted to Mrs. Clark, but what was the motivation behind her devotion?" says Wallace Bock, Huguette's lawyer. What Hadassah learned was that if she simply mentioned her problems to Huguette, her wealthy and healthy patient would reach for her checkbook. "What do you do when you are in the room for twenty years, you talk about your family, what is your life," Hadassah said in a legal deposition, when asked about the unending flow of gifts. "She ask you how your kid is doing, what is the problem. What you going to say—you tell your life story and that's how it begins. We don't ask Madame to give us."

The secret of Hadassah's salesmanship was that she never had to directly ask for anything. All she had to do was discuss her concerns over the high cost of private school (and then college) for her three children; Huguette began paying not only the tuition bills but the cost of after-school activities. When Hadassah's brother Ramon Oloroso and his wife and daughter, Michelle, came from California for a visit and stayed past their welcome, Hadassah confided to Huguette about how crowded her home had become. Huguette bought the nurse a $775,000 Brooklyn house, for use by Hadassah's relatives. A broker called Hadassah when a bungalow, located next to her first home, became available. The nurse mused out loud about how she would love to buy it now for her children to use when they grew up. Huguette made that dream come true, too.

For Hadassah, this was astonishing—the equivalent of dealing with the Make-A-Wish Foundation on steroids. The more Hadassah got, the more she wanted. It was irresistible to see just how far Huguette would go to make her constant companion happy. Hadassah never held back in discussing her problems during her long hours in Huguette's hospital room. When Hadassah's niece Michelle was diagnosed with breast cancer, Huguette paid the medical bills. After Hadassah's middle son reached his teens and had a car accident, the nurse confided in her employer. "We tried to fix the car but Madame said, 'No, it is not safe. You better get a new one,'" Hadassah insisted. Huguette bought David a $21,000 Isuzu.

For Huguette, this was Monopoly money—deriving from her robber-baron father's actual monopolies—and had no meaning for her other than allowing her to buy Hadassah's loyalty and time. During the first five years of their relationship, Huguette wrote checks for $874,000 to Hadassah and her family on top of the real estate and cars. And that was just a taste of the largesse yet to come. Huguette often confided in her friend Suzanne Pierre about "poor Hadassah's" problems and what she was doing to help. Suzanne, who had hired Hadassah, became alarmed that the nurse was taking advantage of her position. Suzanne's granddaughter, Kati Cruz, recalls, "Hadassah was constantly complaining: she needed a summer home, a new car, there was constant bellyaching. It made my grandmother so angry. Hadassah knew that Madame Clark adored her and she wouldn't say no."

Blinded by dollar signs, Hadassah and her husband ignored the warning signs of distress in their own home. For the three Peri children, their lives were forever marked with a dividing line: their mother all but vanished once she began working for Huguette in 1991. Day after day, week after week, year after year, Hadassah was perpetually unavailable to her own children. As much as the children appreciated Huguette's generosity, they missed their mother and resented their stolen childhood.

Geula, who was just four years old when her mother started her unrelenting routine, began weeping years later when asked in a legal deposition about her upbringing, saying, "My mother was always working, so I didn't grow up with my mother." Her oldest brother, Avi, recalls their mother as a fleeting presence, saying, "She was working all the time. I didn't really see her. She had long shifts from early in the morning to late at night. My dad would take care of us at home, or other family members." Asked whether he was upset by his mother's long hours, Avi replied, "She had to do what she had to do. It is what it is. Looking back, what can you say as a kid? My parents came here with nothing—my parents just worked and came to America."

Daniel Peri admits to feeling guilty that his children suffered. "I try my best to give to the family, do everything for the family, but is no mother in the house," he says. "Hadassah is always, always working." The nurse could have asked for—or even insisted on—reduced hours for the sake of her family. It is inhumane to work 365 days a year, with scarcely enough time to sleep between shifts. But if Hadassah had requested time off, she might have risked giving someone else the opportunity to gain Huguette's confidence and affection.

"The suggestion that Mrs. Peri was an uncaring or inferior mother is false," insists Fraser Seitel, a spokesman for the nurse. "Obviously, Mrs. Peri regrets that she couldn't spend more time with her children, but just like lots of parents, she was committed to her work primarily so that her children might enjoy a better life."

Aware of her family's sacrifices, Hadassah felt entitled to every gift that she extracted from Huguette. The petite nurse was later defiant as she described what she did for love—and money. "I dedicate my life to Madame. For almost fourteen years I stayed more in Madame room than in my house," Hadassah insisted. "I work twelve hours, my husband is mother and father while I'm working with Madame. Family vacation I miss when the kids were growing up. She never wants me to take off. She is uncomfortable with other people. I give my life for her..."

———

During the decades that Huguette was home alone on Fifth Avenue, she led a life in the shadows, sheltered from scrutiny. What time she got up in the morning or went to bed at night, whether she spent hours chatting on the phone or practicing her animation techniques, was nobody's business but her own. Her existence played out behind closed doors and out of sight.

Now Huguette's routines were chronicled in meticulous detail by an array of notetakers. Hadassah and night nurse Geraldine recorded their patient's daily life ("listened to radio, conversant and cheerful, settled for sleep @ 3 a.m.") and her ailments. Huguette was in good health during her early years in the hospital, though she suffered through chicken pox and bouts of insomnia.

Unbeknownst to Huguette, many of her offhand remarks to other hospital personnel were being transcribed for posterity. The executives and development officers at Doctors Hospital, which changed its name in 1994 to Beth Israel North, wrote hundreds of candid memos and e-mails describing their behind-the-scenes efforts to cajole Huguette into making donations—memos that in hindsight would be embarrassing for their authors. Hospital CEO Dr. Robert Newman wrote a note acknowledging, "Madame, as you know, is the biggest bucks contributing potential we have ever had...". A Beth Israel development staffer later wrote an e-mail that would subsequently raise red flags about the institution's conduct: "Does Legal know about Mrs. Clark's situation? I guess they do, but my fear is that if we raise the issue with them, they might push the question of whether she should even be living at the hospital. If we were forced to 'evict' her, we'd certainly have no hope of any support." Each time staff members visited or spoke to Huguette, they would race to their computers afterward to analyze her comments and circulate the latest soundings.

The other notetaker chronicling Huguette's life was Chris Sattler. He kept a daily log recording the tasks he performed for his employer, often referred to by her initials, HMC (Huguette Marcelle Clark). His entries included such details as: "Deliver Flowers for Mrs. Clark to Mrs. Pierre"; "Find Missing Photo of HMC's bedroom in Bellosguardo"; "Reassembling Rapunzel House with Newly Discovered Pieces, Photograph and Deliver to the hospital and confer with HMC."

For a woman who treasured privacy, Huguette had put herself into a situation where there was a paper trail charting her moods, her conversations, her spending, her health, and her dawn-to-dusk existence—a rising mountain of documents.

Oblivious to these watchers, Huguette was quietly pursuing a passion that virtually no one in her purview understood. In fact, behind her back, hospital executives mocked her activities. But just like the eighty-eight-year-old Helen Hooven Santmyer, who found late-in-life success with the publication of her best-selling novel, *And Ladies of the Club*, Huguette was still trying to create art.

Huguette continued to commission Japanese miniatures through Marsh and Company. Huguette treated as her bible a book published by the Japanese Board of Tourist Industry in 1935, *Castles in Japan*, by Prof. N. Orui and M. Toba. Enraptured with the Tokugawa Shogunate, she read every English-language book she could find about the era from 1603 to 1867. She was fascinated by the tales of the samurai warriors who unified the country and established the capital, Edo, which would later become Tokyo, as well as the warriors' relationships with the emperors.

But now that she had an assistant, Huguette made an imaginative leap: she wanted to bring her inanimate objects to life. Her artistic vision was to stage scenes using her kabuki theatres and Japanese castles, peopled with miniature costumed characters and accessories. Like a set designer, she would tell Chris Sattler how to arrange these installations at her apartment and instruct him to photograph her choreographed visions. Occasionally he would bring the entire work-in-progress to the hospital for her approval or to enable Huguette to take her own photographs of the scenes.

"She worked on these projects almost every day," says Chris. "Everything had to be perfect. If we were doing a scene of the emperor holding court, she might tell me to move the ladies-in-waiting because they were standing too close to royalty. Sometimes she would get annoyed with me because I didn't know enough about it. She'd send me right back to the house to do it again." Once Huguette was satisfied with the photographs, she would give them back to her assistant, who labeled and stored these projects in closets in her apartment. These were not her only artworks. Huguette envisioned the deconstruction of cartoon television shows as a frame-by-frame investigation and interpretation of the medium. Just as Jeff Koons hired assistants to produce his sculptures and paintings, Huguette relied on Chris Sattler and Daniel Peri to produce her creations, following her discerning directions.

In an art world where Damien Hirst's cow preserved in formalde-hyde sells for millions, it is impossible to know whether Huguette's photographs of staged scenes and her binders of cartoon images would have been embraced or dismissed by critics if shown in a Soho gallery. Art is so subjective that she might have been acclaimed as an origi-nal or ridiculed as a dilettante. Trained by Tadé Styka as a painter, surrounded by Monets and Renoirs on her own walls, Huguette had an eye and a distinct vision. Her mother had been a talented ama-teur photographer, and her art-collector father had marched Huguette through the museums of Europe to see the paintings he was unable to bring home with him. Her parents might not have understood their daughter's works, but they would have applauded Huguette's artistic determination to express herself.

Other than the 1929 show of her paintings at the Corcoran Gallery, Huguette had never sought public acclaim. What continued to give her pleasure even as she headed into her nineties was the act of creation. Up until the year before she died, Huguette spent her days planning and executing new work, slowing down only when her assistant was tempo-rarily sidelined by health problems. She had a reason to wake up each day with anticipation and a sense of purpose that animated her life.

It bothered Chris when others joked that Huguette was "playing" with her doll collection as if she had regressed to childhood. But he did not think it was his place to explain what Huguette was truly up to, and Huguette was certainly not prone to making preten-tious announcements. As Chris puts it, "She would never say, 'I'm making an artistic statement.' She didn't have to say it. She just did it." Huguette's goddaughter, Wanda, adds, "She was an artist and a scholar. That was her whole life. She was astonishingly good. She knew Japanese culture backwards and forwards."

An elderly woman who shows quirky photos of miniature castles to visitors and is fascinated by cartoons can be easily mistaken for a doddering eccentric, rather than treated as an artist in residence. At Beth Israel North, the staff failed to understand their most prized patient. Noting that Huguette had amassed toy soldiers, castles, and dolls in her room, Dr. Henry Singman was patronizing in his description of Huguette's activities, writing in a memo, "She is an excellent photographer and her room is a model occupational therapy setting."

Huguette's relationships with internist Dr. Singman, who supervised her care, and surgeon Dr. Jack Rudick, who continued to visit, were complicated by the financial agendas of both physicians. Not only were the two doctors working closely with the hospital's development staff to convince Huguette to donate money early and often; they were also padding their own pockets with her cash. Grateful for the physicians' care and attention, Huguette gave them bonuses: Dr. Rudick and his wife, Irene, initially received roughly $40,000 per year; Dr. Singman and his wife, Grace, got roughly $50,000, on top of his monthly $2,400 retainer. Those sums would escalate exponentially through the years as the doctors, just like Hadassah, began to mention their problems and desires to Huguette.

At every major hospital, the development staff has a mandate to shake the money tree, but the techniques that executives use to sweet-talk or arm-twist patients are confidential. At Beth Israel North, the staff was willing to take extraordinary measures to convince Huguette to give away her inheritance.

Disappointed by Huguette's initial $80,000 donation in 1991, the staff immediately began to plan a fresh assault. Dr. Rudick had no apparent medical reason to drop by Huguette's room on a regular basis, but he was in attendance so often that he fancied himself an expert on her state of mind. As Cynthia Cromer of the development office wrote in a March 4, 1992, memo: "Dr. Rudick feels she has no 'concept' of money, and that without an amount mentioned, we are likely to receive another five-figure gift. He felt $5 million was the minimum gift we should be asking for."

Dr. Rudick marched into Huguette's room that afternoon and made his pitch, according to notes taken by the development office. Huguette hesitated, saying that she needed to speak to her lawyer. A few days later, she gave $65,000 to the hospital. In a consolation note to the development staff, hospital executive Jane Blumenthal wrote, "I believe that this saga will continue! Here's hoping we end up with even bigger bucks."

To research Huguette's life, a hospital staffer tracked down a copy of the William Mangam book about her family and circulated a CliffsNotes–style summary of the more salacious stories, noting that Huguette was described as having a "mother complex" and as "hopelessly spoiled." Keeping his eyes on this financially prized patient, hospital CEO Dr. Robert Newman convinced his own elderly mother, just a year younger than Huguette, to visit her regularly in an effort to strike up a friendship. The two senior women shared a love for France; the doctor's mother spent part of each year in Nice.

Hospital staffers could not resist joking about Huguette's love of cartoons. On March 4, 1993, development officer Stefanie Steel sent her colleagues a note suggesting asking Huguette for yet another donation: "She hasn't made one in some time and it seems that she should be asked again (even if she changes the subject to the Smurfs or the Flintstones)."

Hadassah seemed to be playing a role as a double agent—as Huguette's confidant and the hospital's advocate. The nurse was recruited by the hospital executives to inform on her patient and use her influence. "Dr. Rudick and I agree that of all the players involved, Hadassah has the closest relationship to Mrs. Clark and has her trust," wrote Cynthia Cromer in 1993. "She has also in the past been supportive of the requests made of Mrs. Clark and there is no reason to think she would not be now." Cromer and Dr. Rudick met with Hadassah privately to discuss how to wheedle a third donation out of Huguette. However, in scripting their proposed pitch, Cromer noted that Dr. Rudick "is very uncomfortable discussing any kind of estate gift with Mrs. Clark because of her reluctance to discuss death."

Ever since Huguette was a young child, death had been a frequent and frightening specter, appearing without warning. One cousin had drowned on the *Titanic*, another young cousin died from appendicitis, her grandmother perished within hours of feeling ill, an airplane crash killed another cousin, and looming above it all was the death of her sister Andrée. Huguette learned early about the unexpected knock on the door, the cries in the night. To hold the heartbreak at bay, she had consistently chosen not to dwell on death. As she passed the milestones—eighty, ninety—she always behaved as if she had a lot of living yet to do. When anyone broached the topic of death, Huguette abruptly changed the subject. Religion is often a comfort to the elderly with death on the horizon, but Huguette was uninterested, rebuffing offers for visits by the hospital chaplain. As an adult she had never embraced faith, although she enjoyed the rituals of celebrating Christmas and Easter.

Like death, estate planning was an unpleasant topic that she declined to discuss. Her lawyer, Donald Wallace, complained repeatedly to Corcoran Gallery director David Levy about Huguette's unwillingness to face the future. The Corcoran hoped to be a major beneficiary in Huguette's will. "The great frustration that Don had with her was that she wouldn't write a will," says David Levy, who joined the museum in 1991. "She wouldn't say the *D* word. Don felt there was going to be a terrible fight, and it would wind up in the wrong hands and half would go to the state of New York, and he thought it was a travesty. But every time he raised it with her, she would shut him down."

In denial about her own mortality, she was confronted with the inevitable every time a friend died. In early June 1993, Dr. Jules Pierre passed away at the age of one hundred. Huguette spent hours on the phone trying to comfort his wife, Suzanne. The tactless hospital staff viewed the death of Dr. Pierre, who had been affiliated with Doctors Hospital, as a moneymaking opportunity. They decided to ask Huguette to make a $1 million donation in the physician's honor. Dr. Singman had the temerity to bring up the subject with Huguette just a week after Dr. Pierre's death. A few days later Cynthia Cromer and Dr. Rudick met with her in the hope of closing the deal. "The very mention of his death appeared to make her uneasy and she refused to be engaged in any further discussion of her gift," Cromer wrote. "She mentioned that she heard of someone who lived to be 120 and that she hopes to do the same." And in a sign that Huguette was reading the newspaper, she came up with another reason to deflect the crass suggestion. Cromer added, "She said she needs to save her money because of Clinton's health plan." Huguette gave the hospital $80,000 that year, a generous gift by most standards but significantly below the hospital's expectations.

Huguette did not want strangers barging into her room and tried to insist that would-be visitors ask for permission in advance. She requested that either Hadassah or Dr. Singman be present when any newcomers including medical personnel wanted to see her. When Patricia Balsamini became the vice president for development at the hospital, Dr. Singman agreed to introduce her to Huguette, but he was vague about her identity. "I spoke to Mrs. Clark and asked if she would mind if this young lady would visit her," Dr. Singman later recalled. "I didn't exactly describe what her position is or that she was going to ask her for any money or donations. I said she ran the public relations at the hospital, and was interested in meeting with her." Dr. Singman had balked at bringing in a psychiatrist to evaluate Huguette without her permission, but had no qualms about being coy about the identity of someone who sought her money.

As a well-bred woman of her era, the ladylike Huguette rarely expressed anger, but two events triggered her ire. After she donated $60,000 to the hospital in 1994, the development staff dropped off a formal thank-you scroll inscribed with her name. That simple gesture set her off. "She said she doesn't want her name printed anywhere," wrote development staffer Tricia McGinley. Turning down an offer by McGinley to retrieve the offending document, Huguette announced that she was "going to tear it into little pieces."

She still cared deeply about her privacy, and the second incident was also provoked by her concerns about loose lips. Like a woman juggling two rival suitors, Huguette took turns giving money to the hospital in the names of Dr. Singman and Dr. Rudick. (These donations give physicians influence, since they can help direct how the money is spent.) But she did not want the men to know that she was playing off one against the other in love-me-love-me-not fashion. Huguette became distressed when the development office alerted Dr. Singman about a $100,000 gift that she had bequeathed in honor of his rival for her affections, Dr. Rudick. Huguette made her anger known to Tricia McGinley, who chronicled the awkward conversation. "She was terribly upset...she did *NOT* want Dr. Singman to know about her donation...I apologized profusely..."

———

Huguette still treasured the memories of her early years in Paris and Montana and frequently reminisced about those times with her nurses. She felt that her Montana pioneer father had never been given his proper due in the history books. So Huguette was pleased to renew her contact with her Clark relative André Baeyens, who had returned to Manhattan in 1992 as the consul-general of France and was working on a biography of her father. With Suzanne playing intermediary, they resumed their phone calls. After Baeyens published his book in France in 1994 about William Andrews Clark, *Le Sénateur Qui Aimait La France*, he sent her a copy. "She was delighted, calling me to say that she was totally delighted that a book had been written about him," Baeyens recalled. She sent him a Christmas card that year with photos enclosed, writing, "Enclosed is a brochure on the living room of Papa who was so francophile."

Suzanne Pierre let slip to André that Huguette was in the hospital, but he never tried to see her, following the protocol that she had established. Huguette also took walks down memory lane with distant cousin Paul Clark Newell Jr., a California Realtor working on his own Clark family history. Newell, a grandson of William Andrews Clark's sister Ella, first wrote to Huguette in October 1994, requesting an interview. Huguette asked André Baeyens whether the Realtor was a legitimate relative, and after the diplomat confirmed Newell's bona fides, she agreed to make herself available by telephone. Newell relied on Huguette's lawyers to set up phone calls. He taped their phone conversations.

At Beth Israel North, the nurses and staff occasionally asked Huguette about her family, since it seemed odd that no relatives visited. She had a stock answer: her half siblings had not been kind to her mother, and she had no desire to see their descendants. Whatever happened years ago, whatever slights occurred, she had long ago closed the door to a rapprochement.

Yet a number of Clark relatives attempted to stay in touch, sending her holiday cards, flowers, and invitations to events that she would never attend, all posted to 907 Fifth Avenue. Huguette still spoke to her California niece, Agnes Albert, every Christmas Eve and chatted with New York relative John Hall and his wife, Erika, once a year to thank them for a Christmas floral arrangement. Huguette shied away from talking about her life and asked about their families instead. "She knew every child by name, and she would ask how the children are, what they are doing," Erika Hall recalled. "I always asked how she was, of course, and she would always say she was fine." Their conversations were noteworthy for ending abruptly. "She would suddenly break off after talking very happily with me for a while, and then she would just say good-bye...it was different than [the way] the normal person would do that." Niceties were not Huguette's strong point with her relatives; she had given all that she was willing to give.

On rare occasions, Huguette sent gifts to family members, but she was much more generous to outsiders. In 1992, she was delighted to receive a letter from Jean-Loup Brusson, the son of the French children's book illustrator Felix Lorioux. Huguette had loved and collected Lorioux's illustrations, corresponding with him and his wife until their deaths (in 1964 and 1972, respectively).

With plans under way for a traveling exhibit of his father's illustrations, Brusson contacted Huguette. She was so enthusiastic about the show that she arranged to reframe and loan her collection. Brusson, an executive with the fragrance company Lancôme, was surprised to receive a large Christmas check from Huguette, which became a yearly event. In return, he would send her one of his father's illustrations for her birthday. At least once a year, Huguette called him in France. As Brusson recalled, "They were very short phone calls, four to five minutes, and she would ask me about the children, if they were growing, if they were good, if they were kind, etc...." Huguette declined to give him a photograph of herself or her phone number. She wanted to remain in control of the means of communication.

———

Although the heiress had a strong constitution for her age, health problems occasionally materialized. In 1998, doctors found a lump in her abdomen. As Dr. Jack Rudick recalled, "I got an emergency phone call late at night at home. I had to see her, and I found that she had an abdominal problem which could have turned out to be life-threatening." Huguette was frightened. "She thought she had cancer," Geraldine Coffey says. "She was worried about the surgery, but she wanted to have the surgery...I worked with her that night and she said to me, 'I haven't made arrangements for you, Geraldine.'" Huguette never mentioned the word *will*. Dr. Rudick operated, and the lump turned out to be noncancerous, allowing Huguette to go back to acting as if she would live forever.

For nearly thirty years, Huguette spoke several times per week with her lawyer, Donald Wallace. She never met him in person but trusted him implicitly. When he suffered a heart attack in early 1997, her longtime accountant, Irving Kamsler, who had always communicated with her by letter, nervously called Huguette. "First time I talked to her was when Don wound up in the hospital in a coma. I was the bearer of bad news," Kamsler recalls. "It was scary on my part to call her. I know she knew my name and who I was. Steps had to be taken. I told her that Wally [Bock] would be handling her affairs until Don came back. She was very polite, surprised, upset, and concerned for Don."

The accountant made a good first impression by phone on Huguette. Kamsler, a Bronx native, came from a hard-luck background. When he was five years old, his carpenter/cabdriver father was permanently disabled in a car accident, and as a result, his mother eked out a living as a billing clerk to support Kamsler and his two older sisters. With tuition to a top college out of reach, Kamsler attended Bronx Community College and then Baruch College, gravitating to bookkeeping as a secure profession. Kamsler had worked for Donald Wallace's other clients, including Jane Bannerman, the wife of Huguette's former lawyer Charles Bannerman. Kamsler began handling Huguette's accounting and taxes in 1977, but all communication up until now had been by mail.

Ever since she had entered the hospital, Kamsler had been taken aback by the size of the bonuses that Huguette was paying to Hadassah, night nurse Geraldine, and others. As early as 1993, he had expressed his concern in a letter to Donald Wallace, writing, "Mrs. Clark appears to be somewhat vulnerable to the influence of people around her. This is evidenced by her extraordinary gifts to her nurses and their families." But this was not the kind of sentiment that Kamsler dared express directly to Huguette.

His new legal counterpart, Wallace Bock, had previously taken care of bits and pieces of Huguette's legal work, but now he was in charge. Although Donald Wallace eventually returned to the office, he was able to work only sporadically until his death in 2002. "I was the guy at the end of the telephone line," says Wallace Bock. "When she needed something, she called me. She was very, very private. I rarely asked questions." Bock and Kamsler, both observant Jews, got along well although their personalities were different: the lawyer was brusque and businesslike, while the voluble accountant liked to schmooze.

Four months after Donald Wallace's heart attack, Bock wrote to Huguette to point out that she was spending $30,000 per month to take care of former staff members (retired cooks, maids, the widow of a caretaker) and that she ought to consider setting up a trust or writing a new will. He cautioned that "should you for some reason be unable to provide the support that these people have to rely upon" they could become "destitute."

Huguette ignored the suggestion, but she did ask for an estimate of her current net worth. Kamsler informed her that she had roughly $300 million in assets, much of them tied up in real estate, paintings, tapestries, jewelry, silver, and antique musical instruments. Reassured that she had plenty of money, she continued to casually spend it. Huguette maintained her own checking account—and frequently wrote checks for tens of thousands of dollars—but did not balance it. She never bounced a check, but that was solely because bank managers would alert her lawyer that she was overdrawn and Bock would transfer cash (as much as $200,000 at a time) into her account.

Huguette's extreme aversion to publicity and confrontation made her a difficult client to represent aggressively. Even when she was wronged, she refused to sue. Citibank had informed the heiress several years earlier that more than five million dollars' worth of jewelry, including her mother's wedding ring and a magnificent bracelet adorned with sapphires and diamonds, had been pilfered from a custodial account at a bank branch. "Somebody walked out of the vault with the jewelry," says Kamsler. "Everything wasn't taken but the majority was taken." Unwilling to file suit for the full amount, she accepted the bank's offer of a $3.5 million settlement. Citibank put the remainder of the jewelry in a safe deposit box in her name, with the agreement not to charge her.

Several years later, Citibank managed to make yet another extraordinary mistake. Citibank listed the box as abandoned. "They opened it up, sold the jewelry at auction, and then realized what they had done," Kamsler recalled. "She wanted them to recover the jewelry. They said, 'Can you describe it?'" Huguette had not seen the gems in decades. Once again, rather than fight, she told Wallace and Kamsler that she would accept significantly less money than the jewelry was worth.

The transition from the gentlemanly and cultured Donald Wallace, an opera and art lover, to the blunt Wallace Bock was jarring for Huguette's inner circle. Acknowledging their personality differences, Bock says, "He was a WASP, I was a Jewish boy from Brooklyn." Agnes Albert, Huguette's niece, was accustomed to relying on Donald Wallace to pass along messages asking Huguette to call her. But after Agnes spoke to Wallace Bock in 1998 requesting a call with Huguette, she got off the phone in tears, complaining to her daughter Karine, "He is a dreadful man." Karine would file that incident away in her memory bank for a later date.

Bock does not recall his conversation with Agnes Albert but says that he was in an awkward position as the middleman. "I probably treated her as I treated everyone who wanted to talk to Mrs. Clark directly," he says. "My usual practice was to call and ask Mrs. Clark if she wanted to speak to that person, and either call them directly or set up something. She did not want to give out her phone number."

Suzanne Pierre tried to intervene to find Huguette another lawyer.

"My grandmother never liked him," said Kati Despretz Cruz of Wallace Bock. "She wanted Huguette to change lawyers. She found lawyers but Huguette said, 'It's too late, I'm going to stay with him.'" Huguette had always been passive about hiring retainers. Rather than switch to a white-shoe full-service firm like Sullivan & Cromwell or use a well-known accounting firm, she accepted without question whoever took over her legal and financial affairs.

However, one constituency was pleased with Huguette's new representatives. Donald Wallace had shied away from overtures by Beth Israel's executives, but Bock and Kamsler proved amenable, charming two members of the hospital development staff during lunch at the kosher restaurant Abigael's on February 17, 1998. In a two-page memo, Patricia Balsamini and Michelle Gelber gushed about the "fascinating" things they had learned about Huguette, from descriptions of her valuables to the fact that she insisted on keeping $8 million in a non-interest-bearing checking account.

The two men blurted out tales of Huguette's generosity: she supported a ninety-year-old bookkeeper at Bellosguardo and gave cash to a temporary secretary who had expressed interest in studying opera in Europe. And they told the hospital staffers that Huguette did not have a current will. "Wally and Irving have been creative in the ideas they have suggested to her, for example turning the Santa Barbara property into a private foundation for scholarly pursuits, such as musical studies," the two women noted in a memo. "The mayor of New Canaan approached them about donating the Connecticut property as a museum. Miss Clark is averse to change and will not follow through on any of these ideas."

It was indiscreet for two of Huguette's lawyers—first Donald Wallace and then Wallace Bock—to tell outsiders that their client refused to update the will that she had signed nearly seventy years ago. Their legal strategy was apparently trying to find allies willing to convince Huguette to reconsider any rational form of estate planning. Part of it was their professional responsibility, but there was also obvious self-interest involved. If she named her lawyer and accountant as executors, they would reap millions in fees after her death.

The money shimmered, just out of reach for so many supplicants.

By then Huguette had given Beth Israel $695,000, a paltry sum given her net worth. After the two development officers reported back on the lunch conversation, hospital CEO Robert Newman immediately called a staff brainstorming session, which was followed by a flurry of e-mails including such suggestions as "we should strategize on how to get Hadassah to help us..."

Development staffer Stefanie Steel sent a cheeky e-mail to Dr. Newman on May 20, 1998: "So, has your mom had a chance to talk to Ms. Clark about the joy of making a will? Please advise." Dr. Newman replied: "Yes, she spent an hour with her. My mother told Mrs. C of the great joy and spiritual satisfaction of preparing her will to 'ensure care of those who loved her.'"

Unwilling to discuss this topic with Dr. Newman's mother, Huguette instead insisted that they watch a tape of *Christmas with the Smurfs*. "I kid you not!" Dr. Newman wrote. "My mom spent thirty minutes watching the Smurfs. She deserves a medal—the lack of outcome not withstanding."

Chapter Fifteen

The Great Giveaway

Huguette had long been a night owl, playing solitaire until 3 or 4 a.m., soothed by the repetitive pleasures of dealing and shuffling. Now during those long hours at night, while the busy hospital was at a standstill, she wrestled with a question that had always been there in the background—what to do with her money. Writing a new will would force Huguette to deal with the troubling sense of her own mortality. She dreaded the legal complexities that would accompany writing a last will and testament to replace the 1929 document bequeathing her entire fortune to her mother.

Yet by 1999, Huguette at age ninety-three was also conscious of the noblesse oblige that comes with vast wealth. People were depending on her, or at least on her money. A shrewd if often ethereal woman, Huguette reveled in the gratitude for what she always referred to as her "little gifts." How pleasurable to see the surprise and glow on the faces of the lucky few—her friends, her nurses, her doctors, and anyone else who wandered into the vicinity and was understanding of her needs.

Why wait for death to spread joy? Huguette decided to write larger checks right now. The beneficiaries would range from her nurses to her hospital, her retainers, and her longtime friends, and as the amounts escalated, the steps that she took to cover her largesse eventually piqued the interest of curious others outside her chosen circle.

At the top of Huguette's beneficiary list was the one woman she could not live without, the person whom she saw every day of the year. Hadassah remained at the center of Huguette's life. A cynic might reduce theirs to a relationship akin to a grifter and her mark, but the relationship was far more complex and tender than that. "They were so good for each other," says Marie Pompei, who had been Huguette's original hospital staff nurse but now visited as a friend. "They were like mother and daughter, daughter and mother."

Suzanne Pierre, the physician's widow who was chauffeured twice a week to the hospital by Christopher Sattler, remained Huguette's closest friend. The two women, closer in age and spirit, spoke several times a day by phone, ending with good-night calls that reassured Huguette. "It was very sweet and precious," recalls Suzanne's granddaughter, Kati Despretz Cruz, who often overheard the conversations. "She'd call to see how my grandmother was doing—'I've been thinking of you, all my affection, we'll talk in the morning.'"

Throughout her life, Huguette had never had to think about having enough money to do whatever she wanted. But she had been running through cash at a rapid rate and did not have enough on hand to give significant sums to her two confidants. For perhaps the first time ever, Huguette would have to sell possessions—treasured objects rich with memories—that had been in her life for decades.

The copper heiress, who had maintained her Fifth Avenue apartment as if she might return tomorrow, was going to have to leave bare spots on the walls. Two Impressionist paintings were consigned to the auction block: Paul Cézanne's *Pichet Des Grès*, a handsome still life of an earthenware jug and fruit, was sent to Sotheby's. The other painting to be deacquisitioned had more personal meaning for Huguette. She had purchased Claude Monet's *Les Trois Peupliers, Temps Gris*—one of a series of lush landscapes featuring poplar trees and a meandering river—at a moment that she needed the comfort of beauty. She had acquired the painting in New York from the Durand-Ruel Galleries in 1930, just as she was heading off to Reno for her divorce. The Sotheby's catalogue for November 1999, detailing the Monet's provenance prior to sale, discreetly listed the last owner as "Mrs. H. C. Gower."

When Huguette learned that the two paintings had sold for $25 million in total, she celebrated by telling Hadassah that she would

receive $15 million and informing Suzanne that $10 million was coming her way. The arithmetic appeared to work perfectly except for the
awkward—but unavoidable—matter of taxes. Huguette, the daughter of a robber baron, did not arrogantly claim like Leona Helmsley
that "taxes are for the little people." But Huguette chose not to dwell
on unpleasant details.

Her accountant Irving Kamsler informed her by letter that she
would owe $10 million in capital gains and $14 million in gift taxes,
plus a generation-skipping transfer tax for the gift to Hadassah of
$8.25 million. (In a quirk of tax law, if the age gap between the giver
and the recipient is more than 37.5 years—a generation—the IRS lev-
ies an additional 55 percent tax.) According to Bock's calculations, if
Huguette wanted to give $25 million from the sale of the paintings
to her friends, she would need to come up with an additional $7.25
million out of her own pocket to deal with the tax consequences.
Huguette's lawyer Wallace Bock urged her to delay or reduce her gifts.

"She wants to give me everything," recalled Hadassah. "But
attorney Bock said installment...there is no cash, said you have to
wait." The nurse was referring to Huguette's decision to stagger the
payments. Ignoring the tax issues raised by the sale of the painting,
Huguette gave $10 million each to Suzanne and Hadassah. But she
was forced to tell Hadassah that the other promised $5 million would
have to come later. To placate the nurse, Huguette wrote an undated
check for $5 million. Hadassah's husband called Wallace Bock to com-
plain. As months and then years passed, Hadassah became frustrated
that the $5 million check was nothing more than a worthless piece
of paper as long as Huguette resisted filling in the date. Huguette's
lawyer was irked, too. "I was upset there was this $5 million check
floating around," Bock said. "I felt that this wasn't the way to do it.
But this is the way Mrs. Clark sought to mollify Hadassah, who felt
she would never collect the money she was promised."

The nurse was not alone in seeing dollar signs above Huguette's
hospital bed; the administrators and doctors running Beth Israel
Hospital wanted their share, too. On Thanksgiving Day in 1999, just
a few weeks after the Sotheby's auction, Beth Israel CEO Dr. Robert Newman stopped by Huguette's hospital room to chat. Visiting

a shut-in is a laudable holiday tradition. But Dr. Newman's goal was not to cheer her up on that occasion but rather to convince her to write a new will. Beth Israel hoped to be among the beneficiaries.

The soft-spoken Huguette listened politely to his warnings about the financial dangers that might flow from a failure to tackle prudent estate planning. Huguette ignored the hospital CEO's advice. But eager to remain in the good graces of the hospital's administrators, a few months later she gave $160,000 to Beth Israel.

By this time, Huguette was writing checks with the same avidity that replicated her father's behavior when he bought out the auction houses of Europe. Huguette was already paying private school tuition for the children of her nurse Geraldine Coffey and had given her $180,000 in bonuses. Now Geraldine asked for financial help to purchase an apartment at the Gatsby, a prewar rental building being converted into a full-service condo near Beth Israel North. Geraldine expressed concern that the condo conversion might not occur because apartments were selling too slowly. Huguette's solution: she gave nearly $100,000 to Geraldine but also spent $1.1 million for a Gatsby apartment to be co-owned by Suzanne Pierre and her granddaughter, Kati Despretz Cruz. Entranced by the convenience of the Gatsby to her hospital room, she also bought an $800,000 two-bedroom there for Hadassah.

Hadassah already owned a home in Brooklyn courtesy of Huguette, a twenty-mile trip home at night. "I work late and Madame is worried. She wants me to have a place to stay every time that I'm late from work," Hadassah said later. That problem was solved by the Gatsby purchase, but Hadassah was disappointed once she settled into the new condo on East Ninety-Sixth Street, between Park Avenue and Madison Avenue.

Her complaint was a familiar one to New Yorkers: the view was dreary from the back of the building, featuring the sight of a city bus terminal. Huguette's solution was to buy Hadassah another $1.4 million apartment in the front of the building, this time with Central Park sightlines. This was one of those rare moments when Huguette's largesse troubled Hadassah's husband, Daniel, who was concerned about paying the monthly maintenance for both apartments. He recalls telling his wife, "We have a view, why do we have to stretch?" But he had no cause to worry. Huguette picked up those costs, too.

Huguette was now writing checks as if there were no tomorrow. She had typically given Wanda checks in the $6,000 to $10,000 range but suddenly a check arrived made out for $60,000. For decades, Huguette had exchanged Christmas cards with Lucy Lyle Tower, the granddaughter of the Clark family's beloved physician, Dr. Gordon Lyle. Lucy's husband, Whitney Tower, a Vanderbilt heir and Saratoga racing enthusiast, died in February 1999; the *New York Times* ran a lengthy obituary. Rather than send a condolence note, Huguette included a little extra something in her Christmas card later that year. While spending her first Christmas as a widow at Jupiter Island, Lucy was sitting on the beach opening holiday cards and was stunned to find a $40,000 check from Huguette. "That blew my mind," says Lucy, who for the next few years received similarly large checks. When Huguette was informed in 1999 that her great-nephew John Hall had died and the Corcoran was putting together a fund in his honor, she sent a check for $50,000.

Huguette retained fond memories of her childhood Spanish tutor, Margarita Vidal, who had traveled to Maine and Hawaii with the Clark family. Each year at Christmas the heiress gave $3,000 to Vidal's college-professor son, Roberto Socas. As he recalls, "I would send her, every Christmas, a box of Whitman chocolates, which she loved for some stupid reason. It was cheap, not Godiva, but that was what she loved. She'd send me back a nice thank-you, or she'd call me up and we'd have a conversation about my kids." Without any explanation, Huguette decided to make his holiday especially memorable with a check for $40,000.

By March 2000, Huguette had completed her ninth year in the hospital. Bill Clinton had survived impeachment and seven melodramatic years in the White House. But other than one trip to see a dentist, Huguette had not left the hospital and had rarely left her room. There was no medical reason for this self-imposed isolation, and no hospital psychiatrist had ever probed her agoraphobia. She could have strolled down the hallway and out to the neighboring park by the East

River to breathe the fresh air at any time. But she did not want to leave the safety of her modest quarters.

People did occasionally try to coax her out on jaunts. Dr. Newman invited Huguette to his home nearby for afternoon tea. "I did suggest to her that she might want to come and visit my apartment, which is five blocks away, just to get out," he recalls, "And she very gratefully and very determinedly thanked me and said no thanks." Her assistant, Christopher Sattler, responded to Huguette's stories about surfing with Duke Kahanamoku in Hawaii by urging her to go to his Long Island neighborhood. "I even tried to get her to Long Beach, get a limo, take her to the beach," he says. "But it was never seriously considered. She laughed about it but never sounded like she was serious."

It was treated as the equivalent of climbing Mount Everest when Huguette ventured out of her room. Hadassah required time off for back surgery in 2000, and at her request, was given a room on the same floor as Huguette at Beth Israel North. While Hadassah was recovering, she had an unexpected visitor: "That's the day everybody in the floor almost dropped dead. They saw Madame coming out of the floor...I never forget that, and everybody had a shock."

Beth Israel's executives made an unusual concession to Hadassah, picking up some of her hospital bills. There was no explicit quid pro quo, but the hospital seemed to be rewarding Hadassah for helping to convince Huguette to make donations. After Hadassah stopped by the development office to drop off her remaining bills to be comped on August 1, 2000, a staffer wrote a memo detailing their conversation. "Hadassah reiterated that Mme. Clark lives in a cocoon and she doesn't even watch the news. She says it makes her too depressed. Hadassah says she is very smart and doesn't miss anything." The memo also paraphrased Hadassah as saying, "Mme Clark is extremely worried about Dr. Newman leaving. She is crazy about him and is also afraid that her position at the hospital might be compromised with him gone."

Worn down by the constant arm-twisting by Beth Israel North, worried that she might be forced out, Huguette opted to pacify the hospital with the gift of a valuable painting. She chose an Édouard Manet, *Pivoines Dans Une Bouteille*, a colorful still life of peonies, and told Chris Sattler to take it off her wall and deliver it to the home of Dr. Newman.

The copper heiress often tried to avoid telling her lawyer, Wallace Bock, when she gave away possessions or promised a large cash gift. Her concern was that he would try to restrain her generosity by lecturing her about the tax consequences and the repercussions on her finances. "I'd get into arguments with her, she shouldn't be doing something," Bock says. "She'd say, 'That's what I want, please do it.'" But Bock had a reluctant spy—Huguette's assistant. Chris Sattler did not want to be held responsible for valuables leaving Huguette's Fifth Avenue apartment without the appropriate paperwork. "I was in the middle," Chris recalls. "It was awkward." Rather than just follow Huguette's orders, he alerted Wally Bock, who reluctantly drew up a document authorizing the gift. "From a tax point of view, giving it to the hospital didn't make sense," Bock says. "If she had given it to a museum, it would have been fully deductible." To avoid taking any chances, Chris hired a bodyguard to accompany him when he dropped off the painting, which had been appraised at $6 million.

At Christie's fall auction in November 2000, the house set a reserve price of $4.2 million for Huguette's painting. But the bidding stopped at $3.5 million and the Manet did not sell. Afterward, Dr. Newman broke the news to Huguette and then wrote a letter on November 15 to hospital chairman Mort Hyman describing her reaction: "She was pleasant and gracious as always. She's keenly aware that our financial problems persist and that the gift she gave has not been converted into a single penny." Of course, had the hospital been willing to sell at the going price, the Manet would have been immediately converted into 350 million pennies.

In a written summary of his conversation with Huguette, Dr. Newman sounded irked that she wanted to discuss topics other than the financial needs of Beth Israel. The nation was riveted by the still unresolved George Bush–Al Gore presidential election as the Florida recount hung in the balance—and that was what Huguette wanted to talk about. Dr. Newman wrote: "She focused on the terribly confused political situation (she's strongly for Gore) and also on the volatile and largely downward spiral of the stock market..."

For a ninety-four-year-old recluse, Huguettte was decidedly in touch with current events. And that extended to the international art market. The heiress, who had spent her entire life surrounded by art and creating it, had strong opinions about current tastes and prices. "She has contempt for the Picasso that went for $50 million—says it's ugly," wrote Newman, referring to a 1938 Cubist painting of Picasso's mistress Dora Maar, *Femme Assise Dans un Jardin*.

Dr. Newman tried to steer the conversation back to what Huguette could do for the hospital, hinting that she ought to make up for the Manet price shortfall. Huguette urged patience, telling him "we should wait until the political situation is stabilized." Dr. Newman grumbled in an e-mail to another colleague that "she didn't take the bait and offer a half dozen more" paintings. The Manet eventually sold for the initial $3.5 million price.

———

Wallace Bock, keenly aware that Huguette was filling every tin cup in sight, decided that he might as well get in line. Rather than request cash for himself, the lawyer sought an expenditure for an unlikely cause that was dear to his heart. His daughter and grandchildren were living in strife-torn Israel, which was facing the uprising known as the second intifada. Huguette asked after the family's well-being whenever another bomb attack made the news.

Bock wrote to Huguette and asked her to pay to improve security for the town of Efrat. He pointed out that "there had been shooting attacks on outlying sections of Town and on buses and cars traveling to and from Town on the main highway to Jerusalem." In November 2000—the same month that the Manet went on sale—Huguette agreed to give $1.85 million to fund the construction of the Israeli emergency command rescue center in Efrat, a security alert system that included a barbed-wire fence, plus cameras and motion and sound detectors to screen vehicles.

The timing of Bock's request may have been dictated by the deteriorating situation on the West Bank, but it made no financial sense. Bock knew that Huguette currently owed $12.5 million in gift taxes—and did not have the available cash to pay. In fact, just five days before he asked her to protect the town of Efrat, Bock wrote to Huguette to remind her of the tax liability stemming from her gifts to Hadassah and Suzanne. On the same day, her accountant, Irving Kamsler, sent Huguette a letter stating that she would need to sell more assets to pay those gift taxes—and copied Bock on the letter. In fact, Huguette was so cash-strapped that Bock gave the $1.85 million to the town of Efrat on the installment plan, in four separate checks over four years. (Bock declined in an interview to discuss the timing of his request.)

Ever since Donald Wallace, her lawyer from 1976 to 1997, had stepped aside due to his failing health, Huguette's financial affairs had become increasingly muddled. The systems to manage cash flow and taxes that he had put in place were no longer operating. In the past, each year Donald Wallace would ask Huguette for a list of her gifts so he could pass along the information to Irving Kamsler, who prepared a gift tax return. Since Huguette wrote her own checks to friends and retainers and her lawyer did not have access to that account, her cooperation was needed to pay gift taxes. But once Donald Wallace no longer managed Huguette's legal affairs, everything came to a standstill.

From 1997 through 2003—at a time when Huguette gave away more than $24 million—no gift tax returns were filed on her behalf.

Part of the problem was that Huguette, even if her sympathies were with liberal presidential candidates like Gore, found it difficult to accept that the federal government should have any say on how she spent her inheritance. After all, her copper mogul father had assembled his fortune before the Sixteenth Amendment was added to the Constitution in 1913 allowing the government to levy taxes. Huguette stubbornly ignored repeated letters from her lawyer and accountant reminding her of the tax consequences of her generosity. But having created this paper trail, Bock and Kamsler did not force the issue.

Wallace Bock would later insist that taxes were not his responsibility, although his monthly bills listed income and gift tax preparation among his legal chores. Bock's explanation: he had carelessly copied the billing language used by his predecessor Donald Wallace. "My position was that Irving was the accountant," says Bock. "Anything to do with taxes, I turned over to him. I really did not know. I knew she owed taxes, but I did not know he was not filing the returns." In civil legal proceedings, Irving Kamsler later took the Fifth Amendment repeatedly in a deposition when asked about why he did not file gift tax returns.

To this day, the behavior of Kamsler as well as Bock—who as her lawyer should have been up-to-date on her obligations—remains baffling since they derived no personal benefit from Huguette's failure to pay gift taxes. In fact, the failure left them open to charges that they had mismanaged her affairs. This was a massive and costly gaffe. The taxes plus penalties quietly multiplied each year.

With so much of Huguette's wealth tied up in real estate and art— which she had not seen in decades—her balance sheet was turning into a bookkeeper's nightmare. Even as her tax obligations ballooned, Huguette's impetuous gift giving resulted in a cash crunch by 2001. Her conservative investments were bringing in only $2.2 million a year, not nearly enough to cover her life at Beth Israel, maintaining three properties, paying for her staff, and passing out large bonuses. Rather than dip into principal, Kamsler wrote a letter urging her to sell more possessions.

First to go was a Stradivarius violin, known as "La Pucelle" or "the Virgin," which she had purchased in 1955 for $50,985. When she had the violin appraised by Sotheby's, Huguette disagreed with the auction house's lowball estimate. Impressed by Huguette's business acumen, Chris Sattler recalled, "The Sotheby's people said the most that has ever been gotten is $2.5 million, we'll start it at that. She said, 'No. Absolutely. Not. That's La Pucelle, the finest violin in the world. I'm not taking less than $6 million.'" She used a private dealer to act on her behalf instead, and the violin sold for $6 million to a Silicon Valley collector.

Huguette also put up for sale two paintings by John Singer Sargent, both sun-dappled scenes featuring European women. At an auction at Sotheby's on May 24, 2001, the Sargent painting *Rosina-Capri*, an 1878 scene of a girl joyfully dancing the tarantella on a rooftop, sold for $5.35 million. But Sargent's haunting 1913 *Girl Fishing at San Vigilio*, showing a young woman in a long white dress at the seaside, did not meet the reserve price. Rather than lower the price or rehang the art at one of her homes, Huguette lent the painting to the Corcoran Gallery.

———

After refusing pleas by three generations of lawyers to make her final wishes known, Huguette finally expressed a willingness to at least discuss her thoughts about potential heirs with Irving Kamsler, who passed her suggestions along to Wallace Bock. Eager to seize the moment, Bock immediately drew up a draft of a will in 2001. That document gives a sense of her priorities at the age of ninety-five: Huguette's most valuable asset, Bellosguardo, was to be turned into an arts foundation.

Her nurse Hadassah and goddaughter, Wanda, were treated as equals in Huguette's heart, each receiving 30 percent of the residue of her estate. Her best friend, Suzanne Pierre, would receive 15 percent. Acknowledging her fond memories of the French marquis whom she almost married, Huguette left 15 percent to his adopted daughter, Marie-Christine DeMarchez. The two women still maintained an ongoing correspondence. Huguette was worth an estimated $300 million, but even after subtracting the value of Bellosguardo (an estimated $100 million) and the mounting tax liabilities, there would still be plenty of cash to spread around.

The missing names on the list were her Clark relatives. She had not seen any family members since 1968, although she had spoken to a few of them sporadically. This draft included a stark paragraph in which Huguette disowned the descendants of her half sisters, Mary and Katherine, and half brother Charles. "I intentionally make no provision in this my Last Will and Testament for any members of my family, whether on my paternal or maternal side, having had minimal contacts with them over the years." Her feelings were unequivocal.

This draft named Wallace Bock and Irving Kamsler as executors, which would guarantee them millions of dollars in fees. The lawyer and accountant would also each receive bequests of $400,000.

Huguette did not sign this will or any of the three follow-up drafts that were sent to her during the next few years. Cynthia Garcia, who began working as a paralegal for Wallace Bock starting in the fall of

2000, prepared many of the drafts and spoke frequently to Huguette by phone. "Wally was obsessed with getting her to sign a will. He would flip out," Garcia says. Every time Huguette received a new will, the heiress would make her feelings known with a quick, one-word reaction. "She'd call me, and say, 'No.' Then she'd hang up," Garcia says. "Wally would say, 'Bring me a Scotch.'"

———

The September 11 attacks did not affect Huguette directly, since she was living in the most protected part of Manhattan, the Upper East Side. Her view out the window across the East River was tranquil, without smoke or debris or obvious signs that anything was amiss. But as in New York and across America, Huguette felt the emotional reverberations from the toppling of the World Trade Center.

Huguette's best friend, Suzanne Pierre, was stranded in Paris, unable to return to New York, so she asked her granddaughter, Kati, to bring food to the hospital for Huguette. Kati had spoken to Huguette by phone, but they had never met before. "My grandmother would bring Huguette asparagus and brioche every Friday, so I did that," she says. "The first time I saw her, she was very tall, white as a ghost, beautiful porcelain skin, piercing blue eyes, lovely white sweater, and she was wearing a light blue cashmere cardigan. She was very happy to see me. She'd answer the door herself, never invited me in. She had a beautiful view of the river but had the shades drawn and the lights low."

Several weeks later on September 30, Huguette called Wanda to talk about what had happened. "I'm so glad I didn't see it," Huguette told Wanda, "It would have been so upsetting. I'm so glad that I didn't see it, live." From the seeming safety of a hospital bed, she was just eight miles from the worst terrorist attack in American history.

For Huguette, the anthrax mailings, which paralyzed the nation in the weeks after September 11, were frightening in a way that transcended terrorism. In a symbolic way, it brought back the death of Andrée, the sanitize-the-door-handles germphobia of her mother and once again, her own intimations of death.

Fear and panic, which many Americans were feeling in the fall of 2001, inevitably made Huguette even more dependant on Hadassah, the nurse whom she saw as her protector. Huguette showed her love in the most tangible way that she could—by writing more checks to Hadassah. Sometimes she would make out two separate five-figure checks to the nurse within one day. No one questioned Huguette's mental acuity, but her behavior made it seem as if she had forgotten by the afternoon what she had given to Hadassah that very morning.

On October 3, 2001, Huguette gave the nurse two checks, each for $35,000. The sequence was repeated on October 26, when the heiress handed Hadassah a $40,000 check followed later that day by a $35,000 check. On November 28, she gave Hadassah checks for $19,500 and then $8,000. Then, of course, there was the nurse's Christmas bonus, a $30,000 check delivered on December 14. Hadassah's husband, Daniel Peri, received his very own checks from Huguette—$25,000, parceled out in two checks written on back-to-back days in early January 2002.

Every gift to the Peri family meant another 55 percent generation-skipping tax obligation for Huguette. The daisy chain of cash gifts during just the three months after the anthrax attacks meant that Huguette owed an additional $125,125 to the federal government, which she displayed not the slightest interest in paying. Her tax-averse father had shut down his New York mansion for five months in 1922 to legally avoid paying New York taxes, but his daughter seemed determined to ignore the pleas of her advisers to pay attention to the tax repercussions of her actions.

As the traumatic year of 2001 drew to a close, Wallace Bock's partners decided to lighten up the law firm's annual December holiday party by playing a practical joke. They gave Bock a beautifully wrapped box as a present: inside was a will purportedly signed by Huguette. "He was so happy, he's thinking that he hit the Lotto," Garcia recalls. "Everyone was laughing. It was a joke. The message was: The firm wants to get this signed. You haven't come through."

Bock's allies at Beth Israel Hospital were not having any luck, either. The following spring, Dr. Robert Newman scolded Huguette in a stern letter on May 1, 2002, for her intransigence on the topic of estate planning. "I feel once more an obligation to raise once more with you an issue about which I spoke to you several years earlier—in fact, it was on Thanksgiving Day 1999," the hospital CEO wrote. He painted an apocalyptic picture: if Huguette did not sign a new will, "all that you possess and that is near and dear to you might be disposed of by some faceless bureaucrat of the Government."

Huguette was smart and obstinate. She hated it when people tried to tell her what she should do: the more they pushed, the more she resisted. For now, she preferred leaving the fate of her father's copper fortune up to a faceless government bureaucrat, rather than surrendering to those harassing her to make up her mind and sign on the dotted line.

———

Huguette had outlived many of her contemporaries, and in 2002, she lost one of her last childhood playmates: her niece Agnes Albert. Agnes, the daughter of Huguette's half brother Charles Clark, died on June 19, 2002, at the age of ninety-four. A lengthy obituary in the *San Francisco Chronicle* praised the music-loving philanthropist for her donations to the San Francisco Symphony and her own talent as a pianist. The symphony's musical director, Michael Tilson Thomas, described Agnes as "witty, charming, vivacious, and full of humor." The article described her exploits, from rafting down the undammed Colorado River in 1941 to picketing the San Francisco Opera to force the group to put up busts of the great composers on the walls.

Ever since Agnes had been Huguette's classmate at Spence, they had shared a special connection. Huguette had cared enough to remember Agnes's ninetieth birthday in 1998 and called to wish her well. Afterward, Agnes sent off a note to her: "It was lovely to speak to you this morning and quite like old times!" But the two women had fallen out of touch in recent years: Agnes stopped leaving messages after what she felt was an acrimonious conversation with Wallace Bock; Huguette did not spontaneously pick up the phone, as had once been the case.

Upon learning of the death of Agnes Albert and the existence of a will, Huguette's accountant tried to use this information as leverage. Irving Kamsler wrote to Huguette: "Your closest relative, Agnes Albert, who passed away last year leaving a substantial Estate, made her wishes known..." He obviously thought that where there was a will, there must be a way. But Huguette paid him no mind.

At ninety-six, an age when many grow fearful, Huguette was worried about being abandoned by her nurses and doctors. Night nurse Geraldine, who had already worked for the heiress for eleven years, recalls that Huguette made a point of specifically asking her to make a commitment to stay. "She didn't say until she died, she said until the end... She also wanted Hadassah Peri to be her nurse until the end. We would both be with her until the end," said Geraldine, adding that Huguette implied that a reward would be forthcoming. "She said she had instructed her counsel to take very good care of me and my husband and my five children."

Geraldine, perhaps naïvely, placed her faith in Huguette's future munificence, while Hadassah followed the credo of "get it while you can." Huguette would still not allow Hadassah to cash the $5 million check yet. But the heiress tried to paper things over by funneling money to Hadassah in smaller increments. Moving beyond two-check days, Huguette put Hadassah into a certain kind of Nursing Hall of Fame by writing her three separate checks ($5,000; $40,000; $5,000) on the same lucrative day, February 5, 2002.

By that date, the nurse with the golden touch had assembled, courtesy of Huguette, a small real-estate empire. Hadassah and her husband owned two Manhattan apartments in the Gatsby, two Brooklyn homes, and a Brooklyn bungalow (plus their original Brooklyn bungalow). But there was a yawning gap in Hadassah's real estate portfolio; she lacked a country house. In the panicked atmosphere after September 11, many wealthy New Yorkers were deciding that rural retreats could serve as a refuge from terrorists.

Hadassah had mastered the art of hinting her wish list into reality. But in this case, Hadassah insists with some plausibility that it was Huguette who suggested that the nurse set out on another house-hunting venture. "Madame said we should have a place to go vacation together as a family," said Hadassah, in her fractured English, "and so if anything happened here, our place, like she did when she bought the Connecticut [house] we have place to go..." Still insistent on tightly controlling Hadassah's schedule, Huguette told the Peris to find a retreat near Manhattan. The couple settled on a $599,000 house in Ocean, New Jersey, in 2002. As Daniel Peri explained, "We are one hour, maybe one hour and a half away in case Madame call for emergency."

Pleased by her good fortune, Hadassah could not resist bragging about her patient's generosity to Dr. Rudick, the plastic surgeon who originally operated on Huguette's skin cancer. His medical services were no longer necessary, but the physician frequently stopped by to visit. Small wonder since Huguette, who appreciated his erudition and plummy South African accent, rewarded him with generous bonuses. "I was on the floor," he later explained. "If you see, for instance, your neighbor's outside gardening, you walk by and you say hello to them, and it was in that same kind of situation."

Dr. Rudick recalls learning from Hadassah that Huguette "had bought her a house and I think she bought an apartment in Manhattan as well." The helpful Hadassah offered to put in a good word with Huguette, suggesting that the surgeon might like an apartment, too. Rudick's reply: "That would be nice."

The physician later insisted that he never asked Huguette for anything, but that much to his surprise, she offered him $1 million with no strings attached. Huguette's attorney, Wallace Bock, has a wildly different recollection. According to Bock, Huguette informed him that Dr. Rudick had financial problems and needed $500,000 to buy out his partners. In September 2001, she loaned the physician the money at 6 percent interest on a one-year promissory note. In March 2002, she threw another $500,000 into the pot on the same terms. Bock drew up the papers; Dr. Rudick never paid interest on either note. In mid-2002, Huguette told her lawyer that the gold-plated physician wanted to open up a new office and needed another $500,000 to buy an apartment.

Convinced that the doctor was taking advantage of the elderly Huguette, Bock became irate after speaking to Dr. Rudick. Bock wrote an impassioned two-page letter to Huguette on December 31, 2002, stressing that the doctor appeared to be issuing a threat: she could either pay up or learn to live without him. According to Bock's letter, Dr. Rudick had explicitly stated that if "you would not give him the money that he needed to buy an apartment in New York City, he would no longer be available to you, as he had in the past." As Bock wrote to Huguette, "I was aghast at his attitude, as was Mr. Kamsler..."

All these questions were later argued in dueling depositions. Dr. Rudick portrayed himself as selfless and misunderstood. In his version, he never had financial problems or partners, never wanted a Manhattan apartment, and certainly never threatened Huguette. As he put it in his deposition, "What I said to her was that since I was retiring, I would not be available to see her frequently." Dr. Rudick retired on December 31, 2002; the day before, Huguette gave $50,000 to the physician and his wife.

Huguette probably had more doctors dancing in attendance than any other aging but healthy woman in America. Dr. Rudick continued to include her on his retirement rounds. "I did not go see any other patients because I was no longer in practice," he admitted. But Huguette was special. She not only forgave the principal and the interest of the $1 million loan to him, but gave Dr. Rudick and his wife, Irene, an additional $280,000 during the next few years.

Huguette's personal physician, Dr. Singman, had also learned that his obliging patient was happy to help out. All he had to do was ask. In May 2003, Huguette gave $25,000 to Dr. Singman's son Paul. "He was having some financial problems," recalled Dr. Singman, who referred to Huguette as his "fairy godmother."

Wallace Bock received a surprising nonfinancial reward in 2003 for his efforts on behalf of his client: Huguette decided to meet with him in person rather than communicate by letter or phone. This was a major concession. For at least a half century, she had refused to meet with any of her lawyers. Bock arrived at Huguette's hospital room with a legal file and brought Irving Kamsler along to notarize some documents.

This would prove to be one of Bock's rare visits to her inner sanctum at Beth Israel. But Huguette took a liking to the shambling Kamsler. Eager to please, the accountant became a frequent visitor, even bringing along his new bride, Judi, to meet the heiress. Huguette called him at night and on weekends, relying on the accountant as a one-man help line. When Huguette needed to appoint a medical proxy, she chose Kamsler. "She was very clear that she wanted to be kept alive by any means possible," Kamsler recalls. "I explained to her, 'You need to understand, I don't want to sound gruesome, but if your heart stops beating they are going to pound on your chest, put tubes into you, hook you up to a machine.' I said, 'If you ever want to change your mind about what you want to happen, it's easy to change.' One of the things she said over the years was, 'I'm not going to die.'"

———

After taking early retirement, Montana reporter Steve Shirley became interested in writing a biography of William Andrews Clark. He had covered the state capital in Helena for many years for the Bee newspapers. Shirley wrote to Huguette at 907 Fifth Avenue requesting an interview, stressing that he believed Senator Clark had been given a raw deal by other authors and portrayed in a one-dimensional way.

Shirley had limited hopes for an interview. So he was startled on April 24, 2003, to receive a phone call from Chris Sattler, who told him, "I've got Mrs. Clark on the line and she wants to talk to you." Huguette began to reminisce with this total stranger about her childhood. "She talked briefly about her father, but she seemed very enamored of her sister, and talked mostly about their time in France," Shirley recalled. "She said her sister was very sorry that they had to leave all of a sudden in 1914 and couldn't spend the summer at the Château." Huguette told that story eighty-nine years after the outbreak of World War I and eighty-four years after Andrée's death. It was a small but telling illustration of the emotional hold that her childhood in France and her sister Andrée still had on Huguette, even after so much time had passed.

The heiress sent the reporter some favorite family photographs— a 1915 photo of Huguette dressed as an Indian with her father, a photo of William Andrews Clark leaving a wreath at the Tomb of the Unknown Soldier, a photo of her aunt Amelia descending the stairs at the Fifth Avenue mansion. She called Shirley three more times during the next few months, eager to talk about her early years.

What was frustrating for Steve Shirley, however, was the one-sided nature of their calls. "It wasn't really a conversation because she was quite hard of hearing," says Shirley, who did not end up writing a book. "When I said I'd like to ask her questions, she did not seem to hear. She did speak softly, had a French accent, seemed articulate."

Huguette's French relative, André Baeyens, had also noticed that phone conversations were becoming increasingly difficult. He was uncertain whether the problem was her age or her hearing. "Starting in 2002 I noticed our calls became more perfunctory as Aunt Huguette began to have difficulty forming full sentences," Baeyens recalled. "Even the forms of politeness became more difficult. Her hearing became impaired. Her telephone conversations consisted of a few polite words...This feebleness became more acute in 2003 and worse in 2004."

Huguette had feared losing her hearing ever since she was a child and watched her mother drag around unwieldy hearing aid boxes with earpieces. Now that her own hearing was failing, Huguette chose to be in denial. She balked at being seen by an audiologist and then resisted using a hearing aid. Her staff purchased an amplified telephone but she refused to use it. In her presence, her nurses and confidants learned to make a point of standing by her left ear. The handful of people whom she spoke to every day—Hadassah, Chris, Wally Bock, and Irving Kamsler—insisted that they could still communicate with her by phone because she was so familiar with their voices. But occasional callers like Steve Shirley and André Baeyens had a more difficult time making themselves understood.

———

Even as her remaining connections with her relatives dwindled away, even as her days were filled with retainers whose services she purchased, Huguette's affection for Wanda Styka remained undiminished. They had a mutual interest in art and history, and never ran out of things to discuss on the phone. Wanda appreciated the chance to talk about her father with someone who had known him well. Whenever Wanda sent a gift package or a note, Huguette brightened at the sight of her goddaughter's distinctive calligraphy-style handwriting, showing it off to her nurses.

For Huguette, her relationship to Wanda kept her implicitly connected to one of the happier periods of her life—the time when she had not only studied painting with Tadé but spent evenings by his side. But now Wanda's mother, Doris, the woman whom Tadé had chosen to marry, was dying. Just as Huguette had hovered protectively over her mother, Anna, in her final years, Wanda was devoted to assisting her mother. Wanda worked as a museum archivist in Stockbridge, Massachusetts, but her real occupation during those years was caretaker. "My mother went to a nursing home, and I went with her and had a bed right in her room," recalls Wanda.

When Doris Styka died in September 2003, Wanda was concerned about how to break the news to her godmother, whom she referred to as Marraine. She was sensitive both because of Huguette's age and because of the bond that Huguette had forged with Doris. Suzanne Pierre recommended that Wanda send a letter. Upon receiving it, Huguette immediately picked up the phone to offer comfort.

Her godmother's emotions were so intense that Wanda felt as if Huguette was reliving her own anguish when Anna Clark passed away. "I knew she was using how devastated she had been and was applying it to me," says Wanda. "She knew that I was very close to my mother. My dear friend mother." In the midst of their shared grief, Huguette offered the hard-won wisdom of experience, telling Wanda, "I know it's going to be very hard for you, the first Christmas and the first Easter."

The next night around 9 p.m., Huguette phoned Wanda again. That was unusual; they did not talk that often. Wanda was so touched by her godmother's concern that she jotted a note in her appointment calendar: "Dearest Marraine called. She said that I ought not to live alone. It was difficult for each of us to hear each other."

Even though the two women were separated by distance and hearing loss, Huguette would not give up on her fears about Wanda's safety. Huguette called again a few weeks later, and Wanda recorded her thoughts in her calendar. "She wishes to know the layout of the property and specifically, how far I am from the people next to me," Wanda wrote. "She said she thinks of me."

———

The emotional thermostat in Huguette's hospital room rarely needed adjusting: she was even tempered and got along with her chosen attendants. Yet roiling emotions lurked beneath the surface. Even though Huguette could have developed writer's cramp from all the checks that she was writing to Hadassah, the nurse was likely becoming frustrated since she was still unable to cash the $5 million check. A promise was a promise, even if by then Hadassah had already received more than $20 million from Huguette. The long hours had begun to grate on Hadassah, as Huguette became frail and needed to be monitored more closely.

Hadassah and Dr. Newman, the CEO of Beth Israel, remained united in what seemed to be a quixotic cause—convincing Huguette to write a new will. On January 4, 2004, Dr. Newman visited Huguette, and when he returned to his office, he jotted down his thoughts. "Stopped to see H. Clark, she seemed same, Hadassah *much* more anxious re lack of will. I'm trying to think of options."

The financially beleaguered Beth Israel Hospital was running out of options, too. Beth Israel was hemorrhaging money as it operated the former Doctors Hospital overlooking the East River. A year earlier, Dr. Robert Newman had written a blunt letter to Huguette alerting her of the "excruciating plight" of the hospital. But after donating her Manet in 2000, Huguette had become less interested in propping up the hospital. Her last check to Beth Israel had been written on Halloween, October 31, 2002, for $35,000—more trick than treat, given what executives expected.

Aware that Huguette abhorred change and that she was firmly attached to her perch at the hospital, in the spring of 2004, Dr. Newman and his colleagues decided to test her I-will-not-be-moved attitude. Consulting with his colleagues, Dr. Newman made an offer that was unusual in the annals of medicine: suggesting that Huguette buy the hospital where she was living. He made it clear that if she balked at writing a nine-digit check, the hospital would be sold to a developer and torn down. On May 11, 2004, Dr. Newman and Beth

Israel chairman Morton Hyman met with Huguette to describe what they had in mind. Afterward, Dr. Newman summarized the conversation in an e-mail.

Mort basically told her exactly where we are at—almost sure to sell the building, offers in hand... Also told her that a contribution in the neighborhood of 125 million would obviate the need to sell. Her only comment: "That's a lot of money." She responded the same way when we asked her for several million a few years ago, and that time she came through with the Manet. We'll see. We also assured her we'd never abandon her...

The executives had suggested that several weeks earlier Huguette make a gift in the form of an annuity, which they promised would pay her more than $1 million each month. But that would have meant selling and handing over all of her stocks and T-bills. Huguette had always been so conservative with her investments that her returns were substandard. Intrigued by the million-dollar number, she called Wallace Bock two days later to ask him about the feasibility of selling her country estate in New Canaan and using those funds to buy the hospital. But the house was not worth that kind of money. At the urging of Bock and her accountant, Irving Kamsler, Huguette refused the hospital's offer.

But after spending thirteen years in the same place, it was wrenching to contemplate relocating to a new neighborhood. The hospital was her home. She had lived on the Upper East Side ever since her father had opened the doors of his mansion in 1911. Beth Israel's main facility was located in a downscale busy commercial neighborhood, at First Avenue and Sixteenth Street. She did not want to go there.

At Huguette's direction, her attorney, her accountant, and Chris Sattler began to research other possibilities on the Upper East Side. Going back to her Fifth Avenue apartment was not on the table. As Bock recalled, she was adamant about one other thing: "She didn't want a nursing home." Huguette talked the situation over with her night nurse, Geraldine. "She wanted quietness and a river view," says Geraldine. "She liked where she was, she just liked the location... the

beauty of it." The Hospital for Special Surgery and New York Hospital, both situated on the East River, were considered as options, but
Mount Sinai, less than a mile from her current abode, seemed to be
the best alternative.

The effort to find a new home for Huguette triggered a new round
of panic along the executive corridors of Beth Israel. On June 2, 2004,
Dr. Newman sent a dejected e-mail to colleagues, lamenting, "I visited HC this afternoon. She was her usual determined self and her
determination is to go to another hospital on the Upper East Side."
Paying lip service to her wishes, Dr. Newman subsequently wrote a
letter of recommendation to New York Hospital on her behalf: "She
is a lovely person, highly educated, totally oriented and in remarkably
good health. She makes almost no demands on the hospital staff, having her own round the clock nursing staff."

But Beth Israel was desperate to hold on to this wealthy patient,
who had proved to be a major profit center for the hospital. She was
about to slip away. Her caregivers tried a startling tactic. Hadassah
and Dr. Singman both announced to Huguette that if she did not
move to Beth Israel's downtown facility, they would cease playing
any medical role in her life. Their threat touched on Huguette's two
great fears: being abandoned and being unable to care for herself.
For Huguette, the prospect of losing her two medical protectors was
terrifying.

Dr. Singman later offered explanations that strained credulity. He
insisted that his threat was motivated by the rigors of a long commute
to Mount Sinai, even though that facility was no more than a five-
minute drive from the old Doctors Hospital.

As he said later, "Apparently Hadassah Peri also told her that she
wouldn't go up to Mount Sinai to see her, and that she would only
come down to Beth Israel, so basically we were like a team..." After
receiving that one-two punch, Huguette had an abrupt change of
heart and agreed to go to Beth Israel's downtown facility after all.
Presumably, she felt she had no choice.

The deft nurse-doctor teamwork between Hadassah and Dr. Singman came in handy six weeks later when Dr. Singman fell down a

flight of stairs during a vacation in Italy and insisted on being mede-vaced back to the United States for treatment of his injuries. He informed Hadassah that the trip cost $65,000. The nurse rushed to tell this hard-luck story to Huguette, who reached for her checkbook.

On July 27, 2004, Huguette left the hospital that had been her round-the-clock home since March 1991. Chris came by the hospital to pack up Huguette's possessions, and then Hadassah escorted her into a waiting ambulance. Concerned that the shock of natural sunlight might be too great after so many years indoors, a staff nurse insisted that Huguette's eyes be covered.

When she arrived at her new room at Beth Israel—an ordinary space rather than the VIP wing—there was little worth opening her eyes for, just a gritty urban scene instead of the serene East River. When her former nurse Marie Pompei came to visit, Huguette plain-tively asked, "Don't you miss the view?"

Chapter Sixteen

The Long Good-bye

In her new environment at the downscale and downtown Beth Israel Hospital, a world away from the serene zip code where she had resided for nine decades, Huguette reestablished her old routines. Perusing the Theriault doll auction catalogues for new acquisitions and working on her photography projects, the ninety-eight-year-old kept busy. She had taken up making jewelry and whiled away the hours stringing beads. But her diminished hearing was now really taking a toll. "She didn't talk on the phone so much anymore," says Chris Sattler. "She was getting old."

Frustrated by her inability to hear, Huguette declined to have a television installed in her new quarters. She began to avoid most phone calls rather than embarrass herself by saying "What?" Huguette ignored messages left by her great-nephew André Baeyens and distant relation Paul Newell. Even Huguette's beloved goddaughter Wanda Styka found herself waiting anxiously by the phone for a call that never came.

The two women had periodically experienced problems hearing each other, but Wanda had no inkling that a conversation on April 12, 2004, would be their last. That night Huguette called to thank Wanda for a box of truffles and two photo books, *Paris from Above* and a volume on Central Park. "Dearest Marraine telephoned at 9:16 p.m.," Wanda wrote in her appointment calendar after the call ended. "We talked about WWI, WWII (Marraine mentioned tragic loss at

Normandy getting up hill) and Iraq War…She asked whether this was a good time to call…When saying good bye, she said, 'Good night my darling.'"

After that call, Wanda became worried when six months passed without further contact. Ever since Huguette had entered the hospital in 1991, she had initiated their calls, either responding to Wanda's letters or spontaneously picking up the phone. Huguette had never acknowledged to Wanda that she was no longer at 907 Fifth Avenue; Wanda finally learned the truth from Suzanne Pierre in 2003. Wanda did not want to intrude but found the silence disquieting.

"I did not hear from her. But I kept writing," Wanda says. "I thought maybe it's too difficult for her to speak. I would write, 'I hope this finds you very well and happy,' but I was a little concerned she might not be feeling well. I hoped she was surrounded by people who were loving." Huguette continued to send affectionate Christmas cards accompanied by checks to Wanda. But Wanda never heard Huguette's whispery French-accented voice again.

Age and illness were taking a toll on Huguette's friendship with Suzanne Pierre. For Suzanne, who lived on Park Avenue at Eighty-Eighth Street, Huguette's new location downtown was inconvenient. Suzanne did not visit as often but remained in contact daily with Huguette by phone. Huguette could still make out her friend's comforting words. But Suzanne was now struggling with her own problems. Chris Sattler became baffled when he noticed that Suzanne's gracious and warm personality seemed to be changing. She was short-tempered, even lashing out at him. She would make plans to go to the hospital and then forget or cancel at the last moment. The mystery was solved after Suzanne became disoriented while on vacation at Disney World with her son and granddaughter. Neurologists discovered that Suzanne was experiencing mini strokes; she was later diagnosed with Alzheimer's disease.

With her goddaughter and best friend on the sidelines, Huguette became even more dependent on her caregiver Hadassah. But although the nurse had pushed for Huguette's move downtown to Beth Israel South, Hadassah was not weathering the transition well. All those years of working eighty-four-hour weeks had finally gotten

to Hadassah. At fifty-four years old, the indefatigable nurse was experiencing excruciating headaches, back pain, and exhaustion. She was
worn out.

By December 2004, Hadassah was finding it increasingly hard to
drag herself to work seven days a week. She put on a good front for
Huguette's sake, but she was having a breakdown. Her husband Daniel explains, "If I say 'breakdown,' that means she is not the same...a
little bit down...You need to get rest, you have to get rest." Their son
Avi recalled, "She was working so hard, no one can work that hard for
that long. She was getting older, so she had those symptoms."

Hadassah was also tired of arguing with the stubborn Huguette.
The heiress had always been high-handed in her attitude toward medical advice, trying to avoid tests and intervention whenever possible.
Now she was increasingly resistant to following medical directions.
On December 21, 2004, Huguette objected when Hadassah wanted
to call a doctor to examine her inflamed right eye. As Hadassah wrote
in her nursing notes: "Patient vehemently refused and was very upset,
states it will heal by itself."

The weary Hadassah took ten days off, from January 3 to January 13, 2005. Huguette was distraught, repeatedly asking substitute
nurses when Hadassah would return. Her distress was so apparent
that Chris called Wally Bock several times to discuss how he could
help. In the seesaw of her relationship with Huguette, Hadassah now
had the upper hand. The copper heiress was bereft.

Not so Hadassah. Life without an alarm clock and the robotic daily
commute, the pleasures of leisurely meals at home, and her family's
company—it was all a revelation. Hadassah realized that she needed
to take care of herself for a change. She could not, would not, work so
hard anymore. Her two sons were at college, and soon she would have
an empty nest. This was her last chance to spend more time with her
teenage daughter, Geula.

In the past, Hadassah had been afraid to cut back her hours for fear
of losing her job, but now she felt secure enough to insist on a civilized
eight-hour day, five-days-a-week schedule. Huguette was so happy to
see Hadassah again that she acquiesced. Once back at work, the nurse

began to press Huguette to finally fill out the date on check #3510 for $5 million, written on Huguette's J. P. Morgan account. On February 7, Huguette and Hadassah jointly called Wally Bock to inquire about coming up with the funds so that the check would clear.

A few days later, Huguette developed a cold that turned into pneumonia, raising fears that death was imminent for the ninety-eight-year-old. On February 15, Bock received back-to-back calls about the health of his wealthiest client. As the lawyer noted in his itemized monthly bill, Chris alerted him that "Mrs. Clark's condition seems to be deteriorating." Then Bock heard from Hadassah, whose priorities were more egocentric—she was worried about getting her $5 million.

The next day, Huguette rallied. She tried to pacify Hadassah with a check for $35,000. But the heiress's illness had made her retainers realize that it was now-or-never time. If Huguette did not sign a new will, they would lose any claim to her fortune. Her entire estate would go to her distant relatives, the descendants of her half siblings, most of whom she had never met.

In her hospital notes, Hadassah wrote on February 22 that Huguette was "sleeping more than usual." Her weight had dropped to eighty pounds—and that included three cashmere sweaters that she was wearing to stay warm. Ever since her mother died in 1963, Huguette had refused the entreaties from her lawyers to write a will. But suddenly the unthinkable occurred: Huguette finally agreed to meet with Bock and Kamsler on Monday, February 28, to discuss writing a new will that would make financial provisions for Hadassah.

The heiress agreed to put her estate in New Canaan, Connecticut, up for sale, acknowledging on paper that Hadassah would be paid $5 million out of the proceeds. Huguette still appeared to be in poor health. On March 2, Dr. Newman visited Huguette, writing in an e-mail to a colleague afterward, "She is indeed weakening and her deafness makes any communication quite agonizing."

Huguette's near-death experience had left her in a contemplative mood. When Dr. Singman went to see her on March 5, she entertained him by reciting a favorite fable—doing so in French and

Spanish—that seemed to explain her decision to lead a reclusive life. This poem had long resonated with Huguette. A half century earlier, she had given Wanda a version of the poem in an illustrated French-language children's book. Only later would Wanda reread that book and understand what her godmother was trying to tell her.

Written by seventeenth-century French poet Jean-Pierre Claris de Florian, "The Little Cricket" describes a cricket hiding in the grass, envying a brilliantly colored butterfly spreading its wings. The self-deprecating cricket laments having no special talent nor alluring appearance to gain the admiration of others. But then rowdy children come along and are entranced by the insect. They chase the butter-fly and capture it—and cruelly rip the gaudy insect apart. The poem ends on this note:

> Oh! Oh! says the little cricket, I am no more sorry.
> It costs too dear to shine in this world.
> How much I am going to love my deep retreat!
> To live happily, live hidden.

For Huguette, who had seen her life dissected in the newspapers from her childhood through her painful divorce, being in the public eye was humiliating. She had hidden from the world, doing everything possible to retain her privacy. She created art out of her own need to do so, not in the hope of recognition or acclaim—she truly believed that it cost too much to shine in this world.

The poem epitomized the sad truths that had dominated her exis-tence. Wounded by the deaths of loved ones, emotionally fragile, and afraid of being hurt, she had allowed very few people to become close. Her father had warned her that people would only want her for her inheritance, and that early parental caution made it hard for her to trust. Her money had purchased loyalty, but had it purchased true friendship or love? "She made it sound like you don't need anybody, you don't need a man in your life," says retired-nurse-turned-friend Marie Pompei. "She didn't seem like the kind of person who would have a close intimate relationship." Even with female friends? "Not many."

On March 7, 2005, two days after she recited the poem, Huguette finally took a step that she had resisted ever since her mother's death in 1963. She signed a minimalist version of a will. Although Wallace Bock had prepared many detailed drafts in recent years—cutting out her relatives, giving cash to specific friends—this document was designed solely to insure that Hadassah got her money. The key paragraph: "Should my dear friend and companion Hadassah Peri not have received from me five million from the proceed of the sale of my property in New Canaan, I give and devise and bequeath to Hadassah the sum of five million." Under this will, Huguette agreed to leave the remainder of her fortune to "my distributees who would share in my estate had I died intestate"—that is, her Clark relatives. Informed that she needed to pick executors, Huguette chose her accountant and her lawyer.

Bock and Kamsler brought the document to the hospital, joined by Lewis Siegel, a lawyer affiliated with Bock's firm. Siegel was aware that this was a significant moment, recalling that Bock had frequently expressed his fear that unless Huguette signed a will "it was going to be a disaster, people grabbing for money." Yet even though this was a momentous occasion, the three men had not brought witnesses with them and needed to recruit two on the spot.

"I was in the hall, waiting to go into my usual meeting with her," Chris says. "I was all flabbergasted that I was asked to come in. They didn't want me to read the will. I just signed it." Chris found a nurse who agreed to serve as the second witness. As executors, Bock and Kamsler stood to earn fees of more than $3 million each.

It was done. Three people could breathe more easily—Hadassah, Wally, and Irving—with the comforting knowledge that they would benefit financially from Huguette's death. It was done—but it wasn't done. There was so much money still on the table, hundreds of millions in real estate, art, and jewels, all of which would now go to her distant relations. Her goddaughter, Wanda, and longtime employees like Chris had been left out.

Just eight days after signing that will, Huguette called Bock and said she wanted to give the entire proceeds of the sale of her Connecticut mansion, priced at $34 million, to Hadassah. Bock, who had become adept at communicating with Huguette despite her hearing problems, told her that this would be a tax nightmare and dissuaded her. Casting around for other possessions that she could sell to raise cash, Huguette authorized her lawyer to sell one of her father's rare collectibles, *The Book of Hours*, an illuminated manuscript dating back to the 1450s. It sold at Sotheby's for $80,000. While Huguette's health had stabilized, she was so cold that she had escalated to wearing six sweaters on top of her hospital gown.

Night after night, as she continued to play solitaire until the wee hours, Huguette had ample quiet time to contemplate what she wanted to do with the rest of her inheritance. Bock and Kamsler would later insist that Huguette's March 7 will was always meant to be temporary, a stopgap measure to resolve Hadassah's anxiety over her $5 million. Kamsler says that he immediately began discussions with Huguette in person and by phone about her true final wishes. Huguette liked her accommodating accountant and found him easier to deal with than her argumentative lawyer, who kept on using the infuriating word *no* to deflect her requests. So she relied on Kamsler to play the middleman in conveying her wishes.

Bellosguardo held a shimmering place in Huguette's memories: those magical summers with her parents, days on the beach and evening concerts on the lawn. She loved her painting studio with canvases and an easel awaiting her return, her peaceful bedroom, the music room adorned with Tadé Styka paintings. Married on the estate overlooking the Pacific Ocean, she could now look back on her brief liaison with equanimity, since she and ex-husband William Gower had ended up as friends. Huguette decided to turn Bellosguardo into an arts foundation. This would be her legacy—the public would be able to enjoy this spot that had once enchanted her family.

Yet drawn by her father's connection to the Corcoran Gallery, she also wanted to leave something to the museum. "We had discussions about various paintings and what she might want to do about the Corcoran," Kamsler recalls. She decided to give the Corcoran a valuable Monet, one of more than 250 in the famous *Water Lilies* series painted by the artist. Huguette nervously asked, "Do you think that will make them happy?" Kamsler's reply: "I think that they will be ecstatic."

Despite the more than $20 million that she had already showered on Hadassah, Huguette wanted to bequeath the nurse the bulk of her estate. But after looking at the numbers and her list of other potential beneficiaries, she agreed to follow the advice of her lawyer and accountant to slightly reduce that amount. Hadassah would receive Huguette's doll collection plus 60 percent of the residue of her estate, after specific bequests had been paid (such as $500,000 for Chris Sattler, $100,000 to Dr. Singman, $1 million to Beth Israel, $500,000 each to Bock and Kamsler). "She wanted to leave substantially more to Hadassah," recalls Kamsler. "We told her that if you do that, nothing will be left to leave for Wanda or to provide for continued upkeep and maintenance of Bellosguardo."

Wanda and Hadassah had been treated as equals in Huguette's 2001 draft, but now the heiress had downgraded her goddaughter, who would receive only 25 percent of the residue of the estate.

One odd thing stood out: Huguette had expressly signed her previous will in March for only one reason, and that was to insure that Hadassah would receive $5 million in case Huguette inconveniently died before her Connecticut estate was sold. But this new document eliminated that clause, making absolutely no mention of that sum or any special obligation to Hadassah. Bock would later admit that this was a mistake, saying, "I had failed to put it in." Pressed on how he could have forgotten such a significant sum and whether he subconsciously intended to thwart the nurse, Bock mused out loud, "It might have very well been subconscious. It's a complete blank to me whether I forgot it or made an assumption that it should be left out because Hadassah was getting so much in the will. I was a little embarrassed, to say the least."

There were other losers: Suzanne Pierre and Marie-Christine DeMarchez, who had both stood to inherit under the 2001 draft of Huguette's will, had been cut from the list. Suzanne had already received $10 million from Huguette. The heiress still exchanged letters with Marie-Christine, the daughter of Etienne de Villermont, but Huguette's emotional tie to that family had lessened.

Huguette never explicitly mentioned her family members by name in any draft of her will. This new will included the primal-scream paragraph disowning her relatives that had initially appeared in the 2001 draft. Just a few weeks earlier, Huguette had signed a new will that gave her distant family members virtually all of her money, by default. But she had apparently had a change of heart.

In memory of the tension between Huguette's mother, Anna, and her stepchildren, Huguette was prepared to punish their descendants. She did not want them to receive any of her inheritance. Huguette had repeated this refrain so often to the members of her circle including Suzanne, Hadassah, and Chris that it was treated as gospel. Irving Kamsler insists that she pointed out to him yet again that she and her half siblings had all received equal shares from William Andrews Clark's estate. "She clearly said that she doesn't want anything to do with her family, hasn't for years. They had been taken care of," he recalls. "Whatever happened or has not happened over the years, they got their money. She felt that certain family members had not treated her or her mother very nicely when she was younger."

On March 30, Dr. Singman suggested to Huguette that she sign a Do Not Resuscitate order. Her recent health woes made this a timely consideration. But Huguette was not receptive. Hadassah, who was present for the conversation, remembers, "She really don't want to hear about this, you know... She wants to be resuscitated." Huguette had a tremendous will to live. She had books to read, dolls to buy, and art projects to work on. She was eager to take another look at her collection of French children's illustrations, to read up on Queen Elizabeth I's coronation, and arrange for a new project using her antique Japanese Hina dolls. She kept Chris running to and from her apartment and the hospital to fulfill her wishes. If she stayed busy enough, she could avoid brooding about the terrifying inevitable. To sign a DNR order would be to give in.

Six weeks after Huguette signed her first new will, Wally Bock, Irving Kamsler, and Lewis Siegel again made their way to Huguette's room on the third floor, document in hand. Siegel was along to supervise the signing ceremony. He would later admit that he had not read the document beforehand and assumed that Huguette already knew what was in it. A copy had been sent to her a few days earlier.

Under estate law, beneficiaries are not supposed to be in the room when someone signs a will, to insure that no arm-twisting or pressure is applied. It is not illegal to stick around, but if the will is later contested, such behavior gives opponents a potent weapon—the ability to charge that undue influence occurred.

Bock's secretary, Danita Rudisill, accompanied him to Beth Israel to serve as a witness, but he would have to recruit a second person from the hospital staff. For a signing ceremony that Kamsler and Bock had been anticipating for years, there was a slapdash quality to the April 19 event.

Hadassah and Chris were chatting with Huguette when the others arrived. Huguette had been up until 4 a.m. the night before, as usual, but appeared alert. "We exchanged pleasantries," Bock says. "I introduced Danita to Mrs. Clark. She had spoken to her many times over the phone, but she had never met her personally."

Since Hadassah, Chris, Wally, and Irving were all slated to receive money from Huguette, they were supposed to make themselves scarce. Hadassah went out into the hallway and recruited nurse Steven Pyram to serve as the second witness. Pyram was preoccupied with other patient responsibilities, but agreed to take a few minutes for the task.

Memories would later differ on what occurred next in Huguette's room. In Wallace Bock's version: "I then asked Mr. Kamsler, Chris, and Hadassah to leave the room, and I left the room and we closed the door and we were out in the corridor."

However, his secretary, Danita Rudisill, who subsequently had a falling out with Bock and left his law firm, would later insist that things played out quite differently. Speaking in a deposition probing the details of the signing ceremony, she stated that Hadassah not only remained in the room but helped guide Huguette's hand when she initialed the pages and signed the will. Rudisill also claimed that Irving Kamsler and Wallace Bock had remained by Huguette's side. Steven Pyram, who was there for less than five minutes, recalled seeing "an Asian" woman and also thought that another man had been present. Hadassah testified that she could not remember whether or not she was in the room, but was certain of one thing: she had not helped Huguette sign the will.

Lewis Siegel later acknowledged in a deposition that if he had read the will and had known that Hadassah was going to inherit, "I might have asked her to leave." He also said that he did not confirm with Huguette that she was aware of all the provisions in the document. She did not study it line by line in front of him and the other witnesses.

Nobody videotaped the signing ceremony, which would have made it easier later on to determine what actually happened. Had a large, established law firm handled the paperwork for a woman leaving a multimillion-dollar estate—especially one who was cutting out her relatives—no doubt this would have been a far more prolonged process. But Wallace Bock was a member of a small firm, and he thought what he had done was sufficient.

"Hindsight is twenty-twenty," Bock said in December 2013. "I should have taken more precautions. I've been writing wills for umpteen years and I have a set procedure. I have the person initial the pages, I ask if they've read it before they initial it. Lewis has observed me doing it." But Bock claims that this situation was unusual for him: he says it was the first time that he prepared a will in which a client left him money, requiring him to leave the room rather than preside over the signing ceremony. If he could have a do-over, Bock says, "I might have made a videotape of it. The witnesses were the male nurse and my secretary. If I had called in a couple of doctors, I would have been better off. I had two independent witnesses who could not remember what happened. In hindsight, I could have done other things."

In Hadassah's official nursing notes that day, she described Huguette as "alert and oriented x 3"—which in nursing shorthand means that she knew who she was, where she was, and what time it was. In other words, Huguette was mentally competent to sign a will enriching Hadassah.

Three days later, Huguette felt the urge to revisit her past; the nursing notes state that she spent a few hours paging through a photo album depicting her childhood in Montana with her parents and Andrée. She gazed at a picture of her sister, her father, and herself putting on hard hats to descend into the mines. Those mines had produced the copper fortune that she had just arranged to give away. Irish and Chinese immigrants working in brutal conditions had wrested the copper from the earth. None of that money would be returning to Montana to benefit the regions ravaged by William Andrews Clark.

———

In the yin and yang of Huguette's relationship with Hadassah, their shifting emotional balance often played out in tangible fashion, as witnessed by the entries in the heiress's check registry. The nurse had become accustomed to receiving large gift checks as often as twice a day, but Huguette had slowed down the pace and now was reaching for her checkbook only twice a month. Hadassah still didn't have her $5 million in hand. Huguette appeared to be holding the money tantalizingly out of reach, shrewdly dangling it in front of the nurse to make sure that she did not quit.

Yet for Huguette, the reverberations lingered from those ten frightening days in January when the nurse had gone AWOL. Huguette was eager to avoid a recurrence. One day that spring, Hadassah came to work wearing a pair of inexpensive but attractive earrings. And that gave Huguette an idea.

She called Chris and asked him to open up her home safe and bring the contents to the hospital. The Cartier and Van Cleef and Arpels boxes were vintage, filled with treasures dating back to Huguette's debutante days—necklaces, rings, bracelets, and earrings that she had either bought for herself or been given as gifts. Huguette opened up the boxes and dumped the contents onto her hospital bed. It was a dazzling display—diamonds, emeralds, rubies, gold, platinum—a shimmering array of colors lighting up the hospital room. This was not even Huguette's "important" jewelry, which remained locked away in a bank vault.

A half century had passed since Huguette had fastened the clasps of the necklaces and bracelets and adorned herself to go out to the opera or a fashion show. The sight of her possessions evoked old times. "She was having so much fun, she loved it," Chris recalls. Huguette not only wanted to show off her jewelry—she wanted to give it away.

Rather than ask Hadassah to pick out a few pieces, Huguette decided to hand it all over to the nurse. But with Chris standing by, Huguette thought that he and his wife and two daughters might like a handful of mementoes, too. Huguette picked up a gold cross with red rubies and said to him, "Hadassah is Jewish now, would you like this? Your girls might like it." Unaware of Huguette's intentions when he brought the jewelry to the hospital, Chris later realized that he had better tell Wallace Bock, recalling, "He always got exasperated when these things happened."

As for Hadassah, she could now be the envy of almost any best-dressed room in Manhattan, dripping in diamonds after receiving eighty-seven pieces of antique jewelry valued at $667,300. The nurse called her husband and urged him to drive over to the hospital immediately to pick up the baubles. "I was afraid to carry it," recalls Daniel Peri. He worried that even just en route back to his car, somebody could "hit me on the head, take it." Back in their Brooklyn home, he waited for his wife to return; they opened up all the boxes together and gazed at the sparkling loot. Daniel Peri then hid the jewelry around the house.

Huguette loved watching Hadassah light up with a smile, overcome with gratitude. Happy days were here again in her hospital room. Why not keep the good mood going? After all, Huguette had two homes full of expensive possessions that she had not seen in years. She called Bock in June and told him that she wanted to give a Renoir to Hadassah. The lawyer recorded his blunt reaction in his monthly bill: "Told her she couldn't." Huguette still owed taxes on her previous gifts to Hadassah; this would just further pile up her indebtedness to the IRS.

Huguette nonetheless was determined to make another grand gesture. She asked Chris to bring a Stradivarius violin from her apartment to the hospital. Crafted in 1686 and known as "the Cremona," the violin was insured at $1.2 million. Fourteen years earlier, Hadassah's six-year-old son David had played a few tunes on an inexpensive violin for Huguette at the hospital. At that time, the heiress had promised him that one day she would give him a gift. But David, now twenty years old, had long since given up the instrument.

Yet Huguette decided to make good on her long-ago promise. Hadassah later insisted that she warned Huguette the instrument would not get much use: "I told Madame that he doesn't play anymore, but she insist maybe he will go back to learn again."

———

In the autumn, Huguette's health deteriorated. Hadassah wrote on October 25 that Huguette was "awake, sitting on bed, confused" and rambling out loud about the sinking of the *Titanic* and the drowning death of her cousin Walter Clark. The 1912 disaster had been one of the defining and frightening events of Huguette's life. She was filled with angst all day, imagining tragedies, fearful of being abandoned. After visiting Huguette, Dr. Singman wrote in his notes that "she was concerned that she heard that I had died in an auto accident as well as her divorced husband." Bill Gower had died in 1974 of an illness, but this imaginary figment so many decades later conveyed what a loss his death had been for Huguette.

That night, night nurse Geraldine Coffey wrote in her notes that Huguette had become "totally delusional" and fearful that there were "people in her room." As if anticipating her death, Huguette was reviewing her life. "Reminisced about older golden days, talked about her family already gone, rest in peace. Patient tried to sleep, looks very tired and worn out."

But two days later, Hadassah wrote that Huguette had bounced back: "No further episodes of confusion, patient doing great." Huguette was so relieved that she picked up the phone and called Suzanne Pierre, Chris Sattler, and Irving Kamsler to let them know that everything was fine again. Huguette's good days would continue to outnumber her bad days, but the ninety-nine-year-old was feeling her age.

She became fretful and ignored medical advice when Hadassah was off duty. Erlinda Ysit, a Filipino aide who worked weekends, would often call Hadassah at home for guidance and then pass along instructions, such as telling Huguette "to do her Central Park"—walk around the room for exercise. One night Huguette missed Hadassah so much that she wanted to call her at midnight, but Erlinda dissuaded her, insisting that the nurse was asleep. Huguette might as well have been singing the Cole Porter song to Hadassah: "Night and day, you are the one."

———

On February 9, 2006, Wallace Bock wrote to Huguette to tell her about a surprising discovery: her long-lost Degas pastel of a dancer, stolen from her apartment more than a decade ago, had been found. "Through a contact in the art world, we have now discovered a reputable collector has somehow acquired ownership of the Degas," the lawyer wrote, "and apparently has entered into a contractual agreement to donate it to a museum."

The collector was Henry Bloch, the founder of the tax preparation firm H&R Block. He lived in Mission Hills, Kansas, and had promised to bequeath the painting to the Nelson-Atkins Museum of Art in Kansas City after his death. Bloch explained that he had purchased the painting in 1993 from a well-known Manhattan dealer, Susan L. Brody, and was unaware that it had been stolen. When Brody was asked how the Degas came into her hands, she replied, "With bad information from the person who sold it." The trail had gone cold; no one was ever charged with the theft.

Huguette wanted her Degas back. Negotiations went on for several years. Even though she had reported the theft to the FBI, she had not filed an insurance claim or listed the Degas on the Art Loss Register. Bloch and his lawyers asserted that by neglecting those steps, she had abandoned the painting. Terrified as always of publicity, Huguette did not want to embark on a fight. "She was a very private person, and it would have meant a lawsuit," says Kamsler. "It would have meant the FBI taking possession of the painting and holding on to it for years as evidence. It was ultimately acknowledged as her painting."

Under a settlement, the wealthy tax maven was allowed to keep the painting on his wall at home, with the promise that it would eventually go to the Nelson-Atkins. "The day we reached an agreement with Ms. Clark was a great day for Kansas City," Bloch boasted in a statement posted on the museum's website. It was, in truth, a great day for Bloch, since he did not have to pay off Huguette and could keep the art for the remainder of his lifetime. Huguette won a small personal victory, insisting on a clause that permitted the Corcoran to borrow the Degas for exhibitions.

———

When Dr. Newman visited Huguette in April 2006, he was so concerned about her health that he wrote to her lawyer and accountant afterward. "She seems considerably more frail than a few weeks ago, lying in bed not able or willing to try to sit up, although she knew I was going to come by. Her hearing has deteriorated to the point that communication is impossible." Others insist that they could still be understood. "Madame is comfortable with my voice, she doesn't really have difficulty with my voice," Hadassah later said.

Huguette had once again regained her zest as she celebrated her hundredth birthday on June 9, 2006, with more than twenty people in her room to honor the occasion. She had been born in Paris but the decorations were as American as could be. Huguette was smitten with the animated cartoon series *SpongeBob SquarePants*, so Chris brought an oversized SpongeBob balloon with wiggly arms and legs. Huguette laughed and tapped it, sending the balloon floating around the room. "She was very quick and clever, she was joking with everybody, she was one hundred but she was saying she was twenty-one," recalls Geraldine Coffey, who had come in early even though she worked the night shift. "She was really happy. She looked great, she was the center of attention. I think she was able to blow out her candles."

———

At Woodlawn Cemetery in the Bronx, William Andrews Clark's family mausoleum was showing the ravages of time. Rodney Devine, the senator's great-great-grandson, noticed the problems with the 1896 structure during a 2007 visit. "It was really in a state of decay," recalls Devine, a retired investment analyst based in Connecticut and a descendant of Clark's oldest daughter, Mary. He discussed the problem with his younger brother, Ian, and other family members including Carla Hall, a great-great-granddaughter of the senator. His mother and his aunt Edith MacGuire, also a Clark descendant, agreed to absorb the $150,000 cost.

But any changes to the mausoleum required the permission of all of William Clark's descendants. Susan Olsen, the family liaison and resident historian at Woodlawn, offered to get in touch with them. Olsen was startled to see the name of William Clark's daughter on the list. The copper mogul had been born in 1839: who could imagine that 168 years later, his child would be still walking the earth? "That was the first time we realized Huguette was still alive," Olsen recalled. "We had no clue." Huguette had succeeded in her quest to be invisible.

Wallace Bock and Irving Kamsler told Huguette about the needed Woodlawn renovations and then broached a verboten topic: where she wanted to be buried when the time came. "We were very delicate about it," Bock recalls. Her reply: "I want to be in the mausoleum with my mother and sister." But there was a structural problem— there was no room. Huguette was adamant, repeating, "I don't care, I want to be in the mausoleum." Engineers determined that since the mausoleum was located on a hill, they could tunnel in from the back without damaging the structure. Susan Olsen, who supervised the efforts on behalf of Woodlawn, recalls, "Floor tiles were removed, a camera set down inside, which exposed that the foundation was made of brick vaults. We knew there was room for a below-ground tomb." Andrée's casket now rested on top of Anna's casket; a space could be made underneath Anna for another coffin.

But to do the work, Bock had to get permission from the Clark descendants, so he needed to ingratiate himself. When Carla Hall wrote to the lawyer and asked to visit Bellosguardo in the summer of 2007, he urged Huguette to let her do so. "This was a visit Mrs. Clark originally refused to consent to, and I convinced her that she should," Bock says. He thought that Carla seemed "to be acting as a spokesman or spokesperson for the cousins, and I thought it was important for Mrs. Clark to accommodate her." Bock wrote to Bellosguardo caretaker John Douglas to stress, "Carla Hall is, in fact, very important to us as a member of the Clark family . . . having her indebted to us cannot hurt."

———

Even now that she was over one hundred, Huguette continued to pursue one of her favorite pastimes: writing checks. She agreed to pay Dr. Singman's malpractice insurance at his request, an unusual doctor-patient arrangement, and bumped up his monthly retainer to $3,000. One day the physician began chatting with her about repairs to his country house, built in 1927, and he spontaneously threw out an invitation. "I told her, why doesn't she come with me and stay at the beach house for awhile, the two weeks, stay by the water, everything would be fine," he recalled. This was about the safest invite ever offered, since at this point Huguette had not left a hospital room for sixteen years. The physician mentioned that the paint job and home improvements were going to cost him $20,000. She promptly sent him a check for that amount. Dr. Singman later said he thought he was doing Huguette a favor by taking her money: "She felt good about it, so I wouldn't want to disappoint her."

Hadassah was facing new financial obligations as well that arose from a serious family crisis. Her oldest son, Avi, an NYU graduate who worked at Goldman Sachs, lost his position, then went into a spiral that landed him in the hospital. Huguette had known Avi since he was a child and was fond of him, paying $35,000 of his medical expenses. When Avi was about to be discharged from the hospital, the doctors insisted that someone needed to be with him for the first two weeks of home recovery. Once again, asked to choose between caring for her own child or assisting her wealthy patient, Hadassah, now a multimillionaire, made a character-revealing decision: she chose to stay with Huguette. Hadassah hired her sister-in-law Nonie Oloroso to keep Avi company. Huguette paid the $10,000 tab.

———

Fire Island is a lovely refuge from New York during the summer, and thanks to its tradition of banning cars, the beach resort has a quaint nineteenth-century feeling. Irving Kamsler and his wife, Judi, spent a relaxing weekend on the island in early September 2007. It was their last carefree interlude for years to come.

The couple had been introduced by a mutual friend at a Manhattan bar; he was divorced with two sons, she was a few years younger, a George Washington University graduate who worked in the garment industry. As Judi recalls, "I'm really into the Grateful Dead and when I met Irving, he had a beard and little round glasses and a bit of ponytail. He looked like Jerry Garcia. He was very polite, a sweet guy, had a little dog, very funny, chivalrous." The couple, who wed in 2000, became involved with a new Bronx synagogue, Shaarei Shalom. As members of the shul's "caring committee," they made home visits to elderly members of the congregation. Irving had recently been named president of the synagogue.

Returning to their Riverdale co-op from Fire Island, Irving parked the car in the garage while Judi went up ahead to the apartment. Opening the door, she was stunned to see a notice from the Nassau County District Attorney's office. The police had entered the apartment with a search warrant and her husband's computer was missing. "The super had let them in," she recalled. "I thought, oh my God, what's going on?" The notice contained a phone number to call for follow-up information. Her husband reached the district attorney's office and learned that prosecutors wanted him to come in for questioning. "I realized we needed to speak to an attorney," he says. "After we'd met with the attorney, I made arrangements to turn myself in the next day."

The charges against him: exchanging sexually explicit e-mails with underage girls in an AOL chat room. In an undercover operation called "Teen Saver," Nassau County investigators had launched a sting, pretending online to be a fifteen-year-old tease who sent out photos. Under his online tax accountant moniker IRV1040, Kamsler had eagerly responded with such comments as "mmmmm nice smile so any sexier pics?"; "have you done anal yet"; and "do you want to set a scene on here for us to imagine meeting and being together" along with other sexually charged remarks. Based solely on his comments, he was charged with endangering the welfare of minors and distributing pornography to minors.

Two weeks passed before the arrest became public. "He didn't tell me immediately," says Wallace Bock. "He told me when it made the papers." The *Riverdale Press* covered Kamsler's arraignment—he pled not guilty and was released on $20,000 bail—prominently featuring a photo of the accountant with his wife by his side. Irving had insisted to Judi that he believed that he was in an adult role-playing chat room online, and she chose to believe him. "I thought, okay, we'll get through this, he has my full support," she recalls. As for her reaction to the racy contents of her husband's messages, she says, "We met when we were both older...People have habits. He didn't try to change me, I didn't try to change him. If he was in a chat room speaking to adults, which is what it turned out to be, as long as it wasn't interfering with our lives, it didn't bother me. He wasn't acting upon it, he was just talking to people."

Kamsler resigned as president of his temple, but at the urging of Rabbi Steven Burton, the couple turned up at temple for the High Holy Day ceremonies, where they were treated like pariahs.

The accountant debated taking his chances with a trial but feared that if he lost, he would end up in jail. As he explains, "The advice that I got was that we're in a conservative county, you mention *child* and *pornography* in the same sentence...even if you can convince people that you were in an adult chat room and you never believed the person was a minor, you have so many counts against you that if you get one count, the judge will throw the book against you."

A year after his arrest, when prosecutors offered him a plea bargain in which he would receive five years probation and a $5,000 fine, the relieved Kamsler agreed to plead guilty, although he would have to register as a sex offender. After his rabbi testified as a character witness, Kamsler received a certificate of relief allowing him to continue to practice as an accountant despite the felony conviction.

———

That October 2008 was the same month that the relatives of William Andrews Clark were enthusiastically gearing up for a family reunion at the Corcoran Gallery. Organized by Carla Hall and Ian Devine, this would mark the first time that many of the descendants of William Clark's oldest children—Mary, Charles, and Katherine—had been in the same room.

In hindsight, Irving Kamsler was not the ideal choice to serve as Huguette's representative at the family affair. Wallace Bock was unable to attend the Friday night and Saturday celebrations and invited Kamsler to go instead. It was a decision the lawyer would regret. "I have an idea that if Irving had not gone, things might have played out differently," says Bock. "He got a lot of people pissed off that night." For Irving Kamsler, the reunion was something to look forward to—a respite from his legal troubles and a chance to be treated with respect.

The descendants of William Andrews Clark had never met Bock or Kamsler, but they had become very curious about the two men who represented Huguette Clark. Some family members felt frustrated that they had lost contact with Huguette, and wondered if their letters and messages were still getting through to her. The sale of Huguette's Renoir in 2003 had piqued their curiosity about how her money was being managed. Bock was the voice on the phone and the name on the letter as Huguette's chosen intermediary. The lawyer insisted that he was passing along to Huguette all communications from her family members, but they didn't know whether to believe him. Irving Kamsler was an unknown to family members, but the accountant was on the party guest list as Huguette's representative.

When Karine McCall, the great-granddaughter of William Andrews Clark, sat in front of her computer and looked up Bock and Kamsler and the stories popped up about Kamsler's criminal record, she was horrified. She had met Huguette as a child, her mother Agnes had been close to Huguette; this was family. Karine felt obligated to tell her Clark relatives about this disturbing news.

That festive night at the Corcoran would launch a titanic clash between two worlds: the privacy-obsessed Huguette and her protective inner circle, and the assertive members of the Clark family, determined to belatedly become involved in Tante Huguette's life and unafraid of a public fight. It began with an abrupt pirouette that evening as Karine threaded her way through the crowd looking for someone to confide in, and found herself artfully veering to avoid coming face-to-face with Kamsler, who had been upgraded to a seat at her table. As Karine recalls, "I wouldn't even shake his hand that night."

But even if the troubled accountant had not been in attendance, Karine would still have met the next day with Carla and Ian, relaying her concerns about whether Tante Huguette was being mistreated or exploited. During the following weeks, as the trio exchanged phone calls and e-mails, they were also getting acquainted.

After spending four decades in Europe, Karine had just moved to Washington, D.C., and she was the newcomer. Karine and her husband, cellist Donald McCall, were grappling with lingering grief over the death of their son Alex, twenty-nine, a talented artist who died of a drug overdose in 2001. The couple's return to the United States was meant to be a fresh start. A novelist and painter with a free-spirited style, Karine had grown up in San Francisco living with her mother, Agnes Albert, and her divorced maternal grandmother, Celia Tobin Clark, who detested both her ex-husband, Charles Clark, and her father-in-law, the senator.

For Carla, twelve years Karine's junior, this was also a period of transition. She was spending her free time painting landscapes and creating abstract sculptures. She was much more attached than Karine to her identity as a Clark, due to family visits to Montana dating back to her childhood, plus her father's and grandmother's experiences as members of the Corcoran's board. As a branding consultant, Carla was aware that the association of a convicted sex offender with William Andrews Clark's daughter was not positive for the family's image. Even though she had never met Huguette, she was eager to get involved.

Ian Devine knew very little about William Andrews Clark, his great-great-grandfather. "I knew the bare bones of his life," he recalls. "My parents never talked about it at any great length." As Ian became drawn into the family drama, the financial marketing consultant became hungry for information to understand his roots. "I was interested in my historical family roots, but also my extended family and getting to know them," he explained. "All these relatives I had met for the first time at the Corcoran." He would prove to be the diplomat when the two strong-willed women disagreed.

All three had grown up with wealth—some of the Clark copper fortune had trickled down—and judging by their real estate, they were all still doing quite well. Ian lived in an Upper East Side co-op and owned a second home in the Berkshires; Carla and her husband had renovated a handsome Upper West Side brownstone and also had a country house. Karine and her husband, Donald, had relocated to a spacious town house in Georgetown. Financially secure, all three insist convincingly that their original motivation in trying to contact Huguette was concern over her well-being and care.

In the months following the Corcoran reunion, the trio embarked on a flurry of activity. "This turned around my life and Ian and Carla's," says Karine. "We were obsessed about doing the right thing." After Carla and Ian tried to visit Huguette twice and were thrown out on the second trip by an angry Hadassah, they endured a contentious meeting with Wallace Bock. But by the summer of 2009, hostilities had ground to a halt. Unsure of how to proceed, the family members temporarily retreated. "We were sort of at a dead end," says Ian. Carla adds, "We were at a loss, like a sailboat in irons. We had no evidence but we had a lot of concerns. What were they doing? Why was she so isolated? Was she ill?" Wallace Bock was still trying to coordinate the construction efforts at Woodlawn Cemetery to make room for Huguette and was eager to resume good relations with the family.

So when Karine asked for permission to take her husband, daughter, and son-in-law to visit Bellosguardo in the summer of 2009, Bock convinced Huguette to authorize the trip. Karine had last been on the premises in 1989, when she had joined her mother and her brother Paul on a tour. As she walked through the grounds this time, she paid close attention to the conversational nuggets dropped by caretaker John Douglas. Karine recalled that the caretaker mentioned that he found Bock "difficult to work for as a boss." She reassured Douglas that she would praise him in a letter to the lawyer, stressing what an exemplary job he was doing taking care of the estate.

———

As much as Huguette hated to acknowledge any frailty, her sight had become so diminished that she scarcely wrote her name legibly on checks. But she put her shaky signature on a document authorizing Wallace Bock on February 2, 2009, to draw upon a promissory note at J. P. Morgan, borrowing $5 million to give to Hadassah "in recognition of her devoted care to me and friendship to me for many years." Finally—finally—she had fulfilled her promise to the nurse.

Hadassah could have quit then, and walked away. But she, in turn, fulfilled her promise to Huguette to continue to care for her and do everything possible to keep her alive. The nurse cajoled Huguette to take her medication, and was seen begging on her knees to get her obstinate patient to comply. Chris Sattler watched her curl up in bed next to Huguette and hug her, comforting her patient with the warmth of human touch. When another nurse asked Huguette if she could be of help, the heiress proudly replied, "Hadassah is my right hand, she can take care of me."

The heiress and the nurse had always been close, but now there was a visible sweetness to their relationship. Others praised Hadassah for her devotion. "Hadassah did everything to keep her healthy and motivated," recalls Marie Pompei, noting that Huguette never suffered from bed sores thanks to Hadassah's care. "Her body was in perfect condition."

At the end of 2009, Huguette turned over her Christmas gift check-writing duties to Wallace Bock. This was a momentous step. She was unusually generous that season, even telling Bock to give himself $60,000, although he had never received a holiday bonus before.

———

With efforts by her Clark relatives to pierce the veil of privacy around Tante Huguette stymied, a journalist was taking the first steps that would shatter the serenity of Huguette Clark's life. Investigative reporter Bill Dedman, of msnbc.com, was scanning upscale real estate listings when he came across a description of Huguette's New Canaan home. "I read in the zoning minutes online that her attorney said it had not been lived in for fifty years," Dedman later recalled in an e-mail exchange published in 2010 by the Poynter Institute, a journalism forum. "Then I saw an online discussion in Santa Barbara about her empty mansion there. And her father's political history was interesting. So I was hooked."

After spending several months gathering photographs and documents, and conducting interviews with Ian Devine, André Baeyens, and others, Dedman published his results online on February 26, 2010, in a forty-eight-page slideshow entitled, "The Clarks: an American story of wealth, scandal and mystery." In captions, he raised such questions about Huguette as: "Where is she? And what will become of her fortune?" By July 29, the reporter had tracked Huguette down at the hospital, and he announced on the *Today* show: "I went there and it's drab, patient names written on the board in a hallway. It couldn't be more ordinary. She wasn't sick. She made Howard Hughes look outgoing."

His stories began a media feeding frenzy. The *New York Daily News* headlined an article: A 42-ROOM EMPTY PALACE SITS ON FIFTH AVE-NUE. 104-YEAR-OLD HEIRESS HAS GORGEOUS MANSES BUT PREFERS TO BE A RECLUSE PLAYING WITH HER DOLLS. In August, Dedman, who had won a Pulitzer Prize in 1989 for a series in the *Atlanta Journal-Constitution*, published a two-part investigative series on nbc.com delving into Huguette's life and her retainers, Bock and Kamsler.

Dedman chronicled his reporting, including showing up unannounced at the apartment building of Suzanne Pierre. Afflicted with Alzheimer's, she had twenty-four-hour care. Dedman told her aide that he wanted an interview, and was admitted an hour later. ("Suzanne was easily distracted by the television and the conversation lagged.") After Irving Kamsler did not reply to Dedman's messages, the reporter turned up at the Kamslers' co-op in the Bronx and called from the doorman's station; Judi answered and hung up.

Dedman went to Beth Israel to try to see Huguette. Arriving at the third floor, Dedman asked for Huguette and a hospital employee inquired, "Who are you to her?" ("That's as far as I got," he wrote. "I wasn't going to barge into her room, and won't divulge the name of the hospital.")

The reporter took on the role of advocate in the story by listing the legal steps that a bank, Huguette's family members, or total strangers could take to investigate her affairs, such as contacting Adult Protective Services or filing a guardianship petition. He helpfully offered questions that they could put to Huguette.

Dedman wrote his stories in a tone that suggested he could not imagine Huguette reading the articles or having them read to her, referring to her as an "old lady" five times in such passages as, "Who protects an old lady who secluded herself from the world, limiting her life to a single room, playing dress-up with her dolls and watching cartoons?"

As other reporters turned up at Beth Israel, trying to get into Huguette's room, a security guard was posted outside to rebuff intruders. Her name was changed to a pseudonym, Harriet Chase, in the hospital computer system. The *New York Post* blared: NY'S HERMIT

HEIRESS & HER SAD SECRETS—CENTURY OF MYSTERIES. Huguette had spent her life trying to avoid attention, but now her divorce, her love for dolls, and her personality quirks were being dished up to a voyeuristic public. She had identified with the unassuming cricket in her favorite fable, but now she had been transformed into the colorful butterfly torn apart by the media.

Huguette's inner circle agonized and decided that the lucid 104-year-old needed to know what was being said about her. Irving Kamsler met with Huguette to tell her about the articles. "She was upset, she did not want to be in the newspapers," Kamsler recalls. He had printed out the series and believes that he left her a copy.

On August 25, the *Post* ominously reported that the Manhattan District Attorney's office had launched a criminal investigation into Huguette's welfare and fortune. The D.A.'s office had received a tip, but Dedman's stories added fuel to the fire. That same day, Gerald Gray, Huguette's great-nephew and a California social worker who specialized in treating torture victims, submitted a request to New York Adult Protective Services for an investigation. Bock and Kamsler went to the hospital to tell Huguette about the D.A.'s legal inquiry, informing her that she would have to answer questions and they would have to hire lawyers for themselves. They asked her to pay their legal fees, and she agreed to pick up the bill.

As the chief of the district attorney's elder abuse unit, Elizabeth Loewy had developed a national reputation as a champion for the elderly after winning the conviction in 2009 of Anthony Marshall for stealing from his mother, Brooke Astor, who suffered from dementia. Ever since then, Loewy had experienced a sharp jump in new cases. The Astor case encouraged more people to report suspected abuse.

After alerting hospital executives that she would be coming and brushing up on her French, Loewy went to see Huguette, bringing along a genial detective, Donald Kennedy, who had worked with her on the Astor case. She met Dr. Newman at his office, and he escorted the prosecutor and detective to Huguette's room. Hadassah was on duty, but Loewy asked the nurse and Dr. Newman to leave the room so that she could have a private conversation.

Loewy took a low-key approach, trying to first ascertain whether the hard-of-hearing centenarian was able to hold a conversation—she was—and then asking whether she was doing well. Sitting up in bed, Huguette responded thoughtfully to each question, conveying that she knew about the allegations but that she was fine and that no one had threatened her in any way. She did not appear to be confused or sad.

Even though the family was aware that the D.A. was investigating, they felt pressure to act. On September 1, Bill Dedman sent an e-mail to Gerald Gray:

> I'm told on good authority that Irving Kamsler was over at the hospital yesterday trying to get Huguette to sign a will.
>
> It's not the place of the police or the DA to, in effect, put a new regime in place to keep a convicted felon from continuing to visit her. But speaking frankly, I have to let you know that this is going on, and to ask, when will the family step up to file a guardianship petition. Is there not, at this point, more than enough smoke?
>
> I realize there's more than enough that I don't know, but this raises questions.

This email was later produced in discovery during the legal battle over Huguette's will. On Friday, September 3, Carla, Ian, and Karine filed legal papers in Manhattan requesting that a guardian be appointed to protect Huguette from potential financial abuse, the same initial step that had been taken in the Astor case. "Her mental abilities are uncertain," the petition stated, "but on information and belief as a result of her physical condition, she has limited ability to understand and manage her financial affairs..."

Wallace Bock called the trio "nothing more than officious interlopers" in his legal response and insisted that Huguette was not mentally incapacitated. A week later, Supreme Court Justice Laura Visitacion-Lewis turned down the guardianship request, ruling that the relatives were acting on "hearsay, conclusory, and speculative assertions."

Huguette was disturbed that her relatives were trying to hijack her life. "It was the first time I ever saw her angry," Chris Sattler recalls. She was convinced that her relatives were motivated by greed. "Why do they want my money?" she asked Chris. Adds Wallace Bock, "She was not the type of person who starts screaming and ranting and raving. She'd show her displeasure in her tone of voice. She might say a few harsh words like, 'What do these people want?'"

On December 9, Ian and Karine tried to visit her at the hospital. Ian called ahead to tell the hospital's legal counsel that they were en route. "There was a security guard," Ian recalls. "We said, 'We're here to see our aunt.' He knocked on the door and Hadassah Peri came out." Karine adds, "She wasn't happy to see us. I found her very confrontational. I was tongue-tied." The nurse berated them for turning up after so many years had passed, demanding, "Why are you here?" Hadassah refused to accept their flowers, but Karine insisted that she take in a note to Tante Huguette, which stressed that the family cared about her and were acting out of concern.

Elizabeth Loewy visited Huguette two more times as her investigation continued. Each time, they spoke in French and Huguette repeated that she had not been coerced by anyone. The prosecutor examined Huguette's financial and medical records and interviewed her employees and her relatives. Some of Huguette's magnanimous gifts raised the specter of undue influence. Loewy kept digging, searching to see if a crime had been committed.

———

Huguette had never been religious, but as she approached the twilight of her life, she fondly remembered the Catholic prayers that she had uttered as a child. When Marie Pompei stopped in to see the heiress, Huguette asked, "Do you know the Our Father? Would you like to sing it with me?" As Marie, a practicing Catholic, recalls, "I've got my arm around her back, she's holding my hand with her other hand, and we're singing Our Father together. See me, God? It was so lovely, so unusual."

On Marie's next visit in early 2011, Huguette teased her about how out of tune they had been. Marie suggested that Huguette come to her grandson's upcoming wedding and they could sing it together. Huguette laughed, replying, "I'm not going to make a fool of myself and you shouldn't, either." She asked questions about the wedding—asking for a description of the bride's gown and inquiring about whether the couple had planned their honeymoon yet.

If not, Huguette had a suggestion. Even now, her birthplace called to her, that romantic and beautiful city of lights where her mother and father had fallen in love, where she and Andrée had played together in the family's apartment on the Avenue Victor Hugo. With a smile that spoke of happy memories, Huguette declared: "They should go to Paris."

―――――

Chris Sattler lingered on a few extra minutes at the end of a hospital visit that winter of 2011 to express his enduring gratitude to his employer. Huguette had given him a satisfying job for twenty years, she had paid his daughters' private school tuition, and when he had health problems, she called him every day to wish him well. He did not know how much longer the 104-year-old would be alive. He leaned over by her good ear to express his thoughts. "Thank you, Mrs. Clark, for all you've done," he told her. She turned her head so she could see him clearly and replied, "No, Chris, I thank you."

That was their last conversation. Huguette suddenly came down with an acute case of pneumonia. "I had a bad feeling about it because she was so frail," recalls Mildred Velazquez, her hospital case manager. "But she told me, 'I'm going to fight this.' I said, 'You never quit, you always a fighter.' She smiled. Then the next time I went to see her she was already in the ICU, intubated... unable to respond."

Huguette lingered on in a comalike state for almost two months. Hadassah sat at her bedside, held her hands, and talked to her. Chris, Marie, and Irving made frequent visits. They hoped their familiar voices would be comforting even if Huguette could not communicate. She had refused to sign a DNR order, and now she was on a respirator with a feeding tube. Kamsler, who had been entrusted as her medical proxy, found himself arguing with hospital officials as the weeks stretched on. "They wanted to pull the plug," he says. The accountant had already been vilified in the press for his felony conviction, and he could imagine the headlines if he signed the equivalent of her death warrant. He says that he insisted Huguette's wishes be respected, even though she was unlikely to regain consciousness.

On May 24 at 3 a.m., Chris got a call from Kamsler, summoning him to the hospital. Huguette was dying. It took Chris an hour to get in from Long Island, and by then Hadassah and Dr. Singman were there, as well as other nurses who had cared for Huguette. Chris found it painful to bear witness, saying, "It's awful to watch someone die." For hours, the small group prayed and reminisced. As Kamsler recalls, "We went in and out of the room. Everyone was talking about their little memories of her and how kind she was to them." At Hadassah's insistence, a priest was called to give Huguette last rites. At 7:35 a.m., she took her last breath.

———

Wanda Styka received the news in an early-morning call from Irving Kamsler. She was grateful for his courtesy and his acknowledgment of her relationship with her godmother. Wallace Bock e-mailed Karine McCall, saying that he had sad news, and asked her to inform the rest of the family. She inquired about funeral services, and was told that Huguette had expressly asked for a private burial and no funeral.

The gates at Woodlawn Cemetery opened briefly at dawn on May 26 to admit the hearse with Huguette's casket, transported by pallbearers from the Frank E. Campbell funeral home, the discreet Upper East Side firm favored by the well-to-do. Susan Olsen, the cemetery's historian, was waiting along with the president of the cemetery and the contractor who had rebuilt the Clark mausoleum. No one else was permitted inside: not Hadassah, Chris Sattler, or any of Huguette's intimates. "High-profile funerals have to be orchestrated out of respect for family and the people you are entombing," Olsen says. "It wasn't about keeping anyone away. She led a very private life and deserved a very private funeral."

The mausoleum's bronze door, with its vision of a mysterious woman, was created more than a century earlier, but now that decorative touch seemed especially apt. In an 1897 article about the much-admired door entitled "The Vision," the *New York Times* wrote, "The face of the figure expresses the sadness of parting from family and friends, while the abundant draperies and the right hand raised to the breast furnish at once a suggestion of modesty and offer a gesture that calls attention to the person represented; in other words, it is an appeal to be remembered by the living."

For a private woman, Huguette received a very public send-off. On her death certificate, her occupation was listed as "artist." The form was filled out by Wallace Bock, who knew she cherished that identity. But this central fact of her life was not what fascinated the journalists and headline writers, who focused instead on her copper fortune and her secretive life.

The *New York Times* played Huguette's obituary on page one (HEIRESS TO THE HIGH LIFE, THEN DETERMINED RECLUSE), and the *Wall Street Journal* weighed in as well (SOCIETY GIRL WHO SPENT 8 DECADES IN SECLUSION). This curious tale was an international sensation, covered by publications from Australia's *Courier-Mail* (POOR LITTLE RICH GIRL'S SAD LIFE) to the *Scottish Express* (AMERICA'S ANTISOCIAL SOCIALITE) and Asian News International (REAL "MISS HAVISHAM").

The Clark family drama would continue to unfold, but without Huguette. The *New York Post* cut directly to the chase: MYSTERY HEIRESS DIES—$500 MILLION FORTUNE AT STAKE. It was the obvious question: what would become of Huguette's money?

Chapter Seventeen

The Battle for Huguette's Fortune

S o many famous New Yorkers are buried at Woodlawn Cemetery, from Mayor Fiorello La Guardia to newspaper baron Joseph Pulitzer to Broadway legends Irving Berlin and George M. Cohan, that caretakers offer visitors a "Hall of Fame" map. William Andrews Clark's mausoleum is not on that list, because the robber baron faded long ago to obscurity, but his daughter's death in the spring of 2011 turned the spot into a tourist destination.

In the weeks after Huguette's death, many people came to gawk, but one woman came regularly to mourn: Hadassah Peri. The nurse who had been by Huguette's side for two decades was now at loose ends without her job, and she missed her confidant. So the nurse made frequent visits to the cemetery, sometimes joined by Huguette's other nurse-turned-friend, Marie Pompei. Hadassah tucked tokens of affection such as plastic flowers and cartoon toys into the side of the grand bronze doors. She knew and remembered Huguette's interests.

But her mourning rituals were at odds with the high WASP way of death. After several Clark family members complained to cemetery officials that these gifts were tacky, Hadassah was asked to discontinue her offerings. Reprimanded, she cut back her visits to the white mausoleum.

For the cast of characters who had populated Huguette's well-compensated but invisible world, their new reality was jarring once her will was filed for probate on June 22. Suddenly, they were in the press. Hadassah became a tabloid favorite when it was revealed that she was the chief beneficiary at the expense of Huguette's relatives. FAMILY STIFFED OUT OF $400 MILLION FORTUNE, announced the *Daily News*. HEIRESS HAD ILL WILL: NURSE $34M, KIN 0, trumpeted the *New York Post*. No one knew, at that time, that Hadassah had already received $31 million from Huguette during her lifetime.

The players in this high-stakes drama chose their attorneys with care, aware that they needed to depend on—and would be judged by—the company they kept. Hadassah hired veterans from the Brooke Astor case. Prominent trusts and estate lawyer Harvey Corn had successfully handled an early legal battle for Astor's son Anthony Marshall; Corn brought in public relations man Fraser Seitel, who had been the spokesman in that case for David Rockefeller and Annette de la Renta.

With her shaky command of English, Hadassah was judged too inarticulate for prime time, although her demure demeanor might have played well before the cameras. The public relations spinning began immediately as Seitel issued a statement on Hadassah's behalf about her now deceased employer: "I am profoundly sad at her passing, awed by the generosity she has shown me and my family, and eternally grateful." This did not sound remotely like the nurse's awkward cadences and inverted sentence structure. In Seitel's release, Hadassah went on to piously vow to devote some of Huguette's money "to making the world a better place."

For Wanda Styka, the publicity surrounding being named as a beneficiary of Huguette's will was an intrusion on her rural idyll in the Berkshires. When her home phone began ringing off the hook from reporters requesting comment, she switched to an unlisted number. Instead of hiring New York legal heavyweights, she chose John Graziano, a small-town Lee, Massachusetts, lawyer who had handled her mother's estate.

As the executors of Huguette's estate, Wallace Bock and Irving Kamsler needed to hire their own legal gladiators to protect their interests, probate the will, and insure that Huguette's wishes prevailed if her will was challenged. Kamsler had previously had professional dealings with John Dadakis, of Holland and Knight, a Manhattan attorney who specialized in high-end estate planning. His firm had just won national acclaim for representing the actor Mickey Rooney in an elder abuse case. By signing on as clients, Bock and Kamsler could hope that some of that legal glow would rub off on them.

All wills filed for probate in New York State are assigned to a judge. Case 1995/1375 landed on the docket of Surrogate's Court Justice Kristin Glen, who had been the dean of City University of New York law school before being elected to the bench in 2008. With a sarcastic sense of humor and forceful persona, the judge was intimidating; lawyers tended to sit up straight in her presence. Early in her career, Glen had worked with crusading liberal lawyer Leonard Boudin on such prominent cases as the Pentagon Papers and viewed herself as an advocate for social justice. In her two and a half years on the bench so far, she had not presided over a trial. Every single case—even the most viciously litigated ones—had settled.

The Huguette M. Clark case had the potential to be the will fight of the decade: hundreds of millions up for grabs, angry disinherited relatives, a scandal-tinged accountant, a nurse whose unemployed husband drove a Bentley, a criminal investigation by the district attorney's office, and a press corps avidly following the action. An army of trained professionals would be hired to deconstruct Huguette's life, including private detectives, psychiatrists, forensic accountants, jury consultants, and PR firms hired to influence public opinion. Holland and Knight alone would employ eighty-five people to work on the case.

Justice Glen made a pivotal decision early on that shaped the battle over Huguette Clark's fortune. After ascertaining that the district attorney's office was still investigating Huguette's affairs for evidence of elder abuse, the judge decided to take protective action. Rather than allow Bock and Kamsler's chosen firm, Holland and Knight, to solely manage the estate, Glen announced that she was appointing the public administrator to jointly handle the job. The public administrator typically presides over estates when a person dies without a will. This development did not bode well for Bock and Kamsler, since it meant that Huguette's tangled finances would be scrutinized in painstaking detail by an independent agency.

On the sunny morning of August 17, 2011, when Justice Glen called the first hearing in Case 1995/1375, a dozen principal lawyers marched up to the front of the room. The penny-pinching William Andrews Clark had traveled by mules through snowstorms in the 1860s to deliver goods to mining camps; now the remnants of his fortune would pay the billable hours of these pin-striped pleaders. In the majestic high-ceilinged courtroom, with marble fireplaces, ornate carved wooden moldings, and red drapes, the lineup included lawyers representing the Corcoran Gallery, Beth Israel Hospital, and the New York State Attorney General's charity bureau, on hand to protect the designation of Bellosguardo as an arts foundation.

Nineteen Clark descendants had filed an objection to Huguette's will. Although Carla, Ian, and Karine had initially been drawn into Tante Huguette's orbit out of altruism, concerned that she was being mistreated, this family quest had morphed into a battle over her money. Clark relatives from three branches of the family, located in multiple time zones from Paris to California, were now involved.

Underscoring long-simmering frictions, two relatives, both grandchildren of the racetrack-loving Charles Clark, had not joined the legal fracas: Timothy Gray, who had been adopted into the Clark family, was so estranged from his three siblings that they did not have an address or a phone number for him. (Holland and Knight hired a private detective to find him, since Gray needed to be informed of his legal rights.) Other Clark siblings also had rocky relations with one another: Karine McCall and her sister Victoria Clare Sujata, seven years younger, had not spoken for two decades. The author of a book about a Tibetan yogi, Sujata declined to be drawn into what promised to be a bruising public probate fight.

To start unraveling Huguette's finances, Justice Glen commanded Wallace Bock and Irving Kamsler to produce Huguette's financial records dating back to 1996, including her canceled checks. After spending decades protecting Huguette's privacy, the lawyer and accountant were troubled that this information would become public. But when their lawyers asked that the files be sealed, Glen denied the request. After the 275-page volume was filed at the Surrogate's Court clerk's office at 31 Chambers Street, reporters were riveted by Huguette's outlandish spending, such as toy and doll purchases ($2.5 million to the Parisian store Au Nain Bleu, $729,000 on Theriault's doll auctions) and the $440,000 she distributed in staff bonuses on November 16, 2009. The *New York Post* was so enraptured by the high-spending Huguette that the newspaper ran two stories on November 20, 2011: ALL DOLLED UP: ECCENTRIC'S OWN TOYLAND and THE HEIRESS AND THE NURSE: HEALTH WORKER BECAME SCION'S BE$T PAL.

A team of lawyers and paralegals descended on Huguette's apartments to examine her files. They were stunned by the sheer accumulation of documents and photographs. If Huguette had not been able to store her things in forty-two rooms, she would have been in danger of rivaling the hoarding Collyer brothers. She had kept everything: 1925 receipts for a Louis XV sofa and Jacobean table, a 1928 Cartier invoice for a $320 gold cigarette case, her 1930 divorce decree, a 1942 order for French chinoiserie satin curtains, Bonwit Teller summer storage bills from 1964 for fur coats (sable, ermine, mink, fox), contractor's estimates for a 1964 kitchen renovation, a January 1968 grocery order of raspberries from Winter Market, sketches for couture clothing from Jean Patou in Paris.

There were hundreds of personal letters and telegrams, including her parents' tender 1923 love letters as well as affectionate letters and telegrams to Huguette from the important men in her life—Tadé, Bill, and Etienne. She kept notes jotted on scrap paper about TV shows she planned to tape (such as the groundbreaking PBS show about the dysfunctional Loud clan, *An American Family*) and yearly reminders of "Daddy's birthday" on January 8. She held on to ancient Christmas apartment tip lists and care labels for her Pringle of Scotland cashmere sweaters. Lawyers' letters dating back to the 1930s included accounts of an argument with her downstairs Fifth Avenue neighbor over a leak and an unsuccessful effort to buy and preserve her childhood home in Butte. It was overwhelming. Paralegals began scanning the vast detritus, the residue of a 104-year life. Eventually, more than seventy-five boxes of documents and photographs were carted out.

The Clark relatives hired a new lawyer that fall, John Morken of the Long Island firm Farrell Fritz. Born in China, the son of an evangelist Christian minister, he had an unconventional background. After dropping out of Swarthmore, he cut broccoli as a farmworker and worked in a steel mill before returning to a white-collar path, finishing at Swarthmore, attending NYU law school, and clerking for an Appellate Court judge. The Clark relatives had contributed money toward his initial retainer, but Morken had taken the case on contingency, gambling that he could win big.

Morken used colorful, outraged prose in legal papers filed on November 28 challenging Huguette's will, charging that Wallace Bock and Irving Kamsler had used "deceit, undue influence and exploitation" and "took control of her life, isolated her from her family, and ultimately stripped her of her free will, as well as millions of dollars." Much more important than the angry rhetoric was the biggest revelation so far in this case. As part of discovery, Kamsler's firm had alerted the other law firms that Huguette had signed the earlier March 7, 2005, will, under which the Clark relatives would have inherited. Morken made this information public. The Associated Press sent out a bulletin: COPPER HEIRESS SIGNED 2 WILLS IN 2 MONTHS.

———

A ticking time bomb had been buried in Huguette's finances for nearly two decades, and the inevitable detonation occurred six months after her death. Two IRS agents contacted Peter Schram, the public administrator's counsel, in November 2011 to say that they had been unable to find gift tax returns filed on Huguette's behalf. Where was the missing paperwork?

So the search began for documents that the lawyers assumed had been misfiled. John Dadakis assigned Holland and Knight staffers to examine records provided by Bock and Kamsler, but the forms did not turn up. A puzzled Dadakis called Bock, who insisted that it was Kamsler's job to prepare gift taxes. After hemming and hawing, Kamsler finally confessed that he had never filed the returns. "We were blindsided," said Dadakis. He had to alert the judge and the other lawyers that there was a huge problem with the Internal Revenue Service. The public administrator's office filed a scorching petition charging that Bock and Kamsler's tax fraud and negligence had led to a stunning $90 million tax bill, including penalties, potentially knocking Huguette's estate down to $210 million.

Justice Glen gave Bock and Kamsler a courtroom tongue-lashing on December 23, calling the two men "unfit to serve by reason of dishonesty...violation of their fiduciary obligations, waste of the estate, dishonesty with respect to authorities, violation of the rules of professional conduct, et cetera, et cetera, et cetera..." Prior to the hearing, Kamsler bowed to the inevitable and withdrew as an executor. Justice Glen made it official, suspending Kamsler as an executor as well as Bock, who continued to proclaim his innocence, even though his itemized legal bills to Huguette listed gift taxes as a responsibility.

That same day, the public administrator's counsel made another surprising announcement: he was planning to demand that Hadassah return the $5 million that she had received in 2009, since he could not find any documents showing that Huguette had authorized the cash transfer. "I can guarantee you," Schram said, "I'm not giving away any secrets, that that gift is going to be the subject of clawback proceedings." Hadassah had now been warned that instead of receiving more of Huguette's money from the will, she was in danger of losing what she already had.

For Bock and Kamsler, who had served Huguette side by side for years, the court hearing resulted in a public rift. Holland and Knight dropped Kamsler as a client while continuing to represent Bock. Bock, who had recently turned eighty, seemed stunned to find himself in the center of a legal firestorm over his work for Huguette. "I figured she would go eventually, and I'd be able to relax. Be the executor of the estate, slowly dispose of the property she had, and collect my commissions," said Bock. Did he ever imagine that this day would come, with his reputation and judgment under attack? "Not in my wildest dreams."

———

The battle for Huguette's estate was becoming a referendum on her character: Who was she, really? Huguette's state of mind was at the center of the case. Her psyche was being dissected at Surrogate's Court as each side argued for the point of view that would make their clients rich.

Attorneys for Hadassah Peri and Beth Israel Hospital insisted that Huguette was smart, well-informed, and independent, while the lawyer for her relatives, who had not seen her in decades, portrayed her as a defenseless centenarian who had been exploited by greedy caretakers. In February 2012, Clark family lawyer John Morken filed legal papers claiming that Huguette had been coerced by Hadassah, Wallace Bock, and Irving Kamsler to sign both of her 2005 wills and was "not of sound mind or memory."

This would be difficult to prove, since there was nothing in Huguette's medical records that indicated she suffered from any form of dementia or senility.

It is a time-honored tactic in a probate fight to charge that an elderly person was incompetent, but this portrayal in legal papers and the tabloids felt disrespectful to those people who had actually known Huguette well. Marie Pompei, who had nothing financially to gain, fondly remembered her final few conversations with Huguette in 2011. She vehemently insisted, "You can't tell me she was out of it."

———

Even as the legal battle lines were being drawn, Huguette's possessions—her New York real estate and her jewelry—were being liquidated. Rarely in high-end Manhattan real estate do apartments come up for sale that have been off the market for eighty-six years, so it was not surprising that Huguette's sprawling Fifth Avenue properties drew tremendous interest. IT'LL BE HUGUETTE! BROKERS LICK THEIR CHOPS OVER CITY'S BIGGEST LISTING, wrote the *New York Observer*. Mary Rutherfurd of Brown Harris Stevens, who sold Laurance Rockefeller's triplex apartment to Rupert Murdoch for $44 million in 2004, landed the listing. She began ushering potential buyers through Huguette's long-unoccupied homes in early March. The furniture had been emptied out, but the vintage wallpaper and fixtures spoke of bygone days, a home trapped in amber. "It was like going back in time one hundred years," one would-be buyer told the *New York Times*.

The Clark family descendants were given a private tour. As Carla Hall recalls, "The most fascinating thing for me was Huguette's paintings, the stained-glass windows, and the view. I thought she was a good painter." Adds Celia Gray, a Clark descendant who had flown in from California, "I was very impressed with her talent." Karine McCall was the only relative present who had been there before and remembered visiting Huguette and her lively mother, Anna, back in the 1950s, a lifetime ago. Karine recalled that every time she saw mother and daughter, the dynamics were the same. "Anna did all the talking, Huguette would sit quietly by. She was very sweet, very shy, didn't say much."

The trophy real estate listing brought in an initial $31.5 million bid for two of Huguette's apartments by the prime minister of Qatar, Sheik Hamad bin Jassim bin Jaber al-Thani. But the exclusive co-op board turned him down. Two Wall Street masters of the universe ultimately won the right to live in Huguette's treasured lairs. She had purchased her twelfth-floor aerie for $31,500 in 1955; hedge fund manager Boaz Weinstein paid $25 million for the space. Frederick Iseman, the founder of a private equity firm, bought most of her two eighth-floor apartments for $22.5 million. Now her heirs—whoever they turned out to be—would reap the rewards.

Huguette's diamonds, emeralds, and pearls, the dazzling daughter-of-a-robber-baron spoils, had been locked away in a safe deposit box at a Chase branch on the Upper East Side for more than fifty years until the estate's lawyers turned the key. To generate interest in an auction of the jewelry, Christie's devoted an entire room to the reclusive Huguette in its ground-floor Rockefeller Center headquarters. Her colorful self-portrait, wearing an artist's smock and carrying a palette, dominated the space. Photographs revealed glimpses of her long-gone public life: Parisian baby pictures, girlish photos with her sister and father, high-spirited deb years, and a vamping, laughing 1930s formal portrait in a floral gown. During the week before the auction, crowds gathered in the small space, speculating out loud about Huguette. This private woman would have been mortified that images of her life were being used to boost sale prices.

Visitors were permitted to try on her jewelry; staffers unlocked the glass cases while security guards warily stood by. Prices went Lucy-in-the-sky-with-diamonds-high during the April 17, 2012, auction. Huguette's rare pink diamond sold for $15.7 million, more than double the estimate; her twenty-carat diamond ring was bid up to $2.7 million; Huguette's pearls brought in $362,000; a ruby, emerald, and sapphire Tiffany bracelet sold for $220,000, more than four times the auction house's estimate. The entire take was $21 million. Karine McCall's daughter, Geraldine, bought a gold child's bracelet for $3,500, explaining, "I wanted a connection to her."

———

The Corcoran Gallery had been overjoyed to receive William Andrews Clark's staggering art collection upon his death in 1925, and it stood to reason that the museum would be equally delighted by Huguette's gift of a Monet *Water Lilies*. It is unheard of for an institution to turn down a painting worth an estimated $25 million.

But executives at the beleaguered Corcoran Gallery had become concerned about landing on the wrong side of history. The museum was in such financial trouble that the board was exploring a sale of its historic building in downtown Washington, including the William Andrews Clark wing. The Corcoran had been cozying up to Clark's descendants for decades. Now the accusations by family members that Huguette's will was tainted left the museum in a very uncomfortable position.

The Corcoran quietly filed a two-page document in April that was the equivalent of tossing Huguette's Monet out the fifth-floor window of Judge Glen's courtroom. So much for Irving Kamsler's prediction to Huguette that the museum would be "ecstatic" over the gift. The Corcoran's lawyers announced that they did not believe Huguette was "mentally capable" of signing the second will and accused Hadassah, Bock, and Kamsler of "moral coercion." By siding with the Clark descendants, the museum was committing financial hara-kiri. If Huguette's will was tossed out, the museum had no claim to the painting.

Hadassah's lawyer, Harvey Corn, later railed that the museum's lawyers were not prudently watching out for their own interests. "They've got a $20 million painting that they are not protecting," Corn said. "This is an institution that's going broke." He accused the Corcoran's attorneys of "doing the bidding of family members." Museum officials insisted to David Montgomery of the *Washington Post* that there was no side arrangement with the family and that the gallery had taken the step out of an obligation to respect the "true intentions" of donors. The Corcoran's legal tactic—giving up the Monet without a fight—was seen as inexplicable by other attorneys involved in the case.

———

Clawbacks entered the common vocabulary following the Bernie Madoff case, as lawyers tried to get back money from one group of people in order to give it to other victims of the Ponzi scheme. Now public administrator's counsel Peter Schram wanted to apply the same approach to Huguette's estate. After examining her financial records and the enormous sums that she had handed over to her nurses, doctors, the hospital, and her lawyer and accountant, Schram had concluded that her trusted retainers had abused her trust.

On May 22, Schram filed a phone-book-sized petition demanding the return of $44 million, with exhibits including Bock's and Kamsler's correspondence with Huguette. More than two-thirds of that sum (nearly $31 million) came from Hadassah and her family, representing every gift that Huguette had given them in the previous twenty years. Schram also asked for $2.1 million from Dr. Jack Rudick and his wife, nearly $1 million from Dr. Singman and his family, $1.1 million from night nurse Geraldine Coffey, and even $500,000 that Huguette had donated to the Corcoran. The public administrator wanted to dun Wallace Bock for the entire $1.85 million that Huguette had donated at his behest to the Israeli security system in the West Bank and force Irving Kamsler to give back $435,000.

Schram did not spare Beth Israel Hospital, heaping special scorn upon the medical facility for its avarice. "At no time did Beth Israel, its staff, or any other physician or expert conduct a neurological examination or psychiatric examination of Mrs. Clark or otherwise ensure that she possessed the capacity required to make a gift to Beth Israel." He demanded that the hospital return the $3.5 million from the sale of the Manet and $135,000 in cash donations.

Beth Israel would later respond in logic-defying fashion. Attorney Marvin Wexler, representing the hospital, pointed out that from 2002 to 2007, Huguette had "repeatedly declined" requests by Beth Israel for donations, "proving that during that time Ms. Clark knew her own mind and acted on her own will…Ms. Clark was a strong-willed individual who did nothing that she did not want to do…" In other words, the hospital now purported to be glad that she had cut them off when she did.

The public administrator's petition was a reputation-killing document. Huguette's longtime retainers were publicly transformed into rapacious villains. Hadassah was seen as Imelda Marcos in a nursing uniform. Now the rewards for the twenty years and the eighty-four-hour weeks that she had invested in Huguette could prove fool's gold. She faced the real possibility of having to give it all back: the Cartier jewelry, the Stradivarius, the six homes, and the $5 million check that had obsessed her for so long.

Forcing Hadassah to return this money would have meant an income transfer to Huguette's other heirs. Yet even though Wanda Styka stood to benefit if additional cash flowed back into the estate, she was troubled by the clawback effort. "My godmother would have been so upset," she said. "Can you imagine? She had given people gifts and now, they're supposed to give them back?"

The legal attack also underscored the shifting undercurrents and alliances in this complicated probate case. Two government agencies were involved, and at times they seemed to be acting at cross-purposes. The public administrator's office, pursuing its mandate to investigate and reconcile Huguette's finances, was busily discrediting the key players in her life: Hadassah, Wally Bock, and Irving Kamsler.

But the New York State Attorney General's office, which sent representatives to the court hearings, was charged with protecting her charitable bequest: establishing an arts foundation at Bellosguardo. If Huguette's second will was thrown out because Hadassah, Wally, and Irving were found to have used undue influence on her or behaved inappropriately, then all of Huguette's assets—including Bellosguardo—would go to her family members.

———

The summer of 2012 was when the case moved from legal posturing to flesh-and-blood witnesses. Closed-door depositions were scheduled for fifty-five witnesses, who would be grilled for as long as three days each about their relationship with Huguette Clark. That number had been whittled down from initial requests for 167 witnesses. For a recluse, Huguette had accumulated a lot of acquaintances.

As is standard practice, Hadassah was prepared in advance for her deposition by her lawyers, but she still stumbled over her lines. Wearing a purple jacket over a crisp white blouse and black pants, the nurse kept protesting that she had never demanded anything: "Madame is very generous, and we don't force her to give us—we don't ask for it, she just know our life." Periodically, she would wail, "I give my life for her." Asked inconvenient questions—such as did she call Wallace Bock and ask for her $5 million when Huguette was deathly ill—Hadassah experienced memory failure. She was inadvertently comic when she complained about her husband's disastrous purchase of a Bentley, using Huguette's money. She advised the lawyers, "So expensive to repair...Any one of you guys to buy this, forget it. It is hell."

These were confrontational sessions as rival lawyers constantly interrupted and scolded one another. Irving Kamsler was nervous when he arrived for his deposition at the Lexington Avenue office of Morken's firm, but his blood pressure jumped when he encountered Carla and Ian, who had come to watch him testify. "I'm trying to be as relaxed as I can under the circumstances and they're staring me down," he recalls. "Ian was sitting there with a smirk on his face." The air-conditioning was not working on this hot day and Kamsler began to sweat, drops rolling down his face. It was Ian who felt compassion and ran out to buy a fan to cool the room down. That was a rare break in an acrimonious day as Kamsler repeatedly took the Fifth Amendment when asked why he had not filed gift taxes for Huguette.

Wallace Bock had an even more extreme reaction to the stress. After his first grueling day of being deposed, he went to the hospital for a long-scheduled knee replacement. Right after that surgery, Bock had a major heart attack and ended up having triple bypass surgery, delaying his return to the witness chair for several months.

During their depositions, the Beth Israel team went to great pains to defend their reputations. Dr. Robert Newman, the president of Beth Israel, insisted that he had been unaware that doctors and nurses at his hospital had accepted hundreds of thousands of dollars from Huguette. But he admitted that gift giving happens: "I believe it probably is done. I think it would be an absurdity to claim that it is never done."

Following the philosophy that the best defense is a good offense, Dr. Jack Rudick used his time in the witness chair to attack the Clark family descendants, claiming that Huguette had felt abandoned by them. "She just said she had no contact with them," he said. "She was very resentful of the fact that none of them had deigned to see her or to contact her . . . She was very upset by that."

For Huguette's relatives, the underlying question during their depositions boiled down to one sentence: where had they been all these years?

"I expected it to be adversarial but it was more so than I expected," Ian Devine says. "It was mentally challenging, these two guys were trying to catch me in everything. 'Did you invite your aunt to your high school graduation? You're a horrible person. Did you invite her to your wedding?' 'No.'"

But both Ian and his brother Rodney had written to Huguette in the 1970s and '80s asking to meet her, and she had kept those notes. Huguette's packrat tendencies served the relatives well, offering tangible proof that her family members had tried intermittently to stay in touch. Huguette had held on to everything: invitations to Carla's 1977 wedding, a 1990s London book party for Karine, and the wedding of Karine's daughter, Geraldine; Christmas cards from a half dozen family members; and numerous letters from Karine's mother, Agnes Albert.

Only a handful of the Clark relatives had ever met Huguette, and their memories were sepia toned. In his deposition, Huguette's great-nephew Gerald Gray recalled spending time on the beach at Bellosguardo with Huguette when he was about nine years old in the mid-1940s. "We were sitting on the sand, maybe very low beach chairs," testified Gray. "She sat behind her mother and didn't participate in the conversation at all... Never said a word. Just stared at me." He recalled that his mother said afterward, "It's so sad that all she can do is play with dolls."

That sole recollection did not stop Gray from issuing a diagnosis of her mental health, based on what he had since read and heard. "Huguette has a schizoid paranoid disorder, possibly complicated later by paranoid ideation, so that she could not have chosen to be private," he said with total confidence about a woman he had last seen as a child. "She was compelled by mental illness to isolate herself." Gray acknowledged that he had never tried to contact Huguette during her lifetime.

But the family depositions proved to be a sideshow to the main event. As multiple witnesses each relived that fateful day when Huguette signed her second will, the accounts resembled an extremely off-key version of "Yes, I Remember It Well" from *Gigi*. Bock, Kamsler, and Lewis Siegel offered their recollections about that day while the other key witnesses—Bock's secretary, Danita Rudisill, and nurse Steven Pyram—gave conflicting testimony. A trial would center on deciphering the extremely hazy events that occurred on that spring afternoon in 2005. Who had actually been in Huguette's room? Had undue influence occurred? Did the heiress read her will, and did she understand the provisions? All these facts were in dispute, which caused major headaches for the beneficiaries of Huguette's will.

"What should have been a basic ministerial act was a huge problem. It was botched," says John Graziano, Wanda's lawyer. "And that became my biggest concern. You don't bring your secretary and grab a nurse off the floor to witness a will you suspect will be challenged." Harvey Corn, Hadassah's lawyer, worried out loud that the wealthy nurse was "a hostage" to the signing ceremony.

If Huguette's will was flawed, however, so were the claims of the Clark relatives. At least that seemed to be the opinion of Justice Glen. She was retiring at the end of 2012 and would not be trying the case, which left her even more free than usual to speak her mind. At a hearing on September 7, when a lawyer for Holland and Knight, the firm representing Bock, demanded to know what evidence the Clark relatives had to prove Huguette was incompetent, the justice interjected with a cynical answer. "I think the way it generally happens here is somebody says, 'Oh my God, my relative died with a lot of money and I didn't get any,'" Glen said. "Goes to see a lawyer and a lawyer says, 'Do you think it's possible that she didn't have capacity or it was the subject of undue influence?' 'Well, it must have been, because I am her relative and why would she leave money to the nurse and not to me?'"

Justice Glen also appeared unimpressed with the arguments painting Beth Israel as unscrupulous in soliciting gifts. "I think it's pretty clear that Beth Israel was a minor player here in terms of how this will turned out," she said, adding a few minutes later, "And, you know, all not-for-profit institutions have their hands out. They have to have their hands out."

————

Settlement talks occurred sporadically as the case dragged on, but all sides were so far apart that the conversations amounted to the equivalent of posturing on Capitol Hill. John Morken took an aggressive stance early on, insisting in a meeting on November 12, 2012, that the Clark relatives should receive 75 percent of Huguette's estate. In a follow-up session a month later, he stated that he wanted Bellosguardo to be sold, with the expected $100 million in proceeds put into a charitable foundation that would include family members on the board.

The protectors of Bellosguardo, Carl Distefano and Jason Lilien of the Attorney General's office charity bureau, rejected that money grab out of hand. They did not offer an alternate proposal. So no settlement talks occurred for months on end, even as the legal bills mounted into the millions.

The Attorney General's office was used to dealing with high-profile cases: Lilien and Distefano had helped settle the complex Brooke Astor probate estate, but this time around the public-service veterans were in an odd position. They would either have to choose a side in a courtroom battle or find a way to broker a settlement. Picking a side meant coming to a conclusion about whether Huguette had the mental capacity to sign her second will, or backing the argument made by the Clark family and the Corcoran Gallery that she had been coerced.

After spending a decade as a corporate lawyer at the New York firm Weil, Gotshal, and Manges, Lilien had joined the AG's office in 2008. He had an understanding of Manhattan politics after working pro bono for five years on the creation of the National September 11 Memorial and Museum. His colleague Distefano, who had worked in the AG's office since 2000, was an NYU law school grad who had clerked at the Appellate Court and was familiar with the nuances of estate and trust law.

For information on the heiress's state of mind, they sought out Elizabeth Loewy, the assistant district attorney who had met with Huguette three times in the fall of 2010. Loewy informed the lawyers from the Attorney General's office that the elderly heiress had been able to answer questions and insisted that no one had forced her to do anything. Loewy's eyewitness account made a strong impression. Loewy had put aside the elder abuse investigation of Huguette Clark's finances, since the findings had not merited a criminal indictment.

The only thing all sides appeared to agree on: Wanda Styka had been genuinely close to her godmother and deserved a bequest. But how much? Huguette had not left Wanda a specific amount, but rather a percentage of the residue, difficult to calculate under the circumstances. Her lawyer, John Graziano, was offended when the paltry sum of $1 million was suggested at a settlement conference. As he recalls, "I got tired of everyone telling me how wonderful

Wanda was, and then in the next sentence, offering far less than she deserved."

———

After a delay of several months following Justice Glen's retirement, the Clark case was transferred to Justice Nora Anderson. She set a trial date for September 17, 2013. All the lawyers publicly claimed that they did not want a costly trial that could eat up Huguette's assets, but no one wanted to give any ground. Summer vacations were canceled at law firms as the billable hours soared.

In Santa Barbara, the voluble former mayor Sheila Lodge had organized a group, Friends of Bellosguardo, to protest the Clark family's efforts to block Huguette's will. Current mayor Helene Schneider had joined her in a press conference to send a message that the city would not quietly stand by. In 2011, Holland and Knight, the firm that Bock had hired to probate the estate, had filed papers creating the foundation. But now in August 2013, officers were named: Sheila Lodge and James Hurley, a Santa Barbara lawyer who had handled California legal matters for Huguette. They promptly demanded a seat at the table in New York in any settlement negotiations or trial.

Just maintaining the twenty-three-acre estate had cost Huguette nearly $1 million per year. The aging plumbing and electrical systems had never been updated. Ample funds would be needed to keep it going as a foundation, much more than Huguette had provided for in her will. The local officials insisted that they could raise the money. Jason Lilien of the Attorney General's office flew out to Santa Barbara in August to meet with the current and former mayors and tour Bellosguardo. "It had a *Downton Abbey* feel," he recalls. "It was a home of remarkable taste and character which was exceptionally well-preserved." After seeing the caretaker's cottage and Huguette's separate beach house and stretch of private beach at Bellosguardo, Lilien theorized that if necessary, these properties could be sold, with the cash used to underwrite the foundation. He came away with the strong sense that a settlement could be structured that would save Bellosguardo, pay off the IRS obligations, and still leave enough cash to divide up among the warring parties.

But time was running out. On August 9, Justice Anderson declined a summary judgment motion that would have allowed Wallace Bock's lawyers to admit Huguette's will to probate and avoid a trial. She made it abundantly clear in her decision that she had real concerns about the validity of Huguette's April 2005 will signing. The justice noted that there were "myriad disputed facts" and spent several pages citing all the conflicting testimony.

Large probate cases almost always settle. Yet this legal behemoth seemed to be moving inexorably toward a jury trial. Finally forced to take a position, the Attorney General's office filed a document on August 22 in support of Huguette's will. Jason Lilien and Carl Distefano had decided that they believed that she had not been coerced, and that her will (creating Bellosguardo as a foundation and giving 60 percent of the residue to Hadassah) represented her true wishes. They sided against Huguette's relatives.

Meanwhile, both sides hired jury consultants in late August to conduct mock trials in front of focus groups. The pricy rehearsals would allow the lawyers to figure out the weak spots in their cases and how best to pounce on their adversaries. Would jurors find the hardworking Hadassah admirable, or greedy? Would Irving Kamsler's felony conviction as an Internet sex predator destroy his credibility on issues involving Huguette? Did the Clark relatives come across as sympathetic or johnny-come-latelys, interested in Huguette only for her money?

Even though Wallace Bock was no longer an executor of Huguette's estate, the firm that he had hired, Holland and Knight, had continued to take on the role of defending her 2005 will. "We felt we had an obligation to make sure that her wishes to create the Bellosguardo Foundation were carried out," said John Dadakis of Holland and Knight. The firm convened three sets of twelve-person focus groups. Participants were given detailed statements presenting both sides of the case. The lawyers needed to vehemently argue the facts both ways; otherwise, the exercise would be a waste of money.

The reactions of these would-be jurors varied so wildly that it seemed impossible to predict a likely verdict. The first focus group upheld the will. The second group wanted to toss it out. The third group was informed that they could uphold Huguette's will but pick and choose who would inherit—as a real jury could do. This group voted to back Huguette's will, as long as Hadassah, Wallace Bock, and Irving Kamsler received absolutely nothing. If that happened, Wanda and Bellosguardo would be the chief beneficiaries.

The demographics and income levels of jurors are a factor in any trial, but the reactions to Hadassah were so intense that all expectations were reversed. The working assumption was that blue-collar workers would relate to the hardworking nurse, believing that she had been rightly rewarded for her devotion. Instead, the lower-income focus group members distrusted Hadassah based on the absurd quantities of cash and possessions that she had already received.

"To me that was surprising," says John Graziano, Wanda's lawyer. "It runs contrary to conventional wisdom." John Dadakis, of Holland and Knight, added, "We thought the jurors with her similar background would have an affinity for her. But it was the college-educated people who believed our case." Indeed, the affluent could appreciate the pleasures of disinheriting relatives and rewarding loyal staffers.

John Morken, representing the Clark relatives, had also conducted focus groups out on Long Island, and he claimed that the results were favorable to his cause. He had kept a tight leash on his clients, urging them not to return calls from reporters, but on September 6, 2013, he arranged for me to meet with Ian Devine, Carla Hall, and Karine McCall in his office along with public relations representative Chris Giglio. Our understanding was that the family's remarks would be embargoed for use until after the case was resolved.

For nearly three hours, Carla, Ian, and Karine poured out their tales of the past few years, finishing each other's sentences at times as if prepped and interrupting at other moments to add details. Five years ago, they had suspected that something had gone wrong with Tante Huguette's life, and now they felt vindicated after learning about the $90 million gift tax debacle and the public administrator's claim that Hadassah, Bock, Kamsler, and the Beth Israel doctors had abused Huguette's trust. "For me, this isn't about money, it's about values," Ian insisted. "This is a family member, whatever her vulnerability and emotional state, she was taken advantage of big time."

Karine, who had initially launched the family's investigation in 2008, added, "It made such a vivid impression, looking into those horrifying charges."

Carla talked enthusiastically about a small fund the family members had created to fight elder abuse, contributing $90,000 to be used for educational grants. If they won the case, they planned to put in additional funds. "We wanted to rally around something positive," she said. "We're self-made, we're interested philanthropists, we have causes we're all interested in, but this has bonded us as a family." With a trial scheduled to start in eleven days, the trio were optimistic about their prospects, but still hoping for a last-minute settlement to avert an ugly public fight.

Media outlets had been clamoring for on-the-record interviews with the Clark family members, and they had scheduled a session with Anemona Hartocollis, the *New York Times* reporter who had been covering the case. But John Morken had second thoughts about being perceived as trying his case in the press, and he canceled the family interview. The reporter went ahead with her story, THE TWO WILLS OF THE HEIRESS HUGUETTE CLARK, on September 13, four days before jury selection was scheduled to start.

Any hopes that the family had of being perceived as the protectors of Huguette's legacy vanished with the article, which painted them as opportunists. "I was very upset," says Carla, with good reason. Dripping with sarcasm, the opening few graphs presented an unflattering portrayal of Carla, noting that she lived "an easy taxi ride or a meandering walk through Central Park from Mrs. Clark...but she never tried to meet her." Hartocollis stated that "huge amounts of energy have been spent establishing whether each of the 19 living relatives contesting the second will had ever met or spoken to Mrs. Clark, and if so, when and for how long. The answers are sometimes comical." The underlying message of the article: these people do not deserve Huguette Clark's money. If public opinion mattered in this case, the story had just tipped the balance.

———

There is nothing like a hanging to concentrate the mind. Even as the *Times* story was going to press, settlement talks finally moved into high gear. After learning about the all-over-the-map responses of the Holland and Knight focus groups, Jason Lilien and Carl Distefano of the Attorney General's office did not want to chance a trial and the possibility of a winner-take-all verdict for the Clark relatives. So they took the lead in brokering a settlement.

After a dozen attorneys—representing Hadassah, the Corcoran Gallery, Wallace Bock, and Irving Kamsler—argued with one another in Holland and Knight's conference room in a Fifty-Second Street office tower, Jason Lilien opted to divide and conquer. On September 11, he called John Morken and asked to meet him at the Bryant Park branch of Le Pain Quotidien, a noisy café right across from the New York Public Library. Lilien sketched out his plan, insisting that Bellosguardo be preserved as a foundation but holding out the offer that there would be enough money left to satisfy the family. Then with Lilien as the negotiator and his colleague Distefano as the expert in the minutiae of estate law, they held separate meetings with the rest of the players. Sensing progress, they convinced Justice Anderson to delay the start of the case for two days.

As is so often the case in settling high-stakes estates, Huguette Clark's wishes steadily moved from the center of the case to a secondary concern. Even though the Attorney General's office now supported the validity of her second will—which shut out the Clark relatives in favor of Hadassah and Wanda and the creation of the Bellosguardo Foundation—many provisions that reflected Huguette's desires had to be abandoned in the quest for a settlement. The legal negotiations now pivoted around the $41 million clawback petition, the financial demands of the disinherited Clark relatives, the debt to the IRS, and the escalating legal fees.

Huguette's lawyer, Wallace Bock, and her accountant, Irving Kamsler, agreed to give up the $500,000 each they had been promised in Huguette's will. In exchange, the clawbacks against them were dropped, and the estate agreed not to sue them for matters such as malpractice. Holland and Knight, the law firm that represented Bock, was paid $11.5 million in legal fees by Huguette's estate.

Hadassah had become terrified of losing the entire $31 million given to her by Huguette. The nurse's lawyer, Harvey Corn, had been insisting in negotiations that she get at least $1 million from Huguette's will, to burnish her reputation. Moreover, for symbolic reasons, Hadassah really wanted Huguette's antique doll collection. Using the threat of the clawback petition, the Attorney General's office forced Hadassah to settle. The nurse grudgingly agreed to return the $5 million that she had spent nine years badgering Madame to pay her. Hadassah also abandoned her claim to the dolls. But the nurse was allowed to keep the rest of the $26 million that she had received before Huguette's death. Her legal bills would be paid for by Huguette's estate; Harvey Corn and his firm received $1.5 million.

The Corcoran Gallery's lawyers came in with high expectations, demanding either the *Water Lilies* or a check for $25 million. But they had lost their leverage by claiming eighteen months earlier that Huguette's will was tainted. The Attorney General's office gave the museum a take-it-or-leave-it $10 million offer. The Corcoran took it. There was a sweetener: if the painting sells at auction for more than $25 million, the museum will get 50 percent of the additional proceeds.

The financially troubled Corcoran announced, several months after the Clark settlement, that it was merging with the National Gallery of Art and George Washington University. The National Gallery planned to acquire 50 percent of the Corcoran's collection, with the rest distributed to other museums. The fate of William Andrews Clark's artworks was uncertain.

Wanda had sent the message through her attorney that what she cared about was abiding by her godmother's desires and that she wasn't in this for the money. The Attorney General's office took Wanda, virtually the only selfless player in this entire drama, at her word. She settled for $3.5 million plus attorneys' fees. "Given the IRS bills and the legal bills, we were afraid we'd win at trial but there would have been nothing left for her or to support Bellosguardo," said her lawyer, John Graziano. Wanda herself was sanguine, saying, "I am so relieved that Bellosguardo will be saved."

The winners in this free-for-all, beyond the lawyers, were the Clark relatives, those blood relations whom Huguette had pointedly cut out of her April 2005 will. Not only did they receive $34.5 million, but John Morken and his firm were awarded $11.5 million in attorneys' fees. The family planned to divide the money along generational lines: the great-nieces and great-nephews such as Karine McCall and her brother, Paul Albert, would receive $2 million each, and the great-greats such as Carla Hall and Ian Devine would get roughly $1 million each. Since the missing Clark relative, Timothy Gray, had died in the course of the litigation, his share would go to his siblings.

Huguette's specific requests—to Chris Sattler, the caretakers at Bellosguardo and her New Canaan estate, Dr. Singman ($100,000), and Beth Israel ($1 million)—were honored under the settlement. But there was a twist: the clawback petition remained in place against Beth Israel, Dr. Singman, Dr. Rudick, and Huguette's night nurse, Geraldine Coffey. Just because the hospital and Singman were slated to receive money from the estate under the settlement, they were not off the hook.

The Clark family's lawyer, John Morken, remained angry that Beth Israel had never tried to address Huguette's psychological issues. "If they had treated her properly, she would have been able to go home and enjoy the last twenty years of her life," he fumed. "This was a reputable hospital that should have been taking care of people rather than exploiting someone who was dependent."

In a coordinated legal maneuver, the public administrator subsequently withdrew the clawback petititon and, on behalf of Huguette's estate, Morken sued Beth Israel, Dr. Singman, Dr. Rudick, and Geraldine Coffey for $105 million in damages. Geraldine Coffey countersued, claiming that she had been promised a bequest by Huguette and should receive money from the heiress's estate, not give it back. A trial date was set for the end of 2014. If any financial settlement comes out of that lawsuit, the proceeds will be divided up three ways: the family members will receive 50 percent, and Bellosguardo and the Corcoran Gallery will each receive 25 percent.

Make no mistake, the attorneys' fees in the Huguette M. Clark probate battle were obscene: the lawyers who lucked into this case were awarded nearly $40 million of her money. But a trial would have sent the meters for billable hours racing into overdrive. "It was a victory for charity," Jason Lilien insisted. "Bellosguardo was created as an arts foundation, and the family received much less than they were seeking."

There was one last dramatic turn left in the case. The negotiations orchestrated by the Attorney General's office had not been wrapped up by the time that jury selection was scheduled to start on Thursday morning, September 19, The largest remaining problem: the Santa Barbara members of the self-named Bellosguardo Foundation were still demanding to be involved. So at 10 a.m., the full squadron of lawyers gathered at a large courthouse room at 60 Centre Street to interview potential jurors. Hadassah arrived wearing an expensive-looking quilted black hunting jacket, skirt, and jaunty scarf, looking as if she'd had a makeover. With a flattering haircut framing her face, she smiled shyly at everyone in the vicinity. Paul Albert, Karine's older brother, had flown in from California for the occasion to see the action firsthand.

For an hour, the lawyers questioned potential jurors about what they knew about Huguette Clark, and whether they would be willing to spend two months or longer at a trial. But the larger message was how damaging the *New York Times* story had been to the Clark family's position. As a middle-class professional Asian man freely admitted, he thought they didn't deserve any money. "She had relatives she hadn't seen who showed up," he said. "Her second will gave a lot to the people around her and her caretakers. I have a bias toward the second will." If the case had gone to trial, perhaps the family would not have made out so well after all.

Suddenly, there was a flurry of activity in the courtroom. The lawyers had received an e-mail from Justice Anderson's clerk, saying that she was about to rule on whether the newly formed Bellosguardo group had legal standing. After turning that group down, the judge agreed to suspend jury selection to allow a few more days for negotiations. Around midnight on Friday, September 20, the *Times* broke the story that a tentative settlement had been reached. The following Tuesday, the lawyers marched before Justice Anderson to present the done deal. The battle over Huguette's fortune was over.

The Clark relatives were jubilant. "Someone tried to take advantage of someone in our family and we stood up to it," Karine said. "I'm so glad we did that." Added Carla, "We came together, this choreography brought us together to become a cohesive family that we never knew we had." They were eager to frame the settlement as a victory for a larger cause rather than financial gain. "We achieved everything we wanted to achieve, we got those guys removed," said Ian, referring to Wallace Bock and Irving Kamsler. Ian, who had been chosen as the family representative to the Bellosguardo Foundation, added, "Hopefully, this whole matter will draw more attention to the issue of elder abuse, which is a serious problem in our country."

In truth, elder abuse had almost nothing to do with the resolution of the last will and testament of Huguette Marcelle Clark. There was no legal finding that anyone had preyed on Tante Huguette. Although even the Attorney General's office believed that Huguette's second will reflected her wishes, nonetheless it might not have stood up during a protracted court fight due to the problematic signing ceremony. In that sense, Wallace Bock won the family's victory for them.

When I interviewed him after the settlement, Bock was relieved that he did not have to make restitution to the estate. "I thank God it's over," says Bock. "To me the most important thing is that I've gotten out clean. I don't have to worry about money I'm losing, money I'm gaining. It's over." Aware of the Clark relatives' enmity, he was equally vitriolic toward them. "I think they're pretty low," Bock said. "They jumped on the bandwagon. They didn't give a damn about her for all these years, then it's all about how much they loved her and want her fortune."

How would Huguette have reacted to the way her millions were parceled out by these lawyers, total strangers who did not know her?

Unlike her money-mad father, who was obsessed with building and preserving his fortune down to quibbling over a lost penny in a gumball machine, Huguette had never cared about her inheritance. She enjoyed living well and was adept at using her money to get what she wanted. But the woman who refused to acknowledge her own mortality never appeared to be concerned about what would happen to her fortune once she was gone. Viewing her inheritance as a mixed blessing, she was forever haunted by the fear implanted by her father that people cared about her only for her fortune. Money, love, and insecurity were forever intertwined.

For forty-two years, dating from her mother's death in 1963 until 2005, she had been told repeatedly by lawyers that if she did nothing, the money would go to her distant Clark relatives. Huguette was a healthy fifty-seven years old when the question was first raised and declined to write a new will. Maybe she felt a connection to these blood relatives, maybe she resented them for ancient grudges, but either way, she knew they stood to inherit and did nothing to stop it.

Only when she was nearly ninety-nine years old, frail and recovering from pneumonia, pressured by virtually everyone in her life, did Huguette finally sign two new wills. And even in the first version of her last testament, her relatives would still have inherited. So it's hard to believe that Huguette would have been terribly bothered by the final outcome in a Manhattan courtroom in 2013, as lawyers divided up the fortune amassed by her father, who was born in 1839.

Huguette loved Hadassah but she had already elevated the nurse to the upper 1 percent of the wealthy. Their relationship over the decades had been a study in mutual manipulation and codependency that has the making of a Tony Award–winning two-hander. Exposed to the light of public scrutiny, their transactional cash-for-affection bond was unappealing to the outside world, but the two women had unequivocally each gotten what they wanted. They mirrored each other and saw what they needed to see.

Born into a moneyed and cosseted existence, Huguette had never felt comfortable with that stultifying world and rebelled against some of the rituals. Rejecting the splendors of Fifth Avenue for a stark hospital room was in keeping with many of her other idiosyncratic life decisions. Belonging to society was important to her parvenu parents, and she honored their spirit each year by retaining her membership in the *Social Register*, but she never wanted to spend her time with Rockefellers, Vanderbilts, and Astors. Rather than lunch at the Colony Club and the Knickerbocker, vacation in Palm Beach, and grace the side of an equally moneyed spouse, she chose solitude and art for most of her adult life.

Bellosguardo mattered to her. For thirty years, she spent her happiest times there. Even when she stopped going west, she could imagine sitting in her studio and painting while gazing out the window at the rosebush that Tadé Styka had bought for her. She could picture her father dozing on a lawn chair overlooking the Pacific, recall the sound of her mother's harp echoing down the halls and the bracing tang of salt water while skinny-dipping in the ocean on a hot afternoon.

She didn't want the place to change, ever. And now she had passed that gift on to others. Artists could be inspired in the future by this serene spot that had given her such joy. Bellosguardo would not fall into the hands of a Russian oligarch or a Chinese billionaire. Huguette had now become William Wordsworth's "phantom of delight"— "a dancing shape, an image gay, to haunt, to startle, and waylay"—and her spirit would forever grace the premises.

———

Chris Sattler had not yet heard about the probate settlement when I called for his reaction, so I had the pleasure of telling him that he would receive $500,000. "Oh, dear God, I'm stunned," he said. "I didn't think it would happen. That's such good news. I have to go tell my wife." A few days later, we spoke again. He had been thinking back to his last few days in Huguette's apartment, before he had been let go in the summer of 2011. He had walked through the cavernous rooms, recalling two decades of listening to Huguette's tales. "I was thinking about how lucky I had been, how fortuitous that we had been put together. I got to meet a very special person from a different epoch."

Huguette had given him photographs to go along with her stories: escaping with her family from France in 1914 on the USS *Tennessee*, surfing with Duke Kahanamoku in Hawaii, picnicking with her mother at the Grand Canyon. Chris had hung the framed pictures in the upstairs family room at his Long Beach home, a tribute to her unique twentieth-century history.

He ended his tour of 907 Fifth Avenue in the twelfth-floor wood-paneled Japanese room, gazing at a picture that Huguette had painted of a geisha smoking an opium pipe, with an inscrutable look on her face. It haunted him. Every detail was perfect, even the ashes on the geisha's hands. It made him wonder what the ethereal Huguette had been thinking and feeling when she painted it. For a woman who seemed so sheltered, Huguette's fascination with the floating world of prewar Tokyo illustrated the complexities lurking within. "She was supposed to be unworldly," he concluded. "But she had so much more knowledge of the real world than people gave her credit for."

As Sattler exited the apartment, he locked the door as he had countless times before, but this time it was different. Madame would never be coming home, and as the deadbolt clicked shut, it bid farewell to a woman who had lived through an era and a lifestyle that no one would ever experience again.

Acknowledgments

When Huguette Clark's obituary appeared on page one of the *New York Times* on May 25, 2011, the executives at Grand Central Publishing—publisher Jamie Raab, editor in chief Deb Futter, and executive editor John Brodie—were so intrigued by Huguette's life that they wanted to know more. Since my first book, *Mrs. Astor Regrets*, centered on the final years of another memorable *Social Register* centenarian, Brooke Astor, they thought of me for this book project. I am very grateful to the three of them for sending me off on an absorbing three-year quest to understand the reclusive, talented, and much-misunderstood Huguette Clark.

As he shepherded this idea into a manuscript, John Brodie has been the dream editor, very supportive and a pleasure to work with. His astute suggestions and advice have made the book so much better. I am grateful to unflappable production editor Carolyn Kurek and savvy senior publicist Caitlin Mulrooney-Lysky for their efforts on my behalf. Also, the efforts of copy editor Mark Steven Long, vetting attorney John Pelosi, and Karen Andrews, Grand Central's senior VP for legal and business affairs, were much appreciated.

I want to thank my agent, Gail Hochman, for her friendship, encouragement, and rapid-fire skill as a negotiator. This was a whirlwind experience from phone call to contract: within weeks I was on a plane to Butte to learn about Huguette's copper-baron father, Sen. William Andrews Clark.

I appreciate everyone who took the time to speak with me. But two people—both close to Huguette Clark—made all the difference in the world, granting me exclusive interviews. Wanda Styka, Huguette's goddaughter, not only discussed in multiple conversations her half-century relationship with Huguette, but spent weeks searching through file cabinets of archival materials from her father, Tadé Styka, who was Huguette's painting teacher and confidant. Wanda found letters, journal entries, and appointment calendars chock-full of information about Huguette, and even translated her father's Polish notes into English on my behalf.

Christopher Sattler, who was Huguette's assistant for twenty years, proved an invaluable source of anecdotes and observations. He spoke to Huguette five days a week; she told him stories about her past. Like Wanda, Chris cared deeply about Huguette, and his memories convey her intelligence, her unwavering passion for perfection, and her thoughtful personality.

Several other people believed in this book early on and were enormously helpful but requested anonymity. I send along my heartfelt thanks for your guidance and friendship.

My book is both a biography of Huguette Clark and the story of the high-stakes fight over her $300 million fortune. I was able to talk to virtually all the key players in this legal battle, and I have tried to explain how Huguette's unusual life choices and complicated relationships led to this public drama. Huguette's embattled accountant, Irving Kamsler, who worked for her for thirty-two years, gave me six hours of exclusive interviews, and Huguette's lawyer, Wallace Bock, who spent twenty-four years on retainer, also spoke to me at length on the record. On the other side of this fight, six of the Clark family members who sued to remove Wallace Bock and Irving Kamsler as executors of Huguette's will granted me interviews. I am especially grateful to the three Clark relatives—Ian Devine, Carla Hall, and Karine McCall—who discussed their lawsuit and family history in several on-the-record sessions.

The lawyers involved in the probate court fight were exceptionally patient with my endless questions. Thanks in alphabetical order to Harvey Corn, John Dadakis, Carl Distefano, John Graziano, Thomas LeViness, Jason Lilien, John Morken, and Peter Schram. I am also grateful to Irving Kamsler's lawyers Marci Goldstein and Robert Giacovas.

Kati Despretz Cruz, the granddaughter of Huguette's closest friend, Suzanne Pierre, offered a wealth of information. The Lyle family—Gordon Lyle Jr.; his sister, Tina Harrower; and his daughter, Lucy Tower—summoned up decades of recollections of Huguette and her mother, Anna. Roberto Socas, whose mother was Huguette's tutor, shared memories and a trove of photographs of the Clark family.

Special thanks to: Ellen Crain and Lee Whitney of the Silver-Bow Historical Society in Butte, Bellosguardo caretaker Mario Da Cunha, Ilde Smilen of Milbank Tweed, art appraiser Beverly Jacoby, psychiatrists Dr. Anna Fels and Dr. Chandler Rainey.

I am grateful to the journalists who graciously provided guidance. Lael Morgan, the author of *Wanton West*, and Montana journalist Steve Shirley both made the ultimate gesture and sent me their notes. Ben O'Connell of C-SPAN gave me a crash course in Montana history; *Washington Post* reporter David Montgomery wrote a terrific piece about the Corcoran and helped with details; Andrew Alpern, the author of *Apartments for the Affluent*, provided information about 907 Fifth Avenue; *New York Post* reporter Julia Marsh kept me on top of breaking news.

My dear friend Jere Couture, copyright lawyer extraordinaire, provided legal advice and endless encouragement. Jere died this past August, a tremendous loss.

Alyson Krueger, a 2011 graduate of NYU's Arthur L. Carter Journalism Institute, has been the ideal meticulous fact-checker. Malika Toure, a 2013 Arthur L. Carter graduate, and Margaret Yang, a graduate of NYU's MA Literary Translation program, translated nearly one hundred letters from French to English. Andre Tartar translated *Le Sénateur Qui Aimait La France* by André Baeyens. NYU MA scholars Kate Beaudoin and Georgette Yacoub provided research assistance. I am very grateful to all of the above for their help, but any mistakes are mine.

I have been blessed with wonderful friends: Jane Hartley, Ralph Schlosstein, Susan Birkenhead, Tom Curley, Michelle and Stephen Stoneburn, Mary Macy, Mandy Grunwald, Benjamin Cooper, Louise Grunwald, Liz Loewy, Paul Giddens, Suzanna Andrews, Tamar Lewin, Gail Gregg, Christine Doudna, Rick Grand-Jean, Susan

Chira, Michael Shapiro, Caroline Miller, Eric Himmel, James Wetzler, Rita Jacobs, Judy Miller, Jason Epstein, Elaine and Tino Kamarck, Joe Klein, Victoria Kaunitz, Swoosie Kurtz, Jenny Allen, Diane Yu, Michael Delaney, Lisa New, Larry Summers, Nancy Leonard, Urban Lehner, Jeff and Christine Rosen, Thea Lurie, Joel Kaye, Josh Gotbaum, Joyce Thornhill, Dotty Lynch, Morgan Downey, Joanne Hubschman, Margo Lion, Kate Feiffer, Chris Alley, Patricia Bauer, Ed Muller, Alexis Gelber, Mark Whitaker, Jeff Greenfield, Dena Sklar, Jill Lawrence, John Martin, Richard M. Cohen, David Weisbrod, Peggy Simon, Hillary Ballon, Orin Kramer, Larry Rockefeller, Wendy Gordon, Nancy and Charlie Kantor, Peggy Noonan. Some friends are gone but remain in my heart: Ron Silver, Henry Hubschman, Wendy Wasserstein, Susannah McCorkle.

For the past five years, Graydon Carter and Aimee Bell of *Vanity Fair* have kept me busy with enjoyable assignments, and I am very grateful. Thanks to my NYU colleagues for their support: Robert Boynton, Perri Klass, Brooke Kroeger, Pamela Newkirk, Adam Penenberg, Mary Quigley, Charles Seife, and Carol Sternhell.

My husband, Walter Shapiro, makes me laugh, critiques my topic sentences, and created an entire imaginary sleep clinic to deal with my middle-of-the-night insomnia. When you're lucky in love, everything else is manageable. I spied Walter in 1972 at the *Michigan Daily* newsroom—what an adventure it has been.

My father, David Gordon, now ninety-one, and my mother, Adelle Gordon, now eighty-eight, are a constant inspiration—engaged with the world, loving, and supportive. The other lights of my life: my nephew Jesse Gordon, his wife, Meghan Wolf, their delightful toddler, Ozzy, my nephew Nate Gordon, and Jenny Rakochy. Special thanks to Nate, a photo editor at *Sports Illustrated*, who organized the photographs for this book. My sisters-in-law, Sarah Cooper-Ellis and Amy Shapiro, remain my close friends. I cherish my uncle Melvin Silverman and aunt Beverly. I miss my brother, Bart Gordon, even more as the years go by.

Sources

My main sources of information for this book consisted of personal interviews with more than one hundred people and a vast array of documents.

I am tremendously grateful to the administrators of Huguette Clark's estate for allowing me to read and quote from material in seventy-six boxes—more than twenty-five thousand documents— that belonged to Huguette Clark and were removed from her Fifth Avenue apartment after her death. This trove included Huguette's 1920 diary; her sister Andrée's 1919 diary; family letters written by Huguette, Andrée, and their parents, Sen. William Andrews Clark and his wife, Anna; hundreds of personal letters and telegrams; and thousands of photographs, receipts, and business letters dating back to 1926; plus items of historic interest, including the 1925 contents of William Andrews Clark's wallet and his Senate briefcase.

At press time, I was the only reporter allowed to see the entire archive: seventy-one boxes stored at the Manhattan offices of the law firm Milbank Tweed plus an additional five boxes at Christie's storage facility in Brooklyn. I was also the first journalist allowed, on January 21, 2014, to tour Huguette's Santa Barbara estate, Bellosguardo. Special thanks to the lawyers who made both possible: Peter Schram, for the public administrator; Carl Distefano of the New York Attorney General's office; and Thomas LeViness, the co-administrator for the estate and trustee for Huguette Clark's intellectual property. The Clark family archival material will eventually go to the William Andrews Clark Memorial Library at UCLA in Los Angeles.

Huguette Clark took painting lessons for thirty years from artist Tadé Styka, who was also her frequent evening escort, taking her to the Ziegfeld Follies, to the 1939 World's Fair, and dancing at the Rainbow Room. His daughter, Wanda Styka—Huguette Clark's goddaughter—generously made exclusively available to me the appointment calendars, journal entries, and letters of her parents, Tadé and Doris Styka, dating from 1935 through 1980. These documents enabled me to reconstruct much of Huguette's life during that period.

Other vital material: William Andrews Clark's letters to his lawyer, W. S. Bickford, and other archival documents at the Montana Historical Society in Helena; William Andrews Clark's letters to *Butte Miner* editor J. S. Dobell, plus bound volumes of Montana newspapers and other archival materials at the Silver-Bow Historical Society in Butte.

I relied on databases for newspaper stories from 1869 through 2013: ProQuest Historical, LexisNexis, Old Fulton NY Post Cards, the Library of Congress's Chronicling America, NewspaperArchive.com, America's Historical Newspapers, Ancestry.com, Genealogy.com. Books are also listed separately in a bibliography.

From August 2011 through September 2013, I attended court hearings for the Huguette Clark probate case and read the voluminous depositions and legal documents, File 1995/1375, Manhattan Surrogate's Court, 31 Chambers Street.

CHAPTER ONE: The Clark Family Reunion at the Corcoran

Interviews: former Corcoran Gallery directors Paul Greenhalgh and David Levy, Ian Devine, Carla Hall, Karine McCall, Wallace Bock, Irving and Judi Kamsler, Cynthia Garcia, Beverly Bonner McCord, Martha FitzSimon, Stanley Pitts.
Depositions: Ian Devine, Carla Hall, Erika Hall, Karine McCall, Paul Clark Newell Jr.
Articles cited: "Mr. Clark of Montana," *Washington Post*, December 3, 1899; "Morris-Clark Wedding," *New York Times*, May 29, 1900; "Fortunes Which Exceed a Hundred Million," *New York Times*, February 24, 1907; "Coolidge Cuts Silken Cord Opening Art Gallery Annex," *Washington Post*, March 11, 1928; "Mrs. John H. Hall," *New York Times*, March 22, 1968; Bob Thompson, "Corcoran Director Quits; Trustees Shelve Gehry Plans," *Washington Post*, May 24, 2005; Katherine Boyle, "Corcoran's Clark Sickle-Leaf Carpet Breaks World Record at Sotheby's Auction," *Washington Post*, June 5, 2013.
Documents: Information on monthly fees of Wallace Bock and Irving Kamsler; Huguette M. Clark probate case; File 1995/1375. Carla Hall speech at the Clark reunion, courtesy of Carla Hall.

Books:
    Laura Coyle and Dare Myers Hartwell, *Antiquities to Impressionism: The William A. Clark Collection*, Corcoran Gallery of Art, 2001.

    Lewis Hall, *The William A. Clark Collection, Treasures of a Copper King*, Corcoran Catalog, 1978.

    Writer's Note: Anna La Chapelle's name is sometimes spelled as LaChapelle, but Anna signed both Huguette's birth certificate and a Montana marriage register using La Chapelle.

CHAPTER TWO: The Quest for "Tante Huguette"

Interviews: Wallace Bock, Ian Devine, Carla Hall, Karine McCall, Irving Kamsler.

Depositions: Hadassah Peri, Dr. Jack Rudick, Christie Ysit.

Articles cited: Tommy Hallissey, "Porno Sting Nabs Temple President," *Riverdale Press*, September 20, 2007; Megan James, "Kamsler Admits Guilt in Child Pornography Case," *Riverdale Press*, October 2, 2008; Carol Vogel, "Art Auctions Buffeted by Events," *New York Times*, April 30, 2003; "A Splendid Hospital on the East Side Has Been Built Largely with Contributions from Poor People," *New York Daily Tribune*, December 28, 1902; Joshua Kosman, "Agnes Albert—Pianist, S.F. Symphony Supporter," *Los Angeles Times*, June 20, 2002; "Alumni Spotlight: Ian Devine, Class of 1968," *Bridge*, Palm Beach Day Academy; Jacqueline Trescott, "A Museum's Fortunes on the Decline," *Washington Post*, January 5, 2011.

CHAPTER THREE: Huguette's Walk in Central Park

Interviews: Wallace Bock, Kati Despretz Cruz, Tina Lyle Harrower, Gordon Lyle Jr., Caterina Marsh, Christopher Sattler, Wanda Styka, Lucy (Lyle) Tower.

Depositions: Geraldine Coffey, Dr. Louise Klebanoff, Paul Newell Jr., Dr. Robert Newman, Hadassah Peri, Dr. Henry Singman.

Documents: Beth Israel Medical Center Statistical Review, average stay 5.5 days; Anna La Chapelle trust; Archives, estate of Huguette M. Clark. Huguette Clark's letters to her father: With thanks to the Estate of Huguette Clark for access to review, and permission to extensively quote from, her letters.

CHAPTER FOUR: The Copper King

Interviews: Irving Kamsler, Daniel Osborne, Christopher Sattler, Erin Sigl.

Speeches: William Andrews Clark speech, 34th Annual Convention, Montana Society of Pioneers, Livingston, September 5, 1917; William Andrews Clark speech, Montana Society of Pioneers, September 9, 1920; William Andrews Clark speech, 41st Annual Convention, Society of Montana Pioneers, August 28, 1924; Montana Historical Society, Helena.

Articles and research: "Whiskaway Brings $125,000," *New York Times*, August 12, 1922; "Rich Men of Montana," *Washington Post*, July 30, 1895; "Fortune His Wedding Gift: A Montana Millionaire's Son Marries," *San Francisco Chronicle*, July 1, 1896; "The Men Behind Bryan," *Hartford Courant*, August 29, 1896; "W. A. Clark Buys Fortuny," *New York Journal*, February 8, 1898; "Columbia Gardens, Butte's Famous Summer Resort," *Butte Miner*, December 22, 1901; "William Andrews Clark," *Cosmopolitan*, February 1903; "Son of Senator Clark Is Sued," *San Jose Evening News*, May 20, 1905; "In the Matter of Chinese: Senator Clark Raises His Voice Against Importing Coolies to Compete with Whites," *Anaconda Standard*, December 9, 1905; "Lost $20,000 on Wheel," *Washington Post*, October 9, 1908; "Senator

Clark's Son Sued," *Christian Science Monitor*, May 2, 1911; Henry R. Knapp; Kenneth Ross Toole, "The Genesis of the Clark-Daly Feud," *Montana Magazine of History*, April 1951; Byron Cooney, "Personal Reminiscences and Side Lights about Senator W. A. Clark," *Montana American*, undated clip, Montana Historical Society archives; "Montana's Political Feud," *New York Times*, January 25, 1899; "A Bronze Door by Bartlett," *New York Times*, November 7, 1897; "Fortunes Which Exceed a Hundred Million Dollars," *New York Times*, February 24, 1907; "Clark Properties Sold to Anaconda," *New York Times*, August 23, 1928; Christopher Gray, "When Spain Reigned on Central Park South," *New York Times*, June 17, 2007; Michael P. Malone, "Midas of the West: The Incredible Career of William Andrews Clark," *Montana, The Magazine of Western History*, Autumn 1983; Mary Montana Farrell, master's dissertation, University of Washington, 1933; Beverly Bonner McCord, "The Senator's Kin," 2008 essay; PITWATCH: Berkeley Pit News 2013; Copper King Mansion Tour Script, 2011.

Books: The following books provided especially valuable background for chapters 4 and 5:

W. A. Clark entry in "Personal History and Reminiscences: Silver Bow County," in *History of Montana 1739–1885*, Warner, Beers, & Co., 1885.

John A. Garraty and Mark C. Carnes, *American National Biography*, vol. 4, Oxford University Press, 1999.

C. P. Glasscock, *The War of the Copper Kings*, Riverbend Publishing, 1939.

Donald MacMillan, *Smoke Wars: Anaconda Copper, Montana Air Pollution, and the Courts, 1890–1920*, Montana Historical Society Press, 2000.

Michael P. Malone, *The Battle for Butte*, University of Washington Press, 1981.

Progressive Men of the State of Montana, A. W. Bowen & Co., date unknown.

Dennis Swibold, *Copper Chorus: Mining, Politics, and the Montana Press, 1889–1959*, Montana Historical Society Press, 2006.

CHAPTER FIVE: The Reinvention of Anna

Interviews: Tina Lyle Harrower, Gordon Lyle Jr.

Articles: "They Knocked Him Out: One of Butte's Fakirs Found Guilty by a Jury," *Anaconda Standard*, November 14, 1890; "Americans in Paris: Brilliant Women Who Live in the French Capital," *Chicago Daily Tribune*, May 6, 1893; "In Fairyland," *Anaconda Standard*, August 28, 1895; "For Honor and a Prize," *Helena Independent*, May 28, 1889; "The Death of Paul Clark," *Anaconda Standard*, March 14, 1896; "Death of Paul Clark: Suddenly Expires at Andover While at School," *Butte Weekly Miner*, March 12, 1896; "Clark's New York Palace," *Chicago Daily Tribune*, February 19, 1899; "Protegee of Copper King," *Boston Daily Globe*, March 20, 1900; "Clark Lucky in Love If Not in Politics," *New York World*, April 27, 1900; "Copper King's Protegee," *Pharos-Tribune Logansport*, May 19, 1900; "Senator Clark, Whose Election Is Being Investigated," *San Francisco Call*, February 27, 1900; "Senate Committee Against Mr. Clark: Decision Based on Bribery," *New York Times*, April 24, 1900; "Another Man Named to Succeed Clark," *New York Times*, May 19, 1900; "Hard Man to Throw Down," *Washington Post*, May 27, 1900; "Clark of Montana," *New York Times*, November 13, 1900; "Gossip of the Capital City," *Chicago Daily Tribune*, November 18, 1900; "W. A. Clark Again a Senator," *New York Times*, January 17, 1901; "Miss Laube in Politics," *Anaconda Standard*, April 18, 1901; "Hattie Rose Laube Can't Prove It by Clark Himself," *Anaconda Standard*, April 21, 1901; "Beauty and Wealth United by Marriage," *Chicago Daily Tribune*, June

20, 1901; "Millionaire Senator Is on the Jump," *Los Angeles Times*, July 28, 1901; "A Rich Father Has Charles Clark," *Los Angeles Times*, July 20, 1902; "Senator Clark to Wed Again?" *Los Angeles Times*, May 4, 1904; "Another Rumor," *Anaconda Standard*, July 1, 1901; "Mrs. W. A. Clark Jr., Dead," *New York Times*, January 2, 1903; "Woman Would Sue Clark in Public," *Los Angeles Times*, April 18, 1903; "Senator Clark in Breach of Promise Suit," *New York Times*, April 19, 1903; "Clark Denies Lady's Soft Impeachment," *Los Angeles Times*, April 19, 1903; "Clark's Daughter Seeks Divorce," *Bellingham Herald*, November 19, 1903; Frederick Ackerman, "The Toil for Millions: Is There Pleasure in It?" *Dallas Morning News*, December 6, 1903; "Senator Clark's Daughter," *Macon Telegraph*, November 25, 1903; "Modern Croesus a Very Sick Man," *Minneapolis Journal*, April 22, 1904; "Senator to Be Married," *New York Press*, May 8, 1904; "Senator Clark Says He Is Not to Be Married," *Omaha World-Herald*, June 19, 1904; "They're Married and Have a Baby," *Anaconda Standard*, July 12, 1904; "Clark Tells Why," July 13, 1904; "Principals in the Wedding Whose Announcement Surprised Butte Yesterday," *Anaconda Standard*, July 13, 1904; "Clark Surprise: Senator's Family Not Apparently Pleased," *Boston Daily Globe*, July 13, 1904; "Mrs. Clark Had Visited Here," *Salt Lake Tribune*, July 13, 1904; "Senator Clark Quarrels with Son," *Des Moines Capital*, July 15, 1904; "Details of Great Love," *Anaconda Standard*, July 21, 1904; "May Marry Senator Clark," *Chicago Daily Tribune*, March 1904; "Having Astonished All Europe, Boy Genius Will Dazzle America," *Atlanta Constitution*, May 15, 1904; "Billionaire Clark to Lead to Altar Poor Girl," *Atlanta Constitution*, June 19, 1904; "W. A. Clark's Ward, Whose Marriage to Him Three Years Ago Is Announced," *Chicago Daily Tribune*, July 12, 1904; "Clark Is Wed Again," *Chicago Daily Tribune*, July 12, 1904; "Mrs. Clark's Mother in Dark," *New York Times*, July 13, 1904; "Senator Clark Tells of Bride," *Washington Times*, July 13, 1904; "Clark Baby a Mystery," *Kansas City Star*, July 15, 1904; "Mrs. W. A. Clark Nee Anna La Chapelle," *Seattle Star*, July 16, 1904; "Romance of the Harp in Senator Clark's Marriage," *Minneapolis Journal*, July 22, 1904; "Senator Clark's Brother-in-Law Has Thrown Money to the Birds," *Tacoma Times*, July 27, 1904; "Why He Kept the Wedding Secret," *Hawaiian Star*, August 22, 1904; "Million-Dollar Babe Is Motherless," *Boston Globe*, January 2, 1905; "Photoplay News," *Washington Post*, March 1, 1914; "Montanans Crash Films," *Los Angeles Times*, June 23, 1929.

Documents: William Andrews Clark letters to W. S. Bickford, Montana Historical Society.

Books:

Christopher P. Connolly, *The Devil Learns to Vote*, J. J. Little, 1938.

Adam Gopnik, *Americans in Paris: A Literary Anthology*, Library of America, 2004.

William Daniel Mangam, *The Clarks: An American Phenomenon*, Silver Bow Press, 1941. Includes Katherine Clark Morris's letter to William Andrews Clark Jr.

David McCullough, *The Greater Journey: Americans in Paris*, Simon & Schuster, 2011.

Lael Morgan, *Wanton West*, Chicago Review Press, 2011.

Mark Twain, *Mark Twain in Eruption*, Harper & Brothers, 1922.

CHAPTER SIX: A Parisian Girlhood

Interviews: Christopher Sattler, Neal Sattler.

Depositions: Geraldine Coffey, Hadassah Peri, Dr. Henry Singman.

Articles: "A Youthful Genius," *Los Angeles Times*, September 24, 1904; "Three Amazing Lads," *Washington Post*, November 6, 1904; "Didn't Bring Clark Baby," *New York*

Times, January 12, 1905; "And Clark Laughs," *Los Angeles Times*, January 12, 1905; "Mrs. Clark Under Knife," *Anaconda Standard*, February 18, 1905; "Slot Machine Couldn't Bunko Senator Clark," *New York Times*, February 20, 1905; "Not Home to Some of Butte's Grand Dames Who Cut Her When She Was Poor," *Pawtucket Times*, June 2, 1905; "Social War in Butte," *Philadelphia Inquirer*, June 3, 1905; "New Mrs. Clark a Home Lover," *Chicago Daily Tribune*, July 30, 1905; "In Expectation," *Anaconda Standard*, April 18, 1906; "Luxury for That Clark Baby," *San Antonio Gazette*, September 22, 1906; "Clark to Quit Politics," *Washington Post*, October 25, 1906; "Children's Party," *Anaconda Standard*, June 16, 1907; "Paris Spring Salon," *New York Tribune*, April 30, 1908; "Clark House," *Colorado Springs Gazette*, November 22, 1909; Vance Thompson, "Palace Not Yet Finished," *Washington Post*, May 29, 1910; "Mr. Clark and Sensitive Architects," *Chicago Daily Tribune*, December 21, 1910; Christopher Gray, "Huguette Clark's Worthless Girlhood Home," *New York Times*, June 2, 2011; "Mistress of Big Mansion," *Oelwein Daily Register*, November 18, 1910; "Ex-Senator Clark's Wife Operated On," *Hartford Courant*, February 21, 1911; "Hunt Two Burglars in Fifth Avenue," *New York Times*, February 22, 1911; "Burglars on Roof of Senator Clark's House," *Hartford Courant*, February 22, 1911; "Tadé Styka Portrait," *Buffalo Courier News*, March 12, 1911; "With Millions to Spend, She Could Not Buy Happiness," *Chicago Daily Tribune*, April 16, 1911; "Senator Clark's Son Sued," *Christian Science Monitor*, May 2, 1911; "Senator Clark and Family Leave for the Coronation," *Oakland Tribune*, June 4, 1911; "W. A. Clark Has Test of $120,000 Organ," *New York Times*, June 10, 1911; "Clark for Art, Not Society," *New York Times*, October 26, 1911; "Would You Let Your Daughter Marry a Man Old Enough to Be Her Father?" *Chicago Daily Tribune*, February 12, 1911; "Mrs. William Clark Ill," *Chicago Daily Tribune*, February 20, 1911; "Clark Plans House Opening," *New York Times*, September 2, 1911; "Organs in Millionaires' Homes," *Wall Street Journal*, October 21, 1911; "Clark to Open Gallery to Gotham Public," *Atlanta Constitution*, December 11, 1911; "Mrs. Wm. A. Clark Back from Europe," *New York Tribune*, December 17, 1911; "Dies Suddenly of Acute Pneumonia," *Anaconda Standard*, January 24, 1912; "Society Not Worthwhile: Says Ex-Senator Clark—His Fifth Avenue Home Open to His Friends," *New York Times*, February 10, 1912; "Fashion's Fads and Fancies," *Washington Post*, March 12, 1912; "They Were Passengers on Board the Ill-Fated Titanic," *Anaconda Standard*, April 17, 1912; "The Fashionable Revivification of the Harp," *Town & Country*, April 20, 1912; "Finest Collection of Jewels in the World," *Los Angeles Times*, July 22, 1912; "Many Notable Persons Return Here from Europe," *New York Sun*, November 12, 1912; Walter Ed Taylor, "The House Montana Copper Built," clip in hanging files, Montana Historical Society; "Senator Clark Safe," *San Francisco Chronicle*, September 6, 1914; "Ex-Senator Clark Home," *Wall Street Journal*, October 23, 1914; "Senator Clark Returns from War Zone," *Anaconda Standard*, October 27, 1914; "Grim Poverty in War's Wake," *Los Angeles Times*, November 20, 1914.

Documents: William Andrews Clark letters to W. S. Bickford, Montana Historical Society.

Books:

T. Bentley Mott, *Myron Herrick, Friend of France*, Doubleday, 1929.

CHAPTER SEVEN: The Fractured Fairy Tale

Interviews: Erika Hall, Gordon Lyle Jr., Roberto Socas, Wanda Styka.
Depositions: Geraldine Coffey.

Articles: "The Aladdin Palace, Home of W. A. Clark," *Kansas City Star*, February 28, 1915; "Senator Clark Indignant," *New York Times*, November 27, 1903; "Photo of Portrait of Andrée Clark," *New York Times*, January 31, 1915; "What Girls May Do: A Teacher Who Teaches Play," *Boston Daily Globe*, February 11, 1915; "Mr. Tartoue Limns Society Delicately," *New York Herald*, 1915; "Will Society Keep Lent?" *New York Times*, February 21, 1915; "An Evening of French Music," *New York Times*, February 23, 1915; "W. A. Clark's Palace Used for Charity," *Anaconda Standard*, March 4, 1915; "Miss Andre and Miss Huguette Clark and Their Six Million Dollar House on Fifth Avenue," *Evening World*, March 6, 1915; "Society Goes Charity Mad and Finds Its Reward," *New York Sun*, March 7, 1915; "American Artists' Committee of 100," *New York Times*, March 21, 1915; "Clark's Grandson Dead: Gerald Clark Kling, Victim of Appendicitis," *New York Tribune*, September 20, 1915; "Some Grand Old Men and What They Do to Stay Well," *Anaconda Standard*, January 1, 1917; "Mrs. Clark and Daughters Will Tour the Yellowstone," *Anaconda Standard*, July 6, 1917; "The Clarks in Butte," *Anaconda Standard*, July 26, 1919; "Miss Clark Dies at Summer Home," *Anaconda Standard*, August 8, 1919; "Beautiful Girl Called to Heavenly Home," *Butte Miner*, August 8, 1919; "Funeral Tomorrow at St. Thomas for Andrée Clark, Dead of Meningitis," *New York Herald*, August 10, 1919; "Montana Pioneers with Sons and Daughters Meet," *Butte Miner*, August 30, 1919; "Ex-Copper King Emerges," *Miami District Daily News*, April 4, 1920; "Camp Site to Perpetuate Girl's Love for Scouts," *New York Tribune*, November 11, 1920; Photo of Senator Clark and Huguette Clark, *Philadelphia Evening Public Ledger*, November 12, 1920; "Miss Alma Guy, 68, Aide to Blind, Dies," *New York Times*, September 30, 1938; "Orchestral Society Aims to Foster American Talent," *New York Tribune*, March 20, 1921.

Documents: Family letters and telegrams: Huguette Clark, Andrée Clark, William Clark, Anna Clark; Diaries of Huguette Clark and Andrée Clark; With thanks to the Estate of Huguette Clark for access to review, and permission to extensively quote from, her letters. William Andrews Clark letters to W. S. Bickford, Montana Historical Society. Interview with Alma Guy and Andrée Clark's letters, Girl Scout National Historic Preservation Center.

Books:

Mary Dillon Edmondson, *Profiles in Leadership: A History of the Spence School 1892–1992*, Phoenix Publishing, 1991.

CHAPTER EIGHT: Beginnings and Endings

Interviews: Andrew Alpern, Lindsay Mican Morgan.
Depositions and interviews: Paul Albert, Karine McCall.
Articles: "Mrs. Kling Gets Divorce," *Oregonian*, May 6, 1922; "Hawaiian Youth, Protege of Copper King's Wife, Sees End of College Dream Here," *San Francisco Chronicle*, September 21, 1921; "Clark Protege May Return to Hawaii," *San Francisco Chronicle*, September 25, 1921; "Sail for Europe Today," *New York Times*, May 30, 1922; "Look Who's Here: Sen. William Clark of Montana," *New York Tribune*, September 17, 1922; "Social Notes," *New York Times*, October 8, 1922; "That Disappointed Admirer of Pola Negri," *Ogden, Utah*, February 23, 1923; "Artist Styka's Heart Heals Slowly," *Los Angeles Times*, February 26, 1923; "Millicent's Diary," *Washington Post*, March 20, 1923; "Social Notes," *New York Times*, May 4, 1923; "Miss Clara B. Spence," *New York Times*, August 10, 1923; "Her Beauty Fires Styka's Genius," *Los Angeles Times*, August 19, 1923; "Bye-the-Bye in Wall Street,"

Wall Street Journal, January 9, 1924; "Wine Cellar in Doll House for Queen Is Protested," *Washington Post*, April 14, 1924; "Queen Mary's Million Dollar Dollhouse," *Washington Post*, May 18, 1924; "Queen's Dolls Have Priceless Library," *New York Times*, August 24, 1924; Byron Cooney, "Personal Reminiscences and Side Lights about Senator W. A. Clark," *Montana American*, undated clip, Montana Historical Society; "New York Society," *Chicago Daily Tribune*, June 6, 1924; "On Art and Artists," *Los Angeles Times*, November 16, 1924; "Mrs. Mary Clark Kling a Bride," *New York Times*, March 2, 1925; "Pneumonia Proves Fatal to Picturesque Montanan at Fifth Avenue Home," *New York Times*, March 25, 1925, "Senator Clark's Vivid Life," *New York Times*, March 8, 1925; "Senator Clark Dies in Gotham," *Los Angeles Times*, March 8, 1925; "Clark Rites Amid His Art Treasures," *New York Times*, March 7, 1925; "Will of W. A. Clark Disposes of Vast Fortune," *Anaconda Standard*, April 7, 1925; "The Clark Gift," *New York Herald Tribune*, April 8, 1925; "Art Lovers Hope Museum Takes Clark Paintings," *New York Herald Tribune*, April 9, 1925; "Museum Refuses $3,000,000 Clark Collection," *New York World*, April 21, 1925; "Masterpieces in the Clark Collection," *New York Times*, March 15, 1925; "How Not to Become Immortal," *Chicago Tribune*, April 22, 1925; "Clark Family Hurt by Metropolitan's Refusal of His Art," *New York Tribune*, April 25, 1925; "W. A. Clark's Widow Resigns as Executrix," *Washington Post*, June 11, 1925; "Corcoran Gallery Takes Clark Art," *New York Times*, August 2, 1925; "Fifth Avenue Losing Fight," *Los Angeles Times*, August 9, 1925; "Divorces Charles W. Clark," *New York Times*, August 17, 1925; "Social Notes," *New York Times*, September 30, 1925; "Clark's $7,000,000 Palace Is Going Begging," *Boston Globe*, October 1, 1925; "Storrs Give a Dinner," *New York Times*, March 4, 1925; "Part of Senator Clark's Art to Be Auctioned; Heirs Also to Part with Fifth Avenue Home," *New York Times*, November 22, 1925; "Clarks Give $700,000 and 210 Art Pieces for Corcoran Wing," *Washington Post*, November 29, 1925; "Druggist Was Father of 3 Clark Claimants," *Washington Post*, February 7, 1926; "Sure Senator Clark Was Former Druggist," *New York Times*, February 7, 1926; "Crowd Gathers for Selection of Jury to Try Clark Case," *Butte Miner*, July 1, 1926; "Charles W. Clark Tells of Life in Deer Lodge Town," *Anaconda Standard*, July 7, 1926; "Anderson Clark Called Father of Missouri Women," *Anaconda Standard*, July 8, 1926; "History of Days of Covered Wagon Trains Is Written in Court Record of Clark Case," *Butte Miner*, July 11, 1926; "Women Lose Claim to Clark's Wealth," *Washington Post*, July 16, 1926; "Takes 45 Minutes for Jury to Rule on Clark Contest," *Butte Daily Post*, July 16, 1926; "Death Bed Confession of William Anderson Clark Factor in Settling Battle over Late W. A. Clark's Fortune," *Three Forks News*, undated, tentative October 12, 1931, Montana Historical Society; "Poor Little Rich Clark Girl—Everybody's after Her $333 a Day," syndicated feature, 1926; "View Clark Home, Due to Be Wrecked," *New York Times*, February 23, 1927; "Clark's Folly Stripped," *New York Times*, March 29, 1927; "Quai D'Orsay Ball Draws Paris Elite," *New York Times*, June 5, 1927; "Clark Estate Wins Against Tax Here," *New York Times*, September 23, 1927; Hilton Kramer, "When Money, Not Taste, Builds a Collection," *New York Times*, June 4, 1978.

Documents: Family letters and telegrams: Huguette Clark, William Andrews Clark, Anna Clark, Charles Clark; Katherine Morris, William Andrews Clark Jr.; courtesy of Estate of Huguette M. Clark. William Andrews Clark's letters to W. S. Bickford, Montana Historical Society. William Andrews Clark's will, Montana Historical Society; Silver-Bow Archives.

Books:

Marshall Bond Jr., *Adventures with Peons, Princes, and Tycoons*, Star Rover House, 1974.

William Daniel Mangam, *The Clarks: An American Phenomenon*, Silver Bow Press. 1941.

David F. Myrick, *Montecito and Santa Barbara, Volume II, The Days of the Great Estates*, Montecito Publishing, 1991.

Writer's Notes: Huguette's essay "Happy Moments," dated December 16, no year, was stored with her high school report cards at Christie's warehouse. Huguette Clark's lessons with Tadé Styka began in the 1920s, but the precise year is uncertain. He mentions seeing her paintings in January 1925; she does not call him "chere maitre" in her letters until 1929.

CHAPTER NINE: Society Girl

Interviews: Kati Despretz Cruz, Gordon Lyle Jr., Tina Lyle Harrower, Christie Merrill, Christopher Sattler.

Articles: "William A. Clark Gives Easter Monday Dance for Debutante Grand-daughter," *New York Tribune*, March 29, 1921; "Sketches Interior of Clark Mansion," *New York Times*, January 24, 1926; "New York Society," *Washington Post*, October 8, 1926; "Debutantes Feted at Two Luncheons," *New York Times*, November 23, 1926; Sunday photo section, *New York Times*, December 5, 1926; "Frank V. Storrs, Advertising Man," *New York Times*, March 9, 1939; "Clark Home Sold Under $3,000,000," *New York Times*, February 2, 1927; "Why Not?" *New York Times*, February 5, 1927; "View Clark Home, Due to Be Wrecked," *New York Times*, February 23, 1927; "Clark Mansion Open to Public," *New York Times*, March 20, 1927; "William MacDonald Gower," *Nassau Herald*, courtesy of Princeton University library; "De-Mun Cuyler Wedding Festivities Set New Records for Gayety," *Omaha World-Herald*, May 15, 1927; "Dinners Given at Ritz," *New York Times*, May 25, 1927; "Clark-Gower," *New York Times*, December 14, 1927; "To Wed Heiress of Clark Riches," *New York Sun*, December 14, 1927; "Princeton Graduate to Wed Heiress," *Trenton Times*, December 15, 1927; "Many Betrothals of Wide Interest," *New York Times*, December 25, 1927; "Jungle Dance for Debs," December 30, 1927; "Give Revue for a Charity," *New York Times*, January 23, 1927; "Lewis L. Clarkes Are Hosts at Dance," *New York Times*, January 27, 1928; "Notes of Social Activities," *New York Times*, February 15, 1928; "The Clark Collection," *Washington Post*, March 11, 1928; "Engaged Couple Honored," *New York Times*, April 11, 1928; "Wedding of William Gower to Miss Clark Occurs Today," undated clip, Santa Barbara Historical Society, August 17, 1938; "Miss Huguette Clark Weds William Gower," *New York Times*, August 18, 1928; "A $30-a-Week Husband for a $50,000,000 Heiress," *Salt Lake City Tribune*, September 16, 1928; "She Shocked the 400 by Marrying for Love and $30 per Week," *Danville Bee*, October 4, 1928; "New York Society Couple to Pass Through Salt Lake," *Salt Lake Tribune*, October 28, 1928; "Tadé Styka Praises American Art Trend," *New York Times*, December 28, 1928; "U.S. Has Loveliest Women, Says Famed Polish Artist," *Lancaster Daily Gazette*, January 19, 1929; "Many Entertained by J. S. Laidlaws," *New York Times*, February 10, 1929; "Mrs. de Brabant Is Hostess," *New York Times*, May 10, 1929; Cholly Knickerbocker, "Gowers Near Divorce Court," *New York American*, May 14, 1929; Eleanor Jewett, "Styka's Paintings Entrance Critic Who Then Reveals Why," *Chicago Daily Tribune*, January 25, 1930; "Mrs. Gower Goes to Reno," *New York Times*, April 15, 1930; "Clark's Daughter Coming to Reno for 3 Months," *Reno Evening Gazette*, April 16, 1930; "Reno Agog over Clark Kin's Move," *Los Angeles Times*, April 17, 1930; "Why America's $50,000,000 Heiress Cast Off Her

$30-a-Week Prince Charming and Ritzed Reno by Renting an Entire Hotel Floor and Moving in with an Array of Servants," *Hamilton Evening Journal*, June 28, 1930; "W. A. Clark's Daughter Gets a Reno Divorce," *New York Times*, August 12, 1930; "Fund for Neediest Nearing 1929 Total," *New York Times*, December 26, 1930; "Mrs. Huguette Clark," Associated Press, September 6, 1931.

Documents: Huguette Clark's letters to Tadé Styka, courtesy of Wanda Styka and Estate of Huguette M. Clark; William Gower letter to Anna Clark and receipts from Cartier and Van Cleef and Arpels, courtesy of Estate of Huguette M. Clark. *Social Register*, 1904–2011, New York Public Library, Bryant Park location. Corcoran Gallery catalogue, exhibit of paintings of Huguette Clark, April 1930.

CHAPTER TEN: Alone Again

Articles: "Duke Denies Plan to Wed," *New York Times*, January 28, 1931; "Clark Sues to Void $10,000,000 Trusts," *New York Times*, July 29, 1931; "Polish Artist Finds Gotham More 'Wicked' Than Paree," Associated Press, November 30, 1931; "Toulmin-Gower," *New York Times*, June 4, 1932; "Beauty Will Tell Story of Gross Cruelty," *San Francisco Chronicle*, September 25, 1907; "Hart M'Kee Only Wanted Wife's Money," *San Francisco Chronicle*, May 5, 1908; "Bitter Words for Husband," *Atlanta Constitution*, April 9, 1908; "Charges of Wife Denied by M'Kee," *Chicago Daily Tribune*, April 16, 1908; "Double Divorce in M'Kee Case," *Atlanta Constitution*, May 8, 1908; "The Clark Millions," *Boston Herald*, June 6, 1932; "Mrs. Constance Toulmin Bride of W. M. Gower," *New York Sun*, June 4, 1932; "Mrs. Toulmin Weds," *New York Times*, June 5, 1932; "W. A. Clark 3d Is Killed in Airplane Crash," *New York Times*, May 16, 1932; "Old Names Missing in New Opera List," *New York Times*, November 14, 1932; "Charles W. Clark, Head of Verde Copper, Dies," *Washington Post*, April 9, 1933; "C. W. Clark Dead; A Copper Magnate," *New York Times*, April 9, 1933; "By the Bye in Wall Street," *Wall Street Journal*, May 3, 1933; Edward Alden Jewell, "Art of Tadé Styka," *New York Times*, February 9, 1934; "Dinner Dance Held by Maytown Club," *New York Times*, May 8, 1934.

CHAPTER ELEVEN: Facts, Fiction, and Betrayal

Interviews: Gordon Lyle Jr., Karine McCall, Jan Perry, Wanda Styka.

Articles: "Asks $123,000 'Gifts' as Social Adviser," *New York Times*, January 20, 1929; "Artist's Wife Ends De Brabant Suit," *New York Times*, January 27, 1929; "Society Tongues Cease Wagging as Suit Fizzles," *Los Angeles Times*, January 27, 1929; "Clark Rites in Abeyance," *Los Angeles Times*, June 10, 1934; "William Andrews Clark, Second Son of Noted Montana Pioneer, Called by Death near Missoula," Associated Press, June 14, 1934; "W. A. Clark Junior," *Los Angeles Times*, June 15, 1934; "30 Others to Get Share of Huge Estate," Associated Press, June 20, 1934; "Clark's Heir Comes of Age, Gets $367,891," Associated Press, March 11, no year, Montana Historical Society; "Clark's Big Estate Now Distributed," Associated Press, August 20, no year, Montana Historical Society; "Film Star's Portrait Disrupts Art Show," *New York Times*, June 23, 1934; "Marion Davies' Portrait Stirs Row in Venice," *Chicago Daily Tribune*, June 23, 1934; "Styka's Davies," *Time*, July 2, 1934; "Clark Will Discloses Further Large Gifts," *Los Angeles Times*, July 23, 1934; "American Girl to Pose for Murals at Vatican," *Chicago Daily Tribune*, November 11, 1934; "Clark Estate Share Is Paid," *Trenton Times*, November 8, 1935; "Night Club Notes," *New York Times*, November 16, 1935; "Cabaret Men Cleared," *New York Times*, February 29, 1936; "Rich Texas Widow Must Pay $30,000 to Wife in Love Theft," *Dallas Morning News*, November 21, 1936; "Styka Brothers Joint Exhibitors," *New York Times*, November 21, 1936; "Marquis Is Winner of Heiress Widow," Associated Press, December 25, 1936; "Wealthy Widow Picks Marquis over Prince," *Los Angeles Times*, February 25, 1936; "Miss Toulmin Will Make Debut in London," *New York Sun*, February 6, 1937; "A Novel of an Age of Innocence: Myron Brinig's The Sisters," *New York Times*, February 7, 1937; "One of the Better Brooks," *Atlanta Constitution*, March 14, 1937; "Says First-Floor Homes Give Women Slim Ankles," *New York Times*, April 3, 1937; "William B. Gower, Leader in Copper," *New York Times*, August 31, 1937; "Tadé Styka Shows Portraits at Tea," *New York Post*, October 30, 1937; "Lady Decies Honored at a Luncheon Here," *New York Times*, February 28, 1938; "La Chapelle Rites Solemnized," *Los Angeles Times*, May 30, 1938; "New Films: 'The Sisters,'" *Daily Boston Globe*, November 18, 1938; "Bette Davis Is Star Errol Flynn in Lead Dates back to 1904 Hit Stage Show," *Washington Post*, November 19, 1938; Walter Winchell column, *Charleston Daily Mail*, November 22, 1938; Walter Winchell column, *Brownsville Herald*, May 31, 1939; "Joins Mother," *Los Angeles Times*, September 6, 1939; Cholly Knickerbocker column, *Cleveland Plain Dealer*, March 16, 1940; "Angelenos Gather," *Los Angeles Times*, August 11, 1941; "Party at Opening of Cotillion Room," *New York Times*, November 1, 1941; "Dress Makes the Woman, Painter Says," *Washington Post*, May 16, 1942; Cholly Knickerbocker column, May 12, 1943; "Famous Cases and Criminals: Velvalee Dickinson, the Doll Woman," FBI, http://www.fbi.gov/about-us/history/famous-cases/velvalee-dickinson-doll-woman; "Bare Knuckles on Bare Bodies," *Atlanta Constitution*, June 15 1902; "Submarine Shells Southland Oil Field," *Los Angeles Times*, February 24, 1942; "Refinery Fired On," *New York Times*, February 24, 1942; "Winchell on Broadway," June 25, 1946; "New Friends Offer Paganini Quartet," *New York Times*, November 4, 1946; "Robert Maas, Led Paganini Quartet, 47," *New York Times*, July 9, 1948; "Tadé Styka, Artist, Dies," *New York Times*, September 12, 1954; Barbara Hoelscher Doran, "Huguette Clark: 1906–2011," *Santa Barbara Independent*, June 9, 2011.

Documents: Affidavit of George Pale, August 27, 1935; letters from William A. Clark Jr. to George Pale, Montana Historical Society. Tadé Styka and Doris Styka appointment calendars, notes, and letters, courtesy of Wanda Styka. Huguette Clark letters, with thanks to the Estate of Huguette Clark for access to review, and permission to extensively quote from, her letters. Henri de Villermont letters to Huguette Clark, courtesy the Estate of Huguette Clark.

Books:

Myron Brinig, *The Sisters*, Grosset & Dunlap, 1937.

George H. Douglas, "Major Bowes," in *American National Biography, Volume 3*, Oxford University Press, 1999.

William Daniel Mangam, *The Clarks: An American Phenomenon*, Silver Bow Press, 1941.

CHAPTER TWELVE: The Lady Vanishes

Interviews: Jane Bannerman, Kathleen Bride, Isabelle Cazeaux, Jacques Despretz, Kati Despretz Cruz, Ann Fabrizio, Anna Fels, Helen Garrett (by e-mail), Geraldine (McCall) Gottesman, Bernard Grandjany, Tina Harrower, Margaret Hoag, Sherry Stockwell Howard, Irving Kamsler, Linda Kasakyan, Joy Knapp, Gordon Lyle Jr., Caterina Marsh, Karine McCall, Jan Perry, Christopher Sattler, Neal Sattler, Wanda Styka, Sarah La Chapelle Thompson, Lucy (Lyle) Tower, Florence Young.

Depositions: Paul Albert, André Baeyens, Carla Hall, Gemma Hall, Karine McCall.

Articles: "Second Benefit Versailles Ball," *New York Times*, October 3, 1954; "Mounts Literary Summit at 20: Polan Banks Kept Age Secret," *Brooklyn Daily Eagle*, 1926; "Maria T. Berry, Niece of School's Founder, Married Here to Prince Alexis Droutzkoy," *New York Times*, December 17, 1944; "Mrs. Frank V. Storrs," *New York Times*, February 10, 1954; "Dr. William G. Lyle," *New York Times*, November 26, 1955; "Mrs. Anna E. Clark, Widow of Copper Multimillionaire," *Newsday*, October 12, 1963; "Anna Clark, Patron of Corcoran Gallery," *Washington Post*, October 13, 1963; "Mrs. Anna Clark, Senator's Widow," *New York Times*, October 12, 1963; "William Gower Obituary," *New York Times*, December 22, 1976; "William Leveson Gower, '25," Princeton Alumni Bulletin; "Charles S. Bannerman, Lawyer Who Specialized in Estates," *New York Times*, September 29, 1976; "Algernon P. Banks, Novelist, Dies at 77," *Richmond Times-Dispatch*, March 4, 1984; Barbara Hoelscher Doran, "Huguette Clark 1906–2011," *Santa Barbara Independent*, June 9, 2011.

Documents: Doris Styka notes, courtesy of Wanda Styka. Huguette Clark letters and telegrams, with thanks to the Estate of Huguette Clark for access to review, and permission to extensively quote from, her letters. Letters and telegrams to Huguette Clark from William Gower, Harry Pepper, Etienne de Villermont, Henri de Villermont, Felix Lorioux, and Donald Wallace, receipts, and notes, courtesy of the Estate of Huguette Clark.

Books:

Bill Dedman and Paul Clark Newell Jr., *Empty Mansions: The Mysterious Life of Huguette Clark and the Spending of a Great American Fortune,* Ballantine Books, 2013.

A. A. Hoehling, *Women Who Spied: True Stories of Feminine Espionage*, Madison Books, 1967.

CHAPTERS THIRTEEN THROUGH SIXTEEN

Interviews: Wallace Bock, Susan Brody, Rabbi Steven Burton, Isabelle Cazeaux, Barbara Cleary, Kati Despretz Cruz, Jacques Despretz, Ian Devine, Cynthia Garcia, Jennifer Gibbins, Paul Greenhalgh, Carla Hall, Kurt Harjung, Irving Kamsler, Judi Kamsler, David Levy, Sheila Lodge, Gordon Lyle Jr., Karine McCall, Marilyn McMahon, Daphne Merkin, Susan Olsen, Marie Pompei, Christopher Sattler, Neal Sattler, Fraser Seitel, Steve Shirley, Roberto Socas, Wanda Styka, Lucy (Lyle) Tower.

Depositions: André Baeyens, Jean-Loup Brusson, Geraldine Coffey, Ian Devine, Rodney Devine, Carla Hall, Erika Hall, Dr. Morton Hyman, Karine McCall, Paul Newell Jr., Dr. Robert Newman, Abraham Peri, Daniel Peri, David Peri, Geula Peri, Hadassah Peri, Steven Pyram, Dr. Jack Rudick, Danita Rudisill, Lewis Siegel, Dr. Henry Singman, Mildred Velasquez, Christie Ysit, Erlinda Ysit.

Articles: Joshua Kosman, "Agnes Albert: Pianist, San Francisco Symphony Supporter," *San Francisco Chronicle*, June 20, 2002; Paul Tharp, "Renoir Auction Scratches 10-Year Itch," *New York Post*, April 3, 2003; Bill Dedman, "The Clarks: An American Story of Wealth, Scandal and Mystery," msnbc.com, March 2010; Tim Trainor, "Where Is Huguette Clark?" *Montana Standard*, March 7, 2010; Steve Myers, "MSNBC Uses Slide Show for In-Depth Narrative Story," Poynter.org, March 9, 2010; Erica Pearson and James Fanelli, "A 42-Room Palace Sits Empty," *New York Daily News*, July 31, 2010; Bill Dedman, "Who Is Watching Reclusive Heiress's Millions?" msnbc.com, August 20, 2010; Doug Auer, Laura Italiano, Dan Mangan, "Princess of Beth Israel," *New York Post*, August 27, 2010; Todd Venezia, "New York's Hermit Heiress and Her Sad Secrets," *New York Post*, August 27, 2010; Rebecca Rosenberg, "D.A. Targets 104-Year-Old Heiress' Gifts to Lawyer," *New*

York Post, August 29, 2010; Jeanne MacIntosh, Ada Calhoun, Dan Mangan, "Heiress Phantom 'Family,'" *New York Post*, August 31, 2010; Dan Mangan, "Heiress Kin to the 'Re$cue,'" *New York Post*, September 4, 2010; "Heiress Wants Kin to Butt Out: Lawyer," *New York Post*, September 8, 2010; Jennifer Peltz, "NY Judge: No Guardian for Copper Heiress, 104," Associated Press, September 9, 2010; Margalit Fox, "Heiress to the High Life," *New York Times*, May 25, 2011; Stephen Miller, "Society Girl Who Spent 8 Decades in Seclusion," *Wall Street Journal*, May 25, 2011; "The Real Miss Havisham," Asian News International, May 25, 2011; "Hermit Heiress from an Era of Excess," *West Australian*, May 27, 2011; Marilyn McMahon, "Recluse, Yes; Cut Off from the World, No," *Santa Barbara News-Press*, July 9, 2011; Marilyn McMahon, "Unraveling a Mystery," *Santa Barbara News-Press*, May 29, 2011; Bill Dedman, "The $10 Million Degas Ballerina, Heiress Huguette Clark and the Tax Man," msnbc.com, March 15, 2012; Alice Thorson, "Painting's Story Touches Blochs, FBI and the Nelson," *Kansas City Star*, March 15, 2012.

Documents: Beth Israel e-mails, letters, and records; Irving Kamsler and Wallace Bock letters, billing records, drafts of wills; nurses' notes; Christopher Sattler time sheets; Huguette M. Clark probate case, File 1995/1375, Manhattan Surrogate's Court; Sotheby's catalogue, November 1999.

CHAPTER SEVENTEEN: The Battle for Huguette's Fortune

Interviews: Paul Albert, Wallace Bock, Harvey Corn, Celia Gray Cummings, John Dadakis, Ian Devine, Carl Distefano, John Graziano, Gerald Gray, Carla Hall, Irving Kamsler, Jason Lilien, Karine McCall, John Morken, Marie Pompei, Christopher Sattler, Wanda Styka.

Depositions: Wallace Bock, Ian Devine, Gerald Gray, Irving Kamsler, Dr. Robert Newman, Hadassah Peri, Dr. Jack Rudick, Danita Rudisill, Christopher Sattler, Lewis Siegel.

Articles: "Family Stiffed out of $400 Million Fortune," *New York Daily News*; "Heiress Had Ill Will: Nurse $34 M, Kin 0," *New York Post*, June 23, 2011; "All Dolled Up," *New York Post*, November 20, 2011; "The Heiress and the Nurse," *New York Post*, November 20, 2011; "Copper Heiress Signed 2 Wills in 2 Months," Associated Press, November 28, 2011; Bill Dedman, "A $400 Million Twist: Huguette Clark Signed Two Wills, One to Her Family," msnbc.com, November 28, 2011; Barbara Ross and Tracy Connor, "It's 400M Battle of the Wills!" *New York Daily News*, November 28, 2011; Jason Sheftell and Erin Durkin, "Sheik-Down at Clark Apts," *New York Post*, May 8, 2012; Elizabeth A. Harris, "Unraveling Some Mystery Surrounding the Homes of a Reclusive Heiress," *New York Times*, March 20, 2012; Anemona Hartocollis, "Hospital Caring for an Heiress Pressed Her to Give Lavishly," *New York Times*, May 30, 2013; David Montgomery, "Will the Corcoran Get the Monet?" *Washington Post*, January 31, 2013; Paul Sullivan, "In the Battle over the Estate of a Wealthy Recluse, Some Lessons," *New York Times*, June 15, 2013; Anemona Hartocollis, "Two Wills, One Private Heiress," *New York Times*, September 15, 2013; Anemona Hartocollis, "Tentative Deal in Battle over the Will of an Heiress," *New York Times*, September 20, 2013; Dareh Gregorian, "$100 Million Suit: Hospital Hid Heiress Away," *New York Post*, November 24, 2013.

Documents: Legal filings, Huguette M. Clark probate case, File 1995/1375, Manhattan Surrogate's Court. Christie's catalogue, April 2012.

Bibliography

Andrew Alpern, *Apartments for the Affluent: Historical Survey of Buildings in New York*, McGraw Hill, 1975.

John Astle, *Only in Butte: Stories Off the Hill*, Holt Publishing Group, 2004.

Gertrude Atherton, *Perch of the Devil*, Stokes, 1914.

André Baeyens, *Le Sénateur Qui Aimait La France*, Scali, 2005.

Marshall Bond Jr., *Adventures with Peons, Princes, and Tycoons*, Star Rover House, 1974.

Joseph L. Brennan, *Duke: The Life Story of Duke Kahanamoku*, Ku Pa'A Publishing, 1994.

Myron Brinig, *The Sisters*, Grosset & Dunlap, 1937.

Christopher P. Connolly, *The Devil Learns to Vote*, J. J. Little, 1938.

Laura Coyle and Dare Myers Hartwell, *Antiquities to Impressionism: The William A. Clark Collection*, Corcoran Gallery of Art, 2001.

Ellen Crain and Lee Whitney, *Images of America: Butte*, Arcadia Publishing, 2009.

Bill Dedman and Paul Clark Newell Jr., *Empty Mansions: The Mysterious Life of Huguette Clark and the Spending of a Great American Fortune*, Ballantine Books, 2013.

George H. Douglas, "Major Bowes," in *American National Biography*, vol. 3, Oxford University Press, 1999.

Mary Dillon Edmondson, *Profiles in Leadership: A History of the Spence School 1892–1992*, Phoenix Publishing, 1991.

Mary Montana Farrell, *William Andrews Clark*, master's dissertation, University of Washington, 1933.

Harry Fritz, Mary Murphy, and Robert R. Swartout Jr., *Montana Legacy: Essays on History, People and Place*, Montana Historical Society Press, 2002.

John A. Garraty and Mark C. Carnes, *American National Biography*, vol. 4, Oxford University Press, 1999.

C. P. Glasscock, *The War of the Copper Kings*, Riverbend Publishing, 1939.

Adam Gopnik, *Americans in Paris: A Literary Anthology*, Library of America, 2004.

William Grimes, *Appetite City: A Culinary History of New York*, North Point Press, 2009.

Lewis Hall, *The William A. Clark Collection, Treasures of a Copper King*, Corcoran Catalog, 1978.

Dashiell Hammett, *Red Harvest*, Vintage, 1929.

A. A. Hoehling, *Women Who Spied: True Stories of Feminine Espionage*, Madison Books, 1967.

Kathleen L. Housley, *Emily Hall Tremaine: Collector on the Cusp*, Emily Hall Tremaine Foundation, 2001.

Gypsy Rose Lee, *Gypsy: Memoirs of America's Most Celebrated Stripper*, Harper, 1957.

Donald MacMillan, *Smoke Wars: Anaconda Copper, Montana Air Pollution, and the Courts, 1890–1920*, Montana Historical Society Press, 2000.

Michael P. Malone, *The Battle for Butte*, University of Washington Press, 1981.

William Daniel Mangam, *The Clarks: An American Phenomenon*, Silver Bow Press, 1941.

James McCabe, *Lights and Shadows of New York*, 1872; reprint, Farrar Straus.

David McCullough, *The Greater Journey: Americans in Paris*, Simon & Schuster, 2011.

Lael Morgan, *Wanton West*, Chicago Review Press, 2011.

Patrick F. Morris, *Anaconda Montana: Copper Smelting Boom Town on the Western Frontier*, Swann Publishing, 1997.

T. Bentley Mott, *Myron Herrick, Friend of France*, Doubleday, 1929.

Werner Muensterberger, *Collecting: An Unruly Passion*, Princeton University Press, 1994.

David F. Myrick, *Montecito and Santa Barbara, Volume II, The Days of the Great Estates*, Montecito Publishing, 1991.

Richard H. Peterson, *Bonanza Rich*, University of Idaho Press, 1991.

Dennis Swibold, *Copper Chorus: Mining, Politics, and the Montana Press, 1889–1959*, Montana Historical Society Press, 2006.

K. Ross Toole, *Montana: An Uncommon Land*, University of Oklahoma Press, 1959.

Mark Twain, *Mark Twain in Eruption*, Harper & Brothers, 1922.

David Wallace, *Capital of the World: A Portrait of New York City in the Roaring Twenties*, Lyons Press, 2011.

Edward Wildman, *Famous Leaders of Industry*, Colonial Press, 1920.

Writers Project of Montana, *Copper Camp: The Lusty Story of Butte, Montana, the Richest Hill on Earth*, Montana State Department, 1943; reprint, Riverbend Publishing, 2002.

Index

About the Author

MERYL GORDON is the author of *Mrs. Astor Regrets: The Hidden Betrayals of a Family Beyond Reproach*. She is an award-winning journalist whose articles have appeared in *Vanity Fair*, the *New York Times*, and *New York Magazine*, and is the director of magazine writing at New York University's Arthur L. Carter Journalism Institute. A native of Rochester, New York, and a graduate of the University of Michigan, she lives on Manhattan's Upper West Side with her husband, Walter Shapiro.